Property Law Perspectives VI

Property Law Perspectives VI

Caroline S. Rupp, Rafael Ibarra Garza and Bram Akkermans

eleven
international publishing

Published, sold and distributed by Eleven International Publishing
P.O. Box 85576
2508 CG The Hague
The Netherlands
Tel.: +31 70 33 070 33
Fax: +31 70 33 070 30
email: sales@elevenpub.nl
www.elevenpub.com

Sold and distributed in USA and Canada
Independent Publishers Group
814 N. Franklin Street
Chicago, IL 60610, USA
Order Placement: +1 800 888 4741
Fax: +1 312 337 5985
orders@ipgbook.com
www.ipgbook.com

Eleven International Publishing is an imprint of Boom uitgevers Den Haag.

ISBN 978-94-6236-904-7
ISBN 978-94-6274-994-8 (e-book)

Table of Contents

PREFACE

In 2009, the Young Property Lawyers Forum was established as an informal platform for young researchers in property law to present their ongoing research and discuss ideas and questions resulting from their projects. In this round-table format, senior researchers take on the role of commentators, supporting and advising the younger scholars who take the main stage. Over the years, these meetings have become a source of fruitful exchange for property law scholars both young in age and young at heart. They have inspired creative projects and instigated various cooperations. But most of all, they have sparked friendship – some might even say, a family atmosphere. The network has expanded considerably and now covers not only Benelux countries, but has members from all over the world. The YPLF continues to strive to bring together young property scholars and – under leadership of those somewhat more advanced – to keep debating cutting edge issues in global property law scholarship.

From its inception, the YPLF's approach has been broad in every respect. Property law is understood in the widest possible sense, comprising not only the classic approaches of property law theory and issues like land or water law, but also focusing strongly on more recent questions like space or virtual property. It is not viewed in isolation, but in its interplay with other areas of law, e.g. environmental or constitutional law. It is explored from various angles, as contributions present national solutions, comparative analyses or regional or international approaches. The presentations reflect the contributors' different backgrounds, ranging from law students to postdocs and practitioners, and legal systems, bringing together researchers from all over the world. Historical developments, current problems, and suggestions for future developments are brought together – with sometimes surprising synergies.

The YPLF's main focus has always been on current developments in property law. Often viewed as a very traditional and backward-looking area of law, property law is very closely connected to matters at the core of society. Many of the challenges society faces need to be reflected and solved in property law – for example, housing or environmental issues. Increasingly, these matters transcend national borders and demand solutions on a larger, international scale. It is a mark of the YPLF that it frequently raises such questions some time before they enter the 'mainstream' of the scholarly debate. The exchange of views from different national and political backgrounds leads to constructive discussions and innovative approaches on these issues. Bringing together expertise on traditional national concepts and theories, comparative work, interdisciplinary studies and the 'fresh eyes' of researchers in the early stages of their careers is sometimes surprising, often bold, and always stimulating.

Since the second edition of the YPLF, selected papers have been published in a conference volume – the Property Law Perspectives book series. This book combines contributions from the VIIth and VIIIth editions of the Young Property Lawyers Forum which continued the tradition of expanding the YPLF geographically, in form and in content.

The VIIth edition of the YPLF – the first to take place in Germany – was held in Hamburg from 21-23 September, 2016, on the generous invitation of the Max Planck Institute for Comparative and International Private Law. Organized by Dr. Caroline Rupp, Arvid Arntz and Dr. Bram Akkermans, the conference united around 50 property law scholars from all continents, with representatives from Australia, China, Chile, Georgia, Kosovo, Mexico, South Africa, and various European jurisdictions. The moving and inspirational dinner speech by Prof. Dr. Dr. h.c. mult. Reinhard Zimmermann, director of the Max Planck Institute, reminded participants that the values of international cooperation, mutual respect, and freedom of ideas should not be taken for granted but need to be carefully nurtured and preserved.

As a kick-off event, the European Property Law Journal (EPLJ) board of editors presented a panel discussion on the subject 'Beyond the Lex Rei Sitae?'. Moderated by Dr. Bram Akkermans, distinguished senior property lawyers Prof. Dr. Dr. h.c. mult. Jürgen Basedow, Dr. Wian Erlank, Prof. Dr. Sjef van Erp, Prof. Dr. Eva-Maria Kieninger, Dr. Eveline Ramaekers and Prof. Dr. Vincent Sagaert shared their views on the current state and potential future of the central rule of international property law. The lively debate set the tone for the two-day conference to follow as many of the issues raised in the course of the opening evening were to return again and again throughout the conference.

With its four panels ('Theory and Dogmatics of Property Law', 'Land Law', 'Property Law and Politics' and 'Current Issues in Property Law'), the Hamburg YPLF continued the tradition of diversity of topics and methods with contributions from all fields of property law, from core subjects (e.g. land registration) to the arcane (e.g. property and theology). As far-ranging as the issues addressed were, some topics kept recurring throughout the debates: examples are the connection between property law and environmental law and the search for alternatives to the traditional property law theories and dogmatic approaches. The challenges digitalization poses for property law were the most strongly debated, with contributions from different angles and many discussions turning towards the subject of 'data' eventually. True to form, the Hamburg YPLF included an interactive session in an innovative format: In the workshop 'How to be a Property Lawyer?', senior researchers submitted themselves to the junior participants' questions on the different aspects of property law research – in a speed-dating scenario.

The VIIIth edition marked new horizons for the YPLF as it moved across the Atlantic Ocean for the first time. Hosted by the Universidad de Monterrey on 23-24 October, 2017, it was organized by Prof. Dr. Rafael Ibarra Garza, and proved to be an exciting and diverse space in which various topics were discussed throughout the course of the event. Gathered underneath the same roof were property law scholars from the Netherlands, South Africa, Brazil, Belgium, Scotland, Colombia, and Mexico.

Highlights were some memorable interventions regarding eminent domain in the United States of America, security interests in Brazil, the challenges brought about by crypto-currencies and domain names, property law constitutional structures in South African law, and a myriad of topics considered by several European jurisdictions such as prescription, immovable and movable assets, and security trusts.

Nurtured by the simple yet effective Q&A format, every panelist had the opportunity to interact on a personal basis with the audience. Undoubtedly, this iteration of the YPLF was of significant learning and research value both in national and international terms.

We are very happy to present some of the contributions from the Hamburg and Monterrey conferences in this volume. This collection showcases the depth of critical analysis, the innovativeness of method, and the wealth of ideas that young scholars bring to the YPLF, and to property law in general. It illustrates once again that property law often reflects and crystallizes the issues that are affecting legal and societal developments in general. We hope that it will contribute to the exchange of ideas on the many challenges, creative solutions and fascinating inspirations property law has to offer if one is willing to approach it with an open mind.

With the approach of its 10th anniversary, the YPLF is reaching a new stage in its development. As it is growing into a world-wide network and the first generation of its young property lawyers is maturing, some organizational changes are needed to accommodate its growing nature. We are very glad that after an interim period of uncertainty, the Property Law Perspectives series has found a new home with Eleven International Publishing, and we are looking forward to a harmonious cooperation with our new publisher.

This 'relaunch' of our series also introduces a major change: starting with this issue, each Property Law Perspectives volume will combine selected contributions from two YPLF editions instead of one. We move towards a much more stringent editing process. Although the editors still include organisers of the YPLF events – to also enable those scholars to gain valuable editing experience – the board of advice strictly oversees the process. Content editing and language editing is brought up to higher standards to produce are more creative and high-level volume of property law contributions. The downside of this is that contributions on very current issues sometimes see publication elsewhere.

The successful and inspiring YPLF meetings in Hamburg and Monterrey would not have been possible without the help and support of many brains, hearts and hands. We thank the host institutions for generously inviting us, the staff members for handling the practical aspects of conference organization, the YPLF board of advice for entrusting us with these events, and all participants (young, old, and in between) for making the YPLF what it is. Our special thanks go to Cynthia Alejandra Sánchez Torres (Universidad de Monterrey) for her invaluable help with the technical aspects of manuscript production, and to Elaine Brook for the language editing.

We hope that in the years to come, the YPLF will continue to flourish as an informal network of young property law researchers and to provide a platform for the discussion of topics at the forefront of property research. Its mission continues: drawing on a broad range of sources to explore the possibilities and shape the outlines of a property law fit for the 21st century.

Caroline S. Rupp
Rafael Ibarra Garza
Bram Akkermans

Part I
General Principles and Fundamental Property Questions

1 The Role of the Numerus Clausus Principle in (Re)Characterizing Property Rights

Ghijsbrecht Degeest[*]

1 Introduction on (Re)Characterization (of Agreements)

The characterization of an agreement can be described as the process of naming the agreement or determining its nature, with the aim of placing it into a specific legal category, a specific legal framework, and thereby giving it the legal effects which the law connects to that specific legal framework.[1] Characterization of an agreement concerns the question of whether the agreement complies with the essential and/or characteristic elements of a certain legal concept, with the aim of determining which set of (supplementary and/or mandatory) rules are applicable.[2] Recharacterization is the process whereby the initial parties' characterization is altered into another characterization, more closely connected to the parties' common intention, which can either be purely factual, resulting from external or internal circumstances (*i.e.* the economic result parties had in mind) or a more juridified or legal common intention (*i.e.* the intention to create a specific right (to use) or agreement above another, because of the legal consequences connected to that specific right or agreement).[3]

---

* PhD Researcher, Institute for Property Law, KU Leuven.

1 Belgium: A. Cruquenaire, C. Delforge, I. Durant & P. Wéry, *Précis des contrats spéciaux: vente, bail, mandat, entreprise, dépôt*, Waterloo, Wolters Kluwer, 2015, p. 37-38, nos. 15-16; P. Van Ommeslaghe, *Les obligations*, I, *Introduction – Sources des obligations (première partie)* Brussels, Bruylant, 2013, p. 638, no. 407; P. Van Ommeslaghe, 'Examen de jurisprudence (1974 à 1982): les obligations', *RCJB* (1986), p. 177, no. 79. France: J.-L. Bergel, *Méthodologie juridique*, Paris, PUF, 2016, p. 101-102, no. 57; J. Ghestin, C. Jamin & M. Billiau, *Traité de droit civil. Les effets du contrat*, Paris, LGDJ, 2001, p. 81, no. 59. Quebec: P. Fréchette, 'La qualification des contrats: aspects théoriques', *Les Cahiers de droit*, 2010, p. 119; M. Cumyn, 'Les catégories, la classification et la qualification juridique: réflexions sur la systématicité du droit', *Les Cahiers de droit*, 2011, p. 369.

2 Belgium: Cruquenaire, Delforge, Durant & Wéry, 2015, p. 38, no. 16. France: see P. Malaurie, P.-Y. Gautier & L. Aynès, *Les contrats spéciaux*, Paris, LGDJ, 2014, p. 7, no. 7. Quebec: P. Fréchette, 'La qualification des contrats: aspects pratiques', *Les Cahiers de droit*, 2010, p. 120.

3 See *i.a.* Belgium: Van Ommeslaghe, 2013, p. 638, no. 407; P. Wéry, *Droit des obligations – Volume 1*, Brussels, Larcier 2011, no. 434; L. Cornelis, *Algemene theorie van de verbintenis*, Antwerp, Intersentia, 2000, p. 275-276. France: Malaurie, Gautier & Aynès, 2014, p. 14, nos. 17-18. Quebec: Fréchette, 2010, p. 151.

The (practical) importance of (re)characterization should not be underestimated: "*L'opération de qualification revêt la même importance en droit que le diagnostic en médécine*".[4] It is through the proper characterization of the factual elements that the proper legal effects come into effect, and thus that the legal system (properly) works. The daily task or occupation of each legal practitioner – be it a lawyer, legal advisor, notary, judge etc. – is to characterize the facts presented to him or her.[5] To be able to apply a certain set of the limited legal rules on the unlimited variations of factual circumstances, these factual elements must be characterized.[6] Application of the law presupposes characterization of the presented facts.[7] Despite this major practical relevance, the issue of (re)characterization is underexplored on a dogmatic level in legal scholarship.[8] That is certainly true for Belgian legal scholarship.[9] In France and Quebec, some legal scholars (started to) discuss(ed) the issue of (re)characterization (of agreements).[10]

4 M. Cumyn & F. Gosselin, 'Les Categories Juridiques et la Qualification: Une Approche Cognitive', *McGill Law Journal*, 2016, p. 331.

5 Cruquenaire, Delforge, Durant & Wéry 2015, p. 37, no. 15.

6 Malaurie, Gautier & Aynès, 2014, p. 7, no. 7.

7 Malaurie, Gautier & Aynès, 2014, p. 7, no. 7. Cruquenaire, Delforge, Durant & Wéry, 2015, p. 37, no. 15.

8 Several explanations are plausible for this. A first reason has to do with one of the cornerstone principles of contract law: the principle of freedom of contract. Over the years the legislator has however introduced more and more rules (mandatory and non-mandatory) applicable to the different named contracts, making the determination of the proper characterization of the agreement more and more important. Another explanation is the idea that in many cases the question of the proper characterization of the agreement poses little problems. However, contractual relations and transactions have become more and more complex to meet the particular needs and demands of (legal) practice. Moreover, even for a 'simple' agreement it is not always easy to determine the proper characterization. That is certainly also true for agreements granting a use right.

9 No in-depth study has been conducted on how to characterize an agreement, let alone on how to characterize an agreement that grants a right to use. Some scholars discuss – albeit in a short and fragmented way – the issue or give some examples of (a potential risk for) (re)characterization of rights to use: see V. Sagaert, 'Goederenrecht' in *Beginselen van Belgisch Privaatrecht*, Mechelen, Kluwer, 2014, nos. 52, 478-482, 696-700, 785-788; N. Carette & J. Del Corral, 'De kwalificatie van het recht van vruchtgebruik: contractuele mogelijkheden en afbakening tegenover opstal, erfpacht en huur' in A.-L. Verbeke & V. Sagaert (Eds.), *Vruchtgebruik: mogelijkheden, beperkingen en innovaties*, Antwerpen, Intersentia, 2012; C. Mostin, 'Emphytéose et superficie', *Rép.not.*, 2015, nos. 29-32; F. De Montpellier, 'Usufruit, emphytéose et superficie – Limites de l'autonomie de la volonté et utilisation combinée' in F. Dierckx (Ed.), *Onroerend goed als beleggingsinstrument*, Brussels, De Boeck & Larcier, 2003, p. 1-46.

10 France: F. Terré, *L'influence de la volonté individuelle sur les qualifications*, Paris, LGDJ, 1957; X. Henry, *La technique des qualifications contractuelles*, unpublished doctoral thesis, university of Nancy II, 1992; M.-E. Ancel, *La prestation caractéristique du contrat*, Paris, Economica, 2002; J.-F. Overstake, *Essai de classification des contrats spéciaux*, Paris, LGDJ, 1969; G. Goubeaux, *La règle de l'accessoire en droit privé*, Paris, LGDJ, 1969; Quebec: Fréchette, 2010, p. 117-158 and 395-424; Cumyn & Gosselin, 2016.

2 Rights to Use: Property and Personal Rights

When it comes to rights to use, there are two large groups or categories of contracts: property rights (e.g. an *emphyteusis*, a *superficies*, a usufruct, a real servitude) and personal rights (e.g. a loan, a lease, a *commodatum*).[11] While a property right would result in a direct relation between the holder of the right and the object, a personal right would only allow its holder to obtain the right to use *from* and enjoy the object *through* the other contracting party.[12] Property rights are 'equipped' with special attributes, such as a right to follow,[13] special protection in insolvency proceedings and real subrogation.[14] Personal rights (to use) do not benefit from these special attributes.

3 The Closed System (Numerus Clausus) of Property Rights and the Open System of Personal Rights

Another difference – and one that is or seems of significant importance for the characterization of agreements granting a right to use – is that property rights are generally characterized by a closed system, a *numerus clausus*, while personal rights are not.[15] Although many legal systems do recognize a *numerus clausus* of property rights,[16] some legal systems do not (e.g. South Africa).[17] That does however not mean that there is a proliferation of

---

11 N. Verheyden-Jeanmart and C. Mostin, 'Jouissance d'immeuble: bail et conventions voisines' *in* P.-A. Forriers (Ed.), *Aspects récents du droit des contrats*, Brussels, Jeune Barreau, 2001, p. 94, nos. 2 and 3.

12 Verheyden-Jeanmart & Mostin, 2001, p. 94, nos. 2 and 3.

13 A property right is connected to the object and runs with it, making it effective against third parties.

14 Sagaert, 2014, p. 31-43, nos. 31-45. See P.-C. Lafond, *Précis de droit des biens*, 2nd ed., Montréal, Éditions thémis, 2007, p. 173 ff., nos. 442 ff.

15 See *i.a.* H.J. Snijders & E.B. Rank-Berenschot, 'Goederenrecht' *in Studiereeks Burgerlijk recht*, 6th ed., Deventer, Wolters Kluwer, 2017, p. 60, no. 78; Sagaert, 2014, p. 13-14, no. 16; T. Struycken, *De numerus clausus in het goederenrecht*, Deventer, Kluwer 2007, p. 245 ff.; H. Vuye & S. Stijns, 'Zakenrecht: tweehonderd jaar oud of tweehonderd jaar jong?' *in* D. Heirbaut & G. Martyn (Eds.), *Napoleons nalatenschap: tweehonderd jaar burgerlijk wetboek in Belgium*, Mechelen, Kluwer, 2005, p. 157; W. van Gerven, *Algemeen deel* In *Beginselen van Belgisch Privaatrecht*, Antwerp, Story-Scientia, 1987, p. 96, no. 34. See P. Heck, *Grundriss des Sachenrechts*, Tübingen, J.C.B. Mohr, 1930.

16 There are several economic reasons for introducing and preserving the *numerus clausus* of property rights, and recently the *numerus clausus* has repeatedly been discussed by law and economic scholars: see *i.a.* H. Hansmann & R. Kraakman, 'Property, Contract and Verification: The Numerus Clausus Problem and the Divisibility of Rights', *Journal of Legal Studies*, 2002, p. 373; T. Merill & H. Smith, 'Optimal Standardization in the Law of Property: The *Numerus Clausus* Principle', *Yale Law Journal*, 2000, p. 1; H. Smith, 'Standardization in Property Law' *in* K. Ayotte & H. Smith (Eds.), *Research Handbook on the Economics of Property Law*, Northampton, Edward Elgar, 2011, p. 148; Y.-C. Chang & H. Smith, 'The Numerus Clausus Principle, Property Customs, and the Emergence of New Property Forms', *Iowa Law Review*, 2015.

17 M. De Waal, 'The Uniformity of Ownership, Numerus Clausus and the Reception of the Trust into South African Law', *European Review of Private Law*, No. 3, 2000, p. 442-443.

property rights in these legal systems; only few 'new'[18] property rights see the light.[19] Even in legal systems without a closed system, creation and recognition of property rights is not entirely free. While not formally recognizing a *numerus clausus* of property rights, there is still a need for criteria in order to separate those rights that (can) have third party effect (*i.e.* property rights) from rights that have effect between the contracting parties only (*i.e.* personal rights).[20] Similar reasoning applies to the American legal system. Although the *numerus clausus* can – in civil law systems – be seen as a reaction against feudal systems,[21] and is therefore not formally introduced or recognized in the American legal system, American legal scholars recently demonstrated that there is a standardization of property rights.[22] This standardization is similar to, yet different from the civil law concept of *numerus clausus*. Both from the perspective of *Typenzwang* and *Typenfixierung* (*cf. infra*), the approach is more 'liberal'.[23]

On the other hand, some legal systems, traditionally characterized by a (strict) *numerus clausus* of property rights (e.g. France and Quebec), show a tendency to open up this closed system to some extent. In France, in the early days following the introduction of the French Civil code, the *Cour de Cassation* seemed reluctant to accept a *numerus clausus* of property rights.[24] However, the existence of a *numerus clausus* of property rights remained heavily

18 South African law 'starts' from the property rights traditionally known in Roman law (e.g. ownership, servitudes, mortgage and pledge) (De Waal, 2000, p. 443).

19 In general: B. Akkermans, 'The Numerus Clausus of Property Rights' *in* M. Graziadei & L. Smith (Eds.), *Comparative property law: global perspectives*, Cheltenham, Edward Elgar Publishing, 2017, p. 101. For South Africa: e.g. lease of land, mineral rights (De Waal, 2000, p. 443).

20 See Akkermans, 2017, p. 101-102. For Instance, in South Africa, the so-called 'subtraction from the *dominium* test' is used to decide whether or not a new property right is accepted (De Waal, 2000, pp. 443-444).

21 See *i.a.* Sagaert, 2014, p. 17, no. 19; Struycken, 2007, p. 753-754.

22 See Hansmann & Kraakman, 2002, S373-S420; Merrill & Smith, 2000, p. 1-70. See also S. Van Erp, 'A *numerus quasi-clausus* of property rights as a constitutive element of a future European property law?', *Electronic Journal of Comparative Law*, Vol. 7.2, 2003, p. 8-9.

23 Although practical reasons have led to the use of a limited number of categories, courts may still recognize (certain) third party effect for rights outside the existing list (*contra Typenzwang*). Moreover, the contents of these categories is not as fixed as it is in civil law (*contra Typenfixierung*) (see Van Erp, 2003, p. 10).

24 See Caquelard v. Lemoine (Cass. *req.* 13 February 1834, *S.* 1834, 1, p. 118): "*les articles 544, 546 et 552 du Code civil sont déclaratifs du droit commun relativement à la nature et aux effets de la propriété, mais ne sont pas prohibitifs. Ni ces articles ni aucune autre loi n'excluent les diverses modifications et décompositions dont le droit ordinaire de propriété est susceptible.*" Later, the same *Cour de Cassation* recognized the right of *superficies* (Cass. civ. 18 May 1858, *S.* 1858, 1, 661).

debated in legal scholarship.[25] With two recent judgements (Maison de poésie I[26] and II[27]), the balance seems to have (definitely?) shifted towards an open system, as the French *Cour de Cassation* recognized the right to create property rights *sui generis.*[28]

The *numerus clausus* has two components: *Typenzwang* and *Typenfixierung.*[29] *Typenzwang* implies that parties cannot create new property rights outside those recognized by law.[30] *Typenzwang* goes so far as to make a formal demarcation between property and personal rights. *Typenfixierung* implies that the law determines the criteria or the framework of the chosen property right, leaving no or at least limited[31] room for freedom of contract.[32]

Because the *numerus clausus* principle limits both the number (*Typenzwang*) and the substance or content (*Typenfixierung*) of property rights,[33] it seems relatively easy to determine whether and, if so, which property right the contracting parties have agreed

25 *Pro* the existence of a *numerus clausus* of property rights: see *i.a.* C. Larroument, *Les biens. Droits reels principaux*, II, 4th ed., Paris, Economica, 2004, p. 33-35; F. Zenati & T. Revet, *Les biens*, 2nd ed., Paris, PUF, 1997, p. 216, no. 196; F. Chabas, *Biens: Droit de propriété et ses démembrements*, II, 8th ed., Paris, Montchrestien, 1994, p. 4-5; Aubry, Rau & E. Bartin, *Cours de droit civil français d'après la méthode de Zachariae*, II, 5th ed., Paris, Librairie Marchal & Billard, 1935, p. 69-74; C. Demolombe, *Traité de la distinction des biens; de la propriété; de l'usufruit: de l'usage et de l'habitation*, I, 4th ed., Paris, Auguste Durand/L. Hachette et Cie, 1870, p. 436-437. *Contra* the existence of a *numerus clausus* of property rights: see *i.a.* C. Atias, *Droit Civil – Les Biens*, 8th ed., Paris, LexisNexis, 2005, p. 47-50; F. Terré & P. Simler, *Droit civil – Les biens*, 5th ed., Paris, Dalloz, 1998; M. Picard, *Traité pratique de droit civil français. Les biens*, III, Paris, LGDJ, 1952, p. 54, no. 48; F. Laurent, *Principes de droit civil français*, VI, 3th ed., Brussels, Bruylant, 1878, p. 107-115. In 1984 the French *Cour de Cassation* recognized a '*droit d'affichage*' as a property right (Cass. 18 January 1984, *D.* 1985, 504), while it did the same for a '*droit de crû et à croître*' in 2012 (Cass. civ. 3e 23 May 2012, n° 11-13.202).

26 Cass. 31 October 2012, *RTD Civ.* 2013, 141.

27 Cass. 8 September 2016, n° 14-26.953.

28 See *i.a.* A. Tadros, 'La liberté d'aménager les droits réels principaux' *in* L. Andreu (Ed.), *Liberté contractuelle et droits réels*, Bayonne, Institut Universitaire Varenne, 2015, p. 87-88, no. 2; W. Dross, 'L'ordre public permet-il que soit créé un droit réel perpétuel?' (annotation under Cass. 31 Oktober 2012), *RTD Civ.*, 2013, p. 141; L. D'avout & B. Mallet-Bricout, 'La liberté de création des droits réels ajoud'hui', *D.*, 2013, p. 53-61.

29 W. Wiegand, '*Numerus clausus* der dinglichen Rechte. Zur Entstehung und Bedeutung eines zentralen zivilrechtlichen Dogmas' *in* G. Köbler (Ed.), *Wege europäischer Rechtsgeschichte – Festschrift Karl Kroeschell*, Frankfurt a.M., Peter Lang, 1987, p. 623-643.

30 Sagaert, 2014, p. 13, no. 16; R. Stevens, 'Party Autonomy and Property Rights' *in* R. Westrik & J. Van Der Weide (Eds.), *Party autonomy in international property law*, München, Sellier European Publishers, 2011, p. 84; B. Akkermans, *The principle of numerus clausus in European property law*, Antwerp, Intersentia, 2008, p. 245.

31 Limitation of the content of the different property rights is required in order to prevent parties from creating new property rights – and thus bypassing *Typenzwang* – by making 'excessive' use of contractual freedom within the framework of a specific property right. Moreover, limitation of the content of the different property rights should prevent that different rights to use are matched to each other.

32 Snijders & Rank-Berenschot, 2017, p. 60, no. 78; Akkermans, 2008, p. 6-7 and 245; T. Struycken, 'The Numerus Clausus and Party Autonomy in the Law of Property' *in* R. Westrik & J. Van Der Weide (Eds.), *Party autonomy in international property law*, München, Sellier European Publishers, 2011, p. 59; Struycken, 2007, p. 757.

33 Akkermans, 2017, p. 100; Van Erp, 2003, p. 8. Because property rights have third party effect – and thus can potentially bind others than the contracting parties – a need is felt to limit both number and content of property rights (Akkermans, 2017, p. 103).

upon. Hence, the question of how to characterize an agreement granting a (property) right to use would appear to have a straightforward answer.

Personal rights, on the other hand, are characterized by an open system, typically leaving much room for party autonomy and freedom of contract.[34] There is no *Typenzwang* for personal rights.[35] The same is true for *Typenfixierung*. Parties are in principle free to shape their contractual relationship in whatever way they deem appropriate and can include any obligation in their agreement, on the sole condition this does not go against public policy (*ordre public*) or accepted principles of morality.[36] Aside from named contracts for which the legislator has developed a specific legal regime, parties are in principle free to create unnamed personal rights or personal rights *sui generis*.[37]

4 The Nuanced Role of the Principle of Numerus Clausus in Characterizing Agreements Granting a Right to Use

The *numerus clausus* principle (in particular *Typenzwang* and *Typenfixierung*) is however not as strict as it seems as a principle. In general, several legal scholars have called for a more flexible *numerus clausus* principle in order to be able to cope with the developments and needs of legal practice.[38]

4.1 Nuancing (the Role in the Characterization Process of) Typenfixierung

4.1.1 Freedom of Contract within the Framework of the Different Property Rights

Typenfixierung does not rule out party autonomy and contractual freedom.[39] Parties are in principle free to agree upon any clause within the framework of a specific property right, as long as they respect and comply with the essential characteristics and provisions of mandatory law connected to that specific property right.[40] Moreover, there are only few

34 Akkermans, 2017, p. 100.

35 Sagaert, 2014, p. 14, no. 16; Verheyden-Jeanmart & Mostin, 2001, p. 95, no. 4.

36 Verheyden-Jeanmart & Mostin, 2001, p. 95, no. 4.

37 Belgium: Cruquenaire, Delforge, Durant & Wéry, 2015, pp. 22 ff., nos. 5 ff.; Sagaert, 2014, p. 14, no. 16; Verheyden-Jeanmart & Mostin, 2001, p. 95, no. 4. France: Malaurie, Gautier & Aynès, 2014, p. 5, no. 3; P. Delebecque & F.-J. Pansier, *Droit des obligations. 1. Contrat et quasi-contrat*, Paris, LexisNexis/Litec, 2010, p. 10, no. 24. Quebec: Fréchette, 2010, p. 375, 401 ff.

38 See *i.a.* Akkermans, 2008, p. 553-563; V. Sagaert, 'Het goederenrecht als open system van verbintenissen? Poging tot een nieuwe kwalificatie van de vermogensrechten', *TPR*, 2005, p. 983.

39 Akkermans, 2017, p. 100; Akkermans, 2008, p. 245.

40 V. Sagaert & R. Jansen, 'Goederenrecht: de gestage groei naar een conventioneel vermogensrecht', *RW*, 2011, p. 68-73. See also Akkermans, 2017, p. 104.

mandatory rules and/or essential characteristics for each property right. Much is thus left to party autonomy and freedom of contract.

On the other hand, from the perspective of the law of obligations, an increasing number of mandatory rules can be observed. Paradoxically, this means that many parties opt for a property right instead of a personal right, just to circumvent mandatory provisions connected to personal rights (e.g. special lease regimes).[41]

These findings lead to the fact that it is not always self-evident to distinguish the different contracts granting a (personal or property) right to use.[42] There is (more and more) overlap between different property rights and even between property rights on the one hand and personal rights on the other hand, making them (to a certain extent) interchangeable.[43]

Let us take an example. X concludes an agreement with Y, allowing Y to use, for a period of 30 years, a piece of land (including the right to build on it) which is owned by X. Y pays a monthly compensation to X. How should this agreement be characterized? The judge could think of a *superficies*, as Y has the right to build and the agreement complies with the mandatory maximum duration of 50 years according to art. 4 of the Belgian *Superficies* act.[44] But the judge could also consider characterization as an *emphyteusis*, as a lease, or as a usufruct, since all these contracts also grant Y the right to use the land, including the right to build on it. The judge could possibly even consider characterization as a personal and unnamed right to use the land, including the right to build on it.

The *numerus clausus* principle, more in particular *Typenfixierung*, does not provide a clear answer for the judge on the question how to determine the proper characterization of the agreement.

4.1.2 Lenient Approach towards Provisions of Mandatory Law and Essential Characteristics

The difficult demarcation and overlap between different property rights, as well as between property rights and personal rights, is further enhanced by the lenient approach that exists and is further developing towards those provisions and elements that are considered mandatory law or essential characteristics of the property right in question, with the result that these provisions and elements are not even always decisive in the (re)characterization process.

41 Sagaert, 2014, no. 464. See for example JP Waver 22 June 2004, *JJP*, 2006, 138.

42 See e.g. JP Kruishoutem 18 November 1949, *JT*, 1950, 177.

43 Sagaert, 2014, no. 52; P. Vits, 'Zakelijke genotsrechten als alternatief voor huur en pacht' in D. Meulemans (Ed.), *Een onroerend goed huren en verhuren*, Leuven, Acco 1996, p. 35-51; Struycken, 2007, p. 624 ff.

44 Art. 4 Belgian Superficies Act of 10 January 1824, *Journal officiel du royaume de Pays-Bas*, 1824, no. 13.

For example, the Belgian *Hof van Cassatie*[45] ruled that the minimum duration of 27 years of an *emphyteusis* – albeit being of mandatory law (art. 2 *juncto* art. 17 *Emphyteusis* act[46]) – does not prevent parties from stipulating the *emphyteusis* can come to an end in case of a liquidation procedure or a dissolution of the holder of the *emphyteusis*. A similar lenient approach is applied towards fulfillment of the duty to pay a (periodical) compensation (*canon*), considered essential to an *emphyteusis*.[47] Traditionally, the *canon* had a symbolic character. Nowadays, it often corresponds with the rental value of the object. Moreover – at least according to some – it is no longer required that the *canon* has a periodical character.[48] Furthermore, it is assumed that it cannot only take the form of a payment in cash, but also of a performance in kind (*in natura*).[49] Note that in Dutch law, the *canon* is not (or no longer) essential, but merely optional for an *emphyteusis*.[50] Another example is the requirement of an objective utility for the dominant land in case of a real servitude, which is interpreted more and more flexible by Belgian case law[51] and which was abolished in the Netherlands.[52]

The same applies to the mandatory maximum duration of the different property rights to use. Suppose that in the example of X and Y, the agreement was concluded for a term of 55 (instead of 30) years; would that rule out characterization as a *superficies* (violation of the mandatory[53] maximum duration of art. 4 Belgian *Superficies* Act)? This would appear to be the case. However, the remedy for concluding a *superficies* for more than 50 years is reduction of the duration to the maximum duration.[54] Hence, the duration of the right to use as such cannot be considered a decisive element in the characterization process.

45 Cass. 30 March 2006, *Arr.Cass.* 2006, 740, Pas., 2006, vol. 3, 720, *RW*, 2006-07 (shortened), 678, annotation K. Vanhove, *TBBR*, 2008, vol. 2, p. 88, annotation V. Waterkeyn, *TBO*, 2006 (shortened), vol. 4, p. 165, annotation S. Snaet, *T.Not.*, 2008, p. 97, annotation V. Sagaert & M. Somers.

46 Belgian *Emphyteusis* Act of 10 January 1824, *Journal officiel du royaume des Pays-Bas*, 1824, no. 14.

47 Sagaert, 2014, p. 573, no. 713; M. Donnay, 'L'emphytéose', *RGEN*, 1974, p. 215; Vits, 1996, p. 46, no. 134. The *ratio legis* (*i.e.* preventing doubt arising about whether the holder of the *emphyteusis* is in fact not the owner) has literally been 'overruled' with the introduction of the Belgian Mortgage Act of 1851.

48 *Pro:* R. Carton De Tournai & A. J. Charlier, 'Quelques considerations d'actualité sur l'emphytéose et la superficie', *JT*, 1971, p. 71. *Contra* (arguing the periodicity is essential): R. Derine, F. Van Neste & H. Vandenberghe, 'Zakenrecht', IIB in *Beginselen van Belgisch Privaatrecht*, Antwerp, Story-Scientia, 1984, p. 876, no. 1006; Donnay, 1974, p. 221, no. 11. Moreover, although art. 1 of the Belgian *Emphyteusis* act states that the compensation has an annual character, it is assumed that another periodicity (e.g. monthly, weekly etc.) is also allowed.

49 See also Sagaert, 2014, p. 574, no. 713.

50 Snijders & Rank-Berenschot, 2017, p. 567, no. 671.

51 A mere added value, an increase in ease of use, a more pleasant use or even a future or potential use is considered sufficient (e.g. Cass. 30 November 2007, *Arr.Cass.*, 2007, 2329, *RW*, 2008-09, 1047, annotation K. Swinnen; Cass. 28 January 2000, *Arr.Cass.*, 2000, 243; Trib. Bruges 23 March 2004, *RJI*, 2004, 164).

52 According to art. 5:70 (1) NBW, the servient land must be burdened 'in favor of' (*ten behoeve van*) the dominant land. See Snijders & Rank-Berenschot, 2017, p. 543, no. 637.

53 Sagaert, 2014, pp. 600-601, no. 753; M. Muylle, *De duur en de beëindiging van zakelijke rechten*, Antwerp, Intersentia, 2012, no. 444; Derine, Van Neste & Vandenberghe, 1984, no. 25.

54 Cass. 15 December 2006, *Arr.Cass.*, 2006, 2643.

(Belgian) legal scholars disagree on the implications and consequences of this lenient approach on the (re)characterization of rights to use. In the view of some, because of this (increased) party autonomy and contractual freedom, it is appropriate to approach the possibility of recharacterization in a restrictive manner.[55] On the contrary, other legal scholars argue it increases the possibility and likeliness of a recharacterization.[56] As a result, according to these legal scholars, the limits of contractual freedom and party autonomy are not only determined by the mandatory rules that the legislator has developed within the framework of the different property rights themselves, but also by the frame itself, by the (legal) definition of the different (property) rights and the legal structure that results from it.[57] Parties are not only bound by rules of mandatory law, but also run the risk of recharacterization if they modulate their agreement in such a way that it no longer corresponds with the nature of the specific (property) right they choose and/or the characteristic or essential elements that follow from the definition of the legal concept itself.[58] Such an approach would be essential to legal certainty.[59]

This (second) line of thinking is particularly present in the context of real servitudes. While the Civil code does not contain many mandatory provisions, the limitation of contractual freedom and party autonomy results from the definition of the concept 'real servitude' itself and the essential characteristics that result from it.[60] If one of these essential characteristics is not met, the agreement is not necessarily null and void, but could be recharacterized as an (unnamed) personal right.[61]

---

55 Sagaert, 2014, nos. 482 and 698.

56 E. Sanzot, *Les droits réels démembrés: aspects civils, fiscaux, comptables et financiers*, Brussels, Larcier, p. 32, no. 6; P. Lecocq, 'Superficie, emphytéose et constructions' *in* P. Lecocq, B. Tilleman & A. Verbeke (Eds.), *Zakenrecht*, Bruges, die Keure, 2005A, p. 288-289, no. 3; P. Lecocq, 'Superficie, servitude et interprétation: une anecdote' *in* C. Biquet-Mathieu, A. Deliège, P. Lecocq, Y.-H. Leleu & M. Vanwijck-Alexandre (Eds.), *Liber amicorum Paul Delnoy*, Brussels, De Boeck & Larcier, 2005B, p. 965-967, no. 2; C. Renard, 'La renunciation à l'accession' (annotation under cass. 13 May 1970), *RCJB*, 1980, p. 22. France: Tadros, 2015, p. 88, no. 3.

57 Lecocq, 2005A, p. 288, no. 3; De Montpellier, 2003, p. 11, no. 18.

58 Sanzot, p. 32, no. 6; De Montpellier, 2003, p. 11, no. 18. See Renard, 1980, p. 22: "*Le fait que, sauf sur le point de la durée, la règlementation de la superficie n'est pas impérative, n'y change rien. La définition d'une structure est intangible même si son organisation est laissée au libre jeu des conventions particulières. Le respect du content des concepts – de leur ipséité – est une exigence première de l'ordre juridique. Baptiser carpe le lapin, prêt le louage, est une imposture et non l'exercice de l'autonomie de la volonté*".

59 Lecocq, 2005B, p. 966, no. 2. See also F. Werdefroy, 'Beschouwingen over de onroerende natrekking, het recht van erfpacht, het recht van opstal, en het verlof tot bouwen', *TPR*, 1983, p. 294, no. 1.

60 Tadros, 2015, p. 94, no. 16. – The characterization as a real servitudes requires a burden on a piece of land (1) for the benefit of another piece of land (2), while both pieces of land belong to different owners (3) (see *i.a.* Belgium: Sagaert, 2014, p. 458-469, nos. 563-575. France: Tadros, 2015, p. 93, no. 14.

61 Sagaert, 2014, p. 469-470, no. 576.

4.2 *Nuancing (the Role in the Characterization Process of) Typenzwang*

Whatever position one is inclined to take, the question remains how a judge will decide on the proper characterization of an agreement granting a right to use. Although the distinction between the different rights to use is of major importance, it is not (always) easy to make.[62] For instance, how will the judge in a specific case decide on characterization of the agreement as an *emphyteusis* or a lease?

To distinguish a lease from an *emphyteusis* (or other property rights), legal scholars often (simply) refer to the proprietary or personal nature of the right to use in question.[63] They refer to *Typenzwang*, which is still relatively strong in Belgian law, although some legal scholars doubt it (still) has a sufficient (legal) ground.[64] Legal scholars (often) also give other differences, but many of these simply refer back to the difference between property and personal rights. E.g.: the fact that the owner has positive obligations (lease) or only negative obligations (*emphyteusis, superficies* or *usufruct*);[65] the fact that a lease has a movable nature, while the nature of a *usufruct* depends on the object of the right; the fact that the holder of an *emphyteusis, superficies* or *usufruct* can mortgage the right, while the holder of a lease does not have that possibility (movable nature); the fact that the holder of an *emphyteusis, superficies* or *usufruct* can transfer the right, while the holder of a lease (in principle) does not have that right.[66]

While the proprietary or personal nature as such – as well as the aforementioned differences that result from it – is of major importance, it does not help to properly characterize a given agreement. In fact, the proprietary or personal nature is a direct *consequence* of the (re)characterization, rather than a judicial standard. In order to be relevant in the characterization process, the proprietary or personal nature of the right to use in question needs to be expressed either internally, within the agreement, or externally, outside the agreement. Internal expression could take the form of a certain clause inserted in the agreement.[67] For example, when parties stipulate that the holder of the right to use can mortgage his right, this clause refers to the proprietary character of the right to use.[68] If

62 See De Montpellier, 2003, p. 13, no. 23. Specifically when the difference between a (long term) lease and an *emphyteusis* is concerned: see S. Van Erp & B. Akkermans (eds.), *Cases, materials and text on national, supranational and international property law*, Oxford, Hart, 2012, p. 273.

63 Sagaert, 2014, pp. 390-391, no. 479, pp. 560-561, no. 696, 622, no. 788; De Montpellier, 2003, p. 15, no. 28, 25, no. 49; Vits, 1996, p. 35, no. 107; Donnay, 1974, pp. 217-218, no. 6; H. De Page & R. Dekkers, *Traité élémentaire de droit civil belge*, VI, Brussels, Bruylant, 1953, p. 155, no. 190. See also trib. Gent 14 July 1950, *JT* 1950, 592; trib. Dendermonde 16 June 1934, *Pas.*, 1935, I, 126.

64 See *i.a.* Vincent Sagaert, "Het goederenrecht als open systeem van verbintenissen?" [2005] TPR 983-1080.

65 De Montpellier, 2003, p. 13, no. 22; Donnay, 1974, p. 218, no. 6; De Page & Dekkers, 1953, p. 155, no. 190.

66 Donnay, 1974, p. 218, no. 7; H. De Page, *Traité élémentaire de droit civil belge*, IV, Brussels, Bruylant, 1972, p. 496, no. 487.

67 See De Montpellier, 2003, p. 13, no. 23.

68 J. Vankerckhove, *Le louage des choses. I. Les beaux en general*, IV, Brussels, Larcier, 2000, p. 19, no. 34.

parties stipulate that the owner undertakes to allow the holder to enjoy a right to use the good, such a clause would refer to the personal character of the right to use. An example of an external expression is the way parties act after concluding the agreement (*cf. infra*). However, even if (internally or externally) expressed, the proprietary or personal nature of the right to use only categorizes the agreement as either *a* property or *a* personal right to use, but does not lead us to the specific characterization.

5 General Remarks Concerning Characterization of Agreements

As property law does not contain any specific rules, and the *numerus clausus* does not provide a clear answer, the characterization of (property and personal) rights to use is governed by the general principles concerning the characterization of agreements. To determine which criteria can be upheld to characterize an agreement, it is useful to recall the basic principles when it comes to characterizing an agreement.

5.1 *The Characterization as a Search for the Parties' Common Intention*

The determination of the proper characterization of the agreement comes down to a search for the parties' *common*[69] intention, a search for what they had in mind and what they intended.[70] The importance of the parties' common intention in the characterization process can be explained by referring to the basic principles of party autonomy and contractual freedom.[71] Subject to public policy (*ordre public*) and accepted principles of morality, parties are in principle free to include any clauses, any rights and obligations in their agreement to shape the legal operation or economic purpose they have in mind.

69 A unilateral intention of one of the parties will not be decisive in the characterization process, as this would seriously undermine the principle of *pacta sunt servanda* (Henry, 1992, p. 93-94, no. 80).

70 Belgium: see Kruishoutem, 1950, p. 177; Van Ommeslaghe, 2013, p. 638, no. 407; P. Wéry, *Droit des obligations, I, Théorie générale du contrat*, Brussels, Larcier, 2010, p. 376, no. 433. France: Cass. Civ. 3e 21 November 1969, *Bull. Civ.* III, n° 744, 564. Quebec: *Carignan c. La visitation de Champlain (Municipalité)*, (1996), J.Q. n° 3964, par. 37 (C.A.) (LN/QL). The Netherlands: M. Hinskens-Van Neck & L. Siemerink, 'Gemengde overeenkomsten. De betekenis van art. 6.215 BW in de praktijk: kwalificatie van overeenkomsten', *MvV*, 2012, p. 5.

71 See Hinskens-Van Neck & Siemerink, 2012, p. 5.

5.2 The Moment of Conclusion as Reference Point

The proper characterization of the agreement is determined by the parties' common intention *at the moment of conclusion* of the agreement.[72] As a result, changed circumstances or behavior, or any element contradicting the characterization at a later stage, cannot in itself justify a recharacterization.

5.3 Necessary Objectification of the Parties' Common Intention

The characterization process must primarily rely on objective, verifiable criteria or elements which must be the same for every agreement (of the same type).[73] In principle,[74] a pure subjective common intention is not taken into account. The (subjective) parties' common intention must be objectified. It must be expressed either internally or externally.[75] This requirement cannot only be explained by the importance of the characterization (process) in a legal system, but also by the basic principles of legal certainty, foreseeability and coherence of the legal system.[76] These principles require that the characterization process is based on objective (characterization) criteria. Relying on the mere subjective and non-expressed parties' intention would lead to legal chaos and legal uncertainty.[77]

---

72 Belgium: Kruishoutem, 1950, 177. France: Cass. Civ. 3^{e} 21 November 1969, *Bull. Civ.* III, n° 744, 564; Ghestin, Jamin & Billiau, 2001, p. 143-144, no. 118. See also Henry, 1992, p. 94, no. 80. Quebec: *Ameublement 640 inc. c. Meubles Canadel inc.*, J.E. 2001-1167, par. 20 (C.S.), REJB 2001-24923; *P.M.R. (Succession de) c. C.G.*, (2001) R.J.Q. 1542, par. 8 (C.S.), (2001) J.Q. n0 2958 (LN/QL). See also Fréchette, 2010, p. 132. The Netherlands: Hinskens-Van Neck & Siemerink, 2012, 5.

73 See *i.e.* also F. Collart Dutilleul & P. Delebecque, *Contrats civils et commerciaux*, Paris, Dalloz, 2015, p. 31, no. 25. Fréchette, 2010, p. 117, 145.

74 That does not mean that the subjective common intention can never be relevant in the characterization process. It can however not be the principal characterization criterion. However, the subjective common intention of the parties – even if not properly and clearly expressed – can be relevant or even decisive when the objective characterization criteria have narrowed the potential characterizations down, for instance, in order to decide whether a given agreement is either a loan or a gift. See Ghestin, Jamin & Billiau, 2001, pp. 112-117.

75 *Carignan c. La Visitation de Champlain (Municipalité)*, 1996, J.Q. n° 3964, par. 37; Fréchette, 2010, pp. 145-146.

76 France: Ghestin, Jamin & Billiau, 2001, p. 114, no. 92. Quebec: Fréchette, 2010, p. 145.

77 Fréchette, 2010, p. 145. The same substantive agreement would one time be characterized as X and on another occasion as Y, depending on the mere subjective mindset of the parties to the agreement (Henry, 1992, p. 64, no. 51).

5.4 *The Objectification of the Parties' Common Intention Can Be Found (Primarily) in Intrinsic and (Secondarily) in Extrinsic Elements*

When determining the characterization of the agreement, the judge may take into account both the intrinsic and the extrinsic elements of the agreement.[78] The intrinsic elements are those that can be found *in* the agreement, in the *instrumentum* itself (the terms, clauses, obligations etc. contained therein).[79] The extrinsic elements are those that can only be found outside the *instrumentum* (e.g. pre-contractual documents, the manner in which the agreement is performed etc.).[80]

In the characterization process, priority is given to intrinsic elements.[81] In principle, extrinsic elements that can supplement and – depending on the circumstances – even contradict the intrinsic elements, must only be considered if the intrinsic elements cannot give one hundred percent certainty as to the proper characterization of the agreement. These extrinsic elements may be indicative for the parties' common intention and – in addition to other elements – even decisive in the characterization process, but do not allow as such, separately and independently, and in a general way, to determine the proper characterization of the agreement.[82]

6 In Search of the Primary Characterization Criterion

The basic principles of legal certainty, foreseeability and coherence of the legal system are served if the characterization process is, for each agreement, always and primarily based on the same (characterization) criterion. This primary characterization criterion should be applied to each given agreement and should ideally allow (in as many cases as possible) to determine the proper characterization of the agreement in itself, or at least reduce the number of potential characterizations to a minimum. The above-mentioned basic principles

78 Belgium: Cass. 3 January 1997, *Pas.*, 1997, I, 4; Cass. 22 October 1982, *Pas.*, 1983, I, 256; Liège 6 June 2011, *TBBR*, 2015, 306; Y. Ninane, 'La requalification du contrat' *in* P. Jadoul (Ed.), *Obligations. Traité théorique et pratique*, Mechelen, Kluwer, 2007, II.1.5-52. France: M. Fabre-Magnan, *Droit des obligations. 1 – Contrat et engagement unilateral*, Paris, PUF, 2016, p. 206, no. 177. Quebec: Fréchette, 2010, p. 117, 132-133.

79 See Quebec: Fréchette, 2010, p. 132.

80 Henry, 1992, p. 93 ff., nos. 80 ff.

81 France: Henry, 1992, p. 93-94, no. 80. See also Fabre-Magnan, 2016, p. 206, no. 177. Quebec: Fréchette, 2010, p. 132. The primacy of intrinsic over extrinsic elements partly results from the priority of objective over subjective elements in the characterization process. While intrinsic elements are objectified and necessarily have approval of all contracting parties because they are found in the *instrumentum* itself, that is not necessarily the same for extrinsic elements. Moreover, intrinsic elements necessarily reflect the parties' intention at the moment of concluding the agreement. That is not necessarily also true for extrinsic elements (e.g. *pre*-contractual documents, conduct of parties *after* conclusion of the agreement).

82 France: Henry, 1992, pp. 93-94, no. 80. Quebec: Fréchette, 2010, p. 132, footnote 64.

of the characterization process allow to determine the requirements that this primary characterization criterion should meet.

6.1 The Requirements for the Primary Characterization Criterion

6.1.1 Permanent

In order to qualify as the primary characterization criterion, this criterion must be permanent and not merely occasional. As it should allow the proper characterization of the agreement in itself to be selected, or to at least reduce the number of potential characterizations to a minimum, it goes without saying that it must be an element or criterion that is present in each and every agreement. This requirement of permanency has as a result that so-called occasional or accidental characterization criteria cannot be upheld as the primary characterization criterion, as these criteria can only be found in some specific contracts, depending on the specific circumstances. They do not have as primary objective giving the proper characterization to an agreement, but serve another specific objective.[83] An example of such an occasional or accidental criterion is the form of the agreement.

In the context of (characterization of) rights to use, the form seems to play an important role. The fact parties opted for a notarial deed serves as an indication that they wanted to create a property – and not a personal – right to use. This can be explained by the fact that property rights must be published, and that this requires an authentic deed.[84] Conversely, the fact that parties did not use a notarial but merely a private deed serves as an indication that they wanted to create a 'mere' personal right to use.

The role of the form of the agreement must however be nuanced. First, the form can at best be a guiding or orientating criterion – merely an element in the general assessment – and is by no means in itself decisive for the characterization of the agreement. Moreover, nothing prevents parties from choosing the notarial form for a mere personal right to use. Furthermore, in several legal systems (e.g. the Belgian[85] and French[86]), any lease concluded for a certain term (*i.e.* more than 9 years in Belgium and more than 12 years in France) – albeit being a personal right – must also be published. Hence, the notarial form is a guiding or orientating characterization criterion for agreements concluded for maximum

83 Such as providing a specific protection to one of the contracting parties, subjecting the agreement to a specific legal regime etc.: see Ghestin, Jamin & Billiau, 2001, p. 88, no. 68.

84 E.g. in Belgian law, any agreement transferring or designating a property right needs to be transcribed into the mortgage register, and only an authentic deed can be transcribed in this register (art. 1 of the Belgian Mortgage Act). A similar publication requirement is present in Dutch law (art. 3:10 and 3:88-89 NBW). The same is true in French law (art. 28, 1° a) Décret n°55-22 du 4 janvier 1955 portant réforme de la publicité foncière).

85 Art. 1, second paragraph of the Belgian Mortgage Act of 16 December 1851, *BS* 22 December 1851.

86 Art. 28, 1° b) of the French Décret n°55-22 du 4 janvier 1955 portant réforme de la publicité foncière.

9 respectively 12 years only. A lease concluded for more than 9 or 12 years respectively must also be published, and thus requires an authentic deed. As a result, the form can in principle not play a role in case there is any doubt between characterization as either a lease or an *emphyteusis*. If the contract is concluded for 9 or 12 years respectively or less, it cannot be characterized as *emphyteusis (bail emphytéotique)* (a violation of the minimum duration). If the contract was concluded for 27 years[87] respectively 18 years[88] or longer, the agreement would in any case (lease or *emphyteusis*) require a notarial deed in order to be published. In case the characterization as another property right (other than an *emphyteusis*) *versus* a lease is on the table, the form might still play a role,[89] albeit a rather limited role.

The importance of the form has yet to be nuanced from another point of view. The fact that parties opted for a private deed (and not a notarial deed) does not necessarily mean that the characterization as a property right has to be rejected. Publication – which presupposes an authentic deed – is no validity requirement, but is only required to make the agreement effective against third parties.[90] Without publication, a property right remains a property right, although the holder of the right will not enjoy the attributes attached to the characterization as a property right (right to follow, protection against insolvency etc.). Nevertheless, since the main reason for establishing a property and not a personal right precisely lies in these attributes, the fact whether or not the parties opted for a notarial deed serves as a relatively important indication for whether or not they wanted to establish a property right. The fact that parties did not opt for a notarial deed, and consequently the agreement was not published, makes it unlikely that they intended to create a property right, as they would miss out on the most important advantages connected to that characterization as a property right.[91] The (lack of) notarial form – as well as the (lack of) publication – has on several occasions been taken into account in Belgian case law to decide on the characterization as either an *emphyteusis* or a lease.[92]

---

87 27 years is the minimum duration of an *emphyteusis* according to Belgian law (article 2 of the Belgian *Emphyteusis* Act).

88 18 years is the minimum duration of an *emphyteusis (bail emphytéotique)* according to French law (article L451-1 of the French Code rural et de la pêche maritime).

89 An *emphyteusis* is the only property right for which a minimum duration is applicable (in Belgian and French law). Note that for example in Dutch law, no minimum duration is applicable to an *emphyteusis* (art. 5:86 NBW).

90 See trib. Kortrijk 18 April 1891, *Pand.pér.*, 1891, 383.

91 This was also taken into consideration by the tribunal of Kortrijk when deciding whether a given agreement should be considered as an *emphyteusis, superficies* or a lease: "*Attendu qu'à la vérité la transcription [...] prescrite par la loi hypothécaire, n'a pour but que de garantir les droits des tiers qui contractent de bonne foi et n'a aucune influence sur la validité du contrat en ce qui concerne les parties contractantes, mais que celui qui acquiert un droit d'emphytéose ou de superficie n'en a pas moins le plus grand intérêt à faire transcrire son titre afin de se garantir contre toute revendication*" (trib. Kortrijk 18 April 1891, *Pand.pér.*, 1891, 383).

92 See trib. Bruges 24 December 2007, *RGEN*, 2008, 306; trib. Dendermonde 26 February 1959, *RW*, 1958-59, 1717; JP Hamoir 26 March 1987, *JJP*, 1988, 54.

6.1.2 Objective

As the characterization of the agreement is guided by the parties' common intention (*cf. supra*), the parties' will or intention plays an important role in the characterization process. The agreement is the direct result of the meeting of the will of the contracting parties. However, the characterization process cannot primarily rely on subjectively colored criteria as the outcome of the same set of facts could then differ depending on the subjective attitude on the part of the parties (which third parties do not (necessarily) know of). The basic principles of legal certainty, equality, foreseeability and coherence of the legal system require that the same set of facts, the same factual situation, lead to the same legal consequences. Equal situations must be treated equally, unequal situations unequally. Therefore, a 'publication', an objectification or an expression of the subjective mindset of the parties (their common intention) is necessary. The characterization process must (primarily) be based on objective criteria.[93]

Nevertheless, the subjective will of the parties cannot be left entirely out of the equation. After all, it is that subjective will on the part of each party that encourages them to conclude the agreement, which in turn serves as the 'engine' to fulfil this subjective will. (Purely) subjective elements may be complementary to other objective primary and secondary characterization criteria, but in principle cannot as such determine the characterization of the agreement.[94] In some (context- or contract-specific) cases, the (pure) subjective intention will be determinant for the characterization of the agreement, after the application of the primary characterization criterion has narrowed the potential characterizations down to a minimum.[95]

6.1.3 Intrinsic

Thirdly, the primary characterization criterion must be an intrinsic element. As explained above, the characterization process should first and foremost rely on intrinsic elements. If this primary intrinsic criterion is insufficient to determine the characterization, then (and only then) secondary characterization criteria must be resorted to, which (can) include extrinsic elements of the agreement.

An example of such an extrinsic element is pre-contractual documentation (a draft agreement, e-mail correspondence on negotiations leading up to the agreement etc.). Since these documents are not intrinsic, they cannot be considered the primary characterization criterion.[96] However, the judge can take these pre-contractual documents into account,

93 Fréchette, 2010, p. 117, 144 ff. See also Collart Dutilleul & Delebecque, 2015, p. 31, no. 25.

94 Ghestin, Jamin & Billiau, 2001, p. 114-116, nos. 92-93.

95 To decide whether an agreement must be characterized as a gift or a loan, the pure subjective will of the parties (the *animus donandi*) will be the (only) relevant – and decisive – characterization criterion (see Quebec: Fréchette, 2010, p. 136. France: Ghestin, Jamin & Billiau, 2001, p. 116, no. 94).

96 Henry, 1992, p. 93-94, no. 80.

but only as either a secondary positive (indicating a certain characterization)[97] or negative (ruling out a certain characterization)[98] criterion.

Another example of an extrinsic element that the judge may take into account when determining the proper characterization is the manner in which the parties have – *in tempore non suspecto* – performed or implemented the (obligations arising or resulting from the) agreement.[99] The parties' behavior after conclusion of the agreement may help to determine their common intention at the time of conclusion of the contract (as a secondary characterization criterion),[100] but cannot in itself determine the proper characterization.[101]

6.1.4 Sufficiently Specific and Selective

As a last requirement, the primary characterization criterion must be sufficiently specific and selective, without however losing its permanent character. This follows from the idea that the primary characterization criterion should (ideally) allow to select the proper

97 See e.g. JP Anderlecht 29 July 1999, unpublished, where the judge took into account the fact that the claimant from the beginning and before signing the agreement had insisted in a letter and some sort of draft agreement to conclude an *emphyteusis*, in order to decide that the agreement was an *emphyteusis* and not a commercial lease.

98 E.g. The court of appeal of Quebec denied the characterization of an agreement as an *emphyteusis* after it compared a pre-contractual document, a draft of the agreement, with the agreement actually concluded by the parties and determined that several changes were made to this draft agreement: "*Il faut souligner que les parties avaient d'abord envisagé de conclure un bail emphytéotique et qu'un projet en ce sens avait été préparé.* [...] *Le bail intervenu entre les parties le 23 octobre 1981, comportait cependant certaines modifications par rapport au projet de bail*" (*Carignan* c. *La visitation de Champlain (Municipalité)*, [1996], J.Q. n° 3964, par. 38 (C.A.) (LN/QL)).

99 Belgium: See Cass. 12 June 1986, *Pas.*, 1986, I, 1284. See also JP Anderlecht 29 July 1999, unpublished. W. van Eeckhoutte, ''Gezag' in de cassatierechtspraak', *NJW*, 2005, p. 10, no. 27; Cornelis, 2000, p. 275; W. Van Gerven & S. Covemaeker, *Verbintenissenrecht*, Leuven, Acco, 2001, p. 57. The Netherlands: Hinskens-Van Neck & Siemerink, 2012, p. 5.

100 France: Henry, 1992, p. 96, no. 80; Terré, 1957, p. 317, no. 365. Quebec: Fréchette, 2010, p. 132, footnote 64.

101 Besides the behavior of the parties after conclusion of the agreement being an extrinsic element, there is also a problem of sequentiality: theoretically, the question of the proper characterization and the answer thereto precedes the performance of the agreement. This element thus does not reveal itself at the relevant point of reference to attribute the proper characterization to the agreement (*i.e.* the time the agreement is concluded (*cf. supra*)). The performance of the agreement necessarily commences *after* the contract has been concluded. One could argue that the criterion of the manner in which parties perform(ed) the agreement also fails to fulfill the necessary requirement of permanence, as the performance takes place *after* the relevant reference point for determining the characterization of the agreement (*i.e.* the time the agreement is concluded). In practice, however, the issue of the proper characterization of the agreement usually only arises at the moment a dispute arises between the contracting parties, thus after the implementation of the agreement has begun. From the foregoing it can be deduced that the manner of performance of the agreement is a more important element in the characterization process depending on whether this performance is closer to the time of conclusion of the agreement. If the implementation started (almost) immediately after conclusion of the contract, this implementation and the moment of assessment of the proper characterization of the agreement (almost) coincide.

characterization of the agreement in itself. However, in a (large) number of cases (an) additional criterion (criteria) will be needed to select the proper characterization amongst the potential characterizations retained on the basis of the primary characterization criterion. Nonetheless, the primary characterization criterion must be sufficiently specific and selective in order to minimize this number of potential characterizations.

6.2 *The Obligations That Result from the Agreement as Primary Characterization Criterion?*

In a legal system characterized by party autonomy and contractual freedom, giving priority to intrinsic over extrinsic elements, it is preferable to look at the obligations that parties included in their agreement to determine the parties' common intention.[102] The intention of the parties is directly apparent from the (principal or characteristic) obligations that each party takes on.[103] The obligations arising or resulting from the agreement form a permanent characterization criterion. Each agreement consists of a(n) (set of) obligation(s). Moreover, the obligations resulting from the agreement serve as an intrinsic (contained in the agreement itself) and objective reflection of the (subjective) parties' common intention. A characterization process that departs from the obligations resulting from the agreement fulfills the necessary guarantees of foreseeability, legal certainty and coherence of the legal system.[104] In addition – and subordinate to the intrinsic expression – the parties' common intention can be expressed extrinsically (e.g. by the manner in which the parties have implemented the agreement).[105]

While fulfilling the first three requirements (permanent, objective and intrinsic), the obligations resulting from the agreement do not seem to be sufficiently specific and selective in order to qualify as primary characterization criterion. However, the condition of sufficient specificity and selectivity is achieved by taking into consideration that:

1. for the purpose of characterizing an agreement not all obligations must be taken into account (on an equal footing).[106] Within the framework of an agreement, a hierarchy can in principle be established between the obligations that result from it.[107] In principle,

102 See Kruishoutem, 1950, p. 177: "*Qu'en vue de résoudre le problème, il importe [...] de rechercher la commune intention des parties contractantes, et de retenir dans le contrat lui-même la nature des droits et obligations qui y sont stipulés*". France: Fabre-Magnan, 2016, p. 206, no. 177; Ancel, 2002, p. 4, no. 4: "*À une vision très subjectiviste du contrat – rencontre de volontés, source de droits personnels –, succède ainsi une conception plus objective, qu'atteste la prestation caractéristique*".

103 See also Ancel, 2002, p. 7, no. 9.

104 Quebec: Fréchette, 2010, p. 136. See also France: Ancel, 2002, pp. 4 and 7-8, nos. 4 and 11.

105 See also K. Nevens, *De arbeidsrelatie, de zelfstandige en de ondernemer*, Bruges, die Keure, 2011, p. 147-149, nos. 209-212.

106 Ghestin, Jamin & Billiau, 2001, p. 96, no. 75.

107 Fréchette, 2010, p. 136.

the characterization of the agreement is guided and determined by the principal obligations that result from it;[108]

2. an agreement is not merely the sum of the individual obligations. In order to attribute the proper characterization to the agreement, it is not sufficient to analyze each obligation separately and individually and to decide on the principal or accessory nature thereof. The analysis of the different individual obligations of the agreement may very well lead to the conclusion that the agreement contains different principal obligations, which refer to different named contracts (*i.e.* characterizations). It is therefore necessary to also examine the relationship and coherence, the link between these obligations.

7 The Internal and External Structure of the Agreement

The determination of the proper characterization of the agreement takes place in two steps. In the first phase (A), the internal structure of the agreement must be determined. The agreement is looked at from a frog's perspective. We walk through the agreement, encountering the different obligations included therein, and distinguish the principal obligations from the accessory obligations of the agreement. In a second phase (B), the external structure of the agreement must be determined. Once the hierarchy between the various obligations included in the agreement has been determined (first phase), the agreement must be looked at from a bird's-eye-view. The agreement is no longer seen as a sum of individual obligations, but as a (coherent) whole. In this phase, it is examined and established how these different individual obligations relate to each other.

7.1 Internal Structure of the Agreement: Principal versus Accessory Obligations

An agreement consists of a set of obligations that result from the meeting of the parties' will. Since it is practically impossible to take all obligations arising from the agreement into account to determine the proper characterization of the agreement, a distinction must be made between the principal obligations and the other accessory obligations.[109] Some obligations are – in light of the agreement at hand – more important than others. These principal obligations are considered to be dominant with regard to the other (accessory) obligations of the agreement.[110] It is a matter of adding a hierarchy. The characterization

108 France: Ghestin, Jamin & Billiau, 2001, p. 97, no. 75. See also J. Raynard & J.-B. Seube, *Droit civil. Contrats spéciaux*, Paris, LexisNexis, 2015, p. 14, no. 15. Quebec: Fréchette, 2010, p. 136.

109 Ghestin, Jamin & Billiau, 2001, p. 96, no. 75; Henry, 1992, p. 396, no. 341.

110 Ancel, 2002, p. 5, no. 5.

process is – logically – controlled by the obligation(s) on top of this hierarchy.[111] The principal obligations are directly decisive for the proper characterization of the agreement, while the accessory obligations – in principle – have no role to play in the characterization process.[112]

7.1.1 The Principal Obligation(s)

7.1.1.1 Notion

While legal scholars disagree on a general definition of the principal obligation for each agreement,[113] there is consensus on two guidelines that help to detect the principal obligation of an agreement:[114]

1. The principal obligation can be modulated and its scope can be restricted to a limited extent, but it cannot be excluded, nor can its scope be limited to the extent it is deprived of any actual content, without this resulting in the denaturation and/or recharacterization of the agreement.[115]
2. Second, the purpose of the principal obligation is not only to define, but also to distinguish and recognize.[116] Therefore, a monetary obligation can – in principle – not be retained as the principal obligation of the agreement, as such an obligation does not sufficiently differentiate between different (named) contracts.[117] However, a monetary obligation can play a(n important) role as a (decisive) context- or contract-specific characterization criterion once the potential characterizations have been narrowed

111 Fréchette, 2010, p. 136.

112 France: Raynard & Seube, 2015, p. 4, no. 5; Malaurie, Gautier & Aynès, 2014, p. 11, no. 12; Ghestin, Jamin & Billiau, 2001, p. 97, no. 75; Henry, 1992, p. 557, no. 504; Goubeaux, 1969, p. 219, no. 147.

113 Some legal scholars assimilate the concept with (the since 2016 in French law abolished) civil law notion of '*la cause*' of the agreement (see P. Jestaz, 'L'obligation et la sanction: la recherche de l'obligation fondamentale' *in Mélanges offerts à Pierre Raynaud*, Paris, Dalloz, 1985, p. 273-280). Others identify the concept with the characteristic performance of the agreement, which in turn would come down to the civil law notion of either the 'subject-matter' or 'object' of the agreement or '*la cause*' of the agreement (see Delebecque & Pansier, 2010, p. 198, no. 323). Others describe the principal obligation as the obligation without which the parties would have never given their consent (J. Mestre, 'Obligations et contrats spéciaux. Obligations en general' *RTD civ.*, 1999, p. 623) or the agreement has no *raison d'être* (Delebecque & Pansier, 2010, p. 198, no. 325).

114 Fréchette, 2010, p. 140.

115 France: N. Cardoso-Roulot, *Les obligations essentielles en droit privé des contrats*, Paris, L'Harmattan, 2008, p. 63, no. 35; Jestaz, 1985, p. 282. Quebec: Fréchette, 2010, p. 141.

116 Cardoso-Roulot, 2008, p. 67-68, no. 41.

117 France: Raynard & Seube, 2015, p. 4, no. 5: Malaurie, Gautier & Aynès, 2014, p. 11, no. 12; P. Malaurie, L. Aynès and P. Stoffel-Munck, *Les obligations*, Paris, LGDJ, 2013, 186, no. 407; Delebecque & Pansier, 2010, p. 198, no. 323; P.-H. Antonmattei & J. Raynard, *Droit civil. Contrats spéciaux*, Paris, LexisNexis/Litec, 2007, p. 4; Ancel, 2002, p. 6, no. 8; Overstake, 1969, p. 32. Quebec: Fréchette, 2010, p. 141. E.g. the obligation to pay a sum of money as such does not allow to distinguish an *emphyteusis* from a lease.

down on the basis of the principal obligation.[118] (Lack of) a monetary obligation can be essential for a specific characterization.[119]

From this second guideline, it results that in contracts that contain a monetary obligation as the most important (and in this sense as the principal) obligation of one of the contracting parties, the principal obligation for characterization purposes is the principal obligation of the debtor who is not the debtor of the monetary obligation.[120] This reasoning can be extended to agreements without a monetary obligation: for characterization purposes, the principal obligation is the principal obligation of the party who is not the party who would normally have been the debtor of the monetary obligation if the agreement would have included a monetary obligation.[121]

7.1.1.2 *The Principal Obligation Is Generally Specified by the Legislator?*

As the principal obligation is generally specified by the legislator,[122] and is thus set out in the law, in the context of rights to use the *numerus clausus* – implying all property rights have a named regime developed by the legislator[123] (*Typenzwang*) – (again) seems to make it easy to determine the proper characterization of a contract granting a (property) right to use. However, three main problems arise:

1. The legislator does not always properly determine the obligations that are principal to a given (property) right to use and legal scholars and case law are often divergent on this point;[124]
2. The fact that an agreement complies with the principal obligation of a specific (property) right to use does not necessarily mean that it cannot comply with those of another (property) right to use (see example above). Principal obligations are not always exclusive to one contract;

118 M.-P. Baudin-Maurin, 'Pour une approche empirique de la notion d'obligations essentielle du contrat (à partir de l'exemple du contrat *Chronopost*)', *RRJ*, 2002, p. 1860. See also Fréchette, 2010, p. 141; Malaurie, Gautier & Aynès, 2014, p. 11, no. 12.

119 Malaurie, Gautier & Aynès, 2014, p. 11, no. 12.

120 Raynard & Seube, 2015, p. 4, no. 5; Delebecque & Pansier, 2010, p. 198, no. 323; Ancel, 2002, p. 6, no. 8; Overstake, 1969, p. 32.

121 Overstake, 1969, p. 32.

122 France: Ghestin, Jamin & Billiau, 2001, p. 97, no. 77. See also Bergel, 2016, p. 109, no. 60. Quebec: C. Deslauriers-Goulet, 'L'obligation essentielle dans le contrat', *Les cahiers de droit*, 2014, p. 939; Fréchette, 2010, p. 141.

123 With the exception of France where the *Cour de Cassation* has occasionally recognized a new property right (e.g. a *superficies*), in civil law systems it is only the legislator who can introduce new types of property rights (Akkermans, 2017, p. 105).

124 E.g. for an *emphyteusis*: obligation to ameliorate and pay a *modest* periodical compensation (Brussels 29 April 1914, *Pas.*, 1914, II, 204; Kruishoutem, 1950, p. 177. *Contra*: trib. Gent 14 July 1950, *Rev.prat.not.b.*, 1951, 45; trib. Dendermonde 16 June 1934, *Pas.*, 1935, I, 126).

3. Contract law acknowledges, aside from named contracts for which the legislator has developed a specific legal regime, also unnamed contracts.[125]

In the circumstances under 1. and 3., it is up to the courts to decide on the principal obligation(s) of the agreement.[126] However, as already mentioned, judges and legal scholars do not always agree on this point.

7.1.1.3 The Role of the Principal Obligation in the Characterization Process

Once the principal obligation(s) of the given agreement has (have) been determined, this (these) obligation(s) must be compared to the principal obligation(s) of the known types of agreements (*i.e.* the named contracts). If both the principal obligation(s) of the given agreement and that (those) of a named contract match, the given agreement in principle receives the characterization of the corresponding named contract.[127] Conversely, a specific characterization must be rejected as soon as (one of) the principal obligation(s) is missing in the given agreement.[128] That does not mean it must necessarily be declared null and void.[129] The judge must investigate whether the agreement can be 'saved' by means of a recharacterization;[130] whether, in view of the principal obligation(s) of the agreement, another characterization is available that allows to give (legal) effect to the parties' agreement.[131] Only if there is an irreparable discordance between the potential characterizations and the parties' common intention,[132] the agreement must be declared null and void.[133]

Determining the principal obligation allows to determine the purpose of or the objective pursued by the contracting parties (their common intention), and thus – in principle – the characterization of the agreement.[134] At least, so far as simple agreements are concerned. In a mixed agreement, the determination of the proper characterization is somewhat more complex. We will turn to this later on. Moreover, even in case of a simple agreement, the

125 Cass. 6 December 2007, *TBO*, 2008, 105 (recharacterization of a commercial lease into a right *sui* generis); trib. Brussels 16 June 1964, *JT*, 1965, 9 (characterization as right to use *sui generis*).

126 Bergel, 2016, p. 109, no. 60; Ghestin, Jamin & Billiau, 2001, p. 98-99, no. 79.

127 Ghestin, Jamin & Billiau, 2001, p. 101, no. 82.

128 Ghestin, Jamin & Billiau.

129 See J. Ghestin, G. Loiseau & Y.-M. Serinet, *La formation du contrat*, Paris, LGDJ, 2013, no. 918; Christian Larroumet, *Droit civil*, III, *Les obligations: le contrat*, Paris, Economica, 1996, 562, no. 575; J. Rochfeld, 'Cause et type du contrat', *LGDJ*, 1999, 388 ff., nos. 433 ff.

130 In France the term "*conversion par réduction*" is used (Ghestin, Jamin & Billiau, 2001, p. 102-104, no. 83).

131 Ghestin, Jamin & Billiau, 2001, p. 103, no. 83.

132 Such irreparable discordance exists for example, if the parties have indicated in the agreement which characterization they have in mind, while excluding the possibility of recharacterization in case the judge decides that the agreement must receive a characterization different from the parties' characterization.

133 Ghestin, Loiseau & Serinet, 2013, no. 918; Terré, 1957, p. 209 ff., nos. 224 ff.

134 R. Sefton-Green, *La notion d'obligation fondamentale: comparaison franco-anglaise*, Parijs, LGDJ, 2000, p. 336, no. 598.

mere determination of the principal obligation is not always enough.[135] In some cases, there is a need for additional characterization criteria.[136]

7.1.2 The Accessory Obligation(s)

The notion 'accessory obligation' is relevant from a double point of view, depending on whether the agreement is either a 'simple agreement' or a 'mixed agreement'.

In a 'simple agreement', where all obligations refer to one single reference category, one named contract, the notion allows to distinguish those obligations that directly influence the characterization (principal obligations) from those that merely modulate the applicable legal regime, but in principle do not affect the characterization (accessory obligations). Determination of the accessory obligations is said to be relatively easy in a simple agreement.[137] There are two types of accessory obligations:

1. natural obligations or elements that result from the nature of the agreement, that are part of the 'default scheme', but that can be excluded without affecting the nature of the agreement;[138] and
2. accidental obligations or elements that are not part of the 'default scheme', but are only part of the agreement if the parties have explicitly or implicitly added them to the agreement.[139,140]

The notion 'accessory obligation' has a different function in 'mixed agreement', wherein the different (principal) obligations refer to different reference categories, different named contracts.[141] Depending on the relationship between these different obligations, there are two possibilities:[142]

1. each obligation – or at least two – contained in or resulting from the agreement, and referring to or derived from different reference categories, different named contracts,

135 Raynard & Seube, 2015, p. 5, no. 5; Ancel, 2002, p. 3, no. 3.
136 Raynard & Seube, 2015.
137 Ghestin, Jamin & Billiau, 2001, p. 104, no. 85.
138 Delebecque & Pansier, 2010, p. 197, no. 319; Ghestin, Jamin & Billiau, 2001, p. 105, no. 86.
139 France: Delebecque & Pansier, 2010; Ghestin, Jamin & Billiau, 2001, p. 105, no. 86.
140 The distinction between principal and accessory obligations can in fact be brought back to the distinction Pothier made in his *Traité des obligations*, where he distinguished between: (1) elements that are the essence of the agreement, without which the agreement cannot (continue to) exist; (2) elements that follow from the nature of the agreement and that do not form part of its essence, but are part of the agreement unless the parties expressed otherwise; and (3) elements that are accidental to the agreement and that are only part of it on the condition that the parties have explicitly added them to the agreement (R. Pothier, *Traité des obligations*, II, Paris, Debure, 1761, p. 6-8, nos. 5-8). As far as the determination of the proper characterization is concerned, only the first category should be taken into account (Henry, 1992, p. 557-558, no. 504).
141 See P. Jadoul, *Obligation. Traité theorique et pratique*, Mechelen, Kluwer, 2007, II.1.2-2.
142 France: Ghestin, Jamin & Billiau, 2001, p. 106-112, nos. 87-89. Quebec: Fréchette, 2010, p. 388 ff.

is/are of equal interest and importance. The agreement must either receive a distributive characterization or a characterization as an unnamed contract (*cf. infra*); or
2. certain obligations resulting from the agreement – albeit principal and not merely accessory – in the given agreement and weighed against the other principal obligations contained therein, must nevertheless be considered accessory to one of the other principal obligations pointing to another named contract. The contract must be given a unitary characterization (*cf. infra*).[143]

While – in principle – the distributive characterization of an agreement that incorporates the obligations of several different named contracts must be the point of departure, a unitary characterization seems – for reasons of simplicity and convenience – to be preferred by Belgian, French and Quebec legal doctrine and jurisprudence.[144] In this case, the principal obligation which, in the context of the given agreement, is considered accessory to another principal obligation referring to another characterization, is not taken into account for the purpose of determining the nature of the agreement. Its role is limited to the adaptation of the legal regime applicable to the agreement.[145] The characterization of the agreement is solely determined by that principal obligation which is regarded as principal with regard to the whole of the agreement, weighed against all other (principal) obligations contained therein. Only when a unitary characterization is not possible, the judge will resort to a distributive or an unnamed characterization.[146] However, this unitary or exclusive characterization must be compatible with the facts presented to the judge. There is a danger that with an exaggerated refuge in a unitary characterization, the complex nature of the contract will be disregarded inadmissibly.[147] In Dutch law (art. 6:215 Dutch

143 Ghestin, Jamin & Billiau, 2001, p. 106, no. 87.

144 France: A. Bénabent, *Droit des* obligations, Paris, LGDJ, 2017, p. 239, no. 290; Raynard & Seube, 2015, p. 4, no. 5; Ghestin, Jamin & Billiau, 2001, p. 106, no. 87. Quebec: Fréchette, 2010, p. 382. See also Henry, 1992, p. 207, no. 167.

145 Ghestin, Jamin & Billiau, 2001, p. 106, no. 87.

146 This preference for a unitary or exclusive characterization can be explained by practical reasons: a judge confronted with a dispute between the contracting parties will much easier find the solution to the dispute if he refers to a single legal regime than if he characterizes the agreement in a distributive way or even as an unnamed contract (Fréchette, 2010, p. 382. See also Goubeaux, 1969, p. 495, no. 360). Moreover, it is argued that a distributive characterization must remain exceptional, given that such a division (*dépeçage*) can be difficult to reconcile with the objective pursued by the parties (Cruquenaire, Delforge, Durant & Wéry, 2015, p. 39, no. 17. See also De Page & Dekkers, 1953, no. 24 C. France: Bénabent, 2017, p. 239, no. 290; Raynard & Seube, 2015, p. 5, no. 5).

147 D. Roskis, 'Les limites des méthodes traditionelles de qualification contractuelle: le parrainage publicitaire', *D.*, 1999, p. 445, par. 12. See also Ghestin, Jamin & Billiau, 2001, p. 124, no. 103. Belgium: P. Brulez, *Koop en aanneming: faux amis?*, Antwerp, Intersentia, 2015, p. 90, no. 109.

civil code),[148] as well as in the *Draft Common Frame of Reference (DCFR)* (art. II.-1:107 (2)),[149] (legal) preference is given to a distributive characterization.

To determine whether an obligation – principal to a certain specific named contract – must – specifically with regard to the given agreement – be considered accessory, weighed against the other principal obligations of the agreement that point to another specific named contract, the adage *accessorium sequitur principale* is used.[150] In order to distinguish '*accessorium*' from '*principale*', traditionally – at least in the first instance – a (purely) quantitative criterion, in the form of the adage '*major pars trahit ad se minorem*', is applied.[151] Determination of the accessory or principal nature of an obligation is, in principle, done by simply comparing the (quantitative) value of these obligations.[152] The fact that a specific obligation is essential for both parties agreeing and entering into the consensus needed for the conclusion of the contract does not mean that the same obligation cannot be merely accessory for characterization purposes.[153] Qualitative equality of the obligations does not prevent the application of the *pars major*-rule.[154] Adherence to the purely objective quantitative criterion of the value of the various obligations of the agreement can however lead to artificial results.[155] The bigger the difference in value between the obligations, the more support for the strict application of this 'hard' quantitative crite-

148 Art. 6:215 DCC: "*Voldoet een overeenkomst aan de omschrijving van twee of meer door de wet geregelde bijzondere soorten van overeenkomsten, dan zijn de voor elk van die soorten gegeven bepalingen naast elkaar op de overeenkomst van toepassing, behoudens voor zover deze bepalingen niet wel verenigbaar zijn of de strekking daarvan in verband met de aard van de overeenkomst zich tegen toepassing verzet*". See P.S. Bakker, 'Samenloop bij gemengde overeenkomsten', *MvV*, 2017, 138; Hinskens-Van Neck & Siemerink, 2012, p. 4. Note that the preparatory works state that the distributive characterization applies merely as a rule of thumb, the exceptions being hardly less important than the main rule (*Parl. Gesch. BW Inv. 3, 5 en 6 Boek 6*, 1990, p. 1432. See also I.S.J. Houben, *Bijzondere overeenkomsten. Deel X. Onbenoemde overeenkomsten*, Deventer, Kluwer, 2015, p. 10, no. 10).

149 Art. II.-1:107 (2) DCFR: "*Where a contract is a mixed contract then, unless this is contrary to the nature and purpose of the contract, the rules applicable to each relevant category apply, with any appropriate adaptations, to the corresponding part of the contract and the rights and obligations arising from it*".

150 Belgium: Cruquenaire, Delforge, Durant & Wéry, 2015, p. 39, no. 17; Wéry, 2011, p. 412, no. 436. France: Ghestin, Jamin & Billiau, 2001, p. 106, no. 87.

151 Malaurie, Gautier & Aynès, 2014, p. 12, no. 13; Ghestin, Jamin & Billiau, 2001, p. 106, no. 87. See also Brulez, 2015, p. 91 ff., nos. 111 ff.; Goubeaux, 1969, p. 452 ff., nos. 329 ff.

152 Ghestin, Jamin & Billiau, 2001, p. 106, no. 87; Goubeaux, 1969, p. 465 ff., no. 338.

153 Ghestin, Jamin & Billiau, 2001, p. 106-107, no. 87; Goubeaux, 1969, p. 213, no. 142.

154 Ghestin, Jamin & Billiau, 2001, p. 106, no. 87; Goubeaux, 1969, p. 207, no. 137.

155 For example, in times labour is one of the main sources of wealth, its application means that an agreement is usually characterized as a service agreement instead of a sales contract, whereas this objective evaluation is not necessarily consistent with the subjective view of the contracting parties (See Brulez, 2015, p. 93, no. 113). Moreover, the criterion can lead to the conclusion that two similar contracts must be regarded as a service agreement on the one hand, and as a sales contract on the other hand, depending on the (objective) value of the materials used (A. Fettweis, 'L'option préliminaire: commande d'un ouvrage ou achat d'un bien à fabriquer ou à construire', *Act.dr.*, 1991, p. 866; Terré, 1957, p. 336).

rion of *pars major trahit ad se minorem*.[156] The objective and quantitative criterion of the *pars major*-rule also ignores the fact that – for the contracting parties – the value of the obligations resulting from the agreement is not always a purely economic fact and cannot always be expressed in monetary value.[157] The judge has some discretion to determine which obligations should be regarded as accessory in a specific agreement.[158] In addition to the objective quantitative criterion, there must be room for subjective criteria that influence the characterization process. The objective and quantitative *pars major*-rule must be combined with the subjective criterion of the purpose or objective pursued by the parties, their (common) intention, in order to determine whether a given obligation is either principal or merely accessory.[159] An obligation that – from an objective point of view – should be considered accessory in a specific agreement, can – by means of the parties' common intention – still have a (subjective) principal character. The question of the accessory or principal nature of an obligation is determined on the basis of the civil law notion of '*la cause*' of the agreement (*i.e.* the purpose of the agreement or the parties' determinant or decisive motives for entering into a contract).[160] Note that in 2016 the notion '*la cause*' has been abolished as a condition for a valid contract in French law.[161] However the concept '*la cause*' did not totally disappear.[162]

156 On the other hand, as the distinction in value becomes small(er), other criteria emerge to distinguish accessory from principal obligations and elements (Goubeaux, 1969, p. 466, no. 339). Some legal scholars suggest to abandon the *pars major*-rule as a general criterion, and to retain its application only for those cases in which the accessory element or obligation represents no or only a very limited value (See R. Pothier, *Traité de louage*, IV, Debure, 1765, no. 394; see Goubeaux, 1969, p. 466, footnote 29). These legal scholars suggest to only apply the *pars major*-rule if the difference in value between the principal elements or obligations on the one hand, and the accessory elements or obligations on the other hand, is so big, that the result is clear in advance (Goubeaux, 1969, p. 466, no. 339). But isn't that just moving the problem? What is a 'very limited value'? What is such a big difference in value that the result is clear in advance? A boundary will have to be drawn somewhere and that boundary or limit (e.g. $1/5^{th}$, $1/10^{th}$ etc.) is just as arbitrary as the limit that the *pars major*-rule sets at half (Goubeaux, 1969, pp. 467-468, no. 340).

157 See Henry, 1992, pp. 407-409.

158 Ghestin, Jamin & Billiau, 2001, p. 107, no. 87; Terré, 1957, p. 100, no. 102.

159 Cass. Fr. req. 25 februari 1908, *Journ. Not. Et av.*, 1908, art. 29415, 687; Ghestin, Jamin & Billiau, 2001, p. 115-116, no. 93. See also Brulez, 2015, p. 100, no. 121.

160 Henry, 1992, pp. 83 and 396, nos. 69 and 341.

161 By l'Ordonnance n° 2016-131 du 10 février 2016 portant réforme du droit des contrats, du régime général et de la preuve des obligations.

162 See J.-L. Albert & F. Collart Dutilleul, *Le contrat. Droit des obligations*, 5th ed., Paris, Dalloz, 2017, 94-96: "*Avec la réforme du droit des contrats réalisée en 2016, la cause a formellement disparu des conditions de validité du contrat (art. 1108, 1131, 1132, 1133 anciens; art. 1128 nouveau C. civ.). Mais elle n'a pas vraiment disparu du fond du droit*".

7.2 *External Structure of the Agreement: Named versus Unnamed Contracts*

An agreement is not a mere juxtaposition of the individual obligations contained therein. To determine the characterization of the agreement, the connection, the link and coherence between these different obligations must also be examined.[163] The external structure of the agreement determines whether an agreement must either be given a named (unitary or distributive) or unnamed characterization.[164]

7.2.1 Named versus Unnamed Structure of the Agreement: Notion

7.2.1.1 *Named Contract*

For a (limited) number of important and frequently used contracts, the legislator has developed its own legal regime – a framework with mandatory and non-mandatory legal rules – in law, inspired by legal practice, economic data and the presumed will of contracting parties.[165] The vast majority of the provisions within the framework of named contracts remain subject to contractual freedom.[166]

The number of named contracts has increased significantly over the years. Because of the very broad range of different named contracts, both contracting parties and judges are – in the characterization process – (unwillingly) directed towards one or another named contract.[167] Instead of starting with the determination of the principal obligation of the given agreement, there is a risk that the judge will first look at the various named contracts, select one, and apply it to the given agreement. Such a process naturally undermines contractual freedom and the possibility of creating unnamed agreements.

The increased number of named agreements has led to an increased complexity of the characterization process.[168] Not only the delimitation of the various named agreements relative to each other is difficult, but also the answer to the question whether in a specific

163 Ghestin, Jamin & Billiau, 2001, p. 117, no. 95; Terré, 1957, p. 311, no. 354. For example (see Terré, 1957, p. 311 ff., nos. 353 ff.), in order to characterize an agreement as a sales contract, three elements must be present: an object (to which the sale relates) (1); a prize (2); and a transfer of ownership (3). However, these elements are not sufficient in themselves to decide on a sales contract. A certain link or connection must also exist between these three elements. The transfer of ownership must relate to the object, while the price must be *quid pro quo*. Only if this link or connection exists between the various elements of the agreement, we can speak of a sales contract.

164 Ghestin, Jamin & Billiau, 2001, p. 117, no. 95.

165 Belgium: Cruquenaire, Delforge, Durant & Wéry, 2015, p. 19, no. 3; Wéry, 2011, p. 86, no. 66; Jadoul 2007, II.1.2-2; De Page & Dekkers, 1953, p. 11, no. 3D. France: Bénabent, 2017, p. 240, no. 292; Raynard & Seube, 2015, p. 3, no. 4; Malaurie, Gautier & Aynès, 2014, p. 3, no. 1; Malaurie, Aynès & Stoffel-Munck, 2013, p. 185, no. 407. The Netherlands Hinskens-Van Neck & Siemerink, 2012, p. 2.

166 Cruquenaire, Delforge, Durant & Wéry, 2015, p. 21, no. 4; De Page & Dekkers, 1953, 11, no. 3D.

167 Ancel, 2002, p. 100-101, no. 144.

168 J. Huet, G. Decocq, C. Grimaldi & H. Lécuyer, *Les principaux contrats spéciaux*, Paris, LGDJ, 2012, p. 24, no. 11.

case we are dealing with a specific named contract or an unnamed contract is not always straightforward.[169]

Not only has the number of *named contracts* increased, there is also an increase in the number of *mandatory* rules within the framework of these different named contracts.[170] As a result, the importance of determining the proper characterization of the agreement increases.[171] The legislator can introduce as many (mandatory) rules as he deems appropriate, without (proper) characterization these rules will serve no purpose.[172] The 'proliferation' of mandatory rules leads to several questions that do not have a straightforward answer:

1. Can – and if so to what extent can – parties reshape a certain contract in such a way that it produces equal or similar legal effects to another contract and thereby avoid application of the mandatory rules the legislator specifically developed for the second contract (*cf. infra*)?
2. Can – and if so to what extent can – parties conclude a 'neighboring' unnamed contract instead of a named contract and thereby avoid application of the mandatory rules of this named contract (*cf. infra*)?

7.2.1.2 Unnamed Contract

Ideally, for each type of agreement there would be a separate named characterization with a legal regime elaborated by the legislator.[173] However, the ingenuity of the parties (read: of their legal advisors), supported by the principle of party autonomy,[174] makes this an impossible task, utopia. In addition to the named contracts, there is a category for which the legislator did not (want to) develop a specific legal regime, which are not subject to specific statutory regulation: the unnamed contracts.[175]

7.2.2 The Characterization of the Agreement as Named or Unnamed

The importance of whether or not a named regime is available is directly related to the importance of the characterization of the agreement. In order to allow the legal rules applicable to the contract to be determined, the legislator gave a name to several (types of) agreements.[176]

---

169 Huet, Decocq, Grimaldi & Lécuyer, 2012.

170 The legislator increasingly sees the need – and increasingly seizes the opportunity – to protect certain interests, albeit an individual or the general interest, within the framework of various contracts and through these mandatory rules (Quebec: Fréchette, 2010, p. 385-386. France: Raynard & Seube, 2015, p. 7-8, nos. 8 en 10; Malaurie, Gautier & Aynès, 2014, p. 17, no. 22).

171 Raynard & Seube, 2015, p. 4, no. 5.

172 See also Terré, 1957, nos. 661-662.

173 Terré, 1957, p. 316, no. 362.

174 Jadoul, 2007, II.1.2-2.

175 Belgium: Cruquenaire, Delforge, Durant & Wéry, 2015, p. 22, no. 5; Jadoul, 2007, II.1.2-2. France: Malaurie, Gautier & Aynès, 2014, p. 5, no. 3. The Netherlands: Hinskens-Van Neck & Siemerink, 2012, p. 2.

176 Huet, Decocq, Grimaldi & Lécuyer, 2012, p. 7, no. 8. See also Raynard & Seube, 2015, p. 4, no. 5.

If the judge characterizes the agreement as a certain named contract, he must – for the resolution of the dispute between claimant and defendant – adhere to: (1) the mandatory legal rules put forward by the legislator for that specific named contract; (2) the non-mandatory legal rules laid down by the legislator for that specific named contract from which the parties did not deviate; and (3) the obligations and elements that the contracting parties have added to their agreement, insofar as these do not infringe the mandatory rules, rules of public policy (*ordre public*) and accepted principles of morality.[177] If the judge, on the other hand, concludes that the agreement must be characterized as unnamed, then it is up to the judge to determine the rights and obligations of the contracting parties.[178]

7.2.2.1 The Characterization of the Agreement as a Named Contract

Once it has been established that the obligations contained in the agreement are (potentially) in line with one or more named contracts, two hypotheses must be distinguished. The approach to the characterization problem is different in both hypotheses.

First, it is possible that the principal obligation(s) of the agreement can be reduced to one specific named contract. In such a case, the agreement will be given a unitary or an exclusive characterization. In the hypothesis that the agreement contains principal obligations that point to several different named contracts, when it is practically impossible – even after application of the adage *accessorium sequitur principale* (*cf. supra*) – or undesirable to reduce these principal obligation to one principal obligation for characterization purposes (unitary characterization), the agreement must in principle receive a distributive characterization.[179] As a result, the agreement will be divided (*dépeçage*) into different parts in function of the different principal obligations contained therein, with each part receiving its own characterization and thus its own legal regime.[180]

7.2.2.2 The Characterization of the Agreement as an Unnamed Contract

Unnamed contracts have in common that they cannot be reduced or brought back to (one of the) existing named contracts.[181] They stem from the creativity of the parties – supported by the principles of party autonomy and freedom of contract – who thereby (usually) endeavor to meet practical necessities or shortcomings in the law. There are three types of unnamed contracts.

First, an agreement is considered to be unnamed if it combines different regimes of different named contracts, while this agreement cannot be reduced or brought back to a

177 Jadoul, 2007, II.1.2-3.
178 Jadoul, 2007.
179 Belgium: see Cruquenaire, Delforge, Durant & Wéry, 2015, p. 39, no. 16. France: Collart Dutilleul & Delebecque, 2015, p. 30, 25; Ghestin, Jamin & Billiau, 2001, p. 118, no. 96.
180 Belgium: Cruquenaire, Delforge, Durant & Wéry, 2015, p. 39, no. 17. France: Bénabent, 2017, p. 239, no. 290; Raynard & Seube, 2015, p. 5, no. 5.
181 Cruquenaire, Delforge, Durant & Wéry, 2015, p. 22, no. 5.

mere *juxtaposition* of those different special legal regimes (complex unnamed contract, *innomé-alliage, l'innomé fusionné ou atypique*).[182] Because it goes beyond a mere *juxtaposition* of the various special named contracts, the agreement cannot be given a distributive named characterization. An example is the contract of leasing, which combines the named regimes of a lease and sale contract with a financing element.[183]

Secondly, a simple agreement can have an unnamed character if it shares certain characteristics or elements with a certain named contract, yet does not fulfil or lacks one or more of the essential elements required for the characterization as that specific named contract (simple unnamed contract or *l'innomé-décomposition*).[184] The agreement of *occupation à titre précaire*, which differs from a lease in the sense that it can be terminated at any time without prior notice, serves as an example.

Finally, an agreement is characterized as unnamed if it is a completely new creation of the parties, which cannot be reduced or brought back to one or more named contracts and has no connection therewith (simple unnamed contract *sui generis, l'innomé-création, l'innomé autonome ou typique*).[185] The term '*sui generis*' makes it clear that this type of agreement must be regarded as autonomous, different from the contracts that already exist.[186] An example is the joint venture agreement, whereby several companies agree to pursue a common commercial goal.[187]

The *numerus clausus* principle in property law implies that all property rights have a named legal regime (*Typenzwang*). However, the mere fact that a named regime (*in casu* a property right) exists and contains mandatory provisions does not prevent parties from concluding a 'neighboring' unnamed contract, unless that must be considered abuse of law.[188] According to Belgian law, such a contract based on or inspired by an existing property right, yet different from it, cannot itself be considered a property right (due to *Typenzwang*). The judge confronted with such an agreement must determine: (1) whether he will convert or recharacterize the agreement into one of the existing and known property rights; (2) whether he will deny the proprietary character of the agreement and consider it an unnamed personal right; or (3) whether he will declare the agreement null and void.

182 Belgium: Cruquenaire, Delforge, Durant & Wéry, 2015, p. 22, no. 5. France: Ghestin, Jamin & Billiau, 2001, p. 127, no. 104; Malaurie, Aynès & Stoffel-Munck, 2013, p. 185, no. 407; Terré, 1957, pp. 456-457, no. 569. Quebec: Fréchette, 2010, p. 411.

183 Cruquenaire, Delforge, Durant & Wéry, 2015, p. 22, no. 5.

184 Belgium: Cruquenaire, Delforge, Durant & Wéry, 2015, p. 22, no. 5. France: Ghestin, Jamin & Billiau, 2001, p. 127, no. 104; Terré, 1957, p. 456, no. 569. See also Quebec: Fréchette, 2010, p. 413.

185 Belgium: Cruquenaire, Delforge, Durant & Wéry, 2015, p. 23, no. 5. France: Malaurie, Aynès & Stoffel-Munck, 2013, p. 185, no. 407; Ghestin, Jamin & Billiau, 2001, p. 127, no. 104; Terré, 1957, p. 457, no. 569. See also J Raynard & Seube, 2015, p. 5, no. 5. Quebec: Fréchette, 2010, p. 414.

186 Ghestin, Jamin & Billiau, 2001, pp. 127-128, no. 105; Fréchette, 2010, p. 414.

187 Fréchette, 2010, p. 414.

188 Terré, 1957, no. 664. See Cass. 6 December 2007, *TBO*, 2008, 105 (recharacterization of a commercial lease into a right *sui* generis); trib. Brussels 16 June 1964, *JT*, 1965, 9 (characterization as right to use *sui generis*).

Recent developments in French and Quebec law show a tendency towards accepting unnamed *property* rights (*cf. supra*),[189] which provides for an additional consideration for the judge when coming to a decision: characterizing the agreement as an unnamed property right. However, the judge is probably well advised not to resort too easily to the characterization as an unnamed property right, because:

1. the characterization as unnamed is subsidiary. The agreement should only be characterized as unnamed if it is impossible to bring it back to one or more of the existing named contracts;[190]
2. it would render the principle of *numerus clausus de facto* inapplicable and could lead to legal uncertainty, especially when there are no clear, transparent and straightforward criteria to decide when an unnamed property right must or can be recognized.

8 Applying the Characterization Criteria on the Given Agreement

We will now apply these characterization criteria to our example of X and Y.[191] Suppose that they opted for a notarial deed. The accidental criterion of the form of the agreement (*in casu* a notarial deed) does not even serve as a guiding or orientating characterization criterion in this case as, according to Belgian law, a lease drawn up for more than 9 years also needs to be published, and thus requires a notarial deed (*cf. supra*). The four potential characterizations therefore still remain: an *emphyteusis*; a *superficies*; a *usufruct*; or a lease. The primary characterization criterion is the principal obligation of X to grant a right to use, which includes the right to build. As a result – based on this principal obligation –, the agreement can be: an *emphyteusis*; a *superficies*; a *usufruct*; but also, a lease.

Hence, even if we apply both the accidental criterion of the form of the agreement and the primary criterion of the principal obligation of the agreement to the given agreement, there are still our four original potential characterizations. Note that if it had been clear that the right to build is the key element of the agreement or that Y even has the obligation to build, then this would be a strong, potentially even a decisive, argument in favor of the characterization as a *superficies*, since the right of *superficies* is specifically created in order to allow a party to build on the land of another.[192]

189 See France. i.a. Tadros, 2015, p. 87-88, no. 2. Quebec. i.a. S. Normand, *Introduction au droit des biens*, Montréal, Wilson & Lafleur Ltée, 2014, p. 34-35, 302-303; Lafond, 2007, pp. 170-172, nos. 436-438.
190 Ghestin, Jamin & Billiau, 2001, p. 132, no. 109; Terré, 1957, p. 153, no. 565.
191 Remember that they concluded an agreement allowing Y to use a piece of land (including the right to build on it) owned by X for a period of 30 years. In turn, Y pays a monthly compensation to X.
192 See e.g. Van Erp & Akkermans, 2012, p. 284.

9 The Necessity of Secondary (Contract- or Context-specific) Characterization Criteria

The above shows that in some cases, once we have generally determined the category into which the agreement fits, we still need additional context- or contract-specific characterization criteria in order to be able to distinguish one right to use from another. The determination of the principal obligation(s) is not always sufficient to determine the proper characterization of the agreement, not even for a simple agreement.[193] For some types of agreements, such as agreements granting a right to use, the principal obligation(s) are (more or less) the same: the obligation to grant a right to use the object. Therefore, there is a need for additional – secondary – characterization criteria[194] or at least for an additional specification of the principal obligation(s) in order to determine the proper characterization of the given agreement. Certain obligations or elements that are considered accessory to the given agreement can turn out to be essential in order to characterize the agreement as contract X or Y.[195] These additional characterization criteria can either be decisive or merely guiding or orientating characterization criteria. The decisive positive characterization criteria can basically be brought back to the essential characteristics of each property or personal right to use. The applicable orientating or guiding characterization criteria will be dependent upon the context, as well as on the potential characterizations that are still left after the aforementioned general (primary and accidental) characterization criteria have been applied to the given agreement.

In what follows, I will briefly elaborate on some secondary and context- or contract-specific characterization criteria that are relevant for the characterization of rights to use.

The first element that should be taken into consideration is the (non-)retributive character of the right to use in question. As already discussed, monetary obligations cannot be upheld as the principal obligation for characterization purposes because of the lack of specificity and selectivity (*cf. supra*). That does not mean that this monetary obligation is irrelevant in the characterization process. Not only will it often serve as *a* principal obligation for one of the contracting parties – albeit not being *the* principal obligation for characterization purposes –, but it can and will in some situations be determinant for the characterization of the agreement as either contract X or contract Y.[196] For example, the monetary obligation would be a decisive characterization criterion in the situation where the potential characterizations have – on the basis of the general (additional and primary)

193 Raynard & Seube, 2015, p. 5, no. 5; Ancel, 2002, p. 3, no. 3. See also De Page, 1972, p. 496, no. 487.

194 Raynard & Seube, 2015.

195 See also Cardoso-Roulot, 2008, p. 71, no. 46.

196 The fact that a monetary obligation cannot qualify as the primary characterization criterion does not change the fact that such an obligation must be present in order to be able to attribute certain characterizations to the given agreement.

characterization criteria – been narrowed down to the characterization as either a lease (essentially retributive character) or a *commodatum* (essentially a non-retributive character). In our example of X and Y, the money payment of Y can at most be an indicative, an orientating or guiding criterion in favor of the characterization of the agreement as either a lease or an *emphyteusis* (as these contracts essentially have a retributive character, while a *usufruct* or a *superficies* have not, unless otherwise agreed).

The duration or term for which the right to use is granted can also be taken into account. If we look at the minimum duration of an *emphyteusis* in Belgian law,[197] a vast majority of legal scholars plead for an 'automatic' recharacterization into a lease in case of violation of the minimum duration.[198] A minority plead – in certain cases, depending on the circumstances – for an extension of the duration to the minimum duration.[199] Usually, a long duration is considered as orientating towards characterization as an *emphyteusis*, while a short term serves as an indication for characterization as a lease. However, nothing prevents parties from concluding a long-term lease. This was recently confirmed in a judgement of the tribunal of Henegouwen (Belgium) where the judge argued a 'residential lease' (*woninghuur*) concluded for 99 years could not be considered an *emphyteusis*, because the property tax was not imposed on the holder of the right and the agreement did not foresee rules on constructions or works established or done during the exercise of the right to use.[200] This judgement also indicated that the agreement must always be analyzed as a whole. Note that some case law and legal scholars consider a long duration even essential to an *emphyteusis*.[201] Other case law and legal scholars do not.[202]

If the holder of the right has been given the possibility to change the purpose or destination of the assets subject to the right to use, this serves as an indication towards characterization as either an *emphyteusis*[203] or a *superficies*, as the holders of these rights are not bound by this purpose or destination, unless otherwise agreed. If this possibility has not been given to the holder of the right to use, this points towards a characterization as a lease or a *usufruct*, as the lessee[204] or usufructuary[205] have to stick to the purpose or destination

197 Note that in some countries (e.g. the Netherlands) a minimum duration for an *emphyteusis* does not exist.
198 Derine, Van Neste & Vandenberghe, 1984, p. 855, no. 1000C; J. Hansenne, *Les biens*, II, Brussels, Larcier, 1996, no. 1219; De Page, 1972, no. 700; Laurent, 1878, no. 368.
199 Mostin, 2015, p. 88, no. 22; Muylle, 2012, no. 254.
200 Trib. Henegouwen (division Bergen) 4 November 2015, *JLMB*, 2016, Vol. 38, 1792-1794.
201 See *i.a.* trib. Dendermonde 16 June 1934, *Pas.*, 1935, I, 126; Kruishoutem, 1950, p. 177; Verheyden-Jeanmart & Mostin, 2001, no. 30.
202 See *i.a.* trib. Gent 14 July 1950, *Rev.prat.not.*, 1951, 45; Brussels 18 February 1854, *Pas.*, 1855, II, 63.
203 The French *Cour de Cassation* ruled that there is a presumption of an *emphyteusis* if the 'lessee' has the right to change the purpose or destination (Cass. fr. 23 February 1931, *D.*, 1931, 249).
204 See art. 1728, 1° of the Belgian Civil code.
205 See art. 578 of the Belgian Civil code.

that has been given to the assets by the lessor respectively bare owner, unless otherwise agreed.[206]

The possibility to mortgage the right serves as an indicative criterion in favor of characterization as an *emphyteusis*,[207] a *superficies* or a *usufruct*. It serves as a decisive negative characterization criterion *contra* characterization as a lease (which has a movable nature and can thus not be subject to a right of mortgage). Again, some Belgian case law and legal doctrine – as well as settled case law of the French *Cour de Cassation*[208] – considers the right to mortgage essential to an *emphyteusis*.[209] Again, others do not.[210] There is a similar discussion on the right to transfer the right to use in question.[211]

In some cases, these additional and secondary characterization criteria will serve as decisive negative characterization criteria, meaning the non-presence thereof leads to the conclusion that the agreement cannot be characterized as such (e.g. the obligation to pay a periodical compensation (*canon*) in case of an *emphyteusis*). The same is true for the characterization as a lease in case the agreement lacks an obligation for the lessee to pay a sum of money. In other cases (e.g. the long duration), these criteria serve merely as a guiding or indicative criterion in the characterization process, but are not in themselves decisive. Moreover, legal doctrine and jurisprudence do not always agree which elements are relevant or essential for the characterization of the agreement as a specific right to use (e.g. the possibility to change the purpose or destination of the assets subject to the right to use, the right to mortgage or transfer the right to use). Judges must take the agreement into account as a whole, and the whole agreement, in order to characterize the agreement.[212] For example, if the agreement has a retributive character, a long duration and gives the holder the opportunity to change the purpose or destination of the assets subject to his right to use, the judge will have a strong(er) case in favor of characterization as an *emphyteusis* (compared to the characterization as a lease).

---

206 Sagaert argues that there is a risk for recharacterization of a usufruct into an *emphyteusis* if the usufruct holder has been given the right to change the destination or purpose (Sagaert, 2014, p. 407). Belgian case law ruled that the impossibility to change the purpose or destination serves as an argument *pro* a lease and *contra* an *emphyteusis* (trib. Bruges 24 December 2007, *RGEN*, 2008, 306-308; JP Waver 22 June 2004, *JJP*, 2006, 138-148).

207 District Court Brussels 17 March 1975, *Pas.*, 1975, III, 43; JP Leuze 16 November 1955, *JT*, 1955, 56.

208 See for example Cass. Fr. civ. 3 15 May 1991, n° 89-20.008.

209 See *i.a.* trib. Dendermonde 26 February 1959, *RW* 1958-59, 1718; Verheyden-Jeanmart & Mostin, 2001, no. 30.

210 See *i.a.* V. Sagaert, 'Oude zakenrechtelijke figuren met nut voor een moderne familiale vermogensplanning' in *XXXste Postuniversitaire Cyclus Willy Delva 2003-2004*, Mechelen, Kluwer, 2004, no. 45; De Montpellier, 2003, footnote 21.

211 Mainly considered essential to an *emphyteusis* by the French *Cour de Cassation*: Cass. Fr. 10 April 1991, n° 89-20.276; Cass. Fr. 3 October 1991, n° 90-15.889; Cass. Fr. 7 April 2004, n° 02-19.870; Cass. Fr. 16 June 2011, n° 10-17.169. *Contra*: Brussels 15 July 1882, *Pas.*, 1882, II, 388; Gent 20 October 1900, *Pas.*, 1901, II, 227.

212 Terré, 1957, p. 231. See also Carette & Del Corral, 2012, p. 7, no. 6

10 Conclusion and Closing Remarks

This article has briefly discussed (the role of the *numerus clausus* in) the characterization of rights to use. What can be concluded is that due to both *Typenzwang* and *Typenfixierung*, there seems to be a major role for the *numerus clausus* principle in the characterization process. However, together with the relativisation of *Typenfixierung*, the role of the *numerus clausus* principle in the characterization process must also be nuanced. This is equally true for *Typenzwang* and the role it plays in the characterization process.

The interpretation and implementation of the *numerus clausus* principle comes down to a balancing exercise between the fundamental principles of legal certainty, foreseeability and transparency – which also serve as the economic rationale behind the principle (*i.e.* lowering transaction and information costs) – and the fundamental principles of party autonomy and contractual freedom. An increasing social desire to grant more party autonomy and contractual freedom can be observed, not only – yet especially – within the sphere of (property) rights to use. In the context of property rights and *numerus clausus*, there are two ways to meet this social desire. Either by a lenient approach towards *Typenzwang* or by a lenient approach towards *Typenfixierung*. The first possibility is to open up the closed system by allowing parties to create property rights *sui generis*. This possibility has been put into practice in France and Quebec for example, where there is a tendency to allow parties to create unnamed property rights.[213] However, characterization problems – and thus also problems concerning legal certainty, foreseeability and transparency – arise if no clear criteria are put forward in order to decide when and to what extent parties can create unnamed property rights. A second possibility to grant more party autonomy and contractual freedom is by 'opening up' *Typenfixierung*. The Belgian legal system is an example of this approach, whereby there is not only a limited amount of mandatory provisions and essential elements for each specific property right, but there is also a lenient approach towards these few mandatory rules and essential elements. It has been demonstrated that this approach – while responding to the social desire for an increased party autonomy and contractual freedom – also leads to problems concerning the determination of the proper characterization of the agreement, and as a result to legal uncertainty. It also leads to a large overlap between different property rights to use, as well as between property rights to use on the one hand, and personal rights to use on the other hand, which in turn makes it a very difficult task to distinguish the rights to use from one another. In the Belgian legal system it has been shown that legal uncertainty is complete without clarity and a unanimous answer on the question which elements are considered essential to a certain

213 While in Belgium *Typenzwang* is still strong, there has been criticism on the "anemia" it creates: see V. Sagaert, 'Volume-eigendom. Een verkenning van de verticale begrenzing van onroerende eigendom', *TPR*, 2009, 50-56.

right to use. In both cases (*i.e.* opening up *Typenzwang* or *Typenfixerung* without clear and transparent criteria), the conclusion for the characterization of rights to use is the same: the *numerus clausus* principle does not give such a straightforward answer to the question of the characterization of rights to use as it would seem at first. In both cases, transaction and information costs increase.

As property law does not contain any specific rules and the *numerus clausus* principle does not provide a straightforward answer, the characterization of rights to use is governed by the general principles on characterization of agreements. In the contemporary legal doctrine (in France and Quebec), there is consensus that the principal obligation is decisive for the proper characterization of the agreement. However, to determine the proper characterization of an agreement, the individual obligations contained in the agreement must not only be analyzed individually, but the connection or link between these obligations must also be determined. If the principal obligation(s) of the agreement can be reduced to one specific named contract, the agreement will be given a unitary or exclusive characterization. If the agreement contains principal obligations that point to several different named contracts, while it is practically impossible – even after application of the adage *accessorium sequitur principale* – or undesirable to reduce these principal obligations to one principal obligation for characterization purposes, the agreement must in principle be given a distributive characterization. However, if such a mixed agreement cannot be reduced or brought back to a mere *juxtaposition* of those different special legal regimes, the agreement must be characterized as an unnamed contract. The agreement should also be characterized as unnamed if it shares certain characteristics or elements with a certain named contract, yet does not fulfil or lacks one or more of the essential elements required for the characterization as that specific type of named contract, or if it is a completely new creation of the parties which cannot be brought back or reduced to one or more named contracts and has no connection therewith.

However, when applying the primary and accidental criteria used to characterize agreements in general on agreements granting a right to use, the principal obligation can be seen to be more or less the same for every right to use: the obligation to grant a right to use. Therefore, we need additional context- or contract-specific characterization criteria to determine the exact characterization of the agreement granting a right to use. These can either be decisive or merely guiding characterization criteria. The decisive positive characterization criteria can basically be brought back to the essential characteristics of each property or personal right to use. The applicable orientating or guiding characterization criteria will be dependent upon the context, as well as on the potential characterizations that are still left after the aforementioned general (primary and accidental) characterization criteria have been applied to the given agreement. Examples of such additional context- or contract-specific characterization criteria in the context of rights to use are the retributive character of the right to use, the (long) duration for which it has been granted, the possibility to change the purpose or destination of the assets, the right to mortgage and transfer the right etc. However, not only do legal doctrine and jurisprudence disagree on which elements must be considered essential or determinant for the characterization of agreements granting a right to use, there is also a lack of consensus on the question if, and if yes to what extent, the different elements have or should have an orientating or guiding role in the characterization process. All this leads to a problematic degree of legal uncertainty.

It is here that an important role could or probably should be played by a 'renewed' – or at least a differently interpreted – *numerus clausus* principle. An optimal balance between legal certainty, foreseeability and transparency on the one hand, and party autonomy and contractual freedom on the other hand, could be reached by slightly opening up *Typenzwang*, combined with a *Typenfixierung* which leaves room for party autonomy and contractual freedom, but which is strongly enforced by clear criteria that have to be fulfilled or complied with within the framework of the different property rights to use. As a result, the closed system would start from the now known limited property rights (*emphyteusis, superficies, usufruct*, real servitudes, right to use and habitation). There is room for parties to create, and for courts to recognize, new property rights but only if they fulfil certain clear, well-defined and transparent criteria. What those criteria are will be the subject of further and future research.[214] The strong *Typenfixierung* that I propose does not mean that the current framework of the different property rights cannot (slightly) be opened up (e.g. where the maximum and minimum duration is concerned, or where the obligatory *canon* in case of an *emphyteusis* is concerned).[215] However, while leaving much to party autonomy and contractual freedom, there have to be clear and transparent mandatory rules and/or essential elements within the framework of the different property rights that the contracting parties cannot touch or undo. This interpretation and implementation of *Typenfixierung* should allow to make a clear distinction between the different (property and personal) rights to use. Which elements or rules should be considered essential or mandatory to the different property rights will also be the subject of further and future research. Inspiration could for instance be drawn from the discussion amongst legal scholars on whether or not certain rules or elements should under current law be considered essential or mandatory. For example, the possibility to transfer and mortgage the right to use, as well as the possibility to change the purpose or destination of the assets subject to the right to use, could be considered essential to an *emphyteusis*, which for instance would allow to make a clear distinction between an *emphyteusis* and a lease. On the contrary, the obligation to respect the purpose or destination could be made essential to a *usufruct*. It

214 The criteria could for instance be inspired by the South African 'subtraction from *dominium* test' (see De Waal, 2000, pp. 443-444). See also Akkermans, 2017, p. 114.

215 The Belgian legal system could look for instance to the Dutch legal system, where there is no minimum or maximum duration and no obligatory *canon* payment for an *emphyteusis*.

would appear that this approach could provide an optimal balance between party autonomy and legal certainty for the parties involved. It could also provide legal certainty to third parties, due to clear and transparent criteria, which in turn could lower transaction and information costs.

Bibliography

Akkermans, B. *The principle of numerus clausus in European property law*, Antwerp, Intersentia 2008.

Akkermans, B., "The Numerus Clausus of Property Rights" in M. Graziadei & L. Smith (eds.), *Comparative property law: global perspectives*, Cheltenham, Edward Elgar Publishing, 2017, 100-120.

Ancel, M.-E., *La prestation caractéristique du contrat*, Paris, Economica, 2002.

Antonmattei, P.-H. & Raynard J., *Droit civil. Contrats spéciaux*, Paris, LexisNexis/Litec, 2007.

Bénabent, A., *Droit des obligations*, Paris, LGDJ, 2017.

Bergel J.-L., *Méthodologie juridique*, Paris, PUF, 2016.

Brulez, B., *Koop en aanneming: faux amis?*, Antwerp, Intersentia, 2015.

Cardoso-Roulot, N., *Les obligations essentielles en droit privé des contrats*, Paris, L'Harmattan, 2008.

Carette, N. & Del Corral, J. 'De kwalificatie van het recht van vruchtgebruik: contractueel mogelijkheden en afbakening tegenover opstal, erfpacht en huur' *in* Verbeke, A.-L. & Sagaert, V. (Eds.), *Vruchtgebruik: mogelijkheden, beperkingen en innovaties*, Antwerp, Intersentia, 2012.

Carton De Tournai, R. & Charlier, A.J., 'Quelques considerations d'actualité sur l'emphytéose et la superficie', *JT*, 1971, 69-72.

Chang, Y.-C. & Smith, H., 'The Numerus Clausus Principle, Property Customs, and the Emergence of New Property Forms', *Iowa Law Review*, 2015.

Collart Dutilleul, F. & Delebecque, P., *Contrats civils et commerciaux*, Paris, Dalloz, 2015.

Cornelis, L., *Algemene theorie van de verbintenis*, Antwerp, Intersentia, 2000.

Cruquenaire, A., Delforge, C., Durant, I. & Wéry, P., *Précis des contrats spéciaux: vente, bail, mandat, entreprise, dépôt*, Waterloo, Wolters Kluwer, 2015.

Cumyn, M. & Gosselin, F., 'Les Categories Juridiques et la Qualification: Une Approche Cognitive', *McGill Law Journal*, 2016, 329-387.

Cumyn, M., 'Les categories, la classification et la qualification juridique: réflexions sur la systématicité du droit', *Les Cahiers de droit*, 2011, 351-378.

De Montpellier, F., 'Usufruit, emphytéose et superficie – Limites de l'autonomie de la volonté et utilisation combinée' *in* Dierckx, F. (Ed.), *Onroerend goed als beleggingsinstrument*, Brussels, De Boeck & Larcier, 2003.

Delebecque, P. & Pansier, F.-J., *Droit des obligations. 1. Contrat et quasi-contrat*, Paris, LexisNexis/Litec, 2010.

Derine, R., Van Neste, F. & Vandenberghe, H., 'Zakenrecht', IIB *in Beginselen van Belgisch Privaatrecht*, Antwerp, Story-Scientia, 1984.

De Waal, M., 'The Uniformity of Ownership, Numerus Clausus and the Reception of the Trust into South African Law', *European Review of Private Law*, No. 3, 2000.

Donnay, M., 'L'emphytéose', *RGEN*, 1974, no. 21803.

Fabre-Magnan, M., *Droit des obligations. 1 – Contrat et engagement unilateral*, Paris, PUF, 2016.

Fréchette, P., 'La qualification des contrats: aspects théoriques', *Les cahiers de droit*, 2010, 117-158.

Fréchette, P., 'La qualification des contrats: aspects pratiques', *Les cahiers de droit*, 2010, 375-424.

Ghestin, J., Jamin, C. & Billiau, M., *Traité de droit civil. Les effets du contrat*, Paris, LGDJ, 2001.

Ghestin, J., Loiseau, G. & Serinet, Y.-M., *La formation du contrat*, Paris, LGDJ, 2013.

Goubeaux, G., *La règle de l'accessoire en droit privé*, Paris, LGDJ, 1969.

Hansenne, J., *Les biens*, II, Brussels, Larcier, 1996.

Hansmann, H. & Kraakman, R., 'Property, Contract and Verification: The Numerus Clausus Problem and the Divisibility of Rights', *Journal of Legal Studies*, 2002.

Henry, X., *La technique des qualifications contractuelles*, unpublished doctoral thesis, university of Nancy II, 1992.

Hinskens-Van Neck, M. & Siemerink, L., 'Gemengde overeenkomsten. De betekenis van art. 6:215 BW in de praktijk: kwalificatie van overeenkomsten', *MvV*, 2012, 1-10.

Huet, J., Decocq, G., Grimaldi, C. & Lécuyer, H., *Les principaux contrats spéciaux*, Paris, LGDJ, 2012.

Jestaz, P., 'L'obligation et la sanction: la recherche de l'obligation fondamentale' in *Mélanges offerts à Pierre Raynaud*, Paris, Dalloz, 1985.

Lafond, P.-C., *Précis de droit des biens*, 2nd ed., Montréal, Éditions thémis, 2007.

Larroumet, C., *Droit civil*, III, *Les obligations: le contrat*, Paris, Economica, 1996.

Lecocq, P., 'Superficie, emphytéose et constructions' in Lecocq, P., Tilleman, B. & Verbeke, A. (Eds.), *Zakenrecht*, Bruges, die Keure, 2005A, 285-334.

Lecocq, P., 'Superficie, servitude et interprétation: une anecdote' in Biquet-Mathieu, C., Deliège, A., Lecocq, P., Leleu, Y-H. & Vanwijck-Alexandre, M. (eds.), *Liber amicorum Paul Delnoy*, Brussels, De Boeck & Larcier, 2005B, 965-973.

Malaurie, P., Aynès, L. & Stoffel-Munck, P., *Les obligations*, Paris, LGDJ, 2013.

Malaurie, P., Gautier, P.-Y. & Aynès, L., *Les contrats spéciaux*, Paris, LGDJ, 2014.

Merill, T. & Smith, H., 'Optimal Standardization in the Law of Property: The *Numerus Clausus* Principle', *Yale Law Journal*, 2000.

Mostin, C., 'Emphytéose et superficie' *in Rép.not.*, 2015.

Muylle, M. *De duur en de beëindiging van zakelijke rechten*, Antwerp, Intersentia, 2012.

Nevens, K., *De arbeidsrelatie, de zelfstandige en de ondernemer*, Bruges, die Keure, 2011.

Ninane, Y., 'La requalification du contrat' *in* Jadoul, P. (Ed.), *Obligations. Traité théorique et pratique*, Mechelen, Kluwer, 2007.

Normand, S., *Introduction au droit des biens*, Montréal, Wilson & Lafleur Ltée, 2014.

Overstake, J.-F., *Essai de classification des contrats spéciaux*, Paris, LGDJ, 1969.

Raynard, J. & Seube, J.-B., *Droit civil. Contrats spéciaux*, Paris, LexisNexis, 2015.

Rochfeld, J., *Cause et type du contrat*, Paris, LGDJ, 1999.

Sagaert, V. & Jansen, R., 'Goederenrecht: de gestage groei naar een conventioneel vermogensrecht', *RW*, 2011, 68-73.

Sagaert, V., 'Het goederenrecht als open systeem van verbintenissen?', *TPR*, 2005, 983-1080.

Sagaert, V., 'Goederenrecht' *in Beginselen van Belgisch Privaatrecht*, Mechelen, Kluwer, 2014.

Sanzot, E., *Les droits réels démembrés: aspects civils, fiscaux, comptables et financiers*, Brussels, Larcier, 2008.

Smith, H., 'Standardization in Property Law' *in* K. Ayotte & H. Smith (Eds.), *Research Handbook on the Economics of Property Law*, Northampton, Edward Elgar, 2011.

Snijders, H.J. & Rank-Berenschot, E.B., 'Goederenrecht' *in Studiereeks Burgerlijk recht*, 6th ed., Deventer, Wolters Kluwer, 2017.

Stevens, R. 'Party Autonomy and Property Rights' *in* Westrik, R. & Van Der Weide, J. (Eds.), *Party autonomy in international property law*, München, Sellier European Publishers, 2011, 83-100.

Strucyken, T. 'The Numerus Clausus and Party Autonomy in the Law of Property' *in* Westrik, R. & Van Der Weide, J. (Eds.), *Party autonomy in international property law*, München, Sellier European Publishers, 2011, 59-82.

Struycken, T. *De numerus clausus in het goederenrecht*, Deventer, Kluwer, 2007.

Tadros, A., 'La liberté d'aménager les droits réels principaux' *in* Andreu, L. (Ed.), *Liberté contractuelle et droits réels*, Bayonne, Institut Universitaire Varenne, 2015.

Terré, F., *L'influence de la volonté individuelle sur les qualifications*, Paris, LGDJ, 1957.

Van Eeckhoutte, W., "Gezag' in de cassatierechtspraak', *NJW*, 2005, 2-17.

Van Gerven, W. 'Algemeen deel' *in Beginselen van Belgisch Privaatrecht*, Antwerp, Story-Scientia, 1987.

Van Ommeslaghe, P., 'Examen de jurisprudence (1974 à 1982): les obligations', RCJB, 1986.

Van Ommeslaghe, P., *Les obligations,* I, *Introduction - Sources des obligations (première partie)*, Brussels, Bruylant, 2013.

Vankerckhove, J., *Le louage des choses. I. Les baux en general*, IV, Brussels, Larcier, 2000.

Verheyden-Jeanmart, N. & Mostin, C., 'Jouissance d'immeuble: bail et conventions voisines' *in* Forriers, P.-A. (Ed.), *Aspects récents du droit des contrats*, Brussels, Jeune Barreau, 2001.

Vits, P., 'Zakelijke genotsrechten als alternatief voor huur en pacht' *in* Meulemans, D. (Ed.), *Een onroerend goed huren en verhuren*, Leuven, Acco, 1996.

Vuye, H. & Stijns, S., 'Zakenrecht: tweehonderd jaar oud of tweehonderd jaar jong?' in Heirbaut, D. & Martyn, G. (eds.), *Napoleons nalatenschap: tweehonderd jaar burgerlijk wetboek in België*, Mechelen, Kluwer, 2005.

Werdefroy, F. 'Bechouwingen over de onroerende natrekking, het recht van erfpacht, het recht van opstal, en het verlof tot bouwen', *TPR*, 1983, 293-342.

Wéry, P., *Droit des obligations - Volume 1*, Brussels, Larcier, 2011.

2 Relative Termination of Immovable Limited Rights *In Rem* in Belgian, French and Dutch Law

*Benjamin Verheye**

1 Introduction

Case law and legal doctrine accept that certain unusual termination grounds of limited rights *in rem* cannot harm third parties that have obtained a real right on those limited rights *in rem*. It is defended that such termination grounds have only 'relative effect'.[1] This fact seems to be inspired by justice: in certain cases, it appears highly unjust that the just trust of a third acquirer is not honored. This relative effect, however, has not been the object of thorough and all-encompassing research. Therefore, such research is the primary goal of this paper.

This contribution also claims, contrary to the classical conception but following recent doctrine, that the resolution of a contract because of violation only has limited effect. A vast number of arguments are provided in this respect. For this termination ground to have relative effect, however, it is necessary for the third acquirer to not be informed of the violation of the contract – purely factual or through the notification in the margin of the action for resolution (art. 3 of the Belgian Mortgage Act) –, nor to have caused this violation himself.

In this contribution, the general principles of the relative effect of certain unusual termination grounds are first laid out. Subsequently, the termination grounds without relative effect and the real subrogation are briefly analyzed, for these constitute the default position. Then a thorough overview of the termination grounds with relative effect is provided. The following grounds are studied: renunciation, termination by mutual consent, denunciation, confusion, deprivation, termination because of changed circumstances (only in Dutch

---

* The author is a member of the Institute for Property Law, KU Leuven (Belgium), where he is currently writing a PhD thesis on real estate publicity systems. A first draft of this paper was presented at the Young Property Lawyers Forum in Hamburg (Germany) on 23 September 2016. For a more elaborate Dutch version of this article: B. Verheye, 'Relatieve beëindiging van onroerende beperkte zakelijke rechten', *TPR* 2017, pp. 455-528.

1 See for instance: V. Sagaert, 'De negatieve werking van hypotheekregisters: een aanklacht', *in* A. De Boeck et al. (Eds.), *Publiciteit in het zakenrecht*, Bruges, die Keure, 2015, p. 190.

law) and, finally, the resolution because of violation of a contract. All this is done by means of an integrated comparative perspective on Belgian, French and Dutch law.

Of course, this contribution has its limitations. First, this research is limited to immovable limited rights *in rem*. Some insights might, *mutatis mutandis*, be applicable to movable limited rights *in rem* – usufruct or pledge –, but this falls outside the scope of this paper. Second, no attention is given to conflicting claims that can arise between acquirers of rights *in rem* on objects that are interrelated, for instance between the creditor of the bare owner of real estate with a mortgage on his bare ownership and the creditor of the usufructor with a mortgage on his usufruct.

2 The Relative Nature of Some Termination Grounds: General Principles 1.0

2.1 The Concept 'Relative Nature of Termination Grounds': Essentials

The underlying question in this paper is what 'relative effect of termination grounds' means. Essentially, this means that the limited rights *in rem* that have been granted by a titular of a limited real right on those same real right to third acquirers are protected, in case the original limited real right is terminated. Thus, a termination ground has relative effect to the extent that it only operates between two parties, but does not harm the interests of third parties.

An example will clarify all this. Suppose person X is the owner of real estate and grants a building lease ('superficies') to person Y. Subsequently, Y encumbers his building lease with a mortgage in favor of Z. The question then is what happens with Z's mortgage right, if Y's building lease is terminated. In principle, the mortgage right is then also terminated, although Z could find out from the land register that Y was the titular of a building lease and could grant him a mortgage right thereon.[2] After all, nobody can transfer more rights than he possesses himself (art. 74 of the Belgian Mortgage Act, *"nemo plus iuris transferre potest quam ipse habet"* and *"resoluto iure dantis, resolvitur ius accipientis"*, *cf. infra*). However, this principle is not fully valid in the case of some termination grounds: these termination grounds have only a relative effect. This means that, even although Y's building lease is terminated, Z's mortgage right is protected and thus remains in existence. A relative termination is not opposable to Z and thus, relative effect of termination grounds functions, in fact, as a rule of third-party protection.

2 E. Dirix & R. De Corte, *Zekerheidsrechten*, Antwerp, Story-Scientia, 2006, pp. 455-456.

Thus, relative effect appears to play a role in case of subsequent constitution of rights *in rem*.[3] The question now is which termination grounds are considered to have only a relative effect. Sagaert defends that such termination grounds must fulfill two requirements: (1) the titular of the first real right must be (one of) the cause(s) of the termination[4] and (2) it must be impossible for the third acquirer to anticipate this termination.[5] The particular termination grounds with relative effect are elaborated below and this will also clarify how Sagaert arrives at these two requirements.

2.2 *Termination Grounds without Relative Effect*

2.2.1 **Introduction**

Before analyzing the termination grounds with relative effect, it would be useful to first look at those without relative effect. The default position is, after all, that a termination ground has effect *erga omnes* and not relative effect. A distinction should be made in this respect: on the one hand, usual termination grounds exist, *ipso facto* without relative effect, and on the other hand, unusual termination grounds without relative effect exist.

Besides, this also provides a perfect opportunity to analyze the basic principles of limited rights *in rem* in French and Dutch law. The differences between these legal systems are, after all, of great importance for the analysis of the termination grounds with relative effect.

2.2.2 **Usual Termination Grounds without Relative Effect**

2.2.2.1 Usufruct

The most common termination ground of a right of usufruct is the end of the term for which the usufruct has been granted. According to article 617 of the Belgian Civil Code, this is the death of the usufructor-natural person, the resolution of the legal person or the end of the fixed period in time for which the usufruct was granted. Article 619 of the Civil

3 See for instance: K. Vanhove & F. Baudoncq, 'Combinatie van beperkt zakelijke rechten. Over de interne grenzen van vruchtgebruik, erfpacht, opstal en erf- dienstbaarheden', *Not.Fisc.M.* 2004, pp. 135-153. In this contribution, the following example will be the standard situation: a titular of limited rights *in rem* grants a mortgage right to a third party on his own limited real right. For this reason, easements (servitudes) are not taken into account: after all, it is impossible to constitute other rights *in rem* on an easement in civil law, as an easement is merely accessory. Second, this paper also presumes that a usufructor, long-lessee or building lessee only constitutes a mortgage on his own rights and not on the buildings that he owns on the basis of his own rights *in rem* or on the real estate that is the object of his own real right. Finally, it is also presumed that the third party-mortgage creditor has fulfilled the requirement of publication of his mortgage right in the mortgage register.

4 This requirement is better rephrased as follows: the third acquirer may not be the cause of the termination. So, both X and Y may be the cause of termination. This becomes clear in the examples below.

5 V. Sagaert, *Goederenrecht*, Mechelen & Kluwer, 2014, pp. 732-733.

Code adds to these the end of a period of 30 years, in case the usufruct has been granted to legal persons. When the term for which the usufruct has been granted comes to an end, the usufruct is terminated.

In principle, limited rights *in rem* that have been constituted on that right of usufruct also end when the usufruct ends.[6]

In French law, articles 617 and 619 of the *Code civil* stipulate the same usual termination grounds.[7]

In the same way as in Belgian law, limited rights *in rem* constituted on the usufruct end when that usufruct ends. Amongst others, this is the case with a mortgage on the usufruct (art. 2414 (former art. 2125) of the French Civil Code, the equivalent of the Belgian art. 74 of the Mortgage Act).[8]

In Dutch law, article 3:203(2) of the Dutch Civil Code stipulates that a usufruct ends with the death of the usufructor, just like in French and Belgian law.[9] The third paragraph of this provision adds that a usufruct granted to a legal person ends in case of resolution of that legal person or, in any case, after 30 years.

If the usufructor has encumbered his right of usufruct with other rights *in rem* (art. 3:223 Dutch Civil Code),[10] then these rights *in rem* end in case of usual termination of the usufruct, just like in Belgian and French law (art. 3:81(2), a) Dutch Civil Code).[11]

2.2.2.2 Long-Lease (Emphyteusis)

A Belgian long-lease must be granted for a period of, minimally, 27 years to, maximally, 99 years (art. 2 Long-lease Act).

When the agreed term ends, the mortgage that the long-lessee has granted on his long-lease right also ends.[12]

---

6 See for instance: Dirix & De Corte, 2006, 455; Sagaert, 2014, p. 445.

7 See also: J.-L. Bergel, M. Bruschi & S. Cinamonti, *Les biens,* Paris, L.G.D.J., 2010, p. 293.

8 See also for instance: Ph. Simler & Ph. Delebecque, *Droit civil. Les sûretés. La publicité foncière*, Paris, Dalloz, 2000, p. 295.

9 See also: C. Asser, F.H.J. Mijnssen, A.A. van Velten & S.E. Bartels, *Zakenrecht. Deel 5. Eigendom en beperkte rechten,* The Hague / Deventer, Kluwer, 2008, pp. 328-330.

10 See for instance: Asser, Mijnssen, van Velten & Bartels, 2008, p. 322.

11 See also: Asser, Mijnssen, van Velten & Bartels, 2008, p. 328 (usufruct on a limited real right); C. Asser, A.I.M. van Mierlo, F.H.J. Mijnssen & AA. van Velten, *Goederenrecht. Deel 3. Zekerheidsrechten*, Deventer, Kluwer, 2003, p. 377 (mortgage on a limited real right).

12 R. Derine, F. Van Neste & H. Vandenberghe, *Zakenrecht*, Ghent, Story-Scientia, 1984, p. 872; S. Snaet, 'Art. 6 Erfpachtwet', *in Bijzondere overeenkomsten – Commentaar met overzicht van rechtspraak en rechtsleer*, Antwerp, Kluwer, 2010, p. 3; K. Vanhove & A. Verbeke, 'Actualia vruchtgebruik, erfpacht, opstal en erfdienstbaarheden, *in Themis Zakenrecht 2002-2003*, Bruges, die Keure, 2003, p. 89; A. Van Oevelen, 'Recente ontwikkelingen inzake het recht van erfpacht en het recht van opstal', *in Zakenrecht: absoluut niet een rustig bezit*, Antwerp, Kluwer, 1992, p. 333; F. Werdefroy, 'Beschouwingen over de onroerende natrekking: het recht van erfpacht', *TPR* 1983, p. 322; F. Werdefroy, 'Beëindiging van de erfpacht', *Not.Fisc.M.* 1994/5, p. 6.

In French private law, two types of long-lease must be distinguished.[13] On the one hand, articles L451-1 ff of the *Code rural et de la pêche maritime*[14] contain the rules concerning long-lease ('*emphytéose*') that is established through the so-called '*bail emphytéotique*'.[15] On the other hand, articles L251-1 ff of the *Code de la Construction et de l'Habitation*[16] concern the '*bail à construction*', a real right with which the titular has the obligation to construct a building.[17]

In French law, too, both forms of long-lease end when the agreed term ends and both must be constituted for a period between 18 and 99 years.[18] Consequent to this termination of the long-lease, rights *in rem* that have been established on it also terminate.[19]

In Dutch law, a long-lease is very similar to that covered by Belgian law. The most important difference is that Dutch law allows parties to determine the duration of the long-lease freely.

The position of third acquirers of limited rights *in rem* on this long-lease depends, in principle, upon the duration of the long-lease: in case of usual termination of the long-lease, limited rights *in rem* thereon also terminate (art. 3:81(2), a) Dutch Civil Code).[20]

---

13 The various kinds of administrative long-lease fall completely outside the scope of this paper.

14 These provisions implement the Act of 25 June 1902 that institutionalised long-lease for the first time in modern French law.

15 See also: J.-L. Bergel, M. Bruschi & S. Cinamonti, 2010, pp. 333-334; J.-L Tixier, *v° Bail emphytéotique*, in *Rép. Dalloz*, 2006, nr. 1 *et seq.*

16 These articles stem from the Act of 16 December 1964, which had as its purpose to enhance urbanisation projects and established long-lease in urban areas. See also: R. Saint-Alary, in *Rép.civ. Dalloz, v° Bail à construction*, 2001, nr. 1-6.

17 See also: Bergel, Bruschi & Cinamonti, 2010, pp. 334-335; Saint-Alary, 2001, integrally.

18 See article L451-1 *C. rural* and article 251-1 *C. de l'Habitation et de la Construction.* See also: Bergel, Bruschi & Cinamonti, 2010, p. 333; L. Josserand, *Cours de droit civil positif français*, I, Paris, Sirey, 2nd edition, 1932, p. 1007; P. Jourdain, *Les biens* in G. Marty & P. Raynaud, *Droit civil*, Paris, Dalloz, 1995, p. 232; H. Mazeaud, L. Mazeaud, J. Mazeaud & F. Chabas, *Leçons de droit civil. II. Biens. Droit de propriété et ses démembrements*, Paris, Montchrestien, 1994, p. 413; M. Planiol & G. Ripert, *Traité pratique de droit civil français. III. Les biens*, Paris, L.G.D.J., 1952, pp. 988-989; R. Saint-Alary, 2001, nr. 46, 63; J.-L Tixier, 2001, nr. 15.

19 See for the *bail à construction*: R. Saint-Alary, 2001, nr. 63. Article L251-6 *C. de l'Habitation et de la Construction* explicitly stipulates: "*Les servitudes passives, autres que celles mentionnées au quatrième alinéa de l'article L. 251-3, privilèges, hypothèques ou autres charges nées du chef du preneur et, notamment, les baux et titres d'occupation de toute nature portant sur les constructions, s'éteignent à l'expiration du bail sauf pour les contrats de bail de locaux d'habitation*". See for the *bail emphytéotique*: Tixier, 2001, nr. 33, 36. Article L451-9 *C. rurale* explicitly stipulates: "*L'emphytéote peut acquérir au profit du fonds des servitudes actives, et les grever, par titres, de servitudes passives, pour un temps qui n'excédera pas la durée du bail à charge d'avertir le propriétaire*".

20 Asser, Mijnssen, van Velten & Bartels, 2008, pp. 274 *et seq.*; H.J. Snijders & E.B. Rank-Berenschot, *Goederenrecht*, Deventer, Kluwer, 2012, pp. 561-562.

2.2.2.3 Building Lease (Superficies)

The usual termination ground of the independent[21] building lease in Belgian law is the ending of the agreed term that cannot exceed 50 years.[22] It is very logical that a mortgage right on that building lease only lasts for the term of the building lease, for the building lessee cannot grant a mortgage for a longer term (*nemo plus*-principle).[23]

French law is not as straightforward as Belgian law. French law has a building lease ('*droit de superficie*'), but for a very long time, there has been no legal framework for this concept. Yet, French case law and doctrine have always acknowledged the existence of the building lease stemming from the refutation of the accession presumption.[24] Over time, this building lease has also been acknowledged outside the *Code civil*.[25] Not only has it been accepted that a contract can grant an independent right to build on someone else's plot of land, but it has also been accepted that some contracts, such as the *bail à construction* or the *bail emphytéotique* (*cf. supra*), *ipso facto* imply a building lease.[26] Eventually, in 2006, the building lease has been explicitly acknowledged in article 2531 of the French Civil Code.[27] Thus, in France, a building lease can be both eternal and limited in time, depending upon the contract by which it is constituted.

21 A dependent building lease exists when another real right, for instance usufruct, implies the right to build on a plot of land or on another building.

22 See articles 4 and 9 of the Building Lease Act. See also: De Page, *Traité du droit civil belge*, VI, Brussels, Bruylant, 1953, nr. 695, 1°.

23 D. Bracke, 'Schoppenboer jagen in het recht van opstal ... Over de vroegtijdige beëindiging van het recht van opstal en enkele valkuilen (annotation onder Gent 12 mei 2005)', *TBBR* 2007, p. 549; H. De Page, *Traité du droit civil belge*, VII, Brussels, Bruylant, 1957, nr. 469; Derine, Van Neste & Vandenberghe, 1984, p. 920; M. Donnay, '*L'emphytéose*', *Rec.gén.enreg.not.* nr. 21.803, nr. 24; A. Kluyskens, *Beginselen van burgerlijk recht. V. Zakenrecht*, Antwerp, Standaard-Boekhandel, 1951, pp. 242 *et seq.*; Van Oevelen, 'Overeenkomsten op basis van het recht van erfpacht en het recht van opstal. Onroerende leasing: een theoretisch kader', *in* KFBN (Ed.), *Oude en nieuwe rechtsfiguren*, Antwerp, Kluwer, 1989, pp. 37, 40-41; A. Van Muylder & J. Verstappen, 'Actuele problemen inzake het recht van natrekking, de verzaking daaraan, en het recht van opstal', *T. Not.* 1992, pp. 281 301; J. Verstappen, 'Een nieuwe kijk op drie oude zakelijke rechten: erfpacht, opstal en vruchtgebruik', in *Zakelijke rechten en fiscaliteit*, Brussels, Maklu, 2004, p. 50.

24 For instance from former article 2133 of the *Code civil* ("*L'hypothèque acquise s'étend à toutes les améliorations survenues à l'immeuble hypothéqué. Lorsqu'une personne possède un droit actuel lui permettant de construire à son profit sur le fonds d'autrui, elle peut constituer hypothèque sur les bâtiments dont la construction est commencée ou simplement projetée; en cas de destruction des bâtiments, l'hypothèque est reportée de plein droit sur les nouvelles constructions édifiées au même emplacement*".) or from the suppletive nature of article 553 of the *Code civil* (concerning immovable accession, "*si le contraire n'est prouvé*").

25 For instance in Décret n° 55-22 du 4 janvier 1955 portant réforme de la publicité foncière.

26 See for instance: Josserand, 1932, pp. 945-946; P. Walet, v° *Superficie* in *Rép. Dalloz*, 2000, nr. 23 *et seq.* See from a Belgian perspective: M. Muylle, *De duur en de beëindiging van zakelijke rechten*, Antwerp, Intersentia, 2012, p. 357.

27 See on the disputed nature of that building lease: C. Aubry & C.-F. Rau, *Droit civil français. II. Des biens*, Paris, Librairies Techniques, 1961, p. 593; Josserand, *1932*, p. 944; Mazeaud, Mazeaud, Mazeaud & Chabas, 1994, pp. 122-123; Planiol & Ripert, 1952, p. 325. For an excellent overview of the discussion: Bergel, Bruschi & Cinamonti, 2010, pp. 328-330. See from a Belgian perspective: Muylle, 2012, pp. 351-352, 354-355.

The question then is what happens with limited rights *in rem* established on a French building lease. If an independent building lease[28] has been constituted for eternity, then French law does not determine any termination grounds.[29] Thus the mortgage creditor cannot be harmed by a (usual) termination of the building lease. However, if the building lease has been independently granted for a limited period,[30] then the same solution must be followed as in Belgian law: if the building lease ends, the mortgage ends as well. Finally, if the building lease has been implicitly granted by means of another contract,[31] for instance a *bail emphytéotique*, the usual (*cf. infra*) and unusual (*cf. infra*) termination grounds of that other real right also affect the building lease and other rights *in rem* thereon.

As far as other termination grounds of the French building lease are concerned – which is a problem on the boundaries of contract law and property law –, it is remarkable that French doctrine scarcely grants attention to these (*cf. infra*). Consequently, possible relative effect of these termination grounds is completely understudied, too. For this reason, all remarks below concerning termination grounds with possible relative effect in relation to the French building lease must be read keeping the *caveat* in mind that these remarks find little to no support in French case law and/or doctrine.

The Dutch building lease is very similar to the Belgian building lease: Dutch law also differentiates between independent and dependent building leases. The most remarkable difference, however, is that Dutch law has no constraint on the duration of an independent building lease: parties can freely determine this duration and even choose an eternal building lease, if denunciation possibilities are excluded.[32]

With the termination of the Dutch building lease, third parties' rights on that building lease also end (art. 3:81(2), a) Dutch Civil Code), just like in Belgian and French law.[33]

2.2.3 Unusual Termination Grounds without Relative Effect

Besides the usual termination grounds, unusual termination grounds also exist that have no relative effect, contrary to those that are analyzed below. Sometimes, there are situations in which the two above-mentioned requirements are not met (*cf. supra*). An example of these is a resolutory condition in an agreement that establishes a limited real right: if this condition is realized and resolves the limited real right, then the mortgage right that has

28 This is called a '*vente de superficie*': Bergel, Bruschi & Cinamonti, 2010, pp. 331-332, 336-337; Walet, 2000, nr. 41-44.

29 Muylle, 2012, p. 367.

30 As is the case in the decision of the French Court of Cassation of 20 May 1958. However, Muylle argues that such a building lease is not possible if the law does not provide this: Muylle, 2012, pp. 363-365.

31 This is called a '*droit de superficie incomplet*'. Bergel, Bruschi & Cinamonti, 2010, p. 338; Walet, 2000, nr. 56-59, 60-65 and 85.

32 See: Asser, Mijnssen, van Velten & Bartels, 2008, p. 314; Snijders & Rank-Berenschot, 2012, pp. 565-566.

33 See also: Asser, van Mierlo, Mijnssen & van Velten, 2003, p. 377.

been constituted on that real right also ends (art. 74 of the Belgian Mortgage Act).[34] This is a literal application of the maxim '*resoluto iure dantis, resolvitur ius accipientis*'.

Other unusual termination grounds without relative effect can be recognized in various nullities. This is for instance the case with vices of consent: if X's consent is withdrawn and the real right of Y is consequently declared null and void, nobody can argue that the rights of third parties on that real right should be protected. However, it could be asked whether this is strictly coherent. After all, although nullity in case of vice of consent has retroactive effect, the resolution because of violation of contract also has retroactive effect and yet, below I defend that this last termination ground has retroactive effect (*cf. infra*). This is clearly a contradiction that has to be solved, which happens below (*cf. infra*).

2.2.4 Real Subrogation as a Remedy

Despite the above-mentioned termination grounds having no relative effect, a third acquirer might still be protected. In some cases, real subrogation can be invoked. In order for real subrogation to be applicable, the following conditions must be fulfilled: 1) the third party has a real right, 2) the original object of that real right has disappeared and is replaced by a new asset, 3) a causal link between the old object and the new asset exists, and 4) real subrogation is the *ultimum remedium* (subsidiarity).[35] The last condition in particular is of the essence for this paper: real subrogation can only play a role if a termination ground has no relative effect.[36] In France[37] and the Netherlands,[38] similar ideas about real subrogation are upheld.

Additional remedies might also exist for the third acquirer, for instance the *actio pauliana*. However, this falls outside the scope of this contribution.

34 K. Byttebier, *Voorrechten en hypotheken*, Antwerp, Maklu, 2005, nr. 639-641; H. De Page, VII, 1958, nr. 472 *et seq.*; E. Genin, 'Traité des hypothèques et de la transcription' *in Rép.Not., X, l. 1*, Brussels, Larcier, 1988, nr. 1276 *et seq.*; F. Laurent, *Principes de droit civil belge, t. 30*, Brussels, Bruylant, 1878, p. 444. See also: Dirix & De Corte, 2006, 455.

35 V. Sagaert, *Zakelijke subrogatie*, Antwerp, Intersentia, 2003, pp. 179-379.

36 See also: Sagaert, 2003, pp. 592-593.

37 Paris 2 February 1832, *S.* 1832, II, 301; Paris 8 February 1892, *D.* 1892, II, 409, annotation M. Planiol. See also: Aubry & Rau, 1961, p. 700; Planiol & Ripert, 1952, pp. 30 *et seq.*

38 Art. 3:229 of the Dutch Civil Code. See also: C. Asser, A.I.M. Van Mierlo, F.H.J. Mijnssen & A.A. Van Velten, 2003, p. 22 *et seq.*; J. De Jong, *Erfpacht en opstal*, Deventer, Kluwer, 2008, p. 65; A. Pitlo, W.H.M. Reehuis & A.H.T. Heisterkamp, *Het Nederlands Burgerlijk Recht – Deel 3. Goederenrecht*, Deventer, Kluwer, 2006, pp. 574-575; J.B. Spath, *Zaaksvervanging*, Deventer, Kluwer, 2010, integrally.

2.3 *Unusual Termination Grounds with Relative Effect*

2.3.1 Renunciation

2.3.1.1 *Usufruct*

A first unusual termination ground with relative effect is the renunciation to usufruct (art. 621-622 Belgian Civil Code): this is a unilateral abdicative legal act[39] with which the usufructor renounces to his right of usufruct.[40] Legal doctrine is semi-unanimous that in this case, a mortgage right on that usufruct persists until the moment in time it would have ended in normal circumstances.[41] This is clearly an example of a termination ground that cannot be anticipated by the mortgage creditor (*cf. supra*).

In French law, the relative effect of renunciation is classically not upheld.[42] Third acquirers must invoke the *actio pauliana* to be protected.[43] However, more recent authors defend that the renunciation has only relative effect.[44]

---

39 Cass. 24 December 2009, *Arr.Cass.* 2009, 3231, *TBBR* 2011, 332-343, annotation S. Jansen.

40 Examples: Cass. 23 February 1880, *Pas.*, 1880, I, 87; Cass. 4 November 1977, *Arr.Cass.* 1978, 284; Brussels 31 March 1988, *Rev.not.b.* 1989, 175; Brussels 21 December 1990, *JT* 1991, 495. See also: Derine, Van Neste & Vandenberghe, 1984, p. 534-536; H. De Page, VI, 1956, nr. 444, A; J. Hansenne, *Les biens. Précis*, Liège, Ed. Collection Scientifique de la Faculté de Droit de Liège, 1996, pp. 1084-1086; Kluyskens, 1951, pp. 227-230; Laurent, t. 7, 1878, pp. 90-96; M. Lefebrvre-Masschelein, *Het verval van een recht in het materieel privaatrecht. La déchéance*, Antwerp, Intersentia, 2010, pp. 173-182; Muylle, 2012, pp. 420-421; Sagaert, 2014, pp. 41-442, 761-763; S. Snaet, 'Alternatieve vormen voor het verwerven van onroerend goed: erfpacht, opstal en vruchtgebruik', *in* X, *Het onroerend goed in de verschillende takken van het recht*, Ghent, Larcier, 2008, p. 95; E. Van Arenbergh, *Traité de l'usufruit*, Brussels, Larcier, 1936, pp. 869-884; P. Van Ommeslaghe, 'Rechtsverwerking en afstand van recht', *TPR* 1980, p. 742; K. Verheyden, 'Voortijdige afstand van onroerende zakelijke rechten', *TFR* 2003, pp. 5, 9-10; J. Verstappen, 'Verzaking aan vruchtgebruik', *Notarius* 1997, pp. 366-368; P. Vits, 'Vruchtgebruik: burgerrechtelijke aspecten', *in* D. Meulemans (Ed.), *Vruchtgebruik, erfpacht en opstal*, Antwerp, Maklu, 1998, pp. 31-32; Werdefroy, 1994, p. 4; L. Weyts, 'De eenzijdige afstand van vruchtgebruik, civiel en fiskaal', *T. Not.* 1989, pp. 64-67. For an excellent general discussion on renunciation, see: Van Ommeslaghe, 1980, pp. 735-791.

41 Byttebier, 2005, pp. 589-590; De Page, VI, 1956, nr. 446-447; VII, nr. 468; Derine, Van Neste & Vandenberghe, 1984, p. 536; Genin, 1988, nr. 1291; Muylle, 2012, p. 670; V. Sagaert, 'Art. 45, 2°, 1e lid', in *Voorrechten en hypotheken – Artikelsgewijze bespreking en commentaar*, Antwerp, Kluwer, 2001, pp. 14-15; Sagaert, 2014, pp. 441-442; Snaet, 2008, p. 95; Van Arenbergh, 1936, nr. 3621 *et seq.*; Vits, 1998, p. 32. *Contra*: Laurent, t. 30, 1878, pp. 187-188.

42 Aubry & Rau, 1961, p. 701 (implicitly); G. Baudry-Lacantinerie, *Traité théorique et pratique de droit civil*, t. 26, Paris, Sirey, 1906, nr. 924-925; Josserand, 1932, p. 1000 (implicitly); Planiol & Ripert, 1952, p. 844 (implicitly, with reference to Aubry and Rau). For a more general analysis of renunciation of usufruct in French law, see for instance: G. Baudry-Lacantinerie, *Traité théorique et pratique de droit civil*, t. 6, Paris, Sirey, 1905, pp. 495-499; Mazeaud, Mazeaud, Mazeaud & Chabas, 1994, pp. 405-406; Josserand, 1932, pp. 1000-1001; Planiol & Ripert, 1952, pp. 843-845. About renunciation in general: A. Breton, 'Théorie générale de la renonciation aux droits réels. Le déguerpissemet en droit civil français', *Rev.trim.dr.civ.* 1928, pp. 261-364.

43 For instance: Planiol & Ripert, 1952, pp. 844-845.

44 Jourdain, 1995, p. 134 ("*La renonciation ne peut porter atteinte aux droits et obligations déjà acquis, lorqu'elle intervient*"); T. Vialatte, 'L'effet extinctif de la réunion sur une même tête de qualités contraires et ses limites', *Rev.trim.dr.civ.* 1978, p. 593. For an early confirmation of this solution, see Breton, 1928, p. 354.

In Dutch law, renunciation – possible under some conditions[45] – undoubtedly has relative effect, according to article 3:81(3) of the Dutch Civil Code.[46] This rule is not only applicable on usufruct, but on all limited rights *in rem*.

2.3.1.2 *Long-Lease*

Traditionally, renunciation to the long-lease right was considered impossible in Belgian law, because the long-lessee is personally liable towards the owner of the land and because he could not redeem himself from that obligation.[47] However, renunciation is recently accepted as a termination ground for long-lease, too.[48] In that case, it has only relative effect.[49]

In French law, renunciation to the right of long-lease stemming from the *bail emphytéotique* is considered impossible, on the basis of article L451-6 of the *Code rural*.[50] As to the *bail à construction*, no specific stipulation exists, nor is this debated in legal doctrine. However, in case renunciation would be accepted in this case, we may uphold that this renunciation only has relative effect, for this is also accepted in case of renunciation to usufruct (*cf. supra*).

For Dutch law, the analysis above is referred to, for the rules for usufruct are *mutatis mutandis* applicable on long-lease (*cf. supra*).[51]

2.3.1.3 *Building Lease*

Renunciation to the building lease is perfectly possible under Belgian law and this must be published in the land register to be opposable to third parties *de bona fide* (art. 1 of the

---

45 See: C. Asser, F.H.J. Mijnssen & P. De Haan, *Goederenrecht I*, Deventer, W.E.J. Tjeenk Willink, 2001, pp. 11 *et seq.*; Asser, Mijnssen, van Velten & Bartels, 2008, p. 22; Pitlo, Reehuis & Heisterkamp, 2006, pp. 467-468; Snijders & Rank-Berenschot, 2012, pp. 394-395, 525.

46 See: Asser, Mijnssen & De Haan, 2001, pp. 13-14; C. Asser, C.C. Van Dam, F.H.J. Mijnssen & A.A. Van Velten, *Goederenrecht II*, Deventer, Kluwer, 2002, pp. 298-299; Asser, Mijnssen, van Velten & Bartels, 2008, pp. 24, 329; Pitlo, Reehuis & Heisterkamp, 2012, pp. 467-468; Snijders & Rank-Berenschot, 2012, p. 395.

47 De Page, VI, 1956, nr. 716, C (*déguerpissement*); Laurent, t. 8, 1878, pp. 480-482 (*déguerpissement*); S. Snaet, 'Art. 18 Erfpachtwet', in *Bijzondere overeenkomsten – Commentaar met overzicht van rechtspraak en rechtsleer*, Antwerp, Kluwer, 2010, pp. 4-5; Van Ommeslaghe, 1980, p. 742; Werdefroy, 1994, p. 4.

48 Derine, Van Neste & Vandenberghe, 1984, p. 883; Hansenne, 1996, p. 1243; Sagaert, 2001, p. 21; Sagaert, 2014, p. 578; H. Vandenberghe & T. Viaene, 'Actuele ontwikkelingen inzake erfpacht en opstal', *TBO* 2006, p. 53; Verheyden, *TFR* 2003, (3) 5. See also: C. Mostin, 'Emphytéose et superficie', *Rép. Not.* 2015, VI[1], p. 131.

49 Derine, Van Neste & Vandenberghe, 1984, p. 883; Mostin, 2015, p. 131; Muylle, 2012, p. 670; V. Sagaert & M. Somers, 'Erfpacht, ontbinding en faillissement: een complexe trilogie' *T.Not.* 2008, pp. 93-94; Sagaert, 2014, pp. 578, 588; Snaet, 2008, p. 57, n. 45; S. Snaet, 'Voortijdige beëindiging van een recht van erfpacht (annotation onder Cass. 30 maart 2006), *TBO* 2006, p. 170; Vandenberghe & Viaene, 2006, p. 54.

50 "*Le preneur ne peut se libérer de la redevance, ni se soustraire à l'exécution des conditions du bail emphytéotique en délaissant le fonds*". See also: Breton, 1928, p. 283; Mazeaud, Mazeaud, Mazeaud & Chabas, 1994, pp. 413-414.

51 See also: Asser, Mijnssen, van Velten & Bartels, 2008, pp. 293-294; A.E. De Vries & A.J.H. Pleysier, *Erfpacht en opstal*, Zwolle, Tjeenk-Willink, 2002, pp. 117-118. See also Snijders & Rank-Berenschot, 2012, p. 564.

Belgian Mortgage Act).[52] Just like renunciation to usufruct (*cf. supra*), the renunciation to building lease has only relative effect.[53]

In French law, it is unclear whether renunciation to building lease is allowed. Arguments in both directions can be made. On one hand, renunciation to the *bail émphytéotique* is impossible (*cf. supra*), but on the other hand, renunciation to the right of usufruct is allowed (*cf. supra*). If renunciation to the building lease is to be accepted, then it must be upheld that this renunciation has only relative effect, as this is also the case for renunciation to usufruct (*cf. supra*).

For Dutch law the analysis above is once again referred to, for the rules for usufruct are *mutatis mutandis* applicable on long-lease (*cf. supra*).

2.3.2 Termination by Mutual Consent

2.3.2.1 Usufruct

A second unusual termination ground that is generally acknowledged to have only relative effect is the termination of the usufruct by mutual consent between bare owner and usufructor.[54] The similarity with unilateral renunciation is undeniable. However, termination by mutual consent is a translative agreement, whereas renunciation is a unilateral abdicative act.[55]

Of course, any third acquirer can also invoke the *actio pauliana* of article 1167 of the Belgian Civil Code. However, if the termination by mutual consent happens against payment, this action can only be successful if the third acquirer proves the bad faith of the contractual party of the usufructor, *i.e.* the bare owner.[56] Nevertheless, this bad faith will be presumed, as the mortgage right of the third acquirer will be published in the land register. In cases where the termination is free, the *actio pauliana* will not depend on this proof. Thus, the *actio pauliana* is, in fact, always possible in this case, if the usufructor wants to deceive the third acquirer, which may be presumed, as he has previously granted

52 G. Blockx, F. Lens & L. Wynant, *Erfpacht, opstal en erfdienstbaarheden*, Antwerp, Kluwer, 2006, p. 94; Bracke, 2007, p. 547; De Page, VI, 1956, nr. 695, 5°; Derine, Van Neste & Vandenberghe, 1984, p. 928; Hansenne, 1996, p. 1258; D. Meulemans, 'Vruchtgebruik, erfpacht en opstal als alternatief voor huur', *in* D. Meulemans (Ed.), *Vruchtgebruik, erfpacht en opstal*, Antwerp, Maklu, 1998, p. 195; Mostin, 2015, p. 190; Sagaert, 2014, pp. 616, 619, 762-763; S. Snaet & P. Truyen, 'Art. 9 Opstalwet', in *Bijzondere overeenkomsten – Commentaar met overzicht van rechtspraak en rechtsleer*, Antwerp, Kluwer, 2010, pp. 4-5; Vandenberghe & Viaene, 2006, p. 53; Van Muylder & Verstappen, 1992, p. 292; Van Oevelen, 1989, p. 47; Van Oevelen, 1992, p. 365; Verheyden, 2003, p. 5; Werdefroy, 1994, p. 4. *Contra*: Van Ommeslaghe, 1980, p. 742.

53 Bracke, 2007, p. 551; Muylle, 2012, p. 670; V. Sagaert, 2014, p. 619; Vandenberghe & Viaene, 2006, p. 54; Werdefroy, 1983, p. 308.

54 De Page, VI, 1956, nr. 442, B, 2°, b), Kluyskens, 1951, p. 228; Laurent, t. 7, pp. 91-92; Van Arenbergh, 1936, p. 872, nr. 2397.

55 Muylle, 2012, pp. 421-422; Van Ommeslaghe, 1980, pp. 738-739.

56 Kluyskens, 1951, p. 229.

a mortgage on his right of usufruct. Thus, it can barely be argued that the termination by mutual consent does not have relative effect, as the same result will be obtained via the *actio pauliana*. Relative effect of the termination is therefore preferable, as this lightens the burden of proof for the third acquirer.

French legal doctrine treats termination by mutual consent in one move with unilateral renunciation.[57] In more recent doctrine, it is defended that termination by mutual consent, too, has only relative effect.[58]

In Dutch law, termination by mutual consent is functionally equal to renunciation: renunciation happens *ipso facto* through an agreement, although this mutuality is, in fact, a formality for usufruct, because the bare owner is obliged to cooperate.[59]

For this reason, it is not useful to analyze termination by mutual consent separately for Dutch law. Below, this termination ground is therefore not mentioned for Dutch law.

2.3.2.2 Erfpacht

Termination by mutual consent is perfectly possible for Belgian long-lease too.[60] This termination ground is generally considered to have relative effect.[61]

In French law, too, termination by mutual consent has relative effect. For the *bail à construction*, this stems from article L251-6(3) of the *Code de l'Habitation et de la Construction*.[62] However, parties need to take a possible requalification into account, if the termination happens before the minimal duration of a *bail à construction* (18 years).

For the *bail emphytéotique*, there is some doubt as to whether termination by mutual consent is possible: legislation and legal doctrine do not mention this termination ground. The French *Cour de cassation* decided in its decision of 15 May 1991[63] that contractual

---

57 See for instance: Aubry & Rau, 1961, p. 701; Planiol & Ripert, 1952, p. 844.

58 Vialatte, 1978, p. 593.

59 Pitlo, Reehuis & Heisterkamp, 2012, pp. 467-468.

60 Examples: Rb. Dendermonde 5 December 2002, *Rec.gén.enreg.not.* 2004, nr. 25.416; Rb. Aarlen 18 December 2001, *Rec.gén.enreg.not.* 2002, nr. 25.399, 505. See also: Mostin, 2015, pp. 130-131; Muylle, 2012, pp. 197-199; Sagaert, 2012, p. 582; Vanhove & Verbeke, 2003, p. 91. Werdefroy analyses the termination by mutual consent jointly with denunciation: Werdefroy, 1994, pp. 3, 7.

61 Mostin, 2015, p. 110; Muylle, 2012, pp. 666-667; Sagaert & Somers, 2008, pp. 89-92, 93; Sagaert, 2014, p. 588; Snaet, 'Art. 18 Erfpachtwet', 2010, 6; Snaet, 2008, p. 57, n. 45; Snaet, 2006, p. 170; Vandenberghe & Viaene, 2006, p. 53; Vanhove & Verbeke, 2003, p. 91 (the authors mention that if parties want to grant retroactive effect (*ex tunc*) to the termination, this only has effect for the future, which has *in casu* the same result as relative effect); Werdefroy, 1994, p. 3.

62 "*Par ailleurs, si le bail prend fin par résiliation judiciaire ou amiable, les privilèges et hypothèques mentionnés au premier alinéa et inscrits, suivant le cas, avant la publication de la demande en justice tendant à obtenir cette résiliation ou avant la publication de l'acte ou de la convention la constatant, ne s'éteignent qu'à la date primitivement convenue pour l'expiration du bail.*" See also: Cass.fr. 24 June 1997, *Rev.dr.imm.* 1998, 191, annotation J.-B. Bergel.

63 Cass.fr. 15 May 1991, *Bull.civ.* 1991, III, nr. 140 = *Rev.dr.imm.* 1991, 322, annotation J.-L. Bergel: "*Qu'en statuant ainsi, alors que les propriétaires s'étaient réservé une faculté de résiliation du contrat pour leur permettre de vendre ou de démolir l'immeuble, ce qui donnait au droit de jouissance du preneur un caractère*

termination grounds are impossible for the *bail emphytéotique*, because these would render this long-lease precarious, which cannot be reconciled with its nature. However, it is rightfully argued that the Court only meant unilateral termination grounds and that termination by mutual consent therefore remains possible.[64] If this is agreed, then it must also be accepted that this termination ground has relative effect, similar to the termination by mutual consent of a *bail à construction*.

2.3.2.3 Opstal

Termination by mutual consent of a Belgian building lease is possible.[65] After all, if one party can unilaterally end the building lease by renunciation, then this must *a fortiori* also be possible for both parties together. This similarity has a logical effect that this termination ground must have relative effect.[66] Judging otherwise would be completely illogical.

In French law, again no information is provided concerning termination by mutual consent of a building lease. There does not seem, however, to be a reason why this would be impossible. Given the fact that the relative effect is defended for renunciation to usufruct (*cf. supra*) and *bail à construction* (*cf. supra*), it is logical that termination by mutual consent of a building lease has relative effect, too.

2.3.3 Denunciation

2.3.3.1 Usufruct

To the extent that the validity of a denunciation clause for a right of usufruct is accepted in Belgian law,[67] I defend that, in a certain situation, this denunciation has only relative effect. When the denunciation stems from the usufructor, this termination cannot be anticipated by the third acquirer.[68] This termination ground is very similar to the renunciation and it cannot be defended that renunciation has relative effect and denunciation does not: in both cases, the third acquirer may trust that the usufructor will do nothing that endangers the mortgage right (which is also sanctioned by art. 1188 Civil Code). Thus, I defend that the denunciation has relative effect in this case.

précaire incompatible avec la constitution d'une hypothèque et excluait le caractère emphytéotique du bail principal, la cour d'appel a violé le texte susvisé".

64 Muylle, 2012, p. 246.

65 Bracke, 2007, p. 547; Muylle, 2012, p. 330. See also: Mostin, 2015, p. 192.

66 Bracke, 2007, p. 551; Muylle, 2012, pp. 666-667; Sagaert, Goederenrecht, p. 619.

67 See concerning this discussion: Muylle, 2012, pp. 125-130. *Pro*: Sagaert, 2014, p. 138.

68 The fact that the third acquirer knows of the possibility for the usufructor to pursue the denunciation does not mean that he can anticipate this. After all, by granting a mortgage right to the third acquirer, the usufructor has created the presumption that he will not invoke the denunciation and the third acquirer may trust on that. The usufrcutor may do nothing that endangers the mortgage right granted by him to a third party.

However, if the denunciation stems from the bare owner, who obtained this possibility in the agreement that constituted the usufruct, then the denunciation does not have relative effect: the third acquirer could perfectly anticipate this denunciation, as he could read in the published act that the bare owner had this opportunity. Contrary to what was the case in the previous hypothesis, the third acquirer cannot trust that the bare owner will not invoke this possibility. One exception exists in this respect: if the bare owner receives the denunciation possibility in a separate deed, which is not published in the land register prior to the acquisition of a mortgage right by the third acquirer, then this denunciation has, again, relative effect. After all, the third acquirer cannot anticipate denunciation, which brings us back to the hypothesis in the previous paragraph.

French law does not contain any information concerning denunciation of usufruct. Therefore, it can be doubted whether this is allowed.[69] It remains to be seen how legal practitioners react when denunciation clauses for usufruct enter French legal practice.

In Dutch law, it is perfectly possible to include a denunciation clause in an agreement constituting usufruct, following article 3:81(2) of the Dutch Civil Code.[70] However, the Civil Code does not mention that this termination ground has relative effect and Dutch legal doctrine therefore argues that it does not.[71] This is justified by the fact that the third acquirer is *ipso facto* aware of the possibility of denunciation, as this must be published in the land register according to article 3:17 Civil Code in order to be opposable to third parties.[72] Contrary to Belgian law, Dutch law does not allow the denunciation possibility to be granted by a later, separate deed, for denunciation is a legal act touching upon the legal situation of the usufruct and must therefore *ipso facto* be published. However, the same remark can be made here as under Belgian law (*cf. supra*).

Besides, the third acquirer can also file the *actio pauliana* according to article 3:45 j° article 3:48 of the Dutch Civil Code. However, this only works in favor of the mortgage creditor and not in favour of third acquirers of other rights *in rem*.[73]

2.3.3.2 Long-Lease

Recent Belgian doctrine accepts the denunciation clause in long-lease agreements, but only if denunciation is not possible before the minimum duration of 27 years has been

69 See also: Muylle, 2012, p. 429.

70 See also: Asser, Mijnssen & De Haan, 2001, p. 14; Asser, Mijnssen, van Velten & Bartels, 329; Pitlo, Reehuis & Heisterkamp, 2012, p. 468.

71 Pitlo, Reehuis & Heisterkamp, 2012, p. 468.

72 Pitlo, Reehuis & Heisterkamp, 2012.

73 Pitlo, Reehuis & Heisterkamp, 2012, p. 468, footnote 8.

attained.[74] Again, I defend that the denunciation has relative effect if it stems from the long-lessee.[75]

However, if the denunciation stems from the long-lessor who was granted this possibility in a deed published anterior to the acquisition by the third acquirer, it does not have relative effect: the third acquirer is perfectly capable of anticipating this denunciation (*cf. supra*).[76]

In French law, a denunciation clause is impossible for the *bail emphytéotique*: this stems from the decision of the French *Cour de cassation* of 15 May 1991.[77] For the *bail à construction*, by contrast, the denunciation clause seems possible, as far as it does not allow parties to escape the minimum duration of 18 years.[78]

The question now is whether this denunciation has relative effect or not. If we apply article L251-6(3), as mentioned above, *mutatis mutandis* here, then it seems logical to grant the denunciation only relative effect, if it stems from the long-lessee. However, if it stems from the long-lessor and the possibility thereto was published in the land register, the relative effect cannot be accepted. This flows from the above-mentioned article L251-6(3) and it shows that the reasoning that I propagate for Belgian law is plausible and possible in practice.

In Dutch law, articles 5:87 and 5:88 of the Civil Code contain the possibility for denunciation in the case of long-lease.[79] No express reference is made to relative effect. On the contrary, both provisions explicitly stipulate that when the denunciation stems from the long-lessor, in case of violation of the contract by the long-lessee, the long-lessor needs to inform third parties about the denunciation.[80] Thus, the third acquirer appears to be harmed *ipso facto* by the denunciation.

---

74 Derine, Van Neste & Vandenberghe, 1984, p. 855; Meulemans, 1998, p. 194; Muylle, 2012, pp. 212-213; Sagaert, 2014, p. 579. If the minimum duration is not respected, the long-lease agreement must be requalified as rent: Vandenberghe & Viaene, 2006, p. 36.

75 See also: Werdefroy, 1994, p. 2-3, 7.

76 See also: Snaet, 2006, p. 170.

77 Cass.fr. 15 May 1991, *Bull.civ.* 1991, III, nr. 140, *Rev.dr.imm.* 1991, 322, annotation J.-L. Bergel.

78 See also: B. Grimonprez, *La Sem.Jur.Not.Imm.* 2003, 1310 *et seq.*: *"Le bail à construction, 'forme moderne et urbaine' du bail emphytéotique, emporte également constitution d'un droit réel au profit du preneur (CCH, art. L. 251-3). Son extinction n'en demeure pas moins régie par le droit commun: rien n'interdit de prévoir une résiliation conventionnelle pour inexécution par une partie de ses obligations conformément à l'article 1184 du Code civil"*. Based on this fact, Muylle argues that denunciation is also possible for the *bail emphytéotique*: Muylle, 2012, pp. 250-251, footnote 932.

79 See also: Asser, Mijnssen, van Velten & Bartels, 2008, pp. 296 *et seq.*; Pitlo, Reehuis & Heisterkamp, 2012, pp. 468, 507; Snijders & Rank-Berenschot, 2012, pp. 563-564.

80 See also: Pitlo, Reehuis & Heisterkamp, 2012, 507.

2.3.3.3 *Building Lease*

In Belgian law, denunciation clauses in the agreement between the building lessor and the building lessee are accepted.[81] This denunciation has the same effects as the denunciation of the right of usufruct (*cf. supra*) and the denunciation of the long-lease (*cf. supra*).[82]

Again, no information is provided concerning this termination ground in French law. To the extent that denunciation is accepted for *bail à construction* (*cf. supra*), we may argue that this is also the case for *superficie* and that it has relative effect.

In Dutch law, article 5:104(2) of the Civil Code declares the provisions concerning denunciation of long-lease (art. 5:87 and 5:88 Civil Code) applicable to building lease. As to the relative effect of that denunciation, I refer to the analysis above (*cf. supra*).

2.3.4 Confusion

2.3.4.1 *Usufruct*

A fourth unusual termination ground with relative effect is the termination[83] of the usufruct by a specific form of confusion ('*consolidatio*'): the bare ownership and the usufruct are united in one hand in a different way than through the extinction of the usufruct by a usual ground (art. 617(3) of the Civil Code).[84] Three different situations exist in which this is the case: the usufructor acquires the bare ownership, the bare owner acquires the usufruct (but not through the extinction of the usufruct), or a third party acquires both.[85] In case of confusion, the mortgage right of the third acquirer does not end: a semi-anonymous legal doctrine argues how the mortgage right persists, but only on that part of the ownership that represents the former part in usufruct.[86] The usufruct persists *ratione hypothecae* until the moment in time that it would have ended in a usual way.[87]

81 Bracke, 2007, p. 550 (implicitly); Meulemans, 1998, p. 195; Muylle, 2012, pp. 334-335; Snaet & Truyen, 'Art. 9 Opstalwet', 2010, p. 7.

82 See also: Bracke, 2007, p. 551.

83 As, for instance, Laurent remarks, this is not really termination of the usufruct, but a suspension thereof: the usufructor is practically incapable of exercising his right, because he is also the bare owner. See Laurent, t. 7, 1878, pp. 72-74. See also Sagaert, 2012, pp. 440-441.

84 See in general: De Page, VI, 1956, nr. 409 *et seq.*; Derine, Van Neste & Vandenberghe, 1984, pp. 536-538; Hansenne, 1996, pp. 1080-1082; Kluyskens, 1951, p. 219; Laurent, t. 7, 1878, pp. 70-74; Sagaert, 2014, pp. 440-441; Snaet, 2008, pp. 95-96; Van Arenbergh, 1936, pp. 840-847; Verstappen, 2004, p. 47; Vits, 1998, p. 32.

85 De Page, VI, 1956, nr. 409. See also De Page, VII, 1957, nr. 468; Hansenne, 1996, nr. 1080.

86 Byttebier, 2005, p. 189; De Page, VI, 1956, nr. 411, B, 413; VII, 1957, nr. 468; Derine, Van Neste & Vandenberghe, 1984, pp. 536-538; Hansenne, 1996, p. 1081; Kluyskens, 1951, p. 220; Laurent, t. 7, pp. 72-73; Sagaert, 2001, pp. 16-17; Sagaert, 2014, p. 440; Snaet, 2008, p. 96; Van Arenbergh, 1936, p. 45. *Contra*: Laurent, t. 30, nr. 212.

87 Examples: Cass. 8 June 1864, *Pas.*, 1864, I, 391; Rb. Bruges 26 October 2001, *RW 2003-04*, 1547, annotation S. Van Overbeke; Brussels 8 March 1988, *RW* 1988-89, 650. See also: Byttebier, 2005, p. 589; De Page, VII, 1957, nr. 468; Genin, 1988, nr. 1293; Muylle, 2012, pp. 669-670; Sagaert, 2001, p. 17; Sagaert, 2014, pp. 440-441.

In French law, the same solution as under Belgian law is traditionally defended.[88] In Dutch law, too, the relative effect of the confusion is accepted (art. 3:81(3) of the Civil Code).[89]

2.3.4.2 Long-Lease

The confusion of the long-lease is, *mutatis mutandis*, identical to the confusion of usufruct.[90] This confusion, too, has only relative effect.[91]

No information is provided concerning confusion of long-lease in French law. Given the fact, however, that the relative effect of the confusion of the right of usufruct is accepted (*cf. supra*), this is probably also the case for long-leases.

As to Dutch law, the analysis of confusion of usufruct (*cf. supra*) is also applicable to confusion of long-lease.[92] After all, article 3:81(3) of the Dutch Civil Code contains a general rule that is also applicable to long-lease.[93]

2.3.4.3 Building Lease

Of course, confusion may also be a termination ground for building leases. Article 9 of the Building Lease Act explicitly concerns this situation. Logically, the confusion again has only relative effect.[94]

88 Examples: Cass.fr. 7 November 1887, *S.* 1890, 442; Cass.fr. 26 January 1972, *JCP* 1972, II, 17104, annotation G. Goubeaux. *Contra*: Montpellier 17 March 1970, *JCP* 1970, II, 16421, annotation G. Goubeaux, rejected by Cass.fr. 26 January 1972. See also: Aubry & Rau, 1961, p. 697; Baudry-Lacantinerie, t. 6, 1905, pp. 479-480, t. 26, 1906, nr. 924; G. Goubeaux, annotation of Montpellier 17 March 1970, *JCP* 1970, II, 16421; G. Goubeaux, annotation of Cass.fr. 26 January 1972, *JCP* 1972, II, 17104; Josserand, 1995, p. 1004; Jourdain, 1995, p. 135; Planiol & Ripert, 1952, p. 850; Vialatte, 1978, p. 594. See on *consolidatio* in general: Vialatte, 1978, pp. 567-596.

89 See also: Asser, Mijnssen & De Haan, 2001, pp. 15-17; Asser, Mijnssen, van Velten & Bartels, 2008, p. 329; Pitlo, Reehuis & Heisterkamp, 2012, pp. 468-470; Snijders & Rank-Berenschot, 2012, pp. 395-396, 525.

90 See also: De Page, VI, 1956, nr. 716, A, 2°, VII, 1957, nr. 470. See also: Kluyskens, 1951, p. 395; Mostin, 2015, p. 129; Sagaert, 2014, p. 579; Snaet, 2008, p. 57, reference 45; Vandenberghe & Viaene, 2006, p. 52; Van Oevelen, 1992, pp. 337-338; Werdefroy, 1994, p. 2.

91 Rb. Brussels 14 July 1950, *Pas.*, 1951, III, 47. The Tribunal says: "*Attendu que, le droit d'emphytéose n'étant éteint que dans son exercice, les droits que les emphytéotes ont consenti à des tiers ne disparaissent pas nécessairement par l'effet de cette consolidation*". See also: De Page, VII, 1957, nr. 470; Derine, Van Neste & Vandenberghe, 1984, p. 882; Mostin, 2015, p. 129; Muylle, 2012, pp. 669-670; Sagaert, 2001, pp. 21-22; Sagaert & Somers, 'Erfpacht, ontbinding en faillissement: een complexe trilogie', 2008, p. 93; Sagaert, 2014, pp. 579, 588; Snaet, 'Art. 18 Erfpachtwet', 2010, p. 2; Snaet, 2006, p. 170; Vandenberghe & Viaene, 2006, pp. 52-54; Van Oevelen, 1992, p. 338; Werdefroy, 1994, p. 2.

92 See also: Asser, Van Dam, Mijnssen & Van Velten, *Goederenrecht II*, 262; Asser, Mijnssen, van Velten & Bartels, *Zakenrecht. Deel 5. Eigendom en beperkte rechten*, 293-294; A.E. De Vries & A.J.H. Pleysier, 2002, p. 117.

93 Snijders & Rank-Berenschot, 2012, p. 564.

94 Blockx, Lens & Wynant, 2006, p. 93; Bracke, 2007, p. 551; De Page, VI, 1956, nr. 695, 2°; Derine, Van Neste & Vandenberghe, 1984, p. 925; Kluyskens, 1951, pp. 243-244; Laurent, t. 8, 1878, p. 514; Mostin, 2015, p. 189; Muylle, 2012, pp. 669-670; Sagaert, 2001, pp. 21-22; Sagaert, 2014, p. 619; Snaet & Truyen, 'Art. 9

In French law, confusion is not mentioned in cases of building lease. Given the fact, however, that the relative effect of the confusion of the right of usufruct is accepted (*cf. supra*), this is probably also the case for building leases.

As to Dutch law, the analysis of confusion of usufruct (*cf. supra*) is also applicable to confusion of building leases.

2.3.5 Deprivation Because of Abuse of Rights

2.3.5.1 Usufruct

A fifth termination ground with relative effect is the deprivation of the right of usufruct because of abuse of the rights inherent to usufruct, which needs to be pronounced by a judge (art. 618 of the Belgian Civil Code) and to be mentioned in the land register (art. 3 of the Belgian Mortgage Act).[95] It is debated whether this deprivation has relative effect.[96]

I defend that the deprivation of usufruct does have relative effect. First, it is not useful to treat this situation any differently from the renunciation to usufruct, that is generally accepted to have only relative effect (*cf. supra*). Both hypotheses are essentially the same: the usufructor ends the usufruct, either through his explicit legal act or through abuse of his rights.[97] Second, it is not useful to make the effects of this termination depend upon the judge. This has nothing to do with a lack of respect for '*l'autorité de la chose jugée*',[98] but everything with logic and coherence of the Belgian law.

One exception exists to this relative effect. If a bare owner has already included his action for deprivation in the land register (art. 3 Mortgage Act) anterior to any acquisition

Opstalwet', 2010, p. 3; Vandenberghe & Viaene, 2006, pp. 52-54; Van Oevelen, 1989, p. 45; Van Oevelen, 1992, p. 363.

95 Examples: Luik, 4 October 2000, *TBBR* 2004, 22, annotation B. Vanbrabant; Luik 12 December 2000, *TBBR* 2004, 26, annotation B. Vanbrabant; Ghent 27 June 2002, *TBBR* 2004, 28, annotation B. Vanbrabant; Rb. Luik 17 March 2014, *RTDF* 2014, 940. See also: De Page, VI, 1956, nr. 434 *et seq.*; Derine, Van Neste & Vandenberghe, 1984, pp. 539-543; Kluyskens, 1951, pp. 224-227; Hansenne, 1996, pp. 1082-1083; Lefebrvre-Masschelein, 2010, pp. 47 *et seq.*; Muylle, 2012, pp. 431-433; Sagaert, 2014, pp. 442-443; Snaet, 2008, p. 97; Van Arenbergh, 1936, pp. 884-902; B. Vanbrabant, 'La déchéance d'un droit d'usufruit, d'usage, d'habitation ou d'emphytéose: causes et effets', annotation of Luik 4 October 2000, Luik 12 December 2000 and Ghent 27 June 2002, *TBBR* 2004, pp. 31-42; Vanhove & Verbeke, 2003, pp. 84-85; See in general concerning abuse of rights: Van Ommeslaghe, 1980, pp. 752 *et seq.*

96 *Pro*: Brussels 2 August 1883, *JT* 1883, 618. The Court refers to the *nemo plus*-principle: "*Attendu que nul ne peut transférer à autrui plus de droits qu'il n'en a lui-même; qu'on ne conçoit pas, d'ailleurs, une hypothèque continuant à frapper un droit d'usufruit qui n'existe plus*". See also: Derine, Van Neste & Vandenberghe, 1984, pp. 542-543; De Page, VI, 1956, nr. 438; VII, 1957, nr. 468, nr. 481, 2°, b); Genin, 1988, nr. 1292; Laurent, t. 7, 1878, pp. 103-105 ("*Nous croyons néanmoins que les créanciers hypothécaires conservent leur hypothèque*"); Muylle, 2012, pp. 667-669; Sagaert, 2014, pp. 442-443; Vanbrabant, 2004, pp. 41-42; Vits, 1998, p. 33. *Contra*: Baudry-Lacantinerie, t. 26, 1906, nr. 926; Hansenne, 1996, p. 1083; Sagaert, 2001, p. 15 (however, this author defends the opposite solution in his more recent work).

97 The similarity between both situations is also remarked by other authors: Van Ommeslaghe, 1980, p. 752.

98 Baudry-Lacantinerie, t. 26, 1906, nr. 926, p. 36. See also: Baudry-Lacantinerie, t. 6, 1905, pp. 492-494.

by the third acquirer, then this deprivation cannot have relative effect. The same is the case when the third acquirer has knowledge of the abuse of rights by the usufructor. In both cases, he could anticipate the deprivation (*cf. supra*).

Under French law, the relative effect of the deprivation of usufruct (art. 618 *Code civil*) is not accepted: it is considered a duty of the judge to determine the exact effects of the deprivation towards third parties.[99]

In Dutch law, the deprivation of the right of usufruct has no longer been an option since 1992. Only the management of the usufruct by the bare owner or the judicial supervision remain possible as a sanction for the abuse of rights by the usufructor (art. 3:221 Dutch Civil Code).[100] Thus the usufruct is not terminated and relative effect is of no importance.

2.3.5.2 *Long-Lease*

Deprivation of long-lease is regulated by article 15 and 16 of the Belgian Long Lease Act. This sanction is very similar to deprivation of usufruct, which is analyzed above (*cf. supra*).[101] In this case, too, the deprivation has only relative effect.[102]

Some authors argue that the deprivation of long-leases has only relative effect, if the third acquirer has not been invited to intervene in the process.[103] However, I do not share this point of view. Article 3 of the Act of 4 May 1955 *ipso facto* requires that third parties be informed in order for the action for deprivation to be accepted by the judge.[104] In addition, I uphold that the relative effect protects the third acquirer, regardless of any prior notice (*cf. supra* and *infra*).

French law does not allow for deprivation *ex nunc* of a *bail à construction* and the *bail emphytéotique*. It only knows resolution, which is analyzed below (*cf. infra*).

---

99 Examples: Cass.fr. 6 August 1872, *S.* 1872, 317 ("*Attendu que la loi ne précise pas les causes de déchéance de l'usufruit, et que, par là même, elle laisse les tribunaux juges de la convenance qu'il peut y avoir à prononcer cette peine civile en tenant compte de la nature et du degré de persistance des abus signalés*"); Cass.fr. 12 March 1970, *D.* 1970, 692; Pau 11 March 1893, *S.* 1893, 119. See also; Aubry & Rau, 1961, p. 699; Baudry-Lacantinerie, t. 6, 1905, p. 494, t. 26, 1906, nr. 926, p. 36; Bergel, Bruschi & Cinamonti, 2010, p. 311; Josserand, 1932, p. 1003; Jourdain, 1995, pp. 136-137; Mazeaud, Mazeaud, Mazeaud & Chabas, 1994, p. 406. For a more general discussion, see: Baudry-Lacantinerie, t. 6, 1905, pp. 491-495; Planiol & Ripert, 1952, pp. 846 848.

100 See also: Pitlo, Reehuis & Helsterkamp, 2012, pp. 531-533.

101 See also: De Page, VI, 1956, nr. 716, B; Hansenne, 1996, pp. 1241, 1243; Kluyskens, 1951, p. 396; Laurent, t. 8, pp. 482-485; Mostin, 2015, pp. 132-133; Muylle, 2012, p. 221; V. Sagaert, 2014, pp. 580-581; S. Snaet, 'Art. 15 Erfpachtwet', in *Bijzondere overeenkomsten – Commentaar met overzicht van rechtspraak en rechtsleer*, Antwerp, Kluwer, 2010, p. 2; Vanbrabant, 2004, pp. 31-42; Vanhove & Verbeke, 2003, p. 91; Van Oevelen, 1992, pp. 339-340; Werdefroy, 1994, p. 4.

102 Mostin, 2015, p. 110; Muylle, 2012, pp. 667-669; Sagaert & Somers, 2008, p. 94; V. Sagaert, 2012, p. 588; S. Snaet, 'Art. 15 Erfpachtwet', 2010, p. 2; Vanbrabant, 2004, p. 41; Vandenberghe & Viaene, 2006, p. 54.

103 Derine, Van Neste & Vandenberghe, 1984, p. 888; Werdefroy, 1983, p. 322.

104 See also: Vandenberghe & Viaene, 2006, p. 54, footnote 250.

Dutch law does not know the deprivation of long-lease either. However, it does know a specific form of denunciation by the long-lessor, in case the long-lessee does not fulfill his duties (art. 5:87(2) Civil Code). This rule has already been analyzed above (*cf. supra*).

2.3.5.3 Building Leases

It is debated whether the deprivation of building leases is possible in Belgian law.[105] Authors who reply negatively to this question argue that the legislator has only provided this sanction for usufruct (*cf. supra*) and long-leases (*cf. supra*), but not for building leases. Thus it would not be allowed to apply this sanction *per analogiam*, especially because article 2 of the Act of 14 May 1955 stipulates that the building lessee can (only) be deprived of his long-lease if he does not pay the retribution (*canon*) as foreseen in article 1 of the Building Lease Act.[106] If, however, the deprivation is accepted – rightfully, in my opinion – then it must also be accepted that this deprivation has only relative effect, to the same extent as the deprivation of usufruct (*cf. supra*). In that case, the rights of third parties *de bona fide* must also be protected.

A specific question in this regard is whether the deprivation of building lease because of non-payment of the retribution (art. 2 of the Act of 14 May 1955)[107] has relative effect. The legislator has provided two specific remedies for the third acquirer of a mortgage right in this case: the mortgaged claim becomes immediately payable – a confirmation of article 1188 of the Civil Code – and the third acquirer may invoke real subrogation on the retributions the building lessor owes the building lessee. Nevertheless, two questions arise in this respect. The first question is whether third acquirers of other rights *in rem* may also claim the remedy of the real subrogation. This is most certainly the case, for a case of unequal treatment would arise otherwise. The second question is whether the deprivation because of non-payment of the retribution has also negative effect. I defend that this is the case: this situation is not different from the hypothesis in the previous paragraph. In addition, in this case, real subrogation is superfluous, because real subrogation can only be invoked subsidiarily (*cf. supra*) and in this case, the mortgage right remains in existence.[108]

105 See concerning this discussion: Blockx, Lens & Wynant, 2006, pp. 95-96; Derine, Van Neste & Vandenberghe, 1984, p. 928; Vanbrabant, 2004, p. 34. *Pro*: Kluyskens, p. 244; Laurent, t. 8, 1878, pp. 514-515. *Contra*: De Page, VI, 1956, nr. 695, 5°; Mostin, 2015, p. 192; Muylle, 2012, pp. 338, 680-682; Snaet & Truyen, 'Art. 9 Opstalwet', p. 5; Van Oevelen, 1989, p. 47; Van Oevelen, 1992, p. 365.

106 See also: Sagaert, 2014, p. 617; Van Oevelen, 1989, p. 47.

107 See for instance: Mostin, 2015, p. 192.

108 This is quite paradoxical, because the legislator has expressly provided real subrogation as a remedy in this case. In my opinion, this is an exception in which real subrogation is not subsidiary: the third acquirer can choose whether he invokes the relative effect of the deprivation or the real subrogation.

Again, French law does not provide any information concerning possible deprivation (*déchéance*) of a building lease. The termination because of a violation of a contract is therefore analyzed in general below (*cf. infra*).

Article 5:104(2) of the Dutch Civil Code declares articles 5:87 and 5:88 of the Civil Code applicable to building lease. Thus, Dutch law does not provide for deprivation, but for a specific form of denunciation. This has already been analyzed above (*cf. supra*).

2.3.6 Termination Because of Changed Circumstances in Dutch Law

Dutch law has a specific termination ground for long-leases and building leases. This ground does not exist in this particular form[109] under Belgian or French law.

Article 5:97 of the Dutch Civil Code stipulates that the judge may terminate the long-lease on the basis of changed circumstances, after a period of minimally 25 years.[110] Once 25 years have passed since the constitution of a long-lease and unforeseen circumstances arise, then the long-lessor or long-lessee may ask the judge to terminate the long-lease. Possible third acquirers must be informed of and engaged in this procedure, in order to control whether the condition of changed circumstances was already met when their right was established.[111] If this is the case, the right of long-lease is terminated. Relative effect of this termination ground is not mentioned anywhere. According to the second paragraph of article 5:97, the judge can subject the termination to certain conditions, but no indication has been found that the relative effect of the termination is sometimes stipulated as a condition.

Article 5:104(2) of the Civil Code declares article 5:97 *mutatis mutandis* applicable to building lease.

2.3.7 Resolution Because of Violation of a Contract

2.3.7.1 Introduction: Resolution Because of Violation of a Contract with Relative Effect

One of the most interesting unusual termination grounds to be discussed in this paper is without any doubt the resolution because of violation of a contractual clause. Intuitively, many people argue that this ground cannot have relative effect: resolution is a sanction with retroactive effect (*ex tunc*), so how could this *not* harm the positions of third parties (*cf. supra*)?[112] Two principles are immediately cited in this respect: the *nemo plus*-principle

109 Other functionally equivalent mechanisms, such as the abuse of rights-doctrine, fall outside the scope of this paper.

110 See: Asser, Mijnssen, van Velten & Bartels, 2008, pp. 294 *et seq.*; De Jong, 2008, pp. 68-69; Pitlo, Reehuis & Heisterkamp, 2012, p. 509; Snijders & Rank-Berenschot, 2012, pp. 562-563.

111 Asser, Mijnssen, van Velten & Bartels, 2008, pp. 295-296; De Jong, 2008; Pitlo, Reehuis & Heisterkamp, 2012, p. 509.

112 See for instance: F. Lepinois, *Traité théorique et pratique de la transcription des privilèges et des hypothèques, IV*, Liège, Jacques Godenne, 1897, nr. 1500.

and the *resoluto iure dantis*-principle (art. 74 of the Belgian Mortgage Act, *cf. supra*). Nevertheless, more recent legal doctrine defends the opposite point of view: in some cases, the resolution because of violation of a contractual clause would have relative effect.[113] Various strong arguments can be invoked in favor of this point of view, that I share.

This unusual termination ground meets the two general requirements that were set out above (*cf. supra*): the usufructor, long-lessee or building lessee is the cause of the termination and the third acquirer cannot anticipate this. Even if the third acquirer knows that certain explicit resolutory clauses have been inserted in the original deed establishing the usufruct, long-lease or building lease, he can still not anticipate the fact that the usufructor, long-lessee or building lessee will effectively violate these contractual provisions. Even more: he may trust that they will not do that, for this would endanger his own right. Two exceptions exist to this rule: either the third acquirer is aware of the contractual violation before he acquires his own right – for instance because the action for resolution has already been mentioned in the land register (art. 3 Belgian Mortgage Act) –, or he actively cooperates in this violation. In these two cases, the resolution is of course opposable to the third acquirer and thus does not have relative effect (*cf. infra*).

Second, the similarities between deprivation because of abuse of rights and resolution because of contractual violation is too big to ignore: they both sanction a violation by the usufructor, long-lessee or building lessee. Given the fact that a violation can, in some cases, be sanctioned by both these sanctions, depending on what the parties invoke, it is not useful to let the faith of third parties depend on which sanction is effectively pronounced. Such different treatment of equal situations without any justification might fall within the scope of the constitutional equality principle.

Third, the last couple of decennia have known the evolution in the direction of the partial resolution, as propagated in case of contracts with a certain duration. The Belgian Court of Cassation has judged that the resolution has only retroactive effect until the moment of violation of the contractual equilibrium – thus: not full retroactive effect until the beginning of the contract –, if the agreement concerned has continuing obligations as an object and the obligations that have already been fulfilled cannot be reasonably restituted.[114] This is, for instance, the case with long-lease.[115]

It could be defended that every agreement that established a limited real right is in fact an agreement with a certain duration, for it creates a relationship of a certain time between

113 For usufruct: Muylle, 2012, pp. 665, 667-669. For long-lease: Muylle, 2012, pp. 665, 667-669; Sagaert & Somers, 2008, p. 94; Sagaert, 2014, pp. 188-189. For building lease: Muylle, 2012, pp. 665, 667-669.

114 Cass. 9 February 1990, *TBBR* 1991, 101, annotation M. Storme; Cass 8 October 1987, RCJB 1990, 379, annotation M. Fontaine; Cass. 24 January 1980, *Arr.Cass.* 1979-80, 592.

115 Sagaert, 2014, p. 586; Sagaert & Somers, 2008, p. 93. See in general: M. Fontaine, 'La rétroactivité de la résolution des contrats pour inexécution fautive', annotation of Cass. 8 October 1987, *RCJB* 1990, pp. 382-401; M. Storme, 'Het ingaan en de terugwerkende kracht van de ontbinding van wederkerige overeenkomsten', annotation of Cass. 9 February 1990, *TBBR* 1991, pp. 101-117.

parties. Consequently, fully retroactive resolution would, in most cases, not be possible anymore and the rights of third parties would be protected. Nevertheless, I believe that all this can be better solved on the basis of the relative effect. After all, it is very artificial to see every contract establishing a real right as a contract with a duration, in which it cannot be reasonably expected that fulfilled obligations are restituted. In addition, it cannot be defended why parties could not mutually agree to resolve such contract with fully retroactive effect. Therefore, partial resolution cannot be accepted in these cases.

Finally, termination grounds without retroactive effect (*ex nunc*) exist, which still do not have relative effect in some circumstances, such as the denunciation (*cf. supra*). Well then, if termination grounds *ex nunc* exist without relative effect, why would it then be impossible for termination grounds *ex tunc* to exist with relative effect?

2.3.7.2 Usufruct

Modern Belgian legal doctrine accepts that the implicit (art. 1184 Civil Code) and explicit resolutory clause is also applicable to usufruct.[116] This termination ground is very similar to deprivation, but its scope is wider: the resolution is applicable every time the usufructor violates the contract in a sufficiently severe or explicitly mentioned way.[117] Because of this similarity, recent doctrine defends that this termination ground has, in principle, relative effect, although it works retroactively.[118]

Nevertheless, the two same exceptions apply as above-mentioned (*cf. supra*). If the third acquirer knows of the contractual violation by the usufructor anterior to his acquisition of a real right, or if he cooperates with the usufructor, then the relative effect of the resolution cannot be upheld. In these cases, the third acquirer could anticipate the resolution.

In French law, the validity of an implicit or explicit resolutory clause has recently been denied in case of usufruct, because deprivation is considered the only sanction for violations of the contract by the usufructor.[119]

Dutch legal doctrine has written remarkably little about the implicit or explicit resolutory clause in case of rights *in rem*. Probably this is related to the very strict separation between contract law and property law that is upheld in the Netherlands. Rank-Berenschot remarks how resolution of an agreement establishing a real right is considered impossible, for this agreement is fulfilled and ends with the establishment of the real right. Thus, no agreement

116 See: Muylle, 2012, pp. 422-425; Sagaert, Goederenrecht, pp. 438-439.

117 Muylle, 2012, p. 424. See also: De Page, VI, 1956, nr. 434, C.

118 Muylle, 2012, pp. 665, 667-669. *Contra*: De Page, VII, 1957, nr. 481 (concerning mortgage on usufruct); Laurent, t. 30, 1878, 446 (concerning mortgage on usufruct).

119 B. Grimonprez, 'La résolution contractuelle tenue en échec par le caractère réel de l'emphytéose', annotation of Cass.fr. 14 November 2002, *La Sem.Jur.Not.Imm.* 2003, pp. 1310 *et seq.* See also: Muylle, 2012, pp. 424-425.

exists anymore to be terminated.[120] However, a more nuanced vision also exists: as far as long-lease and building lease are concerned, van Velten argues how book 6 of the Dutch Civil Code can be applied to rights *in rem*, insofar as no specific regulation (*lex specialis*) exists.[121] This last vision is more deeply analyzed below (*cf. infra*).

As far as the resolution of usufruct is specifically concerned, it can be supposed that a resolutory clause is impossible for usufruct in the first point of view. On the basis of the second point of view, it might be argued that it is possible, but the question then is whether the specific provision concerning denunciation cannot be considered a specific regulation in that case. Whatever the answer may be, relative effect is mentioned nowhere in this respect.

2.3.7.3 Long-Lease

The possibility of resolution on the basis of the implicit resolutory clause of article 1184 of the Belgian Civil Code in case of long-lease is heavily debated, because article 15 of the Long-lease Act (deprivation) would be the only way to sanction violations of the contract by the long-lessee.[122] However, the majority of case law and legal doctrine accepts – rightfully – that resolution on the basis of article 1184 Civil Code is possible for long-lease.[123] If the long-lease is terminated in this way, then it seems logical to grant this judicial resolution, even though it works retroactively, only relative effect.[124] After all, in principle (*cf. supra*), the third acquirer cannot anticipate this resolution, nor is he involved in it himself.

120 Snijders & Rank-Berenschot, 2012, p. 540. See also in general: E.B. Rank-Berenschot, *Over de scheidslijn tussen goederenrecht en verbintenissenrecht*, Deventer, Kluwer, 1992, integrally.

121 A.A. van Velten, *Privaatrechtelijke aspecten van onroerend goed*, Deventer, Kluwer, 2009, pp. 484-486.

122 *Contra* application of art. 1184 Civil Code on long-lease: De Page, VI, 1956, nr. 707, 2°, b), 716, A, 5° (he calls this application '*illogique et rigoureuse*', at least as far as the non-payment of the retribution is concerned; for other contractual violations, thus argues Sterckx, he seems to accept the application of article 1184 Civil Code in nr. 716, A, 5° (see D. Sterckx, 'L'emphytéose et la condition résolutoire tacite', annotation of Brussels 19 February 1986, *Rev.not.b.* 1986, p. 543)); Derine, Van Neste & Vandenberghe, 1984, pp. 887-888; Vandenberghe & Viaene, 2006, p. 37; Werdefroy, 1994, p. 4.

123 Examples: Brussels 19 January 1986, *Rev.not.b.* 1986, 536, annotation D. Sterckx ("*Attendu qu'en l'espèce le législateur de 1924 a rejeté la peine de commise pour défaut de paiement du canon sans pour autant exclure le droit de demander la résolution du bail emphythéotique; que les principes généraux consacrés par les articles 1183 et 1184 du Code civil restent d'application en vertu de la loi de 1824, ce qui en fait restaurait le régime souple déjà coutumier en Belgique*"; "*Attendu qu'aucun argument ne peut être tiré du texte d'une loi du 14 mai 1955 relative à la péréquation des redevances; que cette loi qui organise la déchéance des droits de l'emphytéote, n'est en réalité que l'expression du droit commun appliqué à un contrat particulier*"); Rb. Ghent 13 December 1882, *Pas.*, 1883, III, 211 = *B.J.* 1883, 84 = *J.T.* 1883, 117; Rb. Brussels 13 February 1889, Pas. 1889, III, 228. See also: Kluyskens, 1951, pp. 393, 396; Laurent, t. 8, 1878, pp. 478 *et seq.*; Mostin, 2015, pp. 133-134; Muylle, 2012, p. 203; Sagaert & Somers, 2008, pp. 88-89; V. Sagaert, 2014, pp. 583-584; S. Snaet, 'Art. 15 Erfpachtwet', 2010, p. 1; S. Snaet, 2006, p. 169; D. Sterckx, 1986, p. 544; K. Vanhove, 'Erfpacht: meer contractvrijheid dan gedacht!', annotation of Cass. 30 March 2006, *RW* 2006-07, pp. 681-682; Vanhove & Verbeke, 2003, p. 91; Van Oevelen, 1992, p. 340. For a general overview, see: D. Sterckx, 1986, pp. 542-544.

124 Examples: Rb. Veurne 16 February 1887, *JT* 1887, 657: "*Que la cause de résolution du droit d'emphytéose étant un fait volontaire dans le chef des preneurs, le droit d'hypothèque de la demanderesse n'a pu en souffrir*

Beside the implicit resolutory clause of article 1184 Civil Code, one must also refer to explicit resolutory clauses. The validity of such clauses seems to be generally accepted for long-leases, at least as far as judicial intervention is not excluded and the deprivation grounds of article 15 of the Long-lease Act are confirmed.[125] In fact, however, this is not accepting explicit resolutory clauses: this is merely accepting the contractual confirmation of the already existing resolution possibilities. I share Van Oevelen's view that a true explicit resolutory clause, excluding judicial intervention, is also valid.[126] This point of view is supported by the decision of 30 March 2006 of the Belgian Court of Cassation.[127]

Again, I uphold that this resolution has – in principle – only relative effect.[128]

In French law, again, remarkable differences exist between *bail emphytéotique* and *bail à construction*. As to the former, the implicit and explicit resolutory clause is not accepted: the judgment of the *Cour de cassation* of 14 November 2002 stipulates this for the explicit resolutory clause and the doctrine has expanded this rule to the implicit clause.[129] As to

---

et que ce droit lui est resté avec tous ses effets juridiques". See also: Rb. Ghent 13 December 1882, *Pas.*, 1883, III, 211 = *BJ* 1883, 84 = *JT* 1883, 117: "*Qu'on ne peut objecter que, par suite de la résolution du contrat d'emphytéose et en vertu du commandement du 24 février 1877, les hypothèques sont venues à tomber; qu'en effet, le principe;* "Resoluto jure concedentis resolvitur jus concessum quasi nunquam intercessit", *ne peut s'appliquer lorsque le contrat est résolu par une cause inhérente à l'acte lui-même, mais bien par une cause postérieure au contrat et, dans l'espèce, par le fait des Verstrynge qui ont manqué à toutes leurs obligations.*" See also: Muylle, 2012, pp. 665, 667-669; Sagaert & Somers, 2008, p. 94; V. Sagaert, 2014, 188-189. *Contra*: De Page, VII, 1957, nr. 481; Laurent, t. 30, 1878, p. 446.

125 Derine, Van Neste & Vandenberghe, 1984, p. 888; Kluyskens, 1951, p. 393; Van Oevelen, 1992, pp. 351-352; Vandenberghe & Viaene, 2006, pp. 37-38. *Contra*: De Page, VI, 1956 nr. 707, 2°, c).

126 Van Oevelen, 1992, pp. 351-352. This author is followed by others: Mostin, 2015, pp. 134-135; Muylle, 2012, pp. 200-202; P. Puelinckx and L. Boven, 'Erfpacht en opstal: een actuele erfenis', *in* F. Swennen & R. Barbaix (Eds.), *Over Erven. Liber amicorum Mieken Puelinckx-Coene*, Mechelen, Kluwer, 2006, p. 341; Sagaert & Somers, 2008, p. 88; V. Sagaert, 2014, p. 585; S. Snaet, 'Art. 15 Erfpachtwet', 2010, p. 1; S. Snaet, 2006, pp. 165-170; K. Vanhove, 2006-07, pp. 679-682; A. Verbeke & S. Snaet, 'Meccano-goederenrecht', *in* W. Pintens, A. Alen, E. Dirix & P. Senaeve (Eds.), *Vigilantibus ius scriptum. Feestbundel voor Hugo Vandenberghe*, Bruges, die Keure, 2007, pp. 381 e.v; Werdefroy, 1994, p. 4.

127 Cass. 30 March 2006, *Pas.*, 2006, 720 = *RW* 2006-07, 678, annotation K. Vanhove ("Deze bepaling art. 2 van de Erfpachtwet staat er niet aan in de weg dat de partijen in de erfpachtovereenkomst een beding opnemen waardoor de overeenkomst kan worden beëindigd, ook al is de minimumduur van zevenentwintig jaar niet verstreken, in geval van een insolventieprocedure of ontbinding van de erfpachtersrechtspersoon"; Vanhove argues that, *in casu*, it is an resolutory condition (*contra*: V. Waterkeyn and S. Snaet), but his reasoning is also valid for the resolutory clause) = *TBBR* 2008, 88, annotation V. Waterkeyn = *TBO* 2006, 165, annotation S. Snaet. See also: Luik 22 September 1983, *Pas.*, 1984, II, 7 (implicitly); Luik 9 April 1841, *Pas.*, 1842, II, 49; Rb. Brussels 13 February 1889, *Pas.*, 1889, III, 228; Rb. Veurne 16 February 1887, *JT* 1887, 657; Rb. Ghent 13 December 1882, *Pas.*, 1883, III, 211 = *BJ* 1883, 84 – *JT* 1883, 117; Rb. Hoei 22 November 1855, *Cl. Et B.*, 1854-1855, 697. Critique on this decision: Vandenberghe & Viaene, 2006, p. 38 (this allows to circumvent the minimum duration of 27 years).

128 See also: Muylle, 2012, pp. 661-665, 667-669; Sagaert & Somers, 2008, p. 94; V. Sagaert, 2014, pp. 88-589. *Contra*. De Page, VII, 1957, nr. 480, 3°; S. Snaet, 2006, p. 169.

129 Cass.fr. 14 November 2002, *Rép.Defr.* 2003, art. 37676, annotation R. Libchaber = *La Sem.Jur.Not.Imm.* 2003, 1310, annotation B. Grimonprez – *RDC* 2003, 122, annotation G. Lardeux = *Rev.trim.dr.civ.* 2003, 527, annotation T. Revet: "*Qu'en statuant ainsi, alors qu'une clause de résolution de plein droit confère à la jouissance du preneur une précarité incompatible avec la constitution d'un droit réel, la cour d'appel a violé*

the latter, by contrast, the application of the implicit resolutory clause is accepted: this stems from articles L251-6 and L251-7 of the *Code de l'Habitation et de la Construction*. As Saint-Alary formulates: "*Il est tout aussi certain que cette résiliation peut intervenir par décision de justice au cas de d'inexécution des obligations des parties et notamment du preneur, et même que dans ce dernier cas, le contrat peut prévoir que la résiliation aura lieu de plein droit*".[130] In this case, the resolution has only relative effect according to the third paragraph of article L251-6, insofar as the action for resolution has not been published yet.

Things are quite similar for the explicit resolutory clause. This is impossible for the *bail emphytéotique*,[131] but possible for the *bail à construction*.[132]

Dutch legal doctrine does not like the application of the implicit resolutory clause of article 6:265 of the Civil Code in long-leases. First, it is argued that a contractual remedy cannot be applied to a real right.[133] Second, it is upheld that this application is, in principle, possible, but that book 5 of the Civil Code formulates a *lex specialis* for long-leases and building leases, *i.e.* the denunciation for contractual violation, which makes it impossible to apply the general implicit resolutory clause.[134] Whatever the reason may be, it is clear that the implicit resolutory clause is considered impossible for long-leases under Dutch law.

---

les textes susvisés". This decision has been heavily criticized: Grimonprez, 2003, pp. 1310 *et seq.*; T. Revet, annotation of Cass.fr. 14 November 2002, *Rev.trim.dr.civ.* 2003, pp. 528-529. Approving the decision: G. Lardeux, annotation of Cass.fr. 14 November 2002, *RDC* 2003, p. 122. See also: Bergel, Bruschi & Cinamonti, 2010, p. 333; Tixier, 2006, nr. 15. See from a Belgian perspective: Muylle, 2012, pp. 247-248.

130 Saint-Alary, 2001, nr. 65.

131 E. Calveyra & M. Tournois, 'La clause résolutoire dans les d*ifff*érents types de baux', *Gaz.Pal.* 2007, Doctrine, p. 2386; Grimonprez, 2003, pp. 1310 *et seq.*; Lardeux, 2003, p. 122; Tixier, 2006, nr. 15: "*La précarité résultant d'une clause de résolution de plein droit est incompatible avec la notion même de bail emphytéotique*".

132 However, this distinction is criticized. Calveyra and Tournois formulate this as follows: "*Cette décision est cependant critiquable en ce qu'elle établit une distinction entre le bail emphytéotique et une institutions voisine, le bail à construction, qui confère également au preneur un droit réel, et dans lequel l'insertion d'une clause résolutoire est néanmoins considérée comme licite*". See Calveyra & Tournois, 2007, p. 2384. See also Grimonprez, 2003, pp. 1310 *et seq.*; R. Libchaber, *Rép.Defr.* 2003, art. 37676, p. 243. Libchaber criticizes that the Court identifies the precarity of the agreement with the precarity of the real right itself. In that respect, it must be remarked that French law still strictly distiguishes between the agreement establishing a real right and the real right itself… Libchaber pleads for a more nuanced vision thereon: "*Est-ce qu'au fond, la Cour n'est pas en train de se laisser séduire par une vision impressioniste du système juridique? Celle qui aboutirait à estimer qu'en règle générale, le contrat est une source trop instable pour permettre l'établissement de droits réels immobiliers, par nature susceptibles d'hypothèque. Une telle conception serait à l'évidence inacceptable: d'un contrat peuvent naître des droits réels aussi bien que personnels; et si la Cour vient ici mettre une limite à la génération de l'emphytéose, l'esprit de système exigerait de la ressusciter pour tous les autres contrats constitutifs de droits ou de situations réels, qu'ils débouchent sur un usufruit, un droit de superficie ou une servitude*".

133 Snijders & Rank-Berenschot, 2012, p. 540.

134 van Velten, 2009, p. 485.

As far as the explicit resolutory clause for long-lease is concerned, this may be recognized in the denunciation of article 5:87(2) of the Dutch Civil Code (*cf. supra*). However, this article only allows for the sanctioning of two contractual violations by a long-lessee: not paying the retribution for two subsequent years or not fulfilling the other obligations of the long-lessee.[135] Thus, Dutch law does not have a true explicit resolutory clause for long-leases, contrary to Belgian law.

2.3.7.4 *Building Lease*

Article 1184 of the Belgian Civil Code can perfectly be applied to building lease, insofar as the agreement establishing building lease is against payment.[136] In addition, it is ever more accepted that parties can insert an explicit resolutory clause in the agreement that established the building lease.[137]

To the extent that such clauses are allowed, I argue that the subsequent resolution has only relative effect.[138] The same exceptions apply as above (*cf. supra*). After all, I cannot see the difference with renunciation or deprivation, of which I have defended above that these have relative effect, too (*cf. supra*). In all these cases, in principle, the third acquirer cannot anticipate the termination of the real right on which he has an own real right, nor does he lie at the basis of the termination himself (*cf. supra*).

Under French law, no information is provided concerning this unusual termination ground for building leases. The fact that resolutory clauses are accepted as a termination ground for the *bail à construction* (*cf. supra*) forms an argument to accept this for building leases too. In that case, it could also be argued that the resolution has only relative effect, which is also the case for the *bail à construction* on the basis of the above-mentioned article L251-6 of the *Code de l'Habitation et de la Construction*.

For Dutch law, I refer to the analysis above for long-lease (*cf. supra*). After all, the rules for building lease are based on those for long-leases.

2.3.7.5 *Relation with Unusual Termination Grounds without Relative Effect*

An interesting question – and already discussed above (*cf. supra*) – is how this point of view on the relative effect of the resolutory clause, despite its retroactive effect, relates to the unusual termination grounds with retroactive effect but without relative effect.

---

135 Asser, Mijnssen, van Velten & Bartels, 2008, pp. 297-298; Snijders & Rank-Berenschot, 2012, p. 563.

136 Example: Ghent 12 May 2005, *TBBR* 2007, 541, annotation D. Bracke. See also: Bracke, 2007, p. 548; Laurent, t. 8, 1878, pp. 514-515; Muylle, 2012, pp. 331-334; Sagaert, 2014, p. 617; Snaet & Truyen, 'Art. 9 Opstalwet', 2010, p. 6; Van Oevelen, 1989, pp. 47-48.

137 Example: Ghent 12 May 2005, *TBBR* 2007, 541, annotation D. Bracke. See also: Bracke, 2007, pp. 548 *et seq.*; Mostin, 2015, p. 191; Muylle, 2012, pp. 333-334; Sagaert, 2014, p. 617; Snaet & Truyen, 'Art. 9 Opstalwet', 2010, p. 6; Snaet, 2008, p. 64; Vandenberghe & Viaene, 2006, p. 38; Verbeke & Snaet, 2007, p. 390.

138 See also: Muylle, 2012, pp. 665, 667-669. *Contra*: De Page, VII, 1957, nr. 481; Laurent, t. 30, 1878, p. 446; Snaet & Truyen, 'Art. 9 Opstalwet', pp. 6-7.

The first example I mentioned above was the resolutory condition (art. 74 of the Belgian Mortgage Act, *cf. supra*). The fact that the fulfilment of this condition does have an effect on third parties stems from the publicity of this condition: it is part of the deed establishing the real right and thus integrally published in the land register. Third parties can perfectly anticipate the fulfilment and effects of this resolutory condition.[139]

Second, I mentioned certain nullities, such as those occurring with vices of consent. It is not suggested anywhere that these have relative effect. On the contrary: it is commonly accepted that they also fall within the scope of article 74 of the Belgian Mortgage Act.[140] The question is how the following distinction can be justified: retroactive nullity following a vice of consent does not have relative effect, whereas retroactive resolution because of a contractual violation does have relative effect in this paper's view. In my opinion, the justification is to be found in the fact that vices of consent touch the establishment of the agreement, whereas resolution because of a contractual violation concerns the execution of that agreement. In case of a vice of consent in an agreement establishing a real right, this agreement is *ab initio* precarious, which is not the case for an agreement that is terminated because of a contractual violation. In addition, this precarity is not healed by the fact that the agreement is published in the land register: this is the so-called negative nature of the Belgian land register: *la publicité ne purge pas l'acte de ses vices*.[141] Let me clarify this with the following reasoning. A third party-mortgage creditor may trust that his mortgage debtor does not commit a violation of the agreement establishing the mortgaged real right, because of which that real right would be terminated. This is the justification for the relative effect of, for instance, the deprivation (*cf. supra*). That same third party, however, may not trust that the real right that is the object of his mortgage right is free from all vices. The publicity in the Belgian land register does not alter that fact. This is exactly why the nullity because of a vice of consent does not have relative effect.

3 Conclusion

This paper offers a thorough overview of the termination grounds with relative effect. In order to be clear, first, the termination grounds without relative effect have been briefly analyzed. The real subrogation as an alternative remedy for third acquirers has also received attention in that respect. Subsequently, the following termination grounds with relative effect have been studied: renunciation, termination by mutual consent, denunciation,

139 See also: Muylle, 2012, pp. 661-665; Sagaert & Somers, 2008, pp. 94-95. Examples: Bergen 4 May 1998, *Rec.gén.enreg.not.* 2000, nr. 25.015, *JLMB* 1999, and Bergen 17 May 1999, *Rec.gén.enreg.not.* 2000, nr. 25.016, annotation G.H.

140 Byttebier, 2005, nr. 639-641; De Page, VII, 1957, nr. 479 *et seq.*; Dirix & De Corte, 2006, p. 455; Genin, 1988, nr. 1281; Laurent, t. 30, 1878, p. 445; Muylle, 2012, p. 669.

141 This topic is the subject of the PhD thesis of the author.

confusion, deprivation because of abuse of rights, termination because of changed circumstances in Dutch law and, finally, resolution because of violation of a contractual clause.

As far as this last termination ground is concerned, this paper defends – following recent legal doctrine, but contrary to the classical point of view – that it effectively has relative effect and thus forms an exception to article 74 of the Belgian Mortgage Act. A series of arguments has been presented in this respect. However, in order for the resolution because of contractual resolution to have relative effect, it is required that the third acquirer is not aware of that contractual violation – factually or through the mentioning thereof in the land register (art. 3 Belgian Mortgage Act) – nor lies at the basis of it himself.

On a more abstract level, this paper studies the particularly interesting field of the boundaries between property law and contract law. Whereas in the past, these two branches of law were strictly separated, that separation has in recent decades become more blurred.[142] In this paper, this is exactly proven by the fact that contractual termination grounds are ever more accepted for rights *in rem*, whereas older legal doctrine was more skeptical in that regard. Consequently, research on the grey zone in between contract law and property law is very useful, both from an academic and practical point of view. It is the explicit hope of this paper to contribute to that research.

142 See for instance from a Belgian perspective: V. Sagaert, 'Het goederenrecht als open systeem van verbintenissen? Poging tot een nieuwe kwalificatie van de vermogensrechten', *TPR* 2005, pp. 983-1086. In French law, Libchaber regrets that the separation between these two is still so strictly propagated: Libchaber, 2003, p. 243.

3 The Protection of the Transferee Against Bankruptcy of the Transferor: Towards a Functional Approach for Movables?

Sander Baeyens[*]

1 Introduction

Comparative legal research has devoted much attention to the transfer of ownership of movable assets.[1] European legal scholars traditionally focus on the distinction between consensual systems and delivery systems. The distinction between consensual systems and delivery systems divides 'mainstream' European legal systems into two parts. In consensual systems, the transfer of ownership is effected at the moment of consensus between the parties about the transfer agreement. In delivery systems, ownership is transferred through delivery of the asset. Before delivery, the transferee only has a right to performance of the obligation to deliver.

The distinction between consensual systems and delivery systems has important consequences in the event of bankruptcy of the transferor.[2] This can be illustrated by the following example:

> X sells a movable asset to Y. Y immediately pays an important part of the purchase price. Subsequently, X goes bankrupt before the movable asset is delivered to Y.

---

* PhD Candidate, Institute for Property Law, KU Leuven.

1 See e.g. W. Faber & B. Lurger (Eds.), *Rules for the Transfer of Movables. A Candidate for European Harmonisation or National Reforms?*, München, Sellier, 2008, p. 265; B. Lurger & W. Faber (Eds.), *Acquisition and Loss of Ownership of Goods*, München, Sellier, 2008, p. 1658; J.M. Rainer & J. Filip-Fröschl (Eds.), *Transfer of Title Concerning Movables Part* I, Salzburg, Peter Lang, 2006, p. 210.

2 T. Hastad, 'Derivative Acquisition of Ownership of Goods', *ERPL*, Vol. 17, No. 4, 2009, p. 726; V. Sagaert, 'Consensual versus Delivery Systems in European Private Law – Consensus about Tradition?' *in* W. Faber & B. Lurger (Eds.), *Rules for the Transfer of Movables. A Candidate for European Harmonisation or National Reforms?*, München, Sellier, 2008, pp. 40-42.

Bankruptcy law is considered to be the 'litmus test' of private law.[3] It determines the effectiveness of a particular right. The treatment of a right in the event of bankruptcy is often related to its proprietary or personal nature. Ownership is the most extensive property right. In principle, property rights remain outside the bankruptcy estate. Property rights are not affected by the other contracting party's bankruptcy. Bankruptcy effectiveness is one of the essential qualities of property rights. Personal right holders, by contrast, are subject to the risk of bankruptcy. The position of personal right holders is governed by the *pari passu* principle.[4] The *pari passu* principle means that all creditors in the same position should be treated equally. Personal right holders obtain an equal distribution out of the assets of the bankruptcy estate. The proprietary (right of ownership) or personal (right to performance of the obligation to deliver) nature of the right of X is thus of the utmost importance in case of bankruptcy.[5]

The contribution of this paper to the existing body of knowledge is twofold. First, this paper compares the 'mainstream' European approach to the Scandinavian functional approach. Scandinavian legal systems do not use the transfer of ownership concept. In recent times, the Scandinavian functional approach received some attention in comparative legal literature.[6] However, Scandinavian legal systems are often considered to be diametrically opposed to other European legal systems. This paper will examine whether that is in fact the case and whether the adoption of the Scandinavian functional approach in case of bankruptcy would be desirable. Belgian law will be used as a test tube. Second, this paper aims to add a normative layer to the existing body of knowledge. The question is to which extent the transferee should be protected in the event of bankruptcy of the transferor. In answering this question, the distinction between consensual systems, delivery systems and functional systems will be transcended.

The scope of this paper is limited. First, the scope is limited to the transfer of corporeal movable assets. Movable assets are negatively defined as all assets that cannot be classified as immovable. Corporeal movable assets are movable assets that have a tangible structure.

3 See V. Sagaert, 'Insolvency as Bull in the China Store of Contract and Property' *in* D. Faber, B. Schuijling & N. Vermunt (Eds.), *Trust and Good Faith Across Borders. Liber Amicorum Prof. dr. S.C.J.J. Kortmann*, Deventer, Kluwer, 2017, pp. 153-167.

4 With respect to the *pari passu* principle, see E. Dirix, 'Effect of Security Rights vis-à-vis Third Persons' *in* U. Drobnig, H. Snijders & E.-J. Zippro (Eds.), *Divergences of Property Law, an Obstacle to the Internal Market*, München, Sellier, 2006, pp. 70-75; R.J. Mokal, 'Priority as Pathology: The Pari Passu Myth', *CLJ*, Vol. 66, No. 3, 2004, pp. 581-621.

5 R. Goode, *Principles of Corporate Insolvency Law*, 4th ed., London, Sweet & Maxwell, 2011, p. 101.

6 W. Faber, 'Scepticism about the Functional Approach from a Unitary Perspective' *in* W. Faber & B. Lurger (Eds.), *Rules for the Transfer of Movables. A Candidate for European Harmonisation or National Reforms?*, München, Sellier, 2008, pp. 97-122; C. Martinson, 'How Swedish Lawyers Think about 'Ownership' and 'Transfer of Ownership' – Are We Just Peculiar or Actually Ahead?' *in* W. Faber & B. Lurger (Eds.), *Rules for the Transfer of Movables. A Candidate for European Harmonisation or National Reforms?*, München, Sellier, 2008, pp. 69-95.

Second, this paper only focuses on bankruptcy proceedings. Other insolvency proceedings, e.g. reorganization proceedings, do not fall within the scope of this paper.

2 Transfer of Ownership in 'Mainstream' European Legal Systems

2.1 *The Distinction between Consensual Systems and Delivery Systems*

The right of ownership plays a central role in 'mainstream' European legal systems.[7] Ownership is the most extensive property right. 'Mainstream' European legal systems adhere to the so-called 'unitary' approach.[8] Unitary systems are legal systems under which the right of ownership is connected to a vast array of legal consequences, e.g. the right to use, the right to dispose and protection against the general creditors in the other contracting party's insolvency.[9] Unitary systems share the idea that the ownership question is pivotal for the solution of specific conflict situations.[10]

The ownership question is often discussed with respect to the transfer of ownership. Ownership passes when all legal requirements are satisfied.[11] Unitary systems have in common the fact that they link the transfer of ownership to a particular moment in time.[12] Three specific moments in a transfer process are suitable to effect the transfer of ownership: (1) consensus between parties about the contract, (2) transfer of possession of the asset ('delivery') to the transferee or (3) performance of the exchange obligation by the transferee (e.g. payment of the full purchase price). While the first two moments characterize the main distinction within the unitary transfer systems, the third moment is not endorsed by any European legislator as a default rule.[13] However, parties have the contractual freedom to determine that ownership only passes at the third moment.[14]

7 Hastad, 2009, p. 726.

8 A. Salomons, 'Comparative Law and the Quest for Optimal Rules on the Transfer of Movables for Europe', *EPLJ*, Vol. 2, No. 1, 2013, p. 67.

9 Faber, 2008, p. 100.

10 K.R. Haug, 'The Historical Development of the Scandinavian Functional Approach to Transfer of Ownership. A Tale of Change and Continuity', *EPLJ*, Vol. 6, No. 2, 2017, p. 236; M. Lilja, *Concepts, Functional Approaches, and Argumentation Analysis in the Field of the Transfer of Movables*, Hamburg, Verlag Dr. Kovac, 2015, p. 11.

11 K. Kullerkupp, 'Private Autonomy in Property Law: Can the Parties 'Design' their Transfer?' *in* W. Faber & B. Lurger (Eds.), *Rules for the Transfer of Movables. A Candidate for European Harmonisation or National Reforms?*, München, Sellier, 2008, p. 52.

12 W. Faber, 'Functional Method of Comparative Law and Argumentation Analysis in the Field of Transfers of Movables: Can They Contribute to Each Other?', *EPLJ*, Vol. 2, No. 1, 2013, p. 28.

13 Sagaert, 2008, pp. 9-10, note 2.

14 And parties often make use of this possibility, see e.g. V. Sagaert & D. Gruyaert, 'Retention of Title or the Transfer of Ownership in a Slideway: Ownership in Adultery?', *ERPL*, Vol. 25, No. 2, 2017, p. 421.

The distinction between delivery systems and consensual systems is the main dividing line within unitary transfer systems. It will be demonstrated that the two transfer systems are not diametrically opposed to each other. However, both transfer systems apply a different starting point.[15]

The majority of European legal systems are delivery systems (e.g. German law, Austrian law, Swiss law and Dutch law). In delivery systems, consensus between parties regarding the contract (the 'obligatory agreement') only gives rise to an obligation to transfer ownership of the asset.[16] Subsequently, ownership is transferred through delivery of the asset ('*traditio*'). In most delivery systems, delivery consists of (1) a (usually implicit) 'real agreement' and (2) the actual transfer of possession of the asset.[17] The distinction between the obligatory agreement obliging the transferor to transfer ownership and the real agreement which effects the transfer of ownership is referred to as the principle of distinction ('*Trennungsprinzip*').[18]

In consensual systems, consensus between parties about the obligatory agreement not only generates rights and obligations, but also triggers the proprietary effects of the transaction (e.g. French law, Belgian law, Italian law and the English Sale of Goods Act).[19] Consensus between parties suffices to transfer ownership of the asset ('*solo consensu*').[20]

2.2 *The Relevance of the Distinction between Consensual Systems and Delivery Systems in the Event of Bankruptcy*

The distinction between delivery systems and consensual systems is not merely of a theoretical nature, but also holds practical relevance. The choice between a delivery system and a consensual system has important consequences, e.g. in the event of bankruptcy of the transferor which is the subject of this paper.[21] Two basic principles of bankruptcy law are (1) the fixation principle and (2) the *pari passu* principle. The fixation principle means that the nature and amount of the rights of competing creditors to the debtor's property

---

15 L.P.W. van Vliet, *Transfer of Movables in German, French, English and Dutch Law*, Nijmegen, Ars Aequi Libri 2000, p. 23.

16 J. del Corral, 'The Delivery Requirement in So-called Consensual Transfer Systems', *ERPL*, Vol. 21, No. 5, 2013, pp. 1278-1279; van Vliet, 2000, p. 31.

17 del Corral, 2013, p. 1279; Sagaert, 2008, p. 29, note 2; W. Faber, 'National Report on the Transfer of Movables in Austria' *in* W. Faber & B. Lurger (Eds.), *National Reports on the Transfer of Movables in Europe, 1: Austria, Estonia, Italy, Slovenia*, München, Sellier, 2008, pp. 60-61; Van Vliet, p. 31.

18 Sagaert, 2008, pp. 29-30, note 2; Van Vliet, 2000, p. 31, note 15.

19 Sagaert, 2008, p. 14, note 2; F.M.J. Verstijlen, 'General Aspects of Transfer and Creation of Property Rights including Security Rights' *in* U. Drobnig, H. Snijders & E.-J. Zippro (Eds.), *Divergences of Property Law, an Obstacle to the Internal Market?*, München, Sellier, 2006, p. 18.

20 Van Vliet, 2000, p. 73.

21 Hastad, 2009, p. 726.

are measured and determined at the moment of the opening of the bankruptcy proceeding.[22] Further, the rights of the competing creditors on the assets of the debtor receive third party effect ('proprietary effect'). The *pari passu* principle means that all creditors in the same position should be treated equally.

The fixation principle and the *pari passu* principle do not apply outside bankruptcy or, more correctly, outside a situation of '*concursus creditorum*', i.e. the situation when creditors of the same debtor simultaneously enforce their claim against the estate or a particular asset of the debtor. The debtor is, in principle, free to discriminate between his creditors.[23]

In the event of the transferor being declared bankrupt, the nature of the right of the transferee is determined at the moment of the opening of bankruptcy proceedings. This follows directly from the fixation principle. In delivery systems, the transferee is subject to the risk of the transferor being declared bankrupt if the asset is not delivered before the opening of the bankruptcy proceeding.[24] The transferee has not acquired the right of ownership over the asset which means that the asset is still part of the bankruptcy estate.[25] In other words, the transferee did not obtain an enforceable property right ('right *in rem*'). The transferor's breach of the obligation to transfer ownership will only provide the transferee with an unsecured (often worthless) claim for damages.[26]

In consensual systems, by contrast, the transferee is protected against the bankruptcy of the transferor. The asset has left the bankruptcy estate at the moment of the consent.[27] The transferee will be able to establish control and possession over the asset ('*actio revindicatio*').[28]

The distinction between the delivery approach and the consensual approach leads to major practical differences if the transferee has already paid the purchase price in full, or at least in part, at the moment of the opening of bankruptcy proceedings.[29] In consensual systems, the pre-paying transferee is able to separate the assets from the bankruptcy estate.

22 T.H. Jackson, *The Logic and Limits of Bankruptcy Law*, Washington D.C., BeardBooks, 1986, pp. 26-27. See also E. Dirix, 'Insolventierecht en gemeenrecht' *in* H. De Wulf, R. Steennot, M. Tison & C. Van der Elst (Eds.), *Van alle markten. Liber amicorum Eddy Wymeersch*, Antwerpen, Intersentia, 2008, p. 415.

23 Dirix, 2006, p. 71.

24 del Corral, 2013, p. 1283; Sagaert, 2008, p. 40; By contrast, the general creditors of the transferor are protected against the transaction if the assets are still in the possession of the transferor.

25 Lilja, 2015, pp. 71-72; Sagaert, 2008, p. 40.

26 Sagaert, 2008, p. 40; Verstijlen, 2006, p. 19.

27 Lilja, 2015, p. 72; Sagaert, 2008, p. 40.

28 M. Lilja, *Transfer of Movable Property under U.S. Law. Discussed from a Functional Perspective*, Bern, PL Academic Research, 2014, p. 107

29 R. Gengatharen, 'Protecting the Prepaying Buyer of Goods from the Seller's Insolvency', *Insolv LJ*, Vol. 22, No. 1, 2014, p. 5; Faber, 2013, p. 452; B. Lurger, 'Transfer of Ownership of Movables in Book VIII of DCFR 2009 – With and Without the Transferor's Right to Transfer Ownership' in S. van Erp, A. Salomons & B. Akkermans (Eds.), *The Future of European Property Law*, München, Sellier, 2012, p. 53;' M. Boodman, 'The Prepaying Buyer: Another Perspective', *CBLJ*, Vol. 11, No. 3, 1986, p. 266.

In delivery systems, the pre-paying transferee is an unsecured creditor and finds himself in a detrimental situation. The transferee is not able to fully recover (the part of) the purchase price.[30] According to empirical research, unsecured creditors generally only receive a very small percentage of their claims.[31]

If the transferee has not yet paid the purchase price, the practical distinction between the delivery approach and the consensual approach is relatively small. Under the delivery rule, the transferee is entitled to withhold payment.[32] The administrator of the bankruptcy estate has the choice to either assume or reject the executory transfer agreement. If the administrator opts for the assumption of the transfer agreement, the administrator will have to deliver the asset in exchange for the payment of the purchase price.[33]

3 The Convergence between Consensual Systems and Delivery Systems

3.1 Consensual Systems as 'Fictitious' Delivery Systems

Notwithstanding the contrasting starting points, the distinction between delivery systems and consensual systems is not absolute. This results from the historical background of the consensual systems. Legal history research of French law, the mother law of consensual systems, has demonstrated that consensualism has slowly developed from the Roman delivery system.[34] French law has transformed the delivery requirement from an explicit 'genuine' transfer of possession to an implicit 'fictitious' transfer of possession. Consensual systems presume that the delivery requirement is fulfilled at the moment of consensus between parties.[35] Therefore, the principle of distinction ('*Trennungsprinzip*') also applies in consensual systems.[36] The consensus between parties about the obligatory agreement coincides with the conclusion of the real agreement which effects the transfer of ownership.[37]

30 The transferee is not entitled to claim property rights on the purchase price, see Sagaert, 2008, p. 40; van Vliet, 2000, pp. 26-27.

31 J. Baeck, 'Faillissement: wat blijft nog over voor de schuldeisers?' in J. Baeck (Ed.), *Privaatrecht in actie!*, Brugge, die Keure, 2018, pp. 226-244.

32 Lilja, 2015, p. 99.

33 The assumption of the transfer agreement is likely if the administrator does not expect to collect a higher price in case of an enforced auction.

34 Van Vliet, 2000, p. 201.

35 Sagaert, 2008, pp. 12-14.

36 However, the delivery requirement only consists of the real agreement. The actual transfer of possession is not included in the delivery requirement, see del Corral, 2013, p. 1284.

37 J. del Corral, 'Transfer of Generic Goods in So-called Consensual Transfer Systems', *EPLJ*, Vol. 3, No. 1, 2014, pp. 43-44; C. Lebon, 'Non nudis pactis dominia rerum transferuntur. Kritische bemerkingen omtrent de consensualiteit van de overdracht van eigendom en de vestiging van beperkte zakelijke rechten', *TPR*, Vol. 41, No. 1, 2004, pp. 432-433.

3.2 *Generic Assets and Future Assets*

The gap between delivery systems and consensual systems is not only refined from a theoretical perspective, but also from a practical point of view. First, the effect of the principle of consensualism is limited by the nature of the transferred assets. To this end, 'generic assets' and 'future assets' are referred to. Commercial transactions often have generic assets as object.[38] Generic assets are traditionally defined as assets that are determined on the basis of their weight, number or measure (e.g. 100 kilos of rice or 100 bottles of red wine from a certain brand and year).[39] The specificity principle of property law determines that each object of a property right must be identified or identifiable.[40] Therefore, the transfer of ownership of generic assets only takes place at the moment of identification.[41] Traditionally, legal scholars argued that identification must be effected in a consensual way. More recently, legal scholars and case law have accepted the validity and effectiveness of a unilateral identification.[42] The same line of reasoning applies to future assets. The transfer of ownership only occurs after the coming into existence of the transferred asset.[43]

The foregoing analysis cannot be applied to English law. However, the default rule under English law is the same. Section 16 of the English Sale of Goods Act stipulates that property in the assets is only transferred to the transferee if the assets are identified ('ascertained'). With respect to the transfer of assets ex bulk, the default rule is modified significantly in Sections 20A and 20B.[44] Under certain conditions, a right of co-ownership is granted to the transferee ex bulk. First, it is necessary that the assets form part of a bulk which is identified either in the transfer agreement or by subsequent agreement between the parties. Second, the transferee must have paid the price for some or all of the assets that form part of the bulk. If the transferee has only paid a part of the purchase price, the extent of the right of co-ownership will be limited to the share of the assets that have been paid for.[45]

The limitation of the principle of consensualism has important consequences in the event of bankruptcy. With the exception of the English Sale of Goods Act, the transferee of generic assets is not protected against the transferor being declared bankrupt before the

---

38 Lurger, 2012, p. 53; Boodman, 1986, p. 266; Sagaert, 2008, p. 41.

39 del Corral, 2014, pp. 35-36; van Vliet, 2000, p. 27.

40 del Corral, 2014, p. 36; M. Waelbroeck, *Le transfert de la propriété dans la vente d'objets mobiliers corporels en droit compare*, Brussel, Bruylant, 1961, pp. 22-25.

41 With respect to the transfer *en bloc*, i.e. the transfer of a specific lot of assets for a lump sum, identification takes place immediately upon the conclusion of the obligatory agreement, see del Corral, 2014, p. 38.

42 For further references, see del Corral, 2014, pp. 41-42; Sagaert, 2008, p. 21.

43 Sagaert, 2008, p. 22.

44 Section 61 (1) defines transfers *ex bulk* as the transfer of a mass or collection of goods of the same kind which is contained in a defined space or area and is such that any goods in the bulk are interchangeable with any other goods therein of the same number or quantity.

45 Van Vliet, 2000, p. 99.

identification of the transferred assets. Unlike the transferee of specific assets, the transferee of generic assets will only receive a small dividend, or no dividend at all, from the bankruptcy estate. Some legal scholars argue that there are no compelling reasons for this difference in treatment.[46] They suggest providing the pre-paying transferee of generic assets with an equivalent level of proprietary protection. If there are not sufficient generic assets on stock in the bankruptcy estate to satisfy all pre-paying transferees, the transferees should e.g. be provided with a preference right to be satisfied out of the remaining stock of these assets.[47]

3.3 *Contractual Deviations: Retention of Title and Constructive Delivery*

Finally, parties can contractually deviate from default delivery or consensual rules.[48] In consensual systems, parties can delay the transfer of ownership until the moment of delivery of the assets. However, in most cases, parties will insert a retention of title clause in the transfer agreement to delay the transfer of ownership until the purchase price has been paid in full.[49] A retention of title clause delays the transfer of ownership in both delivery and consensual systems. Although the transferee under retention of title will only obtain the right of ownership at the time of payment, the right of the transferee is bankruptcy effective as of the moment of delivery of the asset. This is the so-called '*Anwartschaftsrecht*' ('expectation right') of the transferee.[50] The bankruptcy administrator cannot recover the asset as long as the transferee pays the purchase price in accordance with the terms of the transfer agreement.[51]

Parties cannot only delay but also advance the transfer of ownership in delivery systems. The transfer of ownership can take place '*constitutum possessorium*' ('constructive delivery').[52] Under a transfer of ownership *constitutum possessorium*, parties agree that the right of ownership is transferred to the transferee before the transferee has acquired physical

46 W. Faber, 'Zur Übereignung nach dem tschechischen Entwurf eines Zivilgesetzbuches von 2005 – Anmerkungen aus rechtsvergleichender Sicht' in J. Svetska, J. Dvorak & L. Tichy (Eds.), *Tagungsband der Diskussionsforen zum Bürgerlichen Gesetzbuch*, Beroun, Eva Rozkotova – IFEC, 2008, p. 63; Comment C37 to VIII.-2:101 of the Draft Common Frame of Reference (DCFR); See for a discussion of this argument Lilja, 2015, pp. 94-97.

47 M. Costa & W. Faber, 'Die Eigentumsübertragung beim Kauf beweglicher Sachen im französischen und belgischen Recht', *ZfRV*, Vol. 50, 2010, p. 272; Faber, 2013, p. 45.

48 Kullerkupp, 2008, pp. 52-53.

49 E.F. Verheul, *Eigendomsvoorbehoud*, Deventer, Kluwer, 2018, p. 2; Sagaert & Gruyaert, 2017, p. 421; U. Drobnig, 'Present and Future of Real and Personal Security', ERPL, Vol. 11, No. 5, 2003, p. 649.

50 For a comparative analysis, see Sagaert & Gruyaert, 2017, pp. 423-437.

51 See § 107 of the German Insolvenzordnung; W.H.M. Reehuis & A.H.T. Heisterkamp, *Goederenrecht*, Deventer, Kluwer 2012, para 132; J. Peter, *Levering van roerende zaken*, Deventer, Kluwer, 2007, p. 141; M.E. Storme, 'Van trust gespeend? Trusts en fiduciaire figuren in het Belgische privaatrecht', *TPR*, Vol. 35, No. 3, 1998, p. 724.

52 Sagaert, 2008, pp. 32-33.

possession over the asset.[53] The act of delivery is effected fictitiously at the moment of consensus about the contract.[54] In the event of a transfer of ownership *constitutum possessorium*, parties agree to replace the delivery rule in favor of the application of the consensual rule.[55] In principle, the transfer of ownership *constitutum possessorium* will be effective in case of bankruptcy of the transferor.[56]

4 THE FUNCTIONAL APPROACH

4.1 *The Functional Approach: Concept*

Scandinavian legal systems adhere to the so-called functional approach.[57] In contrast to 'mainstream' European legal systems, Scandinavian legal systems do not apply the transfer of ownership concept.[58] Legal facts (e.g. delivery or consensus about a contract) are directly linked to legal consequences (e.g. protection in the event of bankruptcy of the transferor) without the need for an intermediate legal concept.[59] The transfer of ownership concept is considered to be a detour for solving specific conflict situations.[60] Functional legal scholars perceive the transfer of ownership concept as a meaningless, fictional and metaphysical concept.[61]

---

53 Van Vliet, 2000, p. 35 and p. 142.

54 del Corral, 2013, pp. 1283-1285.

55 Lurger, 2012, p. 51; J. Hallebeek, 'Transfer of Ownership: Traditionalism or Consensualism?', *Codicillus*, Vol. 45, No. 1, 2004, p. 14; In Book VIII of the DCFR, it can be defended from a functional point of view that a mixed delivery-consensual approach is taken. The right of ownership passes at the moment of delivery, unless the parties have agreed otherwise. See for a critical analysis of this question, L.P.W. van Vliet, 'Boek VIII DCFR: Acquisition and Loss of Ownership of Goods', *NTBR*, Vol. 51, No. 7, 2011, p. 353; A. Salomons, 'Fifteen Questions on the Rules Regarding the Acquisition of Movables in Book VIII Draft Common Frame of Reference', *ERPL*, Vol. 17, No. 4, 2009, pp. 714-716.

56 E. Verheul, 'Hoe relatief is de relativering van de levering c.p. door een bezitter?', *WPNR*, Vol. 148, No. 7171, 2017, p. 914; F. Damsteegt-Molier, *Relativering van eigendom. Een analyse aan de hand van de relativering van de levering c.p., de relatieve werking van de verkrijging op grond van de actio pauliana en van de blokkeringsregel bij beslag op roerende zaken*, Den Haag, Boom Juridische Uitgevers, 2009, p. 45; *Contra*: J. del Corral, *De leveringsplicht bij de overdracht van roerende lichamelijke goederen*, Antwerpen, Intersentia, 2013, pp. 462-464.

57 For a historical overview, see Haug, 2017, pp. 236-271; For an interesting study of the similarities between the Scandinavian functional approach and Art. 9 of the U.S. Uniform Commercial Code (UCC), see Lilja, 2015, p. 13 *et seq.*

58 Martinson, 2008, p. 70.

59 Lilja, 2015, p. 13; Hastad, 2009, pp. 726-727.

60 Martinson, 2008, p. 75.

61 G. Alexander, 'Comparing the Two Legal Realisms – American and Scandinavian', *Am.J.Comp.L.*, Vol. 50, No. 1, 2002, pp. 148-162; M. Martin, *Legal Realism – American and Scandinavian*, Bern, Peter Lang, 1997, para 46; V. Lundstedt, *Legal Thinking Revised: My Views on Law*, Stockholm, Almqvist & Wiksell, 1956, p. 85.

The alternative for the transfer of ownership concept is the application of a conflict-by-conflict approach.[62] First, every identified conflict situation deserves a tailored solution and should therefore be separated.[63] The protection of the transferee against bankruptcy of the transferor should e.g. not be mixed up with the protection of the transferor in the event of bankruptcy of the transferee.[64] It is not necessary to coordinate the solutions. A coordination of solutions is possible, but is not considered to be of primary importance.[65] Second, every conflict situation should be solved on the basis of a balance of interests.[66] Legal scholars e.g. debate about the question whether the transferee should be given priority in case of bankruptcy of the transferor.[67] The interests of the transferee are balanced against the interests of the general creditors of the transferor.[68] The outcome of this balancing test is used to justify the legal consequences. In the next section, we will see that the application of the balancing test does not mean a uniform solution in Scandinavian legal systems.

4.2 *The Functional Approach in Scandinavian Legal Systems*

Under Swedish law, the transferee is protected from the transferor's general creditors if the transferor has delivered the asset before the opening of bankruptcy proceedings. Swedish law applies the 'delivery requirement'.[69] There are three exceptions to the delivery requirement. First, the transferee is protected if the transfer is registered.[70] Second, the delivery rule is abolished in relation to business-to-consumer transactions.[71] Third, the delivery rule does not apply with respect to assets bought at an enforced auction.[72] The main reason for the delivery requirement is the prevention of fictitious and sham transactions.[73] Further, delivery provides the transfer with some form of publicity.[74] However,

62 Hastad, 2009, p. 725.

63 M. Lilja, 'National Report on the Transfer of Movables in Sweden' *in* W. Faber & B. Lurger (Eds.), *National Reports on the Transfer of Movables in Europe. Volume 5: Sweden, Norway and Denmark, Finland, Spain*, München, Sellier 2011, pp. 14-15; Martinson, 2008, pp. 90-91.

64 Hastad, 2009, p. 736.

65 Martinson, 2008, p. 91.

66 Lilja, 2011, p. 15.

67 Lilja, 2015, p. 88.

68 See e.g. Hastad, 2009, pp. 734-737.

69 Lilja, 2011, p. 58.

70 This exception is hardly ever used, see Lilja, 2011, pp. 58-59.

71 Hastad, 2009, p. 735.

72 Lilja, 2011, p. 59.

73 Delivery is also required for security agreements. The delivery requirement aligns the regime of outright sales with the rules on security agreements. This prevents the creation of hidden security rights. See Lilja, 2011, pp. 61-62.

74 It is said that future creditors otherwise could be misled about the creditworthiness of the transferor, see with respect to this argument: Lilja, 2011, p. 66; D. Hamwijk, 'Public Filing with Regard to Non-possessory Security Rights in Tangible Assets as Contemplated by the DCFR: Of No Benefit to Unsecured (Trade) Creditors', *ERPL*, Vol. 19, No. 5, 2011, pp. 613-630; Hastad, 2009, pp. 735-736.

over the last decade, the preservation and the utility of the delivery requirement was fiercely debated in Swedish legal scholarship.[75]

The delivery requirement also applies in Norwegian law. However, the solution adopted under Norwegian law is more lenient than the mandatory delivery rule under Swedish law. Legal scholars argue that the transferee will be protected against the transferor's general creditors if the transferor is prepared to transfer the actual possession of the asset but the transferee asks him to wait (e.g. due to problems of storing the assets). In that case, the risk of fraudulent or simulated transactions would be relatively small and the application of the delivery requirement would be difficult to defend from a functional perspective.[76]

The balancing test does not always lead to the application of the delivery requirement. Based on functional considerations, Danish and Finnish law adhere to a consensual rule.[77] The dichotomy between delivery systems and consensual systems also seems to be embedded in Scandinavian legal systems. The difference is that the preference for a delivery rule or a consensual rule does not follow from the answer to the ownership question, but from the answer to the question as to when the transferee deserves protection against bankruptcy of the transferor.[78]

4.3 *The Functional Approach in 'Mainstream' European Legal Systems: Belgian Law as a Test Tube*

Scandinavian legal scholars tend to distance themselves from the unitary approach of 'mainstream' European legal systems.[79] The unitary approach is seen as a very negative 'hocus-pocus' way of legal thinking.[80] In 'mainstream' European legal scholarship, by contrast, the functional approach does not receive a lot of attention. The basic ingredients of a successful relationship, mutual interest and understanding, are not present between functional legal scholars and unitary legal scholars. This is unfortunate because both legal

75 E.g. the delivery requirement is challenged by Supreme Court Judge Hastad, see Lilja, 2011, pp. 63-68.

76 J.-O. Faerstad & M. Lilja, 'National Report on the Transfer of Movables in Norway and Denmark' *in* W. Faber & B. Lurger (Eds.), *National Reports on the Transfer of Movables in Europe. Volume 5: Sweden, Norway and Denmark, Finland, Spain*, München, Sellier, 2011, pp. 238-245.

77 Faerstad & Lilja, 2011, pp. 245-247; M. Kuusinen, 'National Report on the Transfer of Movables in Finland' *in* W. Faber & B. Lurger (Eds.), *National Reports on the Transfer of Movables in Europe. Volume 5: Sweden, Norway and Denmark, Finland, Spain*, München, Sellier, 2011, pp. 360-363.

78 Haug, 2017, p. 239.

79 See for a recent effort to convince the functional lawyer of the importance of trying to understand the functional ratio behind the unitary approach, J. Sandstedt, *Sakräten, Norden och Europeiseringen – nordisk funktionalism möter kontinental substantialism*, Stockholm, Jure förlag, 2013; For a review of this book in English, see C. Martinson, 'Bridging the Gap. Review of Property Law, the Nordic Legal Culture and the Europeanisation – Nordic Functionalism Meets Continental Substantialism', by Johan Sandstedt', *EPLJ*, Vol. 3, No. 3, 2014, pp. 280-284.

80 Lilja, 2011, pp. 17-19; Faber, 2008, p. 99.

systems could learn from each other about how to cope with several issues. In this section, we will see that 'mainstream' European legal systems are in fact open to the functional approach without leaving the transfer of ownership concept.[81] Belgian law is used as a good example.

Belgian law applies a consensual transfer system. Legal scholars agree that the transfer of ownership is effected between parties ('*inter partes*') at the moment of consensus about the contract.[82] The majority of legal scholars defend that consensus about the contract also provides the transfer of ownership with third party effect ('*erga omnes*').[83] This is in accordance with the traditional consensual approach. The conclusion of the transfer agreement protects the transferee against bankruptcy of the transferor.[84]

According to a more modern view in Belgian legal scholarship ('the modern consensual approach'), the priority conflict between the transferee and the general creditors of the transferor is solved by the transfer of possession.[85] This solution is premised on an extensive interpretation of article 1141 of the Belgian Civil Code.[86] Article 1141 of the Belgian Civil Code deals with the scenario of a double sale. In the event of a double sale, priority is given to the first transferee who has been given actual possession of the asset under the condition that he has acted in good faith.[87] Hence, as long as the actual transfer of possession has not been effected, the right of ownership of the transferee will not be enforceable against a second transferee who also acts in good faith, i.e. who did not know and should not have

81 See Sagaert, 2008, pp. 35-37; S.E. Bartels, 'An Abstract or a Causal System' *in* W. Faber & B. Lurger (Eds.), *Rules for the Transfer of Movables. A Candidate for European Harmonisation or National Reforms?*, München, Sellier, 2008, pp. 59-60.

82 M.E. Storme, *Zekerheden- en Insolventierecht. Deel IV*, Gent, 2017, p. 578; del Corral, 2013, pp. 104-105; Sagaert, 2008, pp. 40-41.

83 G. Beltjens, *Encyclopédie du droit civil belge III*, 3th ed., Brussel, Bruylant, 1905, para 7; F. Laurent, *Principes de droit civil XVI*, 4th ed., Brussel, Bruylant, 1887, p. 429; See also in French law, R. Demogue, *Traité des obligations en général – Effets des obligations VI*, Paris, Librairie Arthur Rousseau, 1931, p. 121.

84 Storme, 2017, pp. 589-592; J. Van de Voorde & N. Carette, 'Is het bezit als publiciteitsmiddel in verval?' *in* A. De Boeck, V. Sagaert & R. Van Ransbeeck (Eds.), *Publiciteit in het zakenrecht*, Brugge, die Keure, 2015, p. 69.

85 P. Wéry, 'L'adage *prior tempore potior iure*: principe général de droit ou simple brocard?' *in Le temps et le droit. Hommage au Professeur Closset-Marchal*, Brussel, Bruylant, 2013, pp. 643-645; Sagaert, 2008, p. 41, note 2; E. Dirix, 'Actuele trends in de zakelijke zekerheidsrechten' *in Het zakenrecht: absoluut niet een rustig bezit*, Antwerpen, Kluwer, 1992, p. 6; M.E. Storme, 'Overdracht van roerende goederen, vestiging van pandrecht, eigendomsvoorbehoud: een poging tot systematisatie' *in Het zakenrecht: absoluut niet een rustig bezit*, Antwerpen, Kluwer, 1992, p. 498; Storme, however, changed his opinion more recently, see Storme, 2017, pp. 589-592.

86 Legal scholars have criticized the modern view from a textual perspective, see Van de Voorde & Carette, 2015, p. 69.

87 Van de Voorde & Carette, 2015, p. 65; Wéry, 2013, p. 643; del Corral, 2013, p. 1292; F. Baudoncq, 'Dubbele verkoop', *NJW*, Vol. 3, No. 86, 2004, pp. 1129-1130.

known about the first transfer agreement.[88] A delivery *constitutum possessorium* does not suffice to make the right of ownership effective against a subsequent transferee.[89]

As mentioned above, the claims of the general creditors of the transferor on the debtor's assets receive third party effect ('proprietary effect') at the moment of the opening of the bankruptcy proceeding. Therefore, from a functional perspective, their position is very similar to the position of the second transferee who is in good faith.[90] Both parties are confronted with an older property right that is not yet perfected through an actual transfer of possession.[91] Furthermore, and with respect to immovable assets, the general creditors of the transferor are generally considered as third parties in the sense of article 1 of the Belgian Mortgage Act. The general creditors are protected against transfer agreements that are not published in the land register before the opening of the bankruptcy proceeding.[92] This modern consensual approach aligns the position of the transferee of a movable asset with the position of the transferee of an immovable asset.

The modern view in Belgian legal scholarship implies that the transferee will not be protected against bankruptcy of the transferor. It is almost impossible for the transferee to prove that all the general creditors of the transferor act in bad faith, i.e. that they all knew or should have known about the transfer agreement. Therefore, some legal scholars defend a functional interpretation of the good faith requirement. The transferee is protected against bankruptcy of the transferor if the transfer was entered into in the normal course of business.[93] In that case, the general creditors could have expected the transfer of the asset.[94]

Both the traditional consensual approach and the modern consensual approach can be defended from a Belgian law perspective. The consensual nature of a transfer system does not exclude a functional, result-based approach. The same applies to delivery systems. The assessment of the enforceability of a transfer *constitutum possessorium* will determine whether or not the transferee is protected against bankruptcy of the transferor. The nature of a transfer system is, in itself, not decisive for the position of the transferee in case of bankruptcy of the transferor.[95] The position of the transferee has to be determined on the

---

88 del Corral, 2013, pp. 1292-1293; Sagaert, 2008, p. 18.

89 del Corral, 2013, p. 1294; Storme, 1992, p. 168.

90 Dirix, 1992, p. 6; Storme, 1992, pp. 490-491.

91 The difference is that the second transferee receives a property right through the conclusion of a transfer agreement, while the personal rights of the creditors of the transferor receive proprietary effect through the opening of a bankruptcy proceeding, see Storme, 2017, p. 589.

92 del Corral, 2013, p. 1296; V. Sagaert & A. Lemmerling, 'The Transfer of Immovable Property in Belgian Law' *in* A. Pradi (Ed.), *Transfer of Immoveable Property in Europe. From Contract to Registration*, Trento, Università degli studi di Trento, 2012, p. 56; E. Dirix, 'Faillissement en lopende overeenkomsten', *RW*, Vol. 67, No. 6, 2003, p. 207.

93 del Corral, 2013, pp. 496-497; Sagaert, 2008, p. 41; Dirix, 2003, p. 208.

94 del Corral, 2013, pp. 496-497.

95 Sagaert, 2008, p. 53.

basis of functional arguments. Elaborating these functional arguments requires taking the criteria of legal certainty, coherence and fairness into account. In the next section, a possible solution will be provided from a bankruptcy theory perspective.

5 FUNCTIONAL ANALYSIS OF THE POSITION OF THE TRANSFEREE IN THE EVENT OF BANKRUPTCY OF THE TRANSFEROR: A BANKRUPTCY LAW PERSPECTIVE

5.1 *The Role of Bankruptcy Law*

Bankruptcy law, at its core, is a collective form of debt-collection law.[96] If a debtor goes into bankruptcy, the question arises what assets in its possession are to be considered available for distribution among its general creditors.[97] In principle, the bankruptcy estate contains all the debtor's assets.[98] However, the creditors must take the assets as "*they come into the hands of the debtor.*"[99] The general creditors are in a no better position than the debtor itself. In other words, the relative value of the rights of the creditors cannot transcend the value of the bankruptcy estate.[100] As a consequence, the general creditors must e.g. respect the fact that certain assets are encumbered with an enforceable property right to the benefit of a third party. Enforceable property rights are bankruptcy effective.

Legal scholars have demonstrated that the enforceability of a property right follows from the general rules of property law. It is not the task of bankruptcy law to decide on the enforceability of a particular property right. Bankruptcy law must, in principle, respect pre-bankruptcy entitlements.[101] If bankruptcy law were to alter pre-bankruptcy entitlements, it would create "*incentives for strategic 'shopping' between the nonbankruptcy and bankruptcy forums.*"[102] The United States Supreme Court has described this reasoning as follows in the 1979 *Butner v. United States* case:

---

96 Jackson, 1986, p. 3.

97 Goode, 2011, pp. 94-95.

98 Storme, 2017, p. 309; C. Saint-Aloury-Houin, *Droit des entreprises en difficulté*, 10th ed., Paris, LGDJ, 2016, p. 803; C.J. Tabb, *The Law of Bankruptcy*, 3th ed., St. Paul, West Academic Publishing, 2014, p. 87.

99 T.H. Jackson, 'Translating Assets and Liabilities to the Bankruptcy Forum', *J.LegalStud.*, Vol. 14, No. 1, 1985, p. 99; See also Goode, 2011, p. 97.

100 M.E. Storme, 'Samenloop en rangschikking van schuldvorderingen bij faillissement: algemene beginselen' *in* H. Braeckmans, M.E. Storme, M. Vanmeenen, B. Tilleman en J. Vananroye (Eds.), *Curatoren en vereffenaars: actuele ontwikkelingen IV*, Antwerpen, Intersentia, 2017, p. 159; Tabb, 2014, p. 409; Dirix, 2008, p. 415.

101 Jackson, 1986, pp. 21-27; See also Goode, 2011, pp. 93-94; C.W. Mooney, 'A Normative Theory of Bankruptcy Law: Bankruptcy as (Is) Civil Procedure', *Wash.&Lee L.Rev.*, Vol. 61, No. 3, 2004, pp. 942-945; D.G. Baird, *Elements of Bankruptcy*, 3rd ed., New York, Foundation Press, 2001, p. 4.

102 Jackson, 1986, p. 27.

> Property interests are created and defined by state law. Unless some federal interest requires a different result, there is no reason why such interests should be analyzed differently simply because an interested party is involved in a bankruptcy proceeding. Uniform treatment of property interests by both state and federal courts within a State serves to reduce uncertainty, to discourage forum shopping, and to prevent a party from receiving a windfall merely by reason of the happenstance of bankruptcy.[103]

5.2 *The Conflict between the Transferee and the General Creditors of the Transferor in the Event of Bankruptcy*

Property rights are enforceable if they are protected by a property rule. Property rights are protected by a property rule to the extent that the property right holder cannot be involuntarily deprived of his property right.[104] Property rules constitute an exception to the so-called efficient breach doctrine. According to the efficient breach doctrine, "*the only universal consequence of a legally binding promise is that the law makes the promisor pay damages if the promised event does not come to pass.*"[105] This can be illustrated by the following examples:

1. X sells a movable asset to Y. After the conclusion of the transfer agreement but before delivery, Z approaches X. Z offers to pay a much higher price for the movable asset. X decides to breach the transfer agreement with Y and to transfer and deliver the movable asset to Z. Under the condition that Z has acted in good faith, Y will only be entitled to damages for breach of the transfer agreement.
2. X sells a movable asset to Y. X delivers the movable asset to Y. After delivery, Z approaches X and offers to pay a much higher price for the movable asset. However, Y is protected by a property rule. Y cannot be involuntarily deprived from his property right.

103 Butner *v.* United States *et al.*, 48 U.S. 440 (Sup.Ct. 21 February 1979), pp. 54-55.

104 G. Calabresi & A.D. Melamed, 'Property Rules, Liability Rules, and Inalienability: One View of the Cathedral', *Harv.L.Rev.*, Vol. 85, No. 6, 1971-72, p. 1092; See also E. Sherwin, 'Property, Rules, and Property Rules' *in Cornell Law Faculty Working Papers*, Ithaca, Cornell Law Library, 2007, p. 5; I. Ayres & J.M. Balkin, 'Legal Entitlements as Auctions: Property Rules, Liability Rules, and Beyond', *Yale L.J.*, Vol. 106, No. 3, 1996-97, p. 704.

105 O.W. Holmes, *The Common Law*, Boston, Little, Brown & Co., 1881, p. 301. See also D. Friedman, 'The Efficient Breach Fallacy', *J.Legal Stud.*, Vol. 18, No. 1, 1989, pp. 1-24.

This pre-bankruptcy situation can be translated into the bankruptcy forum. In bankruptcy law, the transferee also faces the risk of breach of contract.[106] The bankruptcy trustee will breach the transfer agreement if this is beneficial to the bankruptcy estate.[107] The influence of the decision of the bankruptcy trustee on the transferee's property right depends on the enforceability thereof. If the debtor has not delivered the asset before the opening of bankruptcy proceedings, the bankruptcy trustee can breach the transfer agreement by selling the asset on to a third party. This results from the unenforceability of the property right in pre-bankruptcy law. The pre-bankruptcy solution must be extended to the bankruptcy forum.[108] Otherwise, the opening of bankruptcy proceedings would enhance the position of the transferee. This would be incompatible with the aforementioned role of bankruptcy law. From a bankruptcy theory perspective, the fulfilment of the 'delivery requirement' is necessary to provide the property right of the transferee with bankruptcy effectiveness.

6 CONCLUSION

The first research question focused on the desirability of the adoption of the Scandinavian functional approach in 'mainstream' European legal systems. It is concluded that the adoption of the Scandinavian functional approach is desirable, but only to a certain extent. The transfer of ownership concept is strongly rooted in 'mainstream' European legal systems. 'Mainstream' European legal systems should not abolish this concept. The application of the transfer of ownership concept has benefits for legal certainty and, even more so, for the coordination of solutions to legal problems. However, this does not mean that 'mainstream' European legal scholars should ignore the functional way of legal thinking. The use of a functional, result-based approach does not exclude the transfer of ownership concept and vice versa. Belgian law is an excellent example of this. The protection of the transferee in the event of bankruptcy of the transferor ultimately depends on the interpretation of the applicable consensual or delivery rule. This interpretation should be based on functional arguments. The gap between 'mainstream' European legal systems and functional Scandinavian legal systems is not unbridgeable. We have to stop dancing on our own. After all, it takes two to tango.

---

106 The risk of breach of contract is even higher in the event of bankruptcy because the decision of the bankruptcy trustee to breach a contract will only generate an unsecured claim.

107 T.T. van Zanten, *De overeenkomst in het insolventierecht*, Deventer, Kluwer, 2012, pp. 129-132; Dirix, 2003, pp. 203-204; J.L. Westbrook, 'A Functional Analysis of Executory Contracts', *Minn.L.Rev.*, Vol. 74, No. 2, 1989, pp. 231-233; M.T. Andrew, 'Executory Contracts in Bankruptcy: Understanding Rejection', *U.Colo.L.Rev.*, Vol. 59, No. 4, 1988, pp. 895-901.

108 Jackson, 1986, p. 110; See also J.L. Westbrook & K.S. White, 'The Demystification of Contracts in Bankruptcy', *Am.Bankr.L.J.*, Vol. 91, No. 3, 2017, pp. 489-491.

3 *The Protection of the Transferee Against Bankruptcy of the Transferor: Towards a Functional Approach for Movables?*

The determination of the desirable position of the transferee in the event of bankruptcy of the transferor was the subject of the second research question. The answer to this question results from the role of bankruptcy law. Bankruptcy law should, in principle, not alter pre-bankruptcy entitlements. The enforceability of a property right results from the general rules of property law. Before delivery, the transferee finds himself in a precarious situation. The property right of the transferee is subject to the risk of breach of contract. This is no different from the situation under bankruptcy law. Therefore, delivery is necessary to make the position of the transferee bankruptcy proof.

4 The Effect of a Seller's Insolvency on the Transfer of Immovable Property

Tiddo Bos[*]

1 Introduction

In 2017 roughly 390,000 transfers of real estate took place in the Netherlands, an increase of 12% compared to 2016.[1] Immovable property, land in particular, generally constitutes a long lasting asset of considerable financial value.[2] Moreover, immovable property – especially real estate for residential purposes – has a significant social value,[3] which aspect of real estate becomes more important in countries where the right to housing cannot be taken for granted.[4] For this reason, the method of transferring an immovable asset is, in most jurisdictions, more complicated than the method of transferring other kinds of assets. The transfer of immovable property in the Netherlands requires a legal practitioner (a civil-law notary) to sign and submit the deed of transfer to the public land records for registration.

It is essential that these transactions are executed as efficiently, safely and inexpensively as possible, in order to sustain economic growth.[5] In this context, the effects of bankruptcy (on the part of the seller) interfere with the transfer of immovable property on two different levels.

Firstly, it interferes on a direct level; the consequences of the transfer may be (automatically) reversed. This means that no transfer took place and that the buyer has never become the owner of the immovable property. Most jurisdictions have a rule that renders it

* LLM, PhD Researcher at the University of Groningen.

1 KNB (Koninklijke Notariële Beroepsorganisatie), 'factsheet akten, meerjarenoverzicht' www.knb.nl/actueel/factsheets (accessed 19 February 2018).

2 In 2016, the total value of immovable property in the Netherlands was over two trillion euros, *see* CBS Statline: 'Waarde onroerende zaken van woningen en niet-woningen', online, last updated on 9 November 2017.

3 L. Fox, *Conceptualising Home: Theories, Laws and Policies*, 1st ed., Oxford, Hart Publishing, 2006, pp. 28, 122 *et seq.* Fox distinguishes multiple aspects of this social value: the ownership of a house offers a safe haven for friends and family, and a means for participating in social activities such as work and sports.

4 South Africa is a prime example of such a country. *Cf.* K. Tissington, *A Resource Guide to Housing in South Africa 1994-2010: Legislation, Policy, Programmes and Practice* (SERI report 2011), pp. 33 *et seq.* This paper discusses South African law in section 4.

5 High transaction costs may prevent mutually beneficial transactions, *see* J. Torstensson, 'Property Rights and Economic Growth: An Empirical Study', *KYKLOS*, vol. 47, no. 2, 1994, p. 232.

impossible for buyers to acquire immovable property if the seller has gone bankrupt. Subsection 2 elaborates on this mechanism. If this situation occurs, buyers of immovable property find themselves in a position that is not exactly enviable, to say the least. If the buyer has already paid the purchase price, the purchase price forms part of the insolvent estate. The buyer has a claim against the estate of the bankrupt seller, because the bankrupt seller has failed to meet their obligation to transfer the immovable property to the buyer. The legal basis of this claim would therefore be breach of contract. However, this claim is usually unsecured. For this reason, the buyer is likely to receive a refund that makes up only a tiny percentage of the initially paid purchase price, that is, if the buyer receives a refund at all.[6] This situation (the situation where the seller and the purchaser have concluded a contract of sale, but no deed of transfer has been registered, and where the purchaser has paid (a part of) the purchase price) is the case that forms the basis of this contribution.

Secondly, the mere possibility of this reversal might require practitioners involved in the transfer of immovable property to bear the duty to prevent the harmful consequences of the seller's bankruptcy. Buyers that give good and valuable consideration expect to 'own' the immovable property thereafter in exclusion of all others.[7] This expectation should be lived up to. If not, buyers may become hesitant to buy (immovable) property.[8] However, the duty to prevent the negative consequences of the seller's bankruptcy may give rise to higher transaction costs. This context demonstrates the importance of an analysis of (substantive private law regarding) the effects of bankruptcy on the transfer of immovable property.

This analysis contributes to a clearer view on whether the fear of not acquiring the immovable property, and subsequently the higher transaction costs, are justified. This paper aims to conduct this analysis for Dutch law. The abovementioned gives rise to the following research questions:

1. To what extent does bankruptcy and in particular the fixation principle affect one's ability to transfer real estate under Dutch law?
2. Whether and to what extent are the interests of the buyer protected in case the buyer has already paid the purchase price under Dutch law?

Section 2 sets out the substantive law with regard to the transfer of immovable property and the effect of the seller's insolvency on that transfer in the Netherlands. Section 3 discusses whether and to what extent the interests of the buyer are protected in case the buyer has already paid the purchase price. As this contribution reveals, the buyer is protected against this risk in *almost* any situation. However, there is still a possibility that the buyer

6 J.B. Huizink, *Insolventierecht*, 7th ed., Deventer, Kluwer, 2012, pp. 8 *et seq.*
7 D.J. Kochan, 'Dealing with Dirty Deeds: Matching *Nemo dat* Preferences with Property Law Pragmatism', *Kansas Law Review*, vol. 64, no. 1, 2015, p. 6.
8 Secure property rights are in general beneficial for the economy, *see* Torstensson, 1994, pp. 233 *et seq.*

pays the purchase price while he or she does not become the owner of the immovable property. For this reason, section 4 examines how this legal 'gap' is filled in other jurisdictions, i.e. Scots and South African law. Section 5 concludes the paper by providing a summary and a few concluding remarks, in particular on how the listed shortcomings can be overcome.

This paper uses South African law and Scots law in section 4. Dutch law classifies as a civil law system. South African and Scots law, however, are mixed systems when it comes to the civil law/common law distinction.[9,10] As this contribution reveals, this more common law-oriented approach provides refreshing perspectives on the abovementioned problem. The South African solution, for instance, relies on an extensive interpretation of section 9 and 26 of the South African Constitution, made possible by the existence of a constitutional court. The Scots judgment that this paper discusses, on the other hand, uses a legal implant from the United Kingdom (i.e., the distinction between a legal and an equitable interest) to solve this problem.

2 The Transfer of Immovable Property and Insolvency: Substantive Law

2.1 *The Transfer of Immovable Property*

In the Netherlands, in order to transfer an asset, three requirements have to be met (section 3:84 of the Dutch Civil Code (hereinafter: BW)). Firstly, a transfer requires a valid title, i.e. an obligation to deliver; this title is most often a contract of sale that obliges the seller to transfer ownership of the immovable property. Secondly, transfer requires that the seller has the power to dispose of the property.[11] This requirement derives from the Latin adage '*Nemo plus iuris ad alium transferre potest quam ipse haberet*', meaning that no one is capable of transferring more rights than they have. Thirdly, transfer requires delivery of

9 B. Lenel, *The History of South African Law and its Roman-Dutch Roots* (Essay 2012, Thal (Switzerland)) online available on www.lenel.ch/docs/history-of-sa-law-en.pdf (accessed 19 February 2018); T.B. Smith, *Studies Critical and comparative*, Edinburgh, W. Green & Son Ltd, 1962, pp. 116-136.

10 In the context of this contribution, 'common law' must be explained as the opposite of a 'civil law' system. However, common law can also be considered the opposite of 'statutory law'. Especially in South African academic writing, scholars tend to use the phrase 'common law' in the last-mentioned meaning, which is confusing since it refers to the old 'Roman-Dutch-law': the rules of a 'civil law' jurisdiction! *See* C.G. Van der Merwe, B.C. Stoop & P.J. Thomas, *Historic foundations of South-African Private Law*, 2nd ed., Durban, LexisNexis South Africa, 2016.

11 Although it is possible to contractually confer the power to dispose to someone who is not the owner of the property, the most common reason for having the power to dispose of property is by being the actual owner. *See* W.H.M. Reehuis & A.H.T. Heisterkamp, *Goederenrecht*, 13th ed., Deventer, Kluwer, 2012, pp. 108 *et seq.*

the asset. The delivery of immovable property is effected through a notarial deed that must be registered in the public land records (section 3:89 BW).

It must be noted that there is no consensus among academics with regard to (the terminology of) these requirements. For example, Dutch academics are divided over whether a 'real agreement' is required for the transfer of ownership. There is also no consensus among scholars as to whether a 'real agreement' requires (or encompasses) a notarial deed and registration in the public land records.[12] For the sake of practicality and clarity, this paper distinguishes between three relevant requirements for the transfer of immovable property: a) the title, where the seller and the buyer express their intention to transfer the ownership and enter into the obligation to do so, b) power to dispose of the property and c) delivery, which encompasses every step taken to effect the transfer in accordance with the title. This distinction makes it easier to compare the procedural aspects with regard to the transfer of immovable property under Dutch law with these aspects under South African and Scots law. For this reason, this distinction becomes especially relevant in section 4.

2.2 *The Effects of Insolvency in General*

Insolvency intertwines with the transfer of (immovable) property on two levels. Firstly, insolvency impacts the seller's ability to conclude a contract pertaining to the sale of immovable property. Secondly, insolvency impacts on the power to dispose of immovable property that forms part of the insolvent estate. On both of these levels, insolvency interferes in two different ways. Firstly, interference may occur because of the *fixation principle* (see subsection 2.3); this usually occurs on or after the day of the bankruptcy judgment by the court. Secondly, *the rules on transaction avoidance* may affect a person's ability to conclude a contract or deliver immovable property.

The goal of the body of rules on bankruptcy is to facilitate the process of taking recourse against a debtor's assets. Without bankruptcy, a judge would have to decide on the distribution of the proceeds of every individual asset, where debtors no longer fulfil their obligations. However, bankruptcy is all too often perceived as being more of a curse than a blessing.[13] This effect of bankruptcy can constitute an incentive for the debtor and the creditors to conduct juridical acts that are detrimental to the creditors as a whole, or have

12 A.L.M. Keirse & Y.E.M. Beukers, 'Commentary on section 3:84 BW, note 22.2 and 23.4', *in* J. Hijma (Ed.), *Groene Serie Vermogensrecht* (online commentary, www.wolterskluwer.nl/shop/online/groene-serie-vermogensrecht/NPGRSEVMR-OU); *see also* S.E. Bartels & A.I.M. Van Mierlo, 'Goederenrechtelijke overeenkomst (note 223)', *in* S.E. Bartels, A.I.M. Van Mierlo & H.D. Ploeger (Eds.), *Mr. C. Assers Handleiding tot de beoefening van het Nederlands Burgerlijk Recht. 3. Vermogensrecht algemeen. Deel IV. Algemeen goederenrecht*, Deventer, Kluwer, 2013.

13 R.J. De Weijs, *Faillissementspauliana, insolvenzanfechtung & transaction avoidance in insolvencies: naar een geobjectiveerde regeling van schuldeisersbenadeling* (PhD thesis, 2010), available online: https://pure.uva.nl/ws/files/1543809/75480_thesis.pdf, p. 1.

the effect of favouring one creditor over another. Therefore, most jurisdictions have a body of rules for the purpose of avoiding such juridical acts under certain conditions.

This paper focuses on interference by virtue of the fixation principle.

2.3 *Transferring Immovable Property after Bankruptcy: The Fixation Principle under Dutch Law*

As stated before, immovable property is often an asset of considerable financial value. Therefore, it stands to reason that an immovable asset is also a valuable object to take recourse against for creditors who have a claim against the owner of the immovable property. When debtors go bankrupt, it is in the interest of the creditors as a whole that assets remain in the insolvent estate.

The fixation principle plays an important role in this regard. Upon bankruptcy, the insolvent estate is exclusively intended to be liquidated so that the proceeds can be distributed among creditors. The fixation principle, therefore, 'fixes' the insolvent estate on two levels. Firstly, it fixes the assets: upon bankruptcy, the insolvent can no longer dispose of any assets belonging to the insolvent estate (section 23 Dutch Bankruptcy Act (hereinafter: Fw)). This form of fixation prevents the transfer of immovable property that forms part of the insolvent estate. Secondly, it fixes the liabilities: after bankruptcy, the insolvent can no longer incur new liabilities (section 24 Fw). The latter form of fixation is to prevent the insolvent from concluding contracts that could be detrimental to the value of the estate.

The fixation principle serves for the protection of creditors. The debtor has already caused enough harm to the creditors, and should therefore no longer be allowed to conduct acts that have detrimental consequences for the creditor's right of recourse.[14,15] In addition to this, the fixation principle purports to fix the relative position of each creditor. The assets should be liquidated and the proceeds thereof distributed in accordance with the relevant bankruptcy act. A key principle of bankruptcy law that should in general be taken into account is the *paritas creditorium* or *pari passu* rule.[16] This rule entails that all creditors should, in principle, be treated equally. The fixation principle ensures that the *pari passu* rule is taken into account, by fixing the relative position of each creditor. This prevents

14 B. De Clercq, R.G. Evans, W. Abrie & C.R. Graham, *Insolvente boedels*, 8th ed., Durban, LexisNexis South Africa, 2011, p. 16; B. Wessels, 'Beschikken door de failliet en betalen aan de failliet', *Vermogensrechtelijke Analyses*, no. 3, 2008, para. 2.

15 One may note that the fixation principle may serve other purposes as well, depending on the jurisdiction. For instance, the goal of the fixation principle in French and Mexican law is to save the bankrupt business, by giving it a chance to overcome its financial difficulties. However, this contribution focuses on the fixation principle as a mechanism that protects the creditors as a whole and/or the *pari passu* rule.

16 W.W. McBryde, A. Flessner & S.C.J.J. Kortmann, *Principles of European Insolvency Law*, Deventer, Kluwer, 2003, p. 40.

the debtor from performing an act whereby a creditor obtains a better position in the insolvency proceedings than this creditor would otherwise have had.

It should be noted that the purpose of the fixation principle closely resembles that of the rules on transaction avoidance. Furthermore, the fixation principle and the rules concerning transaction avoidance have, to a certain extent, a common nature. These rules share the potential to have a direct influence on the transfer of immovable assets, in order to protect the interests of the body of creditors of the bankrupt seller. It could be argued, therefore, that the fixation principle can be seen as a form of transaction avoidance with a much wider scope. In this view, the fixation principle is a form of transaction avoidance that renders the transfer void, notwithstanding the extent of the detrimental effects for the insolvent estate and notwithstanding the state of mind of the seller and the buyer.[17,18] However, one major difference in nature between these sets of rules must be borne in mind. A transfer in contravention of the fixation principle is void *ab initio*. A transfer that can be avoided by virtue of the rules on transaction avoidance is, in principle, valid, but avoidable afterwards by the bankruptcy trustee, *if* certain other requirements are met.

The distinction between juridical acts (that bring about the transfer of ownership) that are 'avoidable' and that are 'void *ab initio*' may pose a terminological problem. With regard to transfers that are void *ab initio*, it can be argued that this 'transfer' must be held valid unless someone challenges it. On the other hand, one may argue that a void transfer does not constitute a transfer at all.[19] However, for the sake of clarity, this paper refers to these instances as (void) 'transfers' nonetheless.

Under Dutch private law, the fixation principle with regard to the fixation of assets is embodied in section 23 Fw:

> As a result of the declaration of bankruptcy the bankrupt debtor loses the right to dispose of and to administer his assets (property) as far as these belong to the liquidation estate, this with effect from and including the day on which the bankruptcy order is rendered.[20]

Two key elements of this section must be emphasised. The first element is that bankrupt debtors remain the owner of their assets.[21] However, from the moment that the assets are

---

17 De Weijs, 2010, p. 379.

18 'The detrimental effects for the insolvent estate' and 'the state of mind of the seller and the buyer' are criteria that are regularly used to assess whether a transaction conducted prior to bankruptcy can be avoided by the bankruptcy trustee.

19 Reehuis & Heisterkamp, 2012, pp. 81 *et seq.*

20 This translation (and other translations used in this paper) originate from www.dutchcivillaw.com/legislation.

21 In many other jurisdictions, such as South Africa and Scotland, the bankruptcy trustee becomes the owner of the insolvent estate upon bankruptcy. *Cf.* section 20 of the South African Insolvency Act (Act 24 of 1936),

fixed, bankrupt debtors lose their power to dispose of those assets themselves. Secondly, the fixation of assets does not take place following the bankruptcy order by the court. Instead, the fixation has a retroactive effect: the assets are fixed at midnight (0.00 am) on the day that the debtor is declared bankrupt. This may give rise to a situation where the seller has lost his power to dispose of his assets, while the buyer could not have been aware of this because the seller has not yet been declared bankrupt. The following example illustrates this statement. Person A sells immovable property to person B. Both of them visit a notary on May the 10th in order to effect the transfer. The notary examines the Central Insolvency Registry (CIR)[22] for A's insolvency at 10 am (and finds that A is not bankrupt at 10 am), and signs the notarial deed at 11 am. The deed is registered at 11.30 am. However, at 3 pm on the same afternoon, A is declared bankrupt by the court. The legal effect is that A lacked the power to dispose of the immovable property as from 0.00 am that same day. Whether or not B should be protected if he or she is in good faith is still a debated question.[23] Hereinafter, this paper assumes that B is not protected in this situation.

Section 24 Fw expresses the fixation of liabilities:

> The liquidation estate is only liable for obligations of the debtor that have arisen after the declaration of bankruptcy to the extent that the estate benefits from such obligations.

Since the contract of sale does not require the assistance of a legal practitioner, the seller and buyer can always conclude a contract after the bankruptcy of the seller. However, any attempt to do so cannot legally bind the insolvent estate, unless the contract is beneficial for the value of the insolvent estate.[24] Since this paper aims to analyse the situation where the immovable property has already been sold prior to bankruptcy (see section 1), this paper does not elaborate further on the fixation of liabilities.

---

section 31 of the former Scots Bankruptcy Act of 1985 and section 78 of the current Scots bankruptcy Act of 2016. *See also* footnote 37.

22 This is a register that keeps track of bankruptcy judgements of individuals and companies. It is accessible online: https://insolventies.rechtspraak.nl.

23 *See* recently: H.W. Heyman, 'Faillissement en beslag aan de zijde van de verkoper', *WPNR* vol. 7180, 2018; L.C.A. Verstappen, 'De notaris en zijn failliete cliënt', *Tijdschrift voor Insolventierecht*, vol. 13, para. 3; A. Steneker, 'Koper failliet? Geen probleem', *WPNR*, vol. 7107, 2016.

24 *See e.g.* Rb. Den Haag (ktr.) 31 August 2000, ECLI:NL:KTGSGR:2000:AG3762, *JOR 2000/227*, where the acquisition of an asset was held to be beneficial for the value of the insolvent estate.

3 Purchaser Has Already Paid the Purchase Price

So how is the buyer protected against the risk of not acquiring immovable property due to the bankruptcy of the seller, where the buyer has already provided the purchase price? In order to answer this question, it is necessary to look at how a transfer of immovable property is conducted in the Netherlands.

3.1 The Transfer of Immovable Property: The Dutch Procedure

Section 3:89 BW describes how the delivery of immovable property is effected; the delivery takes place through a notarial deed that has to be registered in the public land records. In practice, this requires the parties to the transfer (the buyer and the seller) to appear before the civil law notary in person. The notary will then explain the consequences of the transfer. Often, the notary also informs the buyer of the consequences of creating a right of mortgage on a property. Once done, the parties and the notary sign the deed of transfer. This deed of transfer is submitted to the public land records. Once the deed has been registered, the transfer is complete (see section 3:89 BW). As soon as the deed has been registered, the notary receives a confirmation of the registration (*Bewijs van inschrijving*). It must be noted that only the delivery requires the presence of a legal practitioner (i.e. the civil law notary). A contract of sale can be concluded without any legal practitioner being present.[25] Once the deed of transfer is registered in the public land records, the transfer is complete. If necessary, this process can be completed within several days.

Also, the provided consideration, i.e. the payment of the purchase price, must go through the notary. Section 7:26 subsection 3 BW states:

> Where a notarial deed is required for the transfer of ownership of the sold object, followed by the registration of that deed in the public registers which are kept for this purpose [i.e. when transferring immovable property – TB], then the indebted purchase price must have been brought out of the control of the buyer at the latest at the moment on which this notarial deed is signed and it only needs to be brought under control of the seller after this deed has been registered.

In practice, civil law notaries adhere to this rule, by obliging the buyer to transfer the purchase price to the client account of the civil law notary at least one day prior to the transfer. The client account of the notary is a bank account held and controlled by the

25 However, if the parties want to obtain priority notice, only a notary can submit the selling contract for registration (section 7:3 BW).

notary. However, money in the bank account does not belong to the civil law notary personally. Instead, the money is held in joint ownership by the clients that have transferred money to that account (see section 25 subsection 3 of the Dutch Notaries Act – *Wet op het Notarisambt*). For this reason, the bankruptcy of the civil law notary does not affect the money of the clients in any way.[26] By using the client account in the described manner, the civil law notary protects the interests of the seller. After the buyer has transferred the purchase price to the notary's client account, the payment of the seller no longer depends on the willingness of the buyer. Instead, the notary releases the purchase price to the seller as soon as the transfer has taken place. In this context, the civil law notary acts as an intermediary.

3.2 *The* Baarns Beslag*-Judgment in this Context: A Simultaneous Transfer?*

In the *Baarns Beslag*-judgment,[27] the Supreme Court (*Hoge Raad*) of the Netherlands stated that notaries have a general duty to ensure that both parties to the transfer receive what is due to them. This entails, that a) the seller receives the full purchase price and b) the buyer acquires the full and unencumbered ownership of the property concerned.[28] The civil law notary must see to it that parties to the transfer do not bear risks in this context that are, generally, avoidable.[29] Naturally, this general duty encompasses the duty to ensure that the seller is not insolvent. As set out in subsection 2.3, a bankrupt seller is unable to transfer ownership of immovable property to a buyer. Therefore, an attempt to transfer an immovable by a bankrupt seller will result in the realisation of the risk that the buyer does not acquire the full and unencumbered ownership of the immovable property. Because the realisation of this risk is in the vast majority of instances avoidable (see subsection 3.3), the civil law notary has a duty to avoid the realisation of this particular risk.

Furthermore, in the *Baarns Beslag*-judgment, the Supreme Court held that the payment of the purchase price and the transfer of the immovable property must take place simultaneously.[30] As we have seen above, the transfer of the immovable property is completed as soon as the deed of transfer has been registered in the public land records. But what about payment? One possible approach would be to define payment as the moment when the notary releases the purchase price to the seller. However, it must be stressed that the money

26 A. Steneker, *Kwaliteitsrekening en afgescheiden vermogen* (PhD thesis), Deventer, Kluwer, 2005, p. 220.
27 '*Een beslag*' is the Dutch word for 'an attachment' (of property), and in this case, a dwelling in the city of Baarn has been attached by a creditor.
28 HR 30 januari 1981, ECLI:NL:PHR:1981:AG4140, *NJ* 1982, 56 (*Baarns Beslag*), para. 3; *see also* the Regulation concerning the professional and behavioral conduct of notaries (*Verordening beroeps- en gedragsregels notariaat* 2011) section 3.
29 *Baarns Beslag*-judgment, para. 3.
30 *Baarns Beslag*-judgment, para. 3.

in the client account belongs to the clients only. If the buyer and the seller are the notary's only clients, either the buyer or the seller must be entitled to the money in the client account. Therefore, another viable alternative would be to say that payment takes place when the seller becomes entitled to the purchase price (even though the money is still in the notary's bank account). In line with this opinion, the Dutch Supreme Court has decided that payment takes place at the moment when the "seller may rightfully require the release of the purchase price from the notary".[31]

Of course, this raises the question of when the seller can expect payment. It would make a lot of sense to argue that the seller may want the money to be released as soon as the deed of transfer has been registered, since this is the moment when the buyer becomes the owner of the immovable property. This would also be in accordance with the *Baarns Beslag*-judgment: a simultaneous transfer of the immovable property and the purchase price. However, as the next subsection explains, due to bankruptcy and its consequences, this view cannot be upheld.

3.3 *The Retroactive Effect of the Fixation Principle*

Let us go back to the example used in subsection 2.3. On the day of the transfer (10 May), the notary examines the Central Insolvency Registry (CIR) for A's insolvency at 10 am (and finds that A is not bankrupt at 10 am). Hence, the notary signs and submits the notarial deed at 11 am and receives the confirmation of registration on 11.01 am. However, at 3 pm on the same afternoon, A is declared bankrupt by the court. The legal effect is that A lacked the right to dispose of the immovable property as from 0.00 am on that day. This means that B never acquired the immovable property. In these circumstances, if payment took place simultaneously with the transfer of the immovable property (at 11.01 am), this purchase price would form part of the insolvent estate. This means that B would be left with an unsecured claim against the estate. This result would naturally not be in accordance with the duty of the civil law notary to ensure that the buyer becomes the full and unconditional owner of the immovable property. For this reason, the seller cannot request payment at 11.01 am. Instead, the notary uses a method laid out by the Royal Dutch association for Notaries (*Koninklijke Notariële Beroepsorganisatie:* KNB) in the regulation concerning the delivery of registered property (*Reglement rechercheren registergoederen*). This regulation dictates that the notary, when assisting in the delivery of immovable property, is obliged to examine the CIR three times. The first examination (*eerste recherche*) takes place well before the transfer is conducted. Most often, this examination takes place when the buyer and the seller first establish contact with the notary. The second examination (*herrecherche*) takes place shortly before the transfer, preferably on the day of the transfer itself. In our

31 HR 14 januari 2011, ECLI:NL:HR:2011:BN7887, *NJ* 2011/366 (*Butterman q.q./Rabobank*), para. 4.14.

example, the examination of the CIR at 10 am is the second examination. The third examination (*narecherche*) must be conducted the day after the transfer. By conducting this third examination, the notary will spot A's bankruptcy on the day after the transfer (11 May). The CIR *usually* displays a bankruptcy at the latest on the day after the bankruptcy judgment. If the notary finds that B did not acquire the immovable property due to A's bankruptcy, the notary will not release the money to A. Instead, the notary will reimburse the purchase price to B.

The civil law notary that fails to comply with these provisions is exposed to two risks. First of all, the buyer can successfully hold the notary liable on the basis of breach of contract.[32] Secondly, the notary may receive a disciplinary penalty by the disciplinary court.[33] It must be noted that many insurance policies (for professional liability of notaries) explicitly provide that liability caused by failure to examine in accordance with the prescribed way of conduct (as laid down in the *Reglement Rechercheren Registergoederen*) is not covered by the insurance. It stands to reason that this is a strong incentive for the notary to abide by these rules of conduct.

It should be noted that the retroactive effect of bankruptcy as laid down in section 23 Fw is considered a serious obstacle by notaries. The retroactive effect plays a similar role in the context of trading shares in a company. For this reason, many scholars, the KNB and several other organizations that represent the interests of banks and lawyers, argue that the retroactive effect of bankruptcy should be abolished.[34]

Given the procedure as set out above, the delivery and the payment do not actually take place at the same time. This, despite the fact that the Dutch Supreme Court stated that the delivery of the immovable property and the payment of the purchase price must occur simultaneously. Usually (i.e. in around 99,9% of the cases) the transfer is complete as soon as the notarial deed is submitted to the public land records. However, the earliest possible time for payment is one day later, after the third examination of the public land records and the CIR has shown that the buyer actually became the owner on the day before. This discrepancy gives rise to the question of when the seller is entitled to the purchase price and hence at what moment the creditors of the seller can take recourse on the purchase price by attachment on the notary's client account.[35]

Furthermore, it must be emphasised that there is a possibility that the notary fails to notice that the seller has been declared bankrupt with the third check. One can never be 100% sure that a bankruptcy is publicised in the CIR one day after the debtor has been

---

32 The *Baarns Beslag*-judgment is an example where the notary was successfully held liable.

33 Sections 93 *et seq* of the Notaries Act (*Wet op het Notarisambt* 1998).

34 KNB: 'Abolish the retroactive effect of bankruptcy (*Schaf de terugwerkende kracht van faillissement af*)', comment on legislative proposal 34740 (comment dated from 30 August 2017).

35 *See* H.W. Heyman & S.E. Bartels *Vastgoedtransacties: Koop*, Den Haag, BJu, 2012, pp. 430 *et seq*; W.G. de Vries, 'Notaris, beslag en aansprakelijkheid', *WPNR*, vol. 5557, 1981, and comments on this article in the same journal.

declared bankrupt by the court.[36] In the context of the example in subsection 2.3: there is no guarantee that A's bankruptcy will be published in the CIR on May 11th. This possibility implies that there might be circumstances under which the notary is not capable of reimbursing the purchaser of the immovable property in case the seller was bankrupt at the time of the transfer. This possibility exists, because the notary releases the purchase price on May 11th, whereas A's bankruptcy may only become apparent on May 12th. This is not in accordance with the proper fulfilment of the notary's job to ensure that both parties fully fulfil their obligations as formulated in the *Baarns Beslag*-judgment and the relevant regulations by the KNB. This possibility of misfortune raises the question of if and how B is protected, if this situation occurs. Since there is no case indicating that this situation has already occurred, the only solution is to make an educated guess. In these circumstances, it could be surmised that B would successfully hold the notary liable because the notary would have failed to ensure that B received the full and unencumbered ownership of the immovable property. Furthermore, B would have run the risk that they would not obtain the immovable property and would be left with an unsecured claim on the insolvent estate. This risk could *in principle* have been avoided by the civil law notary (this is the other criterium according to the *Baarns Beslag*-judgment). The risk could have been avoided, because the civil law notary could have waited a few more days before releasing the purchase price to A. However, due to the fact that the notary did adhere to the prescribed rules of conduct (amongst which the regulation provided by the KNB), the insurance company would most likely cover the loss. But what would happen if the insurance company did not? Or what if the notary made a mistake and, for instance, forgot to examine the CIR on the day after the transfer? How is this legal gap filled in other jurisdictions?

4 South African Law and Scots Law

This section analyses South African and Scots law with regard to this problem, in order to see how the abovementioned legal gap is filled in other jurisdictions. The legal effect of bankruptcy on the part of the seller is similar in both these jurisdictions. A buyer cannot acquire ownership of the immovable property, if this property forms part of the insolvent estate.[37] If buyers have already paid the purchase price by then, they run the risk that they have to make do with an unsecured claim against the insolvent estate.

36 P.H. Tieskens, 'De notariële kwaliteitsrekening en risico's van faillissement van een koper of verkoper', *V&O*, vol. 6, 2014, p. 117.

37 Section 20 of the South African Insolvency Act states that "*The effect of the sequestration [bankruptcy – TB] of the estate of an insolvent shall be: (under a) to divest the insolvent of his estate and to vest it in the Master until a trustee has been appointed (…)*". One may note that bankrupt debtors lose their power to dispose (just like under Dutch law), but in a different way. Under Dutch law, the bankrupt debtor stays the owner of the assets in the insolvent estate. South African insolvency law however, provides that the Master or

However, it is crucial to keep in mind that the legal gap in South African and Scots law is much wider than the gap under Dutch law. The reason for this is that in South Africa and Scotland there is no rule that says that the purchase price must run through a notary's bank account (or a similar legal practitioner, such as a conveyancer). Hence, a buyer may decide to pay the actual purchase price years ahead of the actual transfer of the immovable property.[38] If the seller goes bankrupt in the meantime, there is no intermediary that reimburses the purchase price to the buyer. This particular situation (payment of the purchase price far ahead of the transfer) led to the judgments that the upcoming subsections discuss.

It must be noted that the procedure of transferring immovable property in Scotland and South Africa is to a large extent similar to the Dutch procedure. In both jurisdictions, legal practitioners draft a deed of transfer, and this deed must be registered in the land records afterwards.[39]

4.1 *South Africa*

South African insolvency law does not allow the buyer to acquire a proprietary interest in an asset that forms part of an insolvent estate (see footnote 37). This may lead to hardship if the buyer has already paid the purchase price (see section 1). This possibility of hardship led to the enactment of the Alienation of Land Act (Act 68 of 1981, ALA). The prevailing view with regard to this matter is that the described position of the purchaser was unfair when it came to purchase agreements of immovable property between housing corporations (as sellers) and individuals (as buyers). Vulnerable individuals would not normally be able to pay the full purchase price in one go. Therefore, the purpose of the ALA is to strengthen the position of the purchaser who pays the purchase price in instalments.[40] One of the provisions that strengthens the position of the purchaser is section 22 of the ALA. This provision dictates that a purchaser is entitled to receive the title to the immovable property if the seller has gone bankrupt prior to delivery, on two conditions: a) the purchaser must have purchased the land in terms of a 'contract', and b) the purchaser must have made arrangements for the payment of all costs in connection with the transfer of land. A 'con-

---

bankruptcy trustee shall become the owner of the assets of the insolvent estate. Section 31 of the former Scots Bankruptcy Act (of 1985) provided a similar rule.

38 This may occur if, for instance, the seller is a powerful party that has the upper hand over the buyer when it comes to negotiating the terms of the transfer.

39 For South Africa, *see* section 16 Deeds Registries Act (Act 47 of 1937). For Scotland, *see* Land Registration etc. (Scotland) Act 2012, section 50.

40 One may note that instalment buyers in the Netherlands run the same risk, and that they hence receive protection in the Netherlands for the same reason, *see* section 7:104 BW. However, contrary to the Alienation of Land Act, Dutch law requires the contract of sale to be registered in the public land records before the buyer is awarded protection against bankruptcy of the seller.

tract' (in terms of the ALA) is an agreement pertaining to the sale of land in more than two instalments over a period exceeding one year.[41]

However, two years ago the scope of this protection was widened significantly by the Constitutional Court in *Sarrahwitz v Maritz N.O. and Another* (herafter: *Sarrahwitz*).[42] In this case, Ms Sarrahwitz, a poor woman, bought a house from Mr Posthumus. She paid the purchase price in full, by borrowing this amount from her former employer. However, as the years progressed, no delivery of the immovable took place.[43] On 14 April 2006, Mr Posthumus was declared bankrupt and Mr Maritz was appointed as trustee. Under South African private law, both the immovable and the purchase price formed part of the insolvent estate. After several unsuccessful attempts, Ms Sarrahwitz made an application to the Constitutional Court. The Constitutional Court held that the distinction between purchasers that paid the purchase price in instalments and ones who immediately paid the full price was not in accordance with sections 9 (equality) and 26 (right to housing) of the Constitution.[44] The Court therefore applied the remedy of severance and reading in at the end of the definition of a 'contract' in section 1 of the ALA. The words "including residential property paid for in full within one year of the contract, by a vulnerable purchaser" were read in. The Court further defined a 'vulnerable purchaser' as "a purchaser who runs the risk of being rendered homeless by a seller's insolvency".[45] Therefore, under these circumstances, the buyer may acquire the ownership of a dwelling, despite the fixation of assets of the insolvent estate.

4.2 Scotland

In Scotland, in 1995, the Court of Session was confronted with a situation that closely resembled the situation of the *Sarrahwitz*-judgment. Albyn Construction Ltd. (hereinafter: Albyn) created a floating charge over *all* their assets to secure a debt with the Bank of Scotland in 1984. Five years later, on 12 June 1989, Albyn sold an apartment to the Thomsons. The Thomsons immediately paid the purchase price. However, no delivery of the immovable property took place. On 10 August 1991, the charge was fixed and Sharp was appointed as the receiver. This crystallized floating charge (still) encompassed *all* the assets of Albyn including the sold apartment, just like bankruptcy does (see footnote 37). According to the Court of Session, this fixed charge also encompassed the apartment sold to the Thomsons and subsequently, the Thomsons did not acquire the dwelling. However,

41 Section 1(1) ALA.

42 *Sarrahwitz v Maritz N.O. and Another*, [2015] ZACC 14.

43 The delay was caused because a certificate stating that she had paid the municipality rate was wrongfully not issued to her. *Sarrahwitz*-judgment, para. 7.

44 *Sarrahwitz*-judgment, para. 66 *et seq.*

45 *Sarrahwitz*-judgment, para. 69 *et seq.*

the House of Lords was of the opinion that the fixed charge did not relate to the concerned apartment.[46] The fixed charge was only vested in assets of which Albyn was both the legal and the beneficial owner. At the time the charge was crystallized, Albyn was the *legal* owner but the Thomsons were the *beneficial* owner of the sold dwelling. The result of the judgment comes down to or closely resembles a division of ownership,[47] which is in accordance with the common law, but unheard of in Scots law. For this reason, this judgment received a lot of criticism.[48] However, a few years later, the House of Lords was given a second chance in the case of *Burnett's Trustees v Grainger*.[49] The facts of this case are very similar to those in *Sharp v Thomson*, but they differed in one aspect: Burnett went bankrupt prior to the delivery of the immovable property. On the basis of *Sharp v Thomson*, it could be argued that Grainger already acquired a *beneficial* interest in the dwelling and that hence, the immovable property did not form part of the insolvent estate. Just like the Thomsons, Grainger had concluded a contract of sale with the sellers and paid the purchase price beforehand. However, the House of Lords found that the difference between the floating charge and bankruptcy was enough to distinguish *Burnett's Trustees v Grainger* from *Sharp v Thomson*,[50] and thus ruled that the dwelling does not belong to Grainger and instead forms part of the insolvent estate.[51] For the purposes of this paper, the first mentioned case is the most interesting (*Sharp v Thomson*).

Sharp v Thomson and *Sarrahwitz v Maritz* show many similarities. In both instances, the buyer had already paid the purchase price but the seller became unable to transfer the property afterwards due to a poor financial position. Another similarity is that in both instances, the buyer in these particular circumstances lacked any form of statutory protection and as a result was given a (proprietary) interest in the immovable by the court. The only difference in this respect is that South Africa had already provided statutory protection to buyers who paid the purchase price in instalments. The protection offered in *Sharp v Thomson* was therefore more 'out of the blue'. However, neither the South African nor

---

46 *Sharp v Thomson*, 1997 SC (HL) 66; see also K.G.C. Reid, 'Equity Triumphant: Sharp v Thomson', *ELR*, 1997, pp. 464 *et seq.*

47 Although it must be noted that the word 'trust' was never explicitly used in this judgment.

48 *Cf.* J.M. Milo, 'Europese klassiekers: Sharp vs Thomson en Burnett's Trustees vs Grainger; Convergentie van civil law en common law goederenrecht', *NTBR*, vol. 29, 2005, footnote 54.

49 *Burnett's Trustee v Grainger*, 2004 SC (HL) 4.

50 *Cf.* Lord Hoffmann: "I agree with my noble and learned friends that the decision in *Sharp v Thomson* 1997 SC (HL) 66 is distinguishable. But, for the reasons I have given, I think it would have been better if it had not been necessary to distinguish it."

51 One of the arguments for this decision was the poor reception of *Sharp v Thomson* in literature. Lord Coulsfield: "(...) it is legitimate for us to take into account the reception of the House of Lord's decision in Sharp vs Thomson in Scotland". Another argument for distinguishing these two cases was that in *Sharp v Thomson*, the House of Lords submitted that the scope of the floating charge should be kept as small as possible, meaning that it would encompass as few assets as possible. This argument did not play a role in *Burnett's Trustees v Grainger*, where instead of (the crystallization of) a floating charge, the debtor went bankrupt.

the Scots approach are conducive to legal certainty. Both Maritz and Sharp expected to win in court, as is confirmed by the fact that both Maritz and Sharp were proven right by every court but the highest one. It seems as if both the House of Lords and the Constitutional Court were of the opinion that an emergency measure had to be applied, in order to prevent hardship that would arise if the court strictly adhered to the existing private law. However, an extensive discussion on this point falls outside the scope of this paper.[52]

Another thing that both judgments have in common is that the inequitable situation was fixed by awarding a proprietary interest in the immovable property, even though no transfer had taken place at the time. Prior to the fixation of the assets because of bankruptcy, both Sarrahwitz and the Thomsons had a mere contractual claim against the insolvent debtor. Given this information, it could be said that both judgments were not in accordance with the fixation principle or the *pari passu* rule as formulated in subsection 2.3. Both judgments fail to explain why the contractual claim of Sarrahwitz and the Thomsons was promoted into a proprietary claim that could be invoked against the bankruptcy trustee or receiver, while other creditors had to make do with a percentage of their claim. In *Sarrahwitz*, the constitutional court set out that the reason for this exception was the fact that Sarrahwitz would run the risk of being rendered homeless if she did not acquire the dwelling. In *Thomson v Sharp*, the reason was (in short) 'equity'. This point must be seen in the context of the discussion on whether it is preferable to have a sharp distinction between personal and property rights, or to have 'intermediary' rights that can be invoked against a bankruptcy trustee as well. This discussion also falls outside the scope of this paper.[53]

5 Summary and Concluding Remarks

Once bankruptcy has been declared, debtors can no longer dispose of their assets. This also means that the buyer of immovable property can no longer acquire the property, if the seller of immovable property goes bankrupt prior to the delivery of the property. If buyers have already paid the purchase price at this point, they have a case for a breach of contract-based claim against the bankrupt debtor. This claim is, however, generally unsecured and buyers are therefore most likely to receive only a tiny percentage of their claim. The reason for this is the 'fixation principle' that aims to protect the *pari passu* rule. This principle entails that the relative positions of the creditors are fixed upon bankruptcy and that each creditor in principle receives the same percentage of their original claim.

52 *See e.g.* P.H. Neuhaus, 'Legal Certainty versus Equity in the Conflict of Laws', *Law and Contemporary Problems*, vol. 28, 1963, pp. 795-807.

53 *See* on this matter D.L. Carey Miller & M.M. Combe, 'The Boundaries of Property Rights in Scots Law: Report to the XVIIth International Congress of Comparative Law', *EJCL*, vol. 10.3, 2006.

Many jurisdictions consider this a problem and provide a solution to this matter. Under Dutch law, the civil law notary functions as an intermediary. The notary only releases the money to the seller when the notary has ascertained that the buyer has indeed acquired the full and unencumbered ownership of the immovable property. The notary ascertains that the buyer has become the owner, by examining multiple registers such as the public land records and the Central Insolvency Registry (CIR). The notary is obliged to examine the registries and protect the interests of the buyer in a manner prescribed by case law and regulations. Usually, the transfer is complete when the deed of transfer has been registered. However, even when the deed has been registered, it is still possible that bankruptcy on the side of the seller can prevent the transfer of ownership, for the fixation of assets in bankruptcy has a retroactive effect. For this reason, the notary must examine the relevant registers again the day after the transfer, to ensure that the seller was not declared bankrupt on the previous day. The consequence of this is that there is no clarity as to when the seller exactly becomes entitled to the purchase price. For this reason, a simultaneous transfer as prescribed by the Supreme Dutch court in the *Baarns Beslag* judgment, cannot occur under current Dutch private law. Furthermore, there is no guarantee that the CIR will display all the bankruptcies from the previous day. For this reason, there is a small yet noticeable legal gap in the Dutch system of conveyancing. This raises the question of how other jurisdictions deal with similar difficulties.

South African law used to provide protection to the buyer only if the buyer paid the purchase price in instalments. However, recently the scope of this protection was broadened by virtue of the *Sarrahwitz*-judgment. Also, a buyer who paid the purchase price in full can acquire the immovable property from a bankrupt seller, on the condition that the buyer qualifies as a 'vulnerable purchaser'. This means that the purchaser must run the risk of being rendered homeless if he or she does not acquire the dwelling. In Scotland, a different approach was adopted in order to offer protection to the buyer. In *Sharp v Thomson,* the House of Lords held that prior to the delivery of the immovable property, the buyer had already acquired the 'beneficial ownership' of the property and that the immovable property was secluded from other assets. These methods could be used as a source of inspiration to fill the legal loophole that exists under Dutch private law. However, it should be remembered that the likelihood of the events of the abovementioned judgments occurring in the Netherlands is minimal, because the notary already protects the buyer of immovable property in the vast majority of circumstances.

Part II
National Developments

5 Is Company Law a Branch of Property Law Under Belgian Law?

The Company with Legal Personality as a Specific Form of Co-ownership or as a Sui Generis Construction

Johan Van de Voorde[*]

1 Introduction

Property law and company law have numerous common characteristics. They both consider publicity (making information known to interested persons) to be important, tend to bind third parties, prefer a rapid circulation of goods and have a *numerus clausus*. In legal economics, an understanding is growing that companies are not (only) a complex whole of contractual relations, but have also strong foundations in property law.[1] It is therefore natural to wonder if company law has to be considered as a branch of property law. This has been proposed by some legal authors, as shall be analysed later. M. Coipel has been the most recent one in Belgium.[2] He proposed that shareholders be recognised as co-owners of the company patrimony, implying that company law is effectively a branch of property law, in the same way that co-ownership is a part of property law.

How can this problem be tackled? One interesting avenue is the company with a legal personality. A company without a legal personality automatically has to use property law mechanisms (especially the co-ownership of the company assets by all shareholders), and is therefore intrinsically a property law figure. Legal personality, on the other hand, is not a property law concept, which indicates that a company with legal personality may not be reducible to property law mechanisms. If this is the case, company law is at least partially autonomous with regard to property law.

Why is this problem relevant, or in other words, what effects does the Coipel thesis have? In the first place, it answers the controversy about the nature of a share in a company

* PhD (University of Antwerp, Belgium), postdoctoral researcher University of Antwerp, research group Personal Rights and Property Rights, e-mail: johan.vandevoorde@uantwerpen.be, ORCID: https://orcid.org/0000-0002-5740-4167.

1 E.g. J. Armour & M.J Whincop,'The proprietary foundations of corporate law', *Oxford Journal of Legal Studies*, 2007, pp. 429, 429-465.

2 See M. Coipel, 'Le droit de propriété des associés dans les sociétés dotées de la personnalité morale' in *Eigendom – Propriété*, die Keure, 1996, pp. 31, 31-59.

with legal personality: it is identical to a share in a co-ownership, and not a personal right or some other construction in the same way as a 'membership right'. Secondly, a company with legal personality has a trust-like property right on its assets, no full ownership, implying it has a fiduciary duty towards its shareholders, even if the law does not explicitly say so. Thirdly, companies with only one shareholder become quite difficult to conceptualise, as they not only lack any contract (traditionally, companies have a contractual origin) but also a co-ownership. On a more theoretical level, the Coipel thesis implies that property law is to be used as a backstop if company law does not regulate a question.

This contribution will concentrate on Belgian law, though French law will also be taken into account. Although a strong argument can be made that the *Code Napoléon* of 1804/1807 no longer has any legal value in Belgium and has been replaced by a Civil Code of 1830,[3] the overwhelming majority of legal academics and practitioners disregard this problem and continue to apply the *Code Napoléon*. For reasons of brevity, the Civil Code of 1830 will not be analysed.

In the first instance the 'Coipel thesis' will be described and then critically analysed. This will be followed with an analysis of the concept of 'third-party law' as a possible alternative to explain the similarities between property law and company law. The paper will end with a general conclusion.

2 A Company with Legal Personality as a Special Form of Co-ownership (Coipel Thesis)

2.1 *The Traditional Thesis*

Traditionally, it is held that the legal personality of a company effects a total separation between the company patrimony and the patrimonies of the shareholders of the company.[4]

3 J. Van de Voorde, "Zijn de Belgen Napoleons trouwste onderdanen?' Een onderzoek naar de mogelijke opheffing van de *Code Napoléon* in België en zijn vervanging door het Burgerlijk Wetboek van het Verenigd Koninkrijk der Nederlanden', *Pro Memorie* (2017), pp. 232, 232-265. In 1815, the United Kingdom of the Netherlands had started writing its own legal codes (a normal move to confirm the independence vis-à-vis France), which was mostly finished in 1830 (only a Penal Code had not been finished and it was decided not to wait for it). The new codes would enter into force on the first of February 1831, but in August 1830, the Belgian Revolution happened. In such an atmosphere, new codes were not considered to be opportune in Belgium. The Interim Government therefore decreed that the codes of 1830 were abrogated in January 1831, but at this moment, all legislative power had already been transferred to the National Congress, which did not adopt any law abrogating the codes of 1830. Therefore, the Interim Government had acted *ultra vires* and the codes of 1830 had entered into force as had originally been decided. This was not recognised in practice, which continued to use the French (Napoleonic) codes until today (discounting new laws and codes promulgated after 1831).

4 J. Heenen, 'Nature des droits de l'associé sur l'actif d'une société commerciale avant et après la dissolution. – Persistance de la personnalité morale après la dissolution' (annotation under Cass. 2 December 1952),

A company with legal personality is therefore the only owner of its patrimony. This means the autonomy of company law vis-à-vis property law is confirmed, because legal personality is not a property law technique.

Note that in certain cases, shareholders 'share' a property right with their company. This is the case when a shareholder contributes a limited property right to the company: he can contribute a usufruct instead of full ownership. These cases are not relevant for this research, as the contributed right is still the full property of the company.

2.2 *Shareholding as Co-ownership of the Company Patrimony (Coipel Thesis)*

Michel Coipel deviates from the traditional analysis of the relationship between shareholders and their company with legal personality, suggesting that company law is in effect a branch of property law.[5] In his opinion, the shareholders are co-owners of the patrimony of a company with legal personality. This is a particular kind of co-ownership, which resembles the co-ownership of heirs (Belgian law does not have probate procedures in general, though some exceptions do exist): in both cases, an undivided property right exists on a universality,[6] without the existence of a certain and actual co-ownership with regards to the individual goods which are part of the universality.[7]

Coipel mentions a few predecessors of his thesis.[8] Firstly, he names De Page and Dekkers (authors of an authoritative handbook on Belgian private law), who described shareholders as 'collective owners', although they do not analyse this further.[9] He also mentions Planiol and Ripert (authors of an authoritative handbook on French private law), who referred to

---

RCJB (1953), pp. 291, 293, no. 3; J. Vananroye, 'Organisatierecht: werfbezoek aan een onvoltooide piramide', *Intersentia,* no. 6 (2015), pp. 13-14; J. Vananroye, 'Ook de enige vennoot heeft altijd gezelschap', TRV (2014), pp. 425, 426, no. 4; D. van Gerven, 'Les associés commandités sont-ils par nature commerçants lorsque la société en commandite simple l'est? Quelques réflexions sur la personnalité morale des sociétés à responsabilité illimitée' (annotation under Cass. 19 December 2008), *RCJB* (2013), pp. (406) 412, no. 5; Ch. Lyon-Caen, 'Le gage des parts d'associés et des créances' (annotation under Paris 18 August 1881), *Sirey*, II, (1882), p. 25.

5 Coipel, 1996, pp. 31, 34ff, nos. 7ff, *supra* note 2.

6 A universality is a group of goods with a common destination, which therefore is treated – at least in some cases – as one object. Universalities may be factual (a group of goods with a common destination and nothing more; this can be the object of a single property right) or legal (a group of goods which has been made partially autonomous: it has its own rights and debts, which may have exclusive or preferential rights on the assets of the legal universality, but it does not have legal personality). Both the co-ownership of heirs and the co-ownership of a company in the Coipel thesis concern legal universalities.

7 J. Vananroye, *Onverdeelde boedel en rechtspersoon. Technieken van vermogensafscheiding, vermogensovergang en vermogensvereffening in het burgerlijk en ondernemingsrecht*, Biblo, 2014, pp. 224-225, nos. 325-326.

8 Coipel, 1996, pp. 31, 46, no. 24, *supra* note 2.

9 H. De Page & R. Dekkers, *Traité élémentaire de droit civil belge, V, Les principaux contrats usuels.* Deuxième partie. Les biens. Première partie, Bruylant, 1952, pp. 1009, no. 1153, 1010-1011, no. 1155.

an old theory which held that the right of a shareholder '*[est] une propriété d'un genre spécial, [...] une variété de ce qu'on appelle les propriétés incorporelles*' (free translation: 'is a property right of a special kind, [...], a variant of what is called incorporeal properties').[10] As Planiol and Ripert did not give any reference, Coipel could not check if this old theory is a predecessor of his. We found that there was indeed such a theory, defended by eminent authors.[11] Even the French Court of Cassation has followed this theory in 1802 (*an X* of the republican calendar).[12] On the other hand, the authority of this old theory is doubtful. While the legal personality of commercial companies was already accepted in the old French law,[13] there was not much of a commercial doctrine to speak of.[14] The legal personality of commercial companies does not seem to have been problematised while writing the *Code de commerce* of 1807.[15] It therefore does not appear that there has been enough reflection on legal personality and its effects to give much weight to this old theory.

3 Critical Analysis of the Coipel Thesis

3.1 *Arguments pro the Coipel Thesis*

3.1.1 Developing the Company from Co-ownership

Companies with legal personality are the endpoint of an evolution starting with groups which firstly created a joint accounting,[16] subsequently were made more independent by making them into a co-ownership in the property law sense[17] and only finally were made

---

10 Coipel, 1996, pp. 31, 47, no. 26, *supra* note 3; referencing M. Planiol & G. Ripert, '*Traité pratique de droit civil français*, XI', *LGDJ* (1954) p. 294, no. 1019.

11 J-M. Pardessus, *Cours de droit commercial*, II (Tarlier 1836) 491, no. 992 (who explicitly recognises the legal personality of commercial companies at 479, no. 975); P.H.-A. Merlin, *Questions de droit*, I, *A.-C.* (Garnery 1819) *v° Action, actionnaire*, p. 29. See also É. Richard, '«Mon nom est personne»: la construction de la personnalité morale ou les vertus de la patience', *Entreprises et histoire* (2009), pp. 14, 31, no. 44.

12 Cass. 1 ventôse an X, (1810) *Pas.*, 382, annotation.

13 V. Thiry, 'Les sociétés civiles constituent-elles des personnes juridiques distinctes de celles des associés?', *Revue critique de législation et de jurisprudence* (1854), pp. 412, 433-434.

14 J. Guyader, 'Existait-il une doctrine commercialiste dans l'ancienne France? L'exemple des sociétés: titre IV de l'ordonnance sur le commerce de terre du 23 mars 1673' in Y. Poirmeur & A. Bernard (Eds.), *La doctrine juridique*, PUF, 1993), pp. 77, 77-111.

15 F.M Huussen-de Groot, *Rechtspersonen in de negentiende eeuw. Een studie van privaatrechtelijke rechtspersonen in de negentiende-eeuwse lawgeving van Frankrijk, Nederland en Duitsland,* Universitaire Pers Leiden, 1976, p. 58.

16 Richard, 2009, p. 14, 19, no. 12, *supra* note 11.

17 See for more recent examples Cass. 28 February 1985, (1987) *RCJB* 571, annotation A. Meinertzhagen-Limpens, analysed by I. Corbisier, 'Pour une nouvelle dimension contractuelle et une personnalité morale non obligatoire en droit des sociétés', *RPS* (2015), pp. 313, 349, footnote 112.

into separate entities with their own legal personality.[18] The effect is that there are a number of entities which exist '*op de drempel van de rechtspersoon-constructie*' ('on the threshold of the legal person-construct'): they are in certain ways made a person, but they continue to be a co-ownership construction, being the undivided property of several persons.[19]

Even in present-day law, an example of the aforementioned evolution can be seen. Until recently, French tenancy in common ('*indivision*') was *grosso modo* identical with that in Belgian law (note that this is not the same as the *société civile* (France) or the *société de droit commun* (Belgium)[20]), at least insofar the powers of the co-owners are considered. Article 815-3 (old) French Cc decided: '*Les actes d'administration et de disposition relatifs aux biens indivis requièrent le consentement de tous les indivisaires.*' (free translation: 'Acts of administration and of disposition concerning the undivided goods necessitate the accord of all co-owners'). Belgian law is essentially the same (art. 577-2, § 6 Belgian Cc). But since 2006[21] the French co-owners who have at least 2/3 of the undivided rights are empowered to sell the moveable undivided goods to pay the costs of the tenancy in common.[22] Since 2009[23] the same majority can, if authorised by a court, sell immoveable undivided goods.[24] Some French authors see this as an evolution of the tenancy in common towards legal personality, as the tenancy in common develops a proper and independent interest, which is typical of legal personality.[25] The tenancy in common is, however, still a co-ownership.

These developments are quite supportive of the Coipel thesis. While the jump from joint accounts to co-ownership is obviously a qualitative jump (from mere bookkeeping to sharing property rights), the jump from a co-ownership to a company with legal person-

18 See J. Vananroye, *Onverdeelde boedel en rechtspersoon. Technieken van vermogensafscheiding, vermogensovergang en vermogensvereffening in het burgerlijk en ondernemingsrecht*, Biblo, 2014 pp. 1-8, nos. 1-11; R. Savatier, 'Essai d'une présentation nouvelle des biens incorporels', (1958) *Rev.trim.dr.civ.* 331, 347, no. 32; I. Corbisier, 'Pour une nouvelle dimension contractuelle et une personnalité morale non obligatoire en droit des sociétés', *RPS* (2015), pp. 313, 339, footnote 83; L. Brunori, *Societas quid sit. La société commerciale dans l'élaboration de la Seconde Scolastique*, Éditions mare & martin, 2015, pp. 177ff.

19 Vananroye, 2014, pp. 215-217, nos. 316-317, *supra* note 19. See also Vananroye, 2015, p. 41, no. 19, *supra* note 4.

20 The French *société civile* has legal personality, while the Belgian *société de droit commun* does not. A company has a specific and obligatory purpose, this being the search of profit, while a co-ownership does not have a purpose.

21 Law 23 June 2006, no. 2006-728 portant réforme des successions et des libéralités, *JORF* 24 June 2006, 9513.

22 Art. 815-3, lid 1: '*Le ou les indivisaires titulaires d'au moins deux tiers des droits indivis peuvent, à cette majorité: […] 3° Vendre les meubles indivis pour payer les dettes et charges de l'indivision.*'

23 Law 12 May 2009, no. 2009-526 de simplification et de clarification du droit et d'allègement des procédures, *JORF* 13 May 2009, 7920.

24 Art. 815-5-1 Cc: '*Sauf en cas de démembrement de la propriété du bien ou si l'un des indivisaires se trouve dans l'un des cas prévus à l'article 836, l'aliénation d'un bien indivis peut être autorisée par le tribunal de grande instance, à la demande de l'un ou des indivisaires titulaires d'au moins deux tiers des droits indivis, suivant les conditions et modalités définies aux alinéas suivants.*'

25 R. Boffa & P. Chauviré, 'Le changement en droit des biens', *Revue de droit d'Assas* (2015), pp. 67, 71-72, no. 12. Some authors stress that the indivision does not have legal personality: G. Mémeteau, *Droit des biens*, Larcier, 2014, p. 162.

ality is not. It is, after all, perfectly possible to make contractual arrangements for a co-ownership. Some of these contractual arrangements are also company contracts (companies without legal personality are undoubtedly a combination of a co-ownership with a company contract), though they do not create a new legal person. Is the creation of a legal person a qualitative jump? Not necessarily, at least not between the shareholders. Their relationships are still regulated by a contract. As legal personality is mostly meant to simplify the relationship between a company and third parties (replacing the multitude of shareholders with one central entity), it does not appear necessary for the co-ownership to disappear just because the company has acquired legal personality. A French example illustrates this: as tenancy in common acquires a proper and independent interest typical of legal personality, it continues to be a co-ownership. In other words: the company with legal personality developed from a property law mechanism (the co-ownership) and the addition of legal personality need not obscure the property law mechanism, at least in the relations between the shareholders and the company (third parties deal with the legal person).

3.1.2 Case Law

A very old judgement of the French Court of Cassation (made at a moment when Belgium was annexed by France and therefore submitted to the authority of this Court) confirms the Coipel thesis.[26] The shareholders of a weapons manufacturer had decided that the shares would be freely transferable. One of them had sold his shares, which subsequently led to a discussion on whether the buyer was a shareholder. *Procureur-général* Merlin de Douai thought he was. He cited important legal authors, such as chancellor d'Aguesseau (*Mémoire sur le commerce des actions*, art. 1, no. 6), and Voet, who defined a share as a *part d'une société*, a *pars societatis* (a part of a company), which he interpreted as a share in a tenancy in common. The Court of Cassation accepted his reasoning: '*ces actions, dans la main des associés, représentaient leur propriété respective dans les fonds de première mise*' (free translation: 'these shares, in the hands of the shareholders, represented their ownership of the funds which had been contributed to the company').

This was an extremely positive judgement for the Coipel thesis. It confirmed that the 'old law' (law from before the French Revolution) perceived companies as co-ownerships, which confirmed the development phases *supra*. Most interesting is that they wrote about what French practice then termed a *compagnie*, which generally (and also in these cases) denoted a company with legal personality thanks to a royal grant.[27] Legal personality did not seem to hinder co-ownership between shareholders.

26 Cass. 1 ventôse an X, (1810) *Pas.*, 382, annotation, also published in Merlin, 1819, p. 34, *supra* note 11, (Merlin was the *procureur-général* who pleaded the case before the Court of Cassation).

27 Richard, 2009, pp. 14, 26 ff, nos. 44 ff, *supra* note 11.

A second judgement of the Court of Cassation also supports the Coipel thesis.[28] The Court judged that the contract to create a company does indeed create a legal person, but this is purely fictional, and is only meant to clearly delineate the patrimony of the shareholders and the goods which they own together as shareholders, which is important for third parties (especially the creditors, as creditors of individual shareholders and creditors of the company have different rights regarding the company patrimony). Nevertheless, Coipel does not follow this judgement, as he does not accept that companies with legal personality are a mere fiction.[29]

3.2 *Problems of the Coipel Thesis*

Although a number of arguments exist in favour of the Coipel thesis, it also has a number of problems, which we will analyse here.

3.2.1 Terminology and Legal Texts

We will start with a number of problems in relation to the terminology of Coipel and legal texts which at least appear to be contrary to the Coipel thesis.

The right of the company on its patrimony does not have its own name, not even for Coipel. For him, the company is also 'owner' of its patrimony.[30] This is a very strange solution. Either the company is owner of its patrimony, in which case the shareholders are probably not owners. Ownership is generally 'exclusive' and 'unitary', which means that there cannot exist different types of ownership[31] and that there may only be one right of ownership on a specific good. Or else the company is indeed not the owner of its patrimony, but then it is not logical to label two rights with a different nature with the same name.

It follows from the Coipel thesis that the company patrimony is in reality owned by the shareholders, but the company has a limited property right of administration on 'its' patrimony. This real right can be transferred by fusing or splitting the company (artt. 671ff C.soc.). But if all company assets are owned by the shareholders, they also own the limited property right of administration. The company is left with empty hands. This is a logical contradiction in the Coipel thesis: the company has a limited property right and at the same time does not have it, because it is also owned by the shareholders.

28 Cass. 22 June 1855, (1855) *Pas.*, I, 346
29 Coipel, 1996, pp. 31, 33-34, no. 5, *supra* note 2.
30 Coipel, 1996, pp. 31, 49, no. 28, *supra* note 2.
31 Translations of continental law texts in English may obscure this, as 'property right(s)' often is used to indicate both ownership (*dominium*) and limited real rights (such as usufruct or servitudes/easements; to be translated by *droits réels démembrés* in French, *beperkte zakelijke rechten* in Dutch or *beschränkte dingliche Rechte* in German).

Article 529 of the *Code Napoléon* states that shares in certain companies are movables by action of law. Normally shares in universalities (groups of goods, see *supra*) become immovable if the universality contains immovable goods such as land.[32] This means that the share in the universality is abstracted from the contents of the universality. This is generally thought of as an effect of the legal personality of those companies, which the legislator confirmed.[33] The legislator even affirmed that shareholders in a company with legal personality have only a right to the value of the company, while shareholders in a company without legal personality are co-owners. Article 529 C.Nap. has therefore been seen as a problem for the Coipel thesis.[34]

Other legal texts also contradict the Coipel thesis. For example, articles 623 and 625 C.soc. state that certain companies with legal personality can be the owner of their own shares. This is a very strange construction if the Coipel thesis is followed, as it means that the shares are not consolidated in favour of the shareholders (they continue to exist, but they should disappear; in a normal co-ownership, the disappearance of a shareholder means that his part passes on to the others). Another difficult article is article 28 C.soc., which regulates the risk of loss or damage to a good which a shareholder has brought into the company (in French: '*apport*'). It differentiates between the *apport* in full ownership and the *apport* of a limited property right, which is strange if seen from the Coipel thesis viewpoint. All *apports* are in the form of a limited property right, after all. If the Coipel thesis is not followed, this is a logical article, as the rights of the company can be a full ownership or a limited property right, depending on what is brought into the company.

Another example necessitates delving into legal history. Canals were an important source of revenue in the nineteenth century, illustrated by the fact that Napoleon acquired a number of them for his *domaine extraordinaire*. The *domaine extraordinaire* consisted of goods which the French Emperor had acquired by conquest or by international treaty (though buying was also a possibility in practice).[35] Several imperial decrees regulated the canals of the *domaine extraordinaire*. They also contain provisions concerning the share-

32 Coipel, 1996, pp. 31, 43, no. 16, *supra* note 3; F.A Fenet, *Recueil complet des travaux préparatoires du Code civil*, XI, (Videcocq 1836) 25; K. Geens, '200 jaar vennootschapsrecht in perspectief: quo vadis ius societatum?', *TPR*, (2007), pp. 73, 80, no. 6.

33 F.A. Fenet, *Recueil complet des travaux préparatoires du Code civil*, XI, (Videcocq 1836), pp. 15, 45-46; Geens, 2007, pp. 73, 77, no. 2, *supra* note 33; Vananroye, 2014, p. 7, no. 9, *supra* note 18; R. Szramkiewicz, *Histoire du droit des affaires*, Montchrestien, 1989, pp. 308-309, no. 776; Richard, 2009, pp. 14, 30, no. 41, *supra* note 11. *Critical*: L. Michoud, 'La théorie de la personnalité morale et son application au droit français', *LGDJ*, I, no. 69, (1906), p. 165. But see apparently *contra* Liège 19 March 1910, (1910) *Jurisprudence de Liège*, p. 145.

34 J.-P. Marguénaud, *L'animal en droit privé*, PUF, 1992, p. 395.

35 See J. Van de Voorde, 'À la plus grande gloire (juridique) de Napoléon Ier, Empereur des Français, de la part de ses plus fidèles sujets, les Belges. Les majorats napoléoniens analysés du point de vue du droit des biens en raison de leur survie continuée en Belgique', *Revista Internacional de Derecho y Ciencias Sociales* (2017), pp. 29, 37, no. 18 and 43, no. 29 and the references.

holders. These provisions stated first that the canals were a '*propriété indivisible entre les mains des actionnaires*' (free translation: 'an undivided property in the hands of the shareholders'). Then, they backtracked and declared: '*La propriété résidera toujours sous le titre collectif de l'association; il ne pourra en être distrait ni séparé aucune portion par cession, donation, décès, faillite des actionnaires, liquidation, faillite de la société et toute autre cause*' (free translation: 'The ownership [of the canal] will always be held by the company; nothing of it may be taken away by selling, donation, death, bankruptcy of the shareholders, liquidation, bankruptcy of the company or any other cause').[36] The company is even expressly called '*la société propriétaire*' ('the owning company').[37]

These elements demonstrate that the Coipel thesis is not totally convincing, at least when reading the laws and writings on the law. It could still, however, represent the best explanatory model.

3.2.2 The Limited Explanatory Value of the Coipel Thesis

A number of company law principles resemble property law principles, e.g. the *numerus clausus*, although a number of company law principles are clearly different. If this was confirmed, it would mean that company law was still autonomous vis-à-vis property law, as not all rules of company law can be retraced to property law. The for-profit rule ('winstoogmerk', '*but lucratif*') was analysed as well as the company interest rule ('vennootschapsbelang', '*intérêt de la société*') (both in art. 1 C.soc., the company interest rule can also be found in art. 19 C.soc.).

Generally speaking, companies set out to make a profit. They must demonstrate some kind of advantages to the shareholders. Property law does not have a for-profit rule; it is generally neutral as to the ends owners and other actors in property law have (they can use their property for profit, to help other people or even destroy it; they are not obliged to pursue one of these ends but are free to choose). More interestingly, at least some co-ownerships (e.g. between heirs, who in principle are the owners and administrators of the estate of the decedent, without any administrator or executor) are expressly meant to be divided between the co-owners as soon as possible, not to be administered in search of

---

36 Art. 5 imperial decree 10 March 1810 relatif au Canal du Midi, (1838) *Bull.* (not published in 1810, according to a footnote), afl. 595, no. 7517, 236; art. 4 imperial decree 16 March 1810 concernant la Propriété et l'Administration des Canaux d'Orléans et de Loing, cédés au Domaine extraordinaire, (1810) *Bull.*, no. 5355, 325.

37 Art. 7 imperial decree 10 March 1810 relatif au Canal du Midi, (1838) *Bull.* (not published in 1810, according to a footnote), afl. 595, no. 7517, 236; art. 6 imperial decree 16 March 1810 concernant la Propriété et l'Administration des Canaux d'Orléans et de Loing, cédés au Domaine extraordinaire, (1810) *Bull.*, no. 5355, 325.

profit.[38] This is an important distinction between company law and property law and a confirmation of their mutual independence.

The company interest is the collective interest of the actual and future shareholders that the company be profitable (original text: 'het collectief winstbelang van haar huidige en toekomstige aandeelhouders'), so writes the Belgian Court of Cassation.[39] Companies – or more precisely their administrators – are obliged to act in the best interest of the company. This means that the for-profit rule is strongly mixed in the company interest rule; it has been shown that no for-profit rule exists in property law, implying that the company interest rule is also no property law rule.

Co-ownerships appear to have a weak 'common interest rule', which might be taken to be the property law source of the company interest rule. Article 577-2, § 6 CC gives to the judge the power to force a cooperation from co-owners for acts of administration which are necessary. This is often considered to be a legal application of the prohibition on abuse of rights (*abus de droit*).[40] The case law does not follow this analysis, instead preferring a more broad criterion.[41] The necessity of an act is controlled 'objectively', without pondering the interests of the co-owners.[42] This can be said to be a common interest rule, but it has a different structure to the company interest rule. The company interest rule indicates how the administrators of a company have to act,[43] while the common interest rule only prohibits resisting necessary acts of administration – but does not impose those acts.

The Coipel thesis does not sufficiently explain certain aspects of company law and they do not have a suitable parallel in property law for property law to be their source.

3.2.3 Case Law

The Belgian Court of Cassation has had several opportunities to judge whether a company with legal personality is owner of its patrimony (and the goods in it) or not. Each time, it has judged that the company is sole owner of its patrimony, and that the shareholders do not have any real right on the patrimony or its contents.[44] In 1911 it expressed this very

38 J. Vananroye, 'Fifty ways to leave your lover: over verdeling, ontbinding, overdracht en uittreding' (annotation under Cass. 20 September 2013), *Notarieel en Fiscaal Maandblad* (2015), pp. 152, 153-154, nos. 3-4.

39 Cass. 28 November 2013, (2014) *Tijdschrift voor Belgisch Handelsrecht* 854, annotation D. Willermain, *RPS* (2014), p. 41, annotation J. Gollier, *TRV* (2014), p. 286, annotation.

40 H. Vandenberghe & S. Snaet, *Zakenrecht. Mede-eigendom* in *Beginselen van Belgisch privaatrecht,* Story-Scientia (1997), p. 53, no. 23; J. Hansenne, *Les biens*, II, Faculté de droit de l'Université de Liège, 1996, p. 865, no. 862.

41 N. Carette & J. Van de Voorde, 'Rechtsmisbruik in het zakenrecht. *Capita selecta*' in J. Rozie, A. Van Oevelen & S. Rutten (Eds.), *Rechtsmisbruik*, Intersentia, 2015, pp. 71, 109-110, no. 41 and the references.

42 Carette & Van de Voorde, 2015, pp. 71, 110-111, no. 42.

43 Vananroye, 2014, p. 425, no. 1, *supra* note 4.

44 Cass. 30 April 1853, (1853) *Pas.*, I, 287; Cass. 17 May 1906, (1906) *Pas.*, I, 249; Cass. 31 May 1951 (1951) *Pas.*, I, 665 (the sole shareholder of a company which is disbanded because of there being but one shareholder

well: '*que ces immeubles appartiennent en propre à l'individualité juridique, distincte de celle des associés, que constitue toute société commerciale aux termes de l'article 2 de la loi du 18 mai 1873; que le patrimoine de la société ne se confond pas avec celui de l'associé commandité et que ce dernier n'a sur les biens apportés à la société ou acquis par elle aucun droit privatif de propriété*' (free translation: 'that these immoveables are the property of the juristic individuality, which is distinct of that of the associates, that is constituted by all commercial companies in the words of article 2 of the law of 18 May 1873; that the patrimony of the company is not confounded with those of the shareholders and that these have no privative right of property on the goods of the company').[45] It therefore denied the Coipel thesis, even if older case law (see *supra*) was more accommodating to the Coipel thesis.

3.3 *Interim Conclusion*

It can be concluded that a company with legal personality is (in principle) full owner of its patrimony and components. A *sui generis* property right as posited by the Coipel thesis is neither necessary nor desirable. It does not fully explain matters and contradicts most case law, though some older case law supports the Coipel thesis. The Coipel thesis is even logically contradictory, as the *sui generis* property right of the company would itself be the property of the shareholders, not of the company.

This does not, however, mean that company law and property law are completely different. Company law often uses property law techniques, especially co-ownership. This is mostly done for companies without legal personality, where no separate patrimony exists. An example: article 55 of the Belgian *Code des sociétés* makes the rules on liquidating a co-ownership applicable to the liquidation of companies without legal personality, though this does not seem to be followed in practice.[46]

---

becomes owner of the company patrimony), Cass. 2 December 1952, (1953) *RCJB* 288, annotation J. Heenen; Cass. 10 May 1966, (1966) *Pas.*, I, 1152; Cass. 17 March 1972, (1971-72) *RW* 1925.

45 Cass. 10 juli 1911, (1912) *RPS*, no. 2207, 73, annotation, (1911) *Pas.*, I, 434.

46 J. Vananroye, 'Declaratoir, retroactief en anticipatief effect van de verdeling' in R. Barbaix & N. Carette (Eds), *Tendensen vermogensrecht 2017*, Intersentia, 2017, pp. 139, 150, no. 11.

4 Property Law and Company Law as 'Third-Party Laws': A Better Analysis

4.1 Introduction

Although company law and property law are separate and autonomous, they continue to have substantial overlaps. Property rights are 'good against the world', just as the existence of a company is good against the world. Publicity is very important in both cases: property rights often need publicity to be fully effective (if no registration in the land registry is made, third parties often are not bound by them), while many things in company law have to be published also (in Belgian law companies often are obliged to publish a large number of their legal acts in the *Moniteur belge* – the official gazette of Belgium, publishing also all laws – and to have a company file at the local court).

These commonalities and the importance of third parties – both their protection and the way in which they are bound – suggest that property law and company law are both part of a larger category. It is regularly written that property law is a 'third-party law',[47] which finds a faint echo in company law.[48] The nature and function of 'third-party law' is rarely elucidated or systematized.[49] We will analyse a few questions on the nature and function of third-party law.

4.2 Defining 'Third-Party Law'

A third-party law may be described as a branch of law in which third parties are regularly bound by the legal acts of parties, regardless of their knowledge or acceptance of this. A contract transferring a property right has to be respected by third parties as they have to accept that the transferee has become the owner. A legal act nominating or revoking a representative of a company has to be respected by third parties, who have to accept that the representative does or has ceased to act for the company. A contract creating a company implies that certain goods are no longer accessible to creditors or the shareholders; it can also designate the applicable law, which may impose more or less obligations on the parties, including obligations to indemnify third parties for e.g. bad management. Third-party

47 Vananroye, 2015, pp. 39-41, no. 19, *supra* note 5; S. Bartels, S. Stelbaert & B. Valsteens, '20 jaar Nieuw BW en het goederenrecht: er is in die tijd veel/weinig* gebeurd. *Doorhalen wat niet van toepassing is.', (2012) *Ars Aequi* 476, 481; F. Verstulen, '*Paritas creditorum*, voorrang en preferentie', *TPR* (2006), pp. 1157, 1205, no. 63.

48 J. Vananroye & G. Lindemans, 'Schuldeisersbescherming in het vennootschapsrecht: een rouwbericht' in *Recht in beweging. 24ste VRG-Alumnidag 2017*, Maklu, 2017, pp. 291-293.

49 Vananroye, 2015, p. 39, no. 19, *supra* note 4.

laws therefore have an impact on the autonomy of third parties. Property law and company law are third-party laws. Insolvency law and intellectual property law are other examples.

Next to the third-party laws, 'first-party laws' exist. They limit themselves to regulating the juridical relations between parties, leaving third parties out of the equation. Contract law, with its privity of contract (or its continental equivalents), is a prime example of a first-party law.

Branches of law are generally mixtures of first-party and third-party law. Designating a branch of law as a first-party or a third-party law is therefore generally only an approximation, based on the more determining character of either the first-party or the third-party elements.

4.3 *Effects of the Qualification as a Third-Party Law*

4.3.1 A Priori Limited Effects

Qualifying a branch of law as a third-party law is, in and of itself, mostly descriptive and didactic. It only means that a certain branch of law binds third parties. This does not imply certain rules on itself. It is only when other principles are brought into play that 'third-party law' becomes a normative qualification, from which a certain number of rules follow.

The most important of these 'other principles' is the protection of third parties. It is forbidden to intervene in the personal sphere of legal autonomy of third parties, unless one has the necessary contractual, judicial or legal authorisation.[50] Combined with the fact that third parties are to be protected and the fact that third-party laws tend to bind third parties against their will, a number of rules appear at least strongly suggested. Here are some examples.

4.3.2 Limiting Party Autonomy

Party autonomy means that the parties to a legal act – generally a contract – have wide powers to decide whether they will act, how they will act and which rights and obligations they will create. Supposing the parties to be mostly equal, their interests in the negotiations will be discounted. A contract can therefore be presumed to be fair to both parties, even if this has to be assorted with many caveats (which we will not analyse here). Third parties, on the other hand, do not generally have any opportunity to have their interests discounted in the negotiations between the parties. The parties may therefore inadvertently or knowingly externalise costs or otherwise impose disadvantages on third parties. This is normally limited by privity of contract and other mechanisms in first-party laws. In third-party laws,

50 W. Van Gerven, *Algemeen deel* in *Beginselen van Belgisch Privaatrecht*, Standaard Wetenschappelijke Uitgeverij, 1969, p. 89, footnote 5.

such mechanisms are much weaker. It is therefore necessary to limit party autonomy in order to minimise the costs and disadvantages which parties can impose on third parties.

An important limitation of party autonomy is the *numerus clausus*: parties can only conclude legal acts which the law authorises. This *numerus clausus* exists in property law,[51] in company law[52] and even in intellectual property law.[53] The *numerus clausus* operates on two levels, named (first by German authors, hence their German names) *Typenzwang* and *Typenfixierung*.[54] *Typenzwang* implies that only the 'forms' (*Typ*, in German) which law admits may be used. If the law has forms A, B and C, form D may not be used. *Typenfixierung* means that the content of the forms is fixed by law: form A implies the rights 1, 2 and 6; form B implies the rights 1, 3 and 5; form C implies the rights 4 and 6. Parties may not change this content, which means that form A will always entail rights 1, 2 and 6. Note that the *Typenfixierung* may be either strong or weak, depending on the autonomy parties conserve to fix the content of the forms. Belgian property law has a rather weak *Typenfixierung*.[55] Belgian company law is somewhat stricter, at least for companies with legal personality.

4.3.3 Publicity

Publicity means that information which is relevant for third parties is brought to their attention, often by registration in a public registry, though possession has always been rather important in making property rights public.[56] In company law, publicity often also necessitates publishing information in official journals or by joining it to the company file held by a court.

Publicity has a double effect on third parties. If a piece of information has been made public, third parties often have a duty to know it and to act accordingly. For example, if the sale of a house has been duly registered, third parties such as creditors have to accept that they can no longer sell it to settle the debts of the debtor. On the other hand, if a piece of information has not been made duly public, third parties have generally no or only a weak duty of care. The information will only be used against them if they knew or should have known about it. The unregistered sale of a house by a debtor is therefore irrelevant to creditors, unless the debtor has written to his creditors to warn them of the sale.

---

51 S. Ginossar, '*Droit réel, propriété et créance. Élaboration d'un système rationnel des droits patrimoniaux*', *LGDJ* 1960, pp. 146-151, no. 58.

52 Cass. 17 May 1968, (1968-69) *RW* 412, annotation. D. Van Gerven, *Rechtspersonen*, I, *Rechtspersonen in het algemeen. Verenigingen, stichtingen & publiekrechtelijke rechtspersonen* in *Beginselen van Belgisch privaatrecht*, Kluwer, 2007, p. 60, no. 32; Geens, 2007, pp. 73, 78, no. 3, *supra* note 32.

53 H. Vanhees, *Handboek intellectuele rechten*, Intersentia, 2017, p. 5.

54 B. Akkermans, *The Principle of* Numerus Clausus *in European Property Law*, Intersentia, 2008, pp. 6-7.

55 V. Sagaert & R. Jansen, 'Goederenrecht: de gestage groei naar een conventioneel vermogensrecht' (2011-12) *RW*, pp. 68, 71-73, nos. 11-13.

56 See J. Van de Voorde & N. Carette, 'Is het bezit als publiciteitsmiddel in verval?' in A. de Boeck, V. Sagaert & R. Van Ransbeeck (Eds.), *Publiciteit in het zakenrecht*, die Keure, 2015, pp. 51, 51-159.

An obligation to publish information is not always well respected. In Belgian company law, shareholder registries have to be kept by each company. Companies are often very careless with their shareholder registries,[57] while sometimes two versions of the shareholder registry exist in order to mislead the fiscal authorities.[58]

4.3.4 Abuse of Right

Some Dutch authors say that abuse of right (*abus de droit* in French) is less important in property law, *because* it is a third-party law where third parties have to be certain of their obligations.[59] Belgian law is less clear on this. Abuse of right is possible in Belgian property law[60] and in company law,[61] but generally this is in a context where the interests of third parties are not substantially endangered. The most important exception is acquisitive and extinctive prescription, where many authors plead for restraint, as refusing to apply prescription rules impacts third parties.[62]

It therefore appears that third-party laws do not necessarily exclude all applications of abuse of right, but only encourage restraint when the interests of third parties are endangered. This is acceptable, because there is no great difference between third-party laws and first-party laws when no third parties are interested in the outcome of a discussion. The differences only arise when third parties come into play.

4.4 *Interim Conclusion*

It is clear that being a third-party law has substantial influence on a branch of law. Substantial care of the legislator (and other actors such as judges) is necessary to protect third parties from being bound without them at least knowing it, and from having to support costs and risks which parties have externalised.

---

57 E. Spruyt, 'Naar meer rechtszekerheid bij overdracht van aandelen op naam: voorstellen van oplossing', *RW*, (2009-10), pp. 1538, 1553, no. 55.

58 L. Weyts, 'Naar meer formalisering bij de overdracht van aandelen op naam' in *Liber Amicorum Paul De Vroede*, II, Kluwer, 1994, pp. 1561, 1569, no. 8.

59 S.E. Bartels & A.A. Van Velten, *Zakenrecht. Eigendom en beperkte rechten* in *Mr. C. Assers Handleiding tot de beoefening van het Nederlands Burgerlijk Recht*, Kluwer, 2017, p. 3, no. 2a.

60 Carette & Van de Voorde, 2015, pp. 71, 71-114, *supra* note 42.

61 R. Houben, 'Het verbod op rechtsmisbruik als beperking op de uitoefening van aandeelhoudersrechten' in J. Rozie, A. Van Oevelen & S. Rutten (Eds.), *Rechtsmisbruik*, Intersentia, 2015, pp. (149) 149-180. See also art. 64, 3° C.soc.

62 Th. Vansweevelt, 'De verjaring van de buitencontractuele vordering (art. 2262bis BW)' in H. Vuye & Y. Lemense (Eds.), *Springlevend aansprakelijkheidsrecht*, Intersentia, 2011, pp. 350-353, no. 86 (mostly on extinctive prescription); J. Van de Voorde, *De verkrijgende verjaring. De nalatenschap van Rome heroverwogen*, (PhD thesis, University of Antwerp 2017), pp. 610-613, nos. 1735-1742 (mostly on acquisitive prescription).

5 General Conclusion

A company with legal personality cannot be reduced to a property law figure, which means that the Coipel thesis is not correct. Company law is therefore an autonomous branch of law, at least with regard to property law. Nevertheless, company law often uses property law techniques, especially co-ownerships for companies without legal personality. Company law and property law are also both third-party laws, which is another way in which they are linked. They give the power to bind third parties without their knowledge or even against their will, so that special provisions have to protect these third parties and limit the autonomy of the parties.

6 Transfer of Title to Goods by Intent in English Law

Zhicheng Wu[*]

1 Introduction

Like many other jurisdictions, an *inter vivos* voluntary transfer of title to chattels[1] in English law could have a number of (i) underlying obligational bases which explain why title is transferred, and a number of (ii) methods of conveyance which explain how title is transferred. For the former, it could be a contract of sale, a contract of barter, an enforceable gratuitous promise,[2] or other kinds of contract involving transfer of title in exchange for some acts. For the latter, it could be delivery, deed, or "in [cases] of contracts of sale where the *intention* of the parties is that the property shall pass before delivery."[3] Generally speaking, it is the role of property law to determine the method of conveyance while it is the role of the law of obligations, especially contract law, to determine the underlying basis of such conveyance. However, there seems to be an exception to such 'division of labour' in the sense that rules regarding conveyance are carved out from property law and are partly or even entirely incorporated in the law of contract. Such exception is the law of sale of goods, which, as described by professor Bridge, "deals with a hybrid transaction that consists of contract and conveyance."[4] This chapter aims to inquire whether contract and conveyance are genuinely 'hybrid' as a whole in the context of sale of goods. The key

* Assistant Professor, Renmin Law School; Law and Technology Institute, Renmin University of China; DPhil in Law, University of Oxford. Contact: 59 Zhongguancun Avenue, Haidian District, Beijing, 100872, China.

1 Roughly equivalent to the civil law concept of 'transfer of ownership to movables', leaving aside the unique feature in English law regarding the 'relativity of title'. For discussions on relativity of title, *see e.g.*, F. Pollock & R.S. Wright, *An Essay on Possession in the Common Law*, Oxford, Clarendon Press, 1888, pp. 22-24; B. McFarlane, *The Structure of Property Law*, Oxford, Hart Publishing 2008, pp. 144-146; W. Swadling, 'Property: General Principles' in A. Burrows (Ed.), *English Private Law*, 3rd ed., Oxford, OUP, 2013, paras. 4.422-4.425; L. Rostill, 'Relative Title and Deemed Ownership in English Personal Property Law', *OJLS*, Vol. 35, 2014, p. 1; D. Sheehan, *The Principles of Personal Property Law*, 2nd ed., Oxford, Hart Publishing, 2017, pp. 14-15.

2 Although normally a gift promise is not enforceable, thus a 'gift contract' makes no sense in English law, there are two exceptions where a gratuitous promise is enforceable. The first is a gratuitous promise in the form of deed: Law of Property (Miscellaneous Provisions) Act 1989, s. 1. The second is a promise on which the promisee has detrimental reliance: *Central London Property Trust Ltd v. High Trees House Ltd* [1947] K.B. 130.

3 *Cochrane v. Moore* (1890) 25 Q.B.D. 57, 73 (emphasis added).

4 M.G. Bridge, *The Sale of Goods*, 3rd ed., Oxford, OUP, 2014, para. 3.01.

to such an inquiry is: what does the word 'intention' (or 'intent') mean in English law of sale of goods – does it mean the intent to convey or the intent in contract? In other words, is it possible to find a separate intent of conveyance which passes title and distinguish it from the intent of incurring a contractual obligation to convey in cases of sale of goods?

The importance of whether title to goods passes by contract or by a separate intent to convey in English law is not confined to England and Wales or other common law jurisdictions, it is also highly relevant to two major comparative property law topics quite familiar to civilian lawyers. These are, as will be elaborated in section 6 below, first, whether the English law of sale of goods follows a separationist approach in the sense that conveyance and its underlying (contractual) basis are conceptually separate from each other, and second, whether the English law of sale of goods is a causal system or an abstract one in the sense that the validity of conveyance could be infected by a flawed contract of sale. If the answer is that title to goods passes by virtue of contract, just like a number of judges and well-established English law writers say in section 2 below, then it is impossible for the English law of sale of goods to be an abstract system. If the answer is that title to goods passes by a separate intent to convey, as argued in this chapter, then the English law of sale of goods could be and is an interesting area demonstrating the possibility, no matter how counter-intuitive it seems, that a property transfer system can be both consensual and abstract, which is rarely to be found in continental Europe.

Moreover, revisiting the property transfer system in the English law of sale of goods is also of importance to civilian jurisdictions outside Europe such as China, where a new Civil Code is currently under way so that the choice of adopting abstraction or causality is still under debate. Compared to the fact that comparative research on the debate between abstraction and causality has been well developed by Chinese academics regarding jurisdictions on the European continent, little effort has been made with regard to English law. One of the main reasons for this is that most of them assumed that English law of sale of goods has nothing to do with the principle of separation because title passes by contract – if the premise is conceptually no separate stage of conveyance, then surely there is no need to explore the debate between causality and abstraction, because such a system must be causal not abstract. This chapter therefore aims to demonstrate the fallacy of such an assumption that English law of sale of goods cannot be interpreted in a separationist way, so that the debate of causality versus abstraction in English law is also a field needed to be explored in order to base the upcoming Chinese Civil Code on a genuinely comprehensive comparative inquiry. The concrete debate on justifying causality or abstraction is another large topic and will not be dealt with in this chapter.

The main part of this chapter is made up of five sections. It begins with an analysis of the meaning of 'intent' in legislative provisions which provides that title passes by intent, together with confusion created by judges and academics. The second section refers back to an old case regarding exigibility[5] in the fifteenth century which could be said to be the origin of such confusion. The third section casts doubt on the great legal historian Sir William Holdsworth's analysis on why contracts have been a method of conveyance since the fifteenth century. The fourth section explains the oddity of why the draftsman of the Sale of Goods Act 1893 said 'contract passes title' but then drafted the act in a different way. Finally, a further implication follows to show the significance of distinguishing a separate intent to convey from the contract of sale on a bigger picture of comparative property transfer systems. That is to demonstrate the possibility of a transfer system being consensual and abstract.

2 Intent to Convey or Intent in Contract

While the separate status of the intention of conveyance is relatively easy to identify where there is a separate stage of conveyance, as in cases of land transfers, or chattel transfers in the context of gifts or barter and so forth, this is less apparent in cases of sale of goods. Section 17 of the Sale of Goods Act 1979 provides that property passes when parties 'intend' it to pass.[6] The wording of this section leaves open the question as to whether it is possible to have a separate stage of conveyance by deed or delivery in the context of sale of goods. If the meaning of section 17 is that property passes by 'intent', then delivery and deed could possibly convey title, for they could be the carrier of such intent. If the meaning is that property passes by 'contract', then delivery and deed can no longer be the device to pass property to goods after the contract of sale comes into existence. Clarifying this point is important, because assuming the latter is the law, it follows that in the context of sale of goods, a contract serves to be both the underlying obligation to convey and the conveyance itself. In this case the validity of the conveyance strictly depends on the validity of the contract, and the entire English law of sale of goods is not only purely consensual, but also purely causal without any possibility to be abstract. The following analysis will prove that such assumption is not the law.

---

5 Exigibility roughly means the ability to sue. As illustrated by Birks, 'Rights *in personam* and rights *in rem* are differentiated according to their exigibility. Rights *in personam* can be exacted only from the person against whom they first arise, and rights *in rem* are exigible wherever the thing in question is found and hence against anyone who has it or interferes with it.': P. Birks, *Unjust Enrichment*, 2nd ed., Oxford, Clarendon Press, 2005, p. 180. For a civilian lawyer, exigibility is not the cause but the result of a legally defined right; it is not exigibility but *numerus clausus* that determines the nature of such right. However, although English law also has *numerus clausus*, exigibility can at least be used to infer the nature of certain rights. For instance, exigibility was used by McFarlane and Stevens to determine the nature of the beneficial interest under trust: B. McFarlane & R. Stevens, 'The Nature of Equitable Property', *Journal of Equity*, Vol. 4, 2010, p. 1.

6 The predecessor of this section, found in the Sale of Goods Act 1893, s. 17, had exactly the same expression.

The most obvious reason why it is intent not contract that is the method of conveyance lies in the provisions themselves. Apart from section 17(1) which explicitly articulates this point, subsection 2, for example, also implies it by stating that the intent is not necessarily to be ascertained from the terms of the contract, but also the conduct of the parties and surrounding circumstances of the case.[7] Moreover, since in commercial practice it is unusual for the parties to specify their intentions as to the passing of property except for the case of retention of title,[8] section 18 provides some 'rebuttable presumptions'[9] for ascertaining implied intention as to the timing of conveyance.[10] No matter whether the primary fact is either (i) goods already in a deliverable state,[11] (ii) goods subsequently in a deliverable state known to the buyer,[12] (iii) goods subsequently weighed, measured or tested and known to the buyer,[13] (iv) goods delivered on approval with a condition precedent satisfied,[14] or (v) unascertained or future goods or goods forming part of a bulk which are unconditionally appropriated to the contract,[15] the consequence of applying any of these rules is nothing more than to use the secondary fact of intent to convey which passes property. Such an intent inferred from ascertainment or appropriation can factually coincide with the conclusion of the contract; it can also be independently generated after the conclusion of the contract.[16] This is just a matter of timing, but conceptually speaking

7 Sale of Goods Act 1979, s. 17(2).

8 S. Worthington, 'Passing of Property' in E. McKendrick (ed.), *Sale of Goods*, London, LLP Professional Publishing, 2000, para. 2-004.

9 *Kulkarni v. Manor Credit (Davenham) Ltd.* [2010] E.W.C.A. Civ. 69; [2010] 2 All E.R. (Comm.) 1017 [29] (Rix L.J.).

10 However, whether these rules of ascertaining intention are strictly speaking 'presumptions' is not beyond doubt. On the one hand, this can be said to be a presumption in the sense that as long as any of those primary facts listed in rules 1-5 of section 18 can be proven by evidence, the secondary fact of the seller's intent to convey is then 'presumed' to be existent without the need to be proven by evidence. On the other hand, such a 'presumption' does not look like a typical presumption, for there is no clear shift of the burden of proof from one to the other, which at least cannot be inferred from the expression 'unless a different intention appears' in this section.

11 Sale of Goods Act 1979, s. 18, r. 1.

12 Sale of Goods Act 1979, s. 18, r. 2.

13 Sale of Goods Act 1979, s. 18, r. 3. According to these three rules, it was rightly summarised that '[i]n the absence of any particular agreement, the moment of transfer of property will be, loosely speaking, the first moment when the goods are *ready for delivery*': M.C. Blair, *Sale of Goods Act 1979*, Oxford, Butterworths, 1980, p. 14.

14 Sale of Goods Act 1979, s. 18, r. 4.

15 Sale of Goods Act 1979, s. 18, r. 5. That such an unconditional appropriation with the seller's intent to convey may be clearly distinctive from the contract of sale itself can also be seen from the wording of Sale of Goods Act 1979, s. 19: 'the seller may, by the terms of the *contract or appropriation*, reserve the right of disposal of the goods until certain conditions are fulfilled.' This section, which 'provides one of the legislative foundations for reservation of title at least in so far as the simple reservation of title clause is concerned' (G. McCormack, *Reservation of Title*, 2nd ed., London, Sweet & Maxwell, 1995, p. 16), demonstrates that for a contract of sale of goods with a retention of title clause, property also passes by intent not contract.

16 To pass property in the context of sale of goods without deed or delivery, there could be either a pre-existing ascertainment of the goods, or a subsequent ascertainment (by e.g. appropriation of the goods to the contract) with 'an intention to attach the contract irrevocably to those goods': *Carlos Federspiel & Co v. Charles Twigg*

it is still the intent of the seller not the contract between the seller and the buyer that passes property.

Although the wording of sections 17 and 18 is all based on 'intent' which seems to support the former notion that 'intent passes property' as illustrated in the previous paragraph, the latter notion that 'contract passes property' is, however, the prevailing view as could be found in many textbooks. For instance, it is commonly understood that "an agreement of sale is both a contract and a conveyance [...] property passes by virtue of the contract itself."[17] Such a general statement was further explained in a way where the transferor makes a contract of sale, he is indicating that he does not intend to transfer the property by ways other than contract, and therefore:

> [title] cannot then pass again by reason of delivery, nor, usually would the parties intend it to. Even if, under the contract, property is to pass on delivery, this is still as a result of the contract and not otherwise.[18]

The logical consequence, as the authors point out later on, is that if a transferor delivers the property under a void contract of sale or a voidable contract of sale which is rescinded, the law would say that there must be no valid intention from him to transfer the property even in a subsequent act of physical delivery.

What is certain is that, given the codification nature of the Acts which is to represent the previous law relating to the sale of goods whether found in statute or common law,[19] where the statute is ambiguous or silent on this question, we could at least try to find the answer from pre-1893 laws. In *Simmons v. Swift*, Bayley J. used the word 'bargain' to describe the method of passing of property:

> Generally speaking, where a bargain is made for the purchase of goods, and nothing is said about payment or delivery, the property passes immediately [...] If anything remains to be done on the part of the seller, until that is done the property is not changed.[20]

& Co [1957] 1 Lloyd's Rep. 240, 255 (Pearson J.). However, it should be noted that strictly speaking it is ascertainment not appropriation that is the necessary condition for passing of property by parties' mere intent: *Karlshamns Oljefabriker v. Eastport Navigation Co* [1982] 1 All E.R. 208, 215 (Mustill J.).

17 R. Goode, *Goode on Commercial Law*, 4th ed. (edited and fully revised by E. Mckendrick), London, Penguin, 2010, p. 147. Similar expression in E.L.G. Tyler & N.E. Palmer, *Crossley Vaines' Personal Property*, 5th ed., London, Butterworths, 1973, p. 325. A.L. Diamond, 'When Is a Gift ... ?', *Modern Law Review*, Vol. 27, 1964, pp. 357, 360, citing *Ramsey v. Margrett* [1894] 2 Q.B. 18.

18 M. Bridge *et al.*, *The Law of Personal Property*, London, Sweet & Maxwell, 2013, p. 352.

19 M. Bridge *et al.* (Eds.), *Benjamin's Sale of Goods*, 9th ed., London, Sweet & Maxwell, 2014, pp. 3-6.

20 *Simmons v. Swift* (1826) 6 B. & C. 857, 862; 108 E.R. 319, 321.

In *Tarling v. Baxter*,[21] Bayley J. used the word 'immediate sale':

> The rule of law is, that where there is an immediate sale, and nothing remains to be done by the vendor as between him and the vendee, the property in the thing sold vests in the vendee.[22]

In *Gilmour v. Supple*, Sir Cresswell said, "by a contract for the sale of specific ascertained goods, the property immediately vests in the buyer."[23] On the contrary, Blackburn, who wrote the first textbook specifically on the English law of sale of goods, clearly stated the pre-1893 law in a different way that it is the intent that passes property: "the property does not pass unless there be an intention to pass it."[24] Such ambiguity remained so; even the case law on the eve of 1893 did not show a clear and consistent line with respect to this question. On one side, Lord Cairns stated that:

> if the property in the goods in question passed, it could only pass by way of contract; there is nothing else which could have passed the property. [...] that [the case namely in which the contract never comes into existence] being so, it is idle to talk of the property passing.[25]

Accordingly, as the intent to convey title is strictly attached to the contract of sale as a part of it, there can be no valid intent to pass property where the contract is void, because the contract itself is the method of conveyance. On the other hand, and as has been cited several times in this thesis, Fry L.J. stated that:

> according to the old law no gift or grant of a chattel was effectual to pass it [...] unless accompanied by delivery: that on that law two exceptions have been grafted, one in the case of deeds, and the other in that of contracts of sale where the intention of the parties is that the property shall pass before delivery.[26]

---

21 (1827) 6 B. & C. 360, 108 E.R. 484.

22 *Tarling v. Baxter* (1827) 6 B. & C. 360, 364; 108 E.R. 484, 486.

23 *Gilmour v. Supple* (1858) 11 Moo. P.C. 551, 566; 14 E.R. 803, 809.

24 C. Blackburn, *A Treatise on the Effect of the Contract of Sale on the Legal Rights of Property and Possession in Goods, Wares, and Merchandise*, London, 1845, p. 147. Surprisingly, in the second edition of this book written not by Blackburn himself, the author added his own remarks without citing any authority in the next chapter of this part II, that '[i]n the English law a contract of sale has two effects. It operates as a contract giving rise to obligations or rights in personam ... and it also, in some cases, operates as a conveyance of property': J.C. Graham, *A Treatise on the Effect of the Contract of Sale on the Legal Rights of Property and Possession in Goods, Wares, and Merchandise*, 2nd ed., London, Stevens & Sons, 1885, p. 243.

25 *Cundy v. Lindsay* (1877–78) L.R. 3 App. Cas. 459, 466. Similar statement in *Tarling v. Baxter* (1827) 6 B. & C. 360, 108 E.R. 484.

26 *Cochrane v. Moore* (1890) 25 Q.B.D. 57, 72-73. Followed by Harman L.J. in *Re Cole* [1964] Ch. 175, 187.

It logically follows that even in the context of sale of goods, at least there could be a valid intent incorporated in conveyance (whatever the method is), not in the contract itself. Furthermore, this means we have to resort to the old rules in common law to find the answer. The following paragraphs will demonstrate that the latter is the more accurate proposition, and that the 'contract' itself has never been the method of conveyance in the context of sale of goods throughout English legal history.

3 Implication from Exigibility

Despite the lack of any decisive authority regarding this point to be found among pre-1893 cases, it is suggested that insights could be gained through a closer look at the relation between sale of goods and the law of detinue.[27] For example, legal historians elucidated the available claims against vendors for non-delivery of goods in the context of sales of chattels under early English law, including the circumstance that:

> If the purchase price were paid, or the buyer's sealed obligation for the price delivered, Detinue would lie from early times. The buyer's right was extended in 1442 or thereabouts, so that he could claim the specific property though he had not paid the price [...][28]

The authority for such radical change around 1442 mentioned by him came from Fortescue C.J.'s illustration during Henry VI's reign:

> If I buy a horse of you, the property is straightway in me, and for this you shall have a writ of debt for the money, and I shall have detinue for the horse on this bargain.[29]

27 Detinue, apart from technical explanations in the following paragraphs, can be understood by civilian lawyers roughly as a form of claim similar to the Roman *vindicatio* in the sense that both normally require pre-existing possession. Indeed, conversion, trespass, detinue, replevin (whether abolished in all or some common law jurisdictions) can all be understood roughly as common law versions of the civilian vindication claim. Notably however, as Douglas pointed out, there are two technical differences between the two. First, detinue requires both the claimant's possession of the movable thing and the defendant's intentional interference of such thing, while vindication does not require the interference being intentional. Second, detinue alone enables the claimant not only to get back possession of the thing, but also to get damages for consequential loss, while vindication alone does not provide for the latter: S. Douglas, *Liability for Wrongful Interferences with Chattels*, Oxford, Hart Publishing, 2011, p. 90.

28 W.T. Barbour, 'The History of Contract in Early English Equity' in P. Vinogradoff (Ed.), *Oxford Studies in Social and Legal History*, Vol. IV, Oxford, Clarendon Press, 1914, pp. 114-115.

29 Y.B. 20 Hen. VI Trin. pl. 4. Translation from Law French to Modern English is in J.B. Ames, *Lectures on Legal History and Miscellaneous Legal Essays*, Cambridge, Havard Uiversity Press, 1913, p. 77.

But why could the purchaser maintain a claim of detinue? What is the underlying rationale of the legal position? As an old form of writ and later a form of action, the content of detinue is that "a person claimed the specific return of goods wrongfully detained from him,"[30] and the effect is to "command the sheriff to order the defendant to yield up to the plaintiff the chattels which he unjustly detained from him."[31] The elements of the action are:

i. a *property* in the plaintiff, either *absolute or special* [...] in personal goods, which are capable of being ascertained;
ii. a possession in the defendant by bailment, finding, etc.;
iii. an unjust detention on the part of the defendant.[32]

Parties usually involved in detinue were described in Comyn's Digest, that detinue "lies by him who has property in a thing certain, against him who detains it."[33] Accordingly, a classic example of such an action could be where A lends B a horse, and B then refuses to return it. In this case, A could be the one holding the highest title, or could be a mere finder, or a bailee authorised by the title-holder holding the higher title under the English system of relativity of title. What the defendant unjustly detains and refuses to return could not be the title, but the thing. As concluded by Holdsworth, "the proper sphere was the recovery of a possession which had formerly belonged to the plaintiff."[34] Simon Douglas also implies that as a species of tort, the precondition for maintaining detinue is to breach a kind of legal duty which is:

> [...] that the claimant's *property right* in his chattel (which could be ownership, a possessory security interest or a reversionary interest) imposes a legal duty on others not to interference with the chattel [...][35]

The gist that 'a pre-existing better title is a prerequisite for maintaining detinue' is plain in the above circumstances because A (the owner/finder/authorised possessor) already has a pre-existing title beforehand, at least as compared to B (the custodian). But when it comes to the vendor-purchaser scenario, the purchaser's right to maintain detinue seems anomalous because it is very rare there would be a pre-existing title, i.e. a better right to

30 W.J. Byrne, *A Dictionary of English Law*, London, Sweet and Maxwell, 1923, p. 301.
31 J.H. Baker, *An Introduction to English Legal History*, 4th ed., London, Butterworths, 2002, p. 391.
32 A.S. Oppe, *Wharton's Law Lexicon*, 14th ed., London, Stevens and Sons, 1938, p. 326; D. Greenberg (Ed.), *Jowitt's Dictionary of English Law*, Vol. I, 3rd ed., London, Sweet and Maxwell, 2010, p. 697 (emphasis added). Element (i) is also described in another way: 'a right to immediate possession' according to M. Jones *et al.* (Eds.), *Clerk & Lindsell on Torts*, 21th ed., London, Sweet & Maxwell, 2014, para. 17-03. All materials are secondary due to the fact that no case law ever gave a definition for 'detinue'.
33 J. Comyns, *A Digest of the Laws of England*, Vol. III, 5th ed., London, 1822, p. 378.
34 W.S. Holdsworth, *A History of English Law*, Vol. III, 5th ed., London, Sweet & Maxwell, 1942, p. 355.
35 Douglas, 2011, p. 89 (emphasis added).

immediate possession against the vendor by the moment when the purchaser pays money. One possible answer could be that the prerequisite to maintain detinue has extended to a person without title to goods. Another possible answer could be that the purchaser got the title with the vendor's consent. If the real answer is the latter, a crucial implication follows: the contract on its own could pass title to the purchaser after the 1442 rule; and even before 1442, 'contract plus payment' could also achieve this.

4 HISTORICAL EXPLORATION OF THE RULES

Since the reasoning above shows that at some earlier stage there could have been a rule to the effect that property passed if the purchase price was paid, and that there must have also been a time even earlier when there was a rule to the effect that it did not pass without delivery, we now turn to an investigation of the original rules regarding chattel transfer under a sale.

Perhaps the earliest evidence in the history of the common law regarding a separate step of chattel conveyance could be found in early textbooks, though writers such as Glanvill, the great twelfth-century jurist, did not make things clear enough at the outset:

> The cause of a debt may also be purchase or sale [...] A purchase and sale is effectively complete when the contracting parties have agreed on price, provided that this is followed by delivery of the thing purchased and sold, or by payment of the whole or part of the price, or at least by the giving and receipt of earnest.[36]

This is ambiguous, for the phrase 'a sale is complete' may imply transfer of title,[37] or merely concern the contract itself and imply nothing on the transfer of title.[38] Fortunately, Bracton gave his answer a century later. When he was discussing the old rule in his era on acquiring title to goods by purchase, he pointed out that:

> There is another *causa* for acquiring the dominion of things which is called that of purchase and sale. When one sells his property to another [...] as we may be seen above in the portion of gifts, without *delivery* dominion over things is not transferred. [...] [T]he risk attending the thing bought and sold both before delivery and after it, falls generally upon him who has it in his possession,

36 R. de Glanvill, *The Treatise on the Laws and Customs of the Realm of England*, London, Nelson, 1965, p. 129.
37 See Baker, 2002, p. 384.
38 See J. Hudson, *The Oxford History of the Laws of England*, Vol. II, Oxford, OUP, 2012, p. 688.

> [...] for obviously he who has not yet delivered the thing to its buyer will still himself be its *owner* [...][39]

Several decades later in the late thirteenth century, *Fleta*, anonymously written by an imprisoned judge, also reaffirmed the position that "dominion over things is not transferred without delivery."[40] Pollock and Maitland also hold the same opinion that in the thirteenth century, it is fairly certain that the ownership of a chattel could not be transferred from one person to another, either by way of gift, or by way of sale, without a '*traditio rei*' (delivery of the thing).[41]

Holdsworth, after a review of previous works, concluded that, before the reign of Henry VI, the purchaser could not sue on detinue for the goods that the vendor had yet to deliver,[42] as the only remedy for the purchaser on payment was a writ of debt in *detinet* — an action simply alleging that the vendor was wrongfully withholding the money, and that "the purchaser on payment could *not* sue for the goods by action of detinue [...] because he could not allege that the things were his."[43] Yet he believed that this changed at some point between Edward III's and Henry VI's reign.

What could be drawn from such a leap of faith regarding detinue? Can the implication truly be that the alteration of the conveyance rule is the reason for the alteration of detinue, just as some legal historians described? The answer is no. It is submitted that detinue changed only because its eligibility[44] changed, and no implications relating to the conveyance rule can be drawn from it. Since Holdsworth's view is the most popular one and the one often cited in other historians' works on this point, we will examine the flaw in his reasoning below.

According to Holdsworth, the reason why the vendor could, even before his performance, sue on debt for payment is because he had provided a sufficient *quid pro quo* for this right – namely, the grant of the right to the purchaser to sue for delivery of goods. It apparently follows from this that the converse should also be true – i.e. the purchaser could, by his contractual promise of performance, sue on detinue for the delivery of the goods since he had provided also a sufficient *quid pro quo* – namely, the grant of the right to the

39 H. de Bracton, *Bracton on the Laws and Customs of England*, Vol. II, Cambridge, Belknap Press, 1968, pp. 181, 183 (footnotes omitted, emphasis added). As for the 'portion of gifts', it is on page 124, that 'A gift is not valid unless livery follows.' Bracton also cited the *Codex Justinianus* to support his view: 'The ownership of property is transferred by delivery ... but not by naked pacts.' (C. 2.3.20) See F.H. Blume, '*Annotated Justinian Code*' www.uwyoedu/lawlib/blume-justinian/ajc-edition-2/book-2html (accessed 07 November 2013).

40 H.G. Richardson & G.O. Sayles (Eds.), *Fleta*, Vol. II, London, Selden Society, 1955, p. 194.

41 F. Pollock & F.W. Maitland, *The History of English Law before the Time of Edward I*, Vol. II., 2nd ed., Liberty Fund, 2010, p. 179.

42 Holdsworth, 1942, pp. 353–355.

43 Holdsworth, 1942, p. 355, citing Y.B. 50 Ed. III Tri. pl. 8.

44 *I.e.*, one of the constituent elements as to who is eligible to maintain detinue against the 'detainer'.

vendor under the contract to sue for payment. Though this is a flawless explanation as to why the parties could sue on the actions of debts and detinue respectively, it is irrelevant as to the passing of property. The fact that the vendor could sue in debt has no logical bearing as to the passing of the *property in money*. The right to get that amount of money (right *in personam*) and the right to vindicate title to that amount of money (right *in rem*) are two different things. The vendor only acquires the former before the purchaser actually makes payment. Unfortunately, by insisting that such right is a property right, Holdsworth in turn stated that:

> [t]his being the case, it is not difficult to see how the idea arose that the property *passes* upon an agreement to sell a specific chattel. [...] A can bring debt [...] because he has *a right to it* by virtue of B's grant [...] B can bring detinue for the horse because he has *a right to the possession* by virtue of A's grant. [...] [T]his right to possession is very often called 'property' in the Year Books. [...] [I]t took upon itself more of the characteristic of ownership. [...] If, therefore, a contract of sale were made which gave the purchaser the right to bring detinue for the thing sold, it was easy to say that he had the property as the result of the sale.[45]

Consequently, there is a logical confusion between property rights and personal rights regarding the nature of 'the right to possession' in Holdsworth's reasoning, although he might have been misled by the old, ambiguous use of the word 'property' in the Year Books. Regardless, it is this misconception that led him to the argument that the extension of detinue altered the nature of the rights held by the purchaser. Yet, this extension of the scope of detinue did not alter the property rights of the purchaser, but rather, it was merely an extension of the availability of detinue to those which have not yet acquired such property rights. This was done through changing the eligibility to sue from a requirement of a 'pre-existing title' to a 'right to possess', which covers both (i) a pre-existing title and (ii) a subsequent right to acquire title from the owner. In other words, the action of detinue had come to be multi-causal, in the sense that it could not only be brought by *title-holders* out of possession to assert their right to *possession*, but also be brought by *non-title-holders* to assert their right to possession, and thereby acquire *title*. This being the case, it follows that the reason why the purchaser could maintain detinue after the fifteenth century was not because he was the owner (right *in rem*) before he entered into the contract, but because he acquired a right to receive the property right (right *ad rem*), which is in essence still a right *in personam*. In this case, the subject-matter of reciprocal grants between contractual parties was simply the right to acquire the property – i.e. money for the vendor, and goods

45 Holdsworth, 1942, p. 356 (emphasis added, footnotes omitted).

for the purchaser. The vendor did not acquire property rights in money, nor did the purchaser acquire property rights in goods. Thus, such radical change of the scope of detinue cannot be regarded as historical evidence for the position that property passed by way of contract suggested by Holdsworth, who omitted the possibility that the reason may well be that the scope of detinue has been extended to a person without title to goods.

Other findings regarding the unstable exigibility of detinue by legal historians also cast doubt on Holdsworth's reasoning and could be used as evidence to support the submitted proposition that detinue has nothing to do with passing of property by contract. As discovered by Milsom, a passing reference in 1347 labelled the buyer's action as detinue, "but this may have been just because the goods were *specific* [...] If so, the earlier *casual* naming of the action may have been partly responsible for the passing of property idea."[46] Indeed, if we look beyond the sale of goods, we can find clues in 1308 when a son could bring a writ of detinue against his father's executors who refused to transfer certain goods to him after the death of his father.[47] Of course the fact that the son could claim in detinue does not imply that title to goods in question passed to him immediately upon his father's death. In fact, the fluctuating scope of detinue throughout English legal history renders it impossible to determine the passing of property through the law of detinue. As illustrated by Fifoot, at the outset detinue was even a part of the writ of debt, and even though they became distinct from each other by the close of the thirteenth century, the test dividing these two was simply whether the claim is for fungibles or specific chattels.[48] Obviously, the test of 'specific chattels' included both those chattels the title to which belongs to the claimant and those that do not. From these historical findings, it can be inferred that what happened in the mid-fifteenth century led by Fortescue's judgment regarding detinue does not suffice to deny the existence of a separate intent to convey recognised in the 1893 Act. Strictly speaking, despite loose talk in numerous cases using 'contract', 'bargain', 'sale' and 'intent' interchangeably, contract has never become a method of conveyance throughout English legal history.

46 S.F.C. Milsom, 'Sale of Goods in the Fifteenth Century', *L.Q.R.*, Vol. 77, 1961, pp. 273–274 (emphasis added), citing Y.B. p. 21 Ed. III pl. 2. It should be noted that Milsom, in surveying the vicinity of the landmark when the '*real* (passing of property) nature of contracts' came into being, also tried to connect this point to constructive delivery, bailment, and conversion against bailees. But he found no direct authority confirming this point. By contrast, the meaning of conversion in the old days 'seems to have meant no more than appropriation' which an owner could also be liable for, and does not necessarily infer a pre-existing property right in the claimant: A.W.B. Simpson, 'The Introduction of the Action on the Case for Conversion', *L.Q.R.*, Vol. 75, 1959, p. 364. For instance, an executor can be liable for 'conversion' in the old days for misappropriating the deceased's goods and exposing his own to execution. This does not mean that title to the deceased's goods is immediately divested from the executor to the successors upon the testator's death. Thus, even if the seller is liable for so-called 'conversion' akin to a bailee in that era, it did not infer that title to goods passed to the buyer upon contract.

47 Y.B. 1 & 2 Ed. II pl. 10, *Anon.* (1308) 17 S.S. 39.

48 C.H.S. Fifoot, *History and Sources of the Common Law: Tort and Contract*, London, Stevens & Sons, 1949, pp. 25–28.

5 The Draftsman's Assertion

Among numerous cases in the field of sale of goods, there was one case cited by the draftsman of the 1893 Act, Sir Chalmers, to reach the conclusion that it is an 'undoubted' rule as old as the year books that 'by English law the property may pass by the contract itself' can be tested.[49] This is *Dixon v. Yates*,[50] but did this case genuinely deliver such an idea? It is suggested that the answer should be in the negative. The plaintiffs in this case purchased of the defendant, one Yates, several puncheons of rum and then sold 46 of those on to one Collard. As those puncheons had been placed in Yate's warehouse at all times prior thereto, the plaintiffs issued Collard an invoice, specifying the marks and numbers of each puncheon, in exchange of Collard's two bills. After two of these puncheons were taken out by Collard, both of the bills became dishonoured due to Collard's insolvency. As a result, the plaintiffs were no longer willing to issue a delivery order to Collard and also ordered Yates not to deliver these 44 puncheons. Later on, Collard sold on 26 of those to one Kaye, and the remaining 18 to two other sub-vendees. Upon the request made from Collard and the sub-vendees, Yates finally allowed Kaye to gauge all the 26 puncheons and delivered three of the 18 puncheons to the other two sub-vendees. Such conduct by Yates was alleged by the plaintiff to be liable for allowing Collard to deal on his own account. The plaintiffs asked for confirmation of the right of lien to these puncheons of rum and ordering the aforementioned sub-vendees to deliver these puncheons in question back to the plaintiffs. These claims were successful.

The ratio of this case is, based on unpaid sellers' lien, that the plaintiffs never had the intent to deliver the aforementioned 46 puncheons of rum to the purchaser, Collard, regardless of the fact that there was a delivery order for the first two puncheons. This was due to, as explained by Denman CJ, the lack of the sellers' intent to hand over possession to the purchaser, which is the prerequisite for the extinction of the seller's right of lien: "[i]t is said that the delivery of a part operates in law as a constructive delivery of the whole; but that is so only where the delivery of part is *intended* to be delivery of the whole."[51] It is based on the sellers' exercise of their right of lien which allowed them to win the case. In other words, this case is about the matter of delivery as a method of changing possession, not as a method of passing property; delivery in this case has nothing to do with the right to exclusive possession forever, but just has something to do with the right of lien. It follows

49 M. Mark & J. Mance, *Chalmers' Sale of Goods Act 1979: Including the Factors Acts 1889 & 1890*, 18th ed., London, Butterworths, 1981, pp. 144-145. Such 18th edition did not make any change to this point compared to the first edition, which was written by Sir Chalmers himself: M.D. Chalmers, *The Sale of Goods Act 1893, Including the Factors Acts, 1889 & 1890*, London, W Clowes, 1894, p. 37.

50 (1833) 5 B. & Ad. 313, 110 E.R. 806.

51 *Dixon v. Yates* (1833) 5 B. & Ad. 313, 336; 110 E.R. 806, 815 (emphasis added).

that what was discussed in the judgment of the case with respect to the issue of passing of property is, technically speaking, not the ratio decidendi but the obiter dictum.

Even assuming those statements regarding passing of property in the judgment is ratio, a closer look at the statement of Parke J regarding passing of property can also reveal that what Parke J meant was not the notion that 'contract passes property'. Before his Lordship delivered his opinion on the issue of lien, he first stated his proposition as to a preliminary issue, i.e. the passing of property:

> I take it to be clear that by the law of England the sale of a specific chattel passes the property in it to the vendee without delivery. The general doctrine that the property in chattels passes by a contract of sale to a vendee without delivery is questioned [...] but I apprehend the rule is correct as confined to a bargain for a specific chattel. Where there is a sale of goods generally, no property in them passes till delivery, because until then the very goods are sold are not ascertained [...] The very *appropriation* of the chattel is equivalent to *delivery* by the vendor, and the *assent* of the vendee to *take* the specific chattel [...] is equivalent to his accepting possession. The effect of the contract, therefore, is to vest the property in the bargainee.[52]

According to such a quotation, the findings which lead to the aforementioned conclusion are as follows. (i) That the rule of passing property in the context of a sale of goods contract derives from the rules of passing property by delivery.[53] (ii) That the ascertainment of goods is a necessary condition for passing property in the context of a sale of goods contract. (iii) That the transferor's act of appropriation is an alternative for his act of delivery. (iv) That the transferee's assent is an alternative for his consent of accepting the delivery. Adding up all these four findings, it follows that the reason why only 'a contract for sale of specifically ascertained goods which are appropriated by the transferor with the assent of the transferee' passes title is because of two elements, i.e. (i) a contract (either general or specific) plus, more importantly, (ii) the transferor's declaration of intention of ascertainment and appropriation together with the transferee's declaration of intention of taking. It is the former that set the scene (so that no actual delivery or execution of deed is required for conveyance in this context); and it is the latter which conveys the right to exclusive possession forever. This must be so, because when Parke J said 'appropriation being equivalent to delivery', it makes no sense if it means that the *physical* appropriation equals the *physical* aspect of delivery (i.e., change of possession), for the location is not changed

52 *Dixon v. Yates* (1833) 5 B. & Ad. 313, 340; 110 E.R. 806, 816.

53 Such finding was also discussed in W. Swadling, 'Rescission, Property, and the Common Law', *L.Q.R.*, Vol. 123, 2005, n. 18.

to the transferee's place by physical appropriation. The only explanation that makes sense should be that it is the transferor's *intention* accompanied by such appropriation that equals to the *mental* aspect of delivery (i.e., the intent to convey title by delivery).

If this is the correct way of understanding Parke J's statement of law, it then follows that his Lordship's conclusion at the end of the paragraph above that the 'effect of contract ... is to vest the property' does not mean what it says. Rather, it is merely a loose way to say that 'intent, which in normal case is the effect of contract ... is to vest the property' in the transferee. Based on these analyses on the role and the essence of Parke J's statement of law, it can be concluded, with respect, that *Dixon v Yates* cannot serve as a support for understanding Sir Chalmers' statement that it is an old and undoubted rule that "by English law the property may pass by the contract itself, if such to be the intention of the parties. Contract may include a conveyance"[54] in an anti-separationist way. Rather, *Dixon v Yates* demonstrated that property may pass by intent to convey which, although sometimes it is understood as an effect of the contract, is nevertheless conceptually independent of the (intent to) contract itself. It might seem odd that Sir Chalmers said 'contract passes property' but then draft the statute of 1893 in a different way, recognising it is literally the 'intent' not 'contract' that passes title. It is submitted that an explanation to this could be that it is reasonable to assume that when Sir Chalmers said so in the book, the distinction between contract and intent in the sense of their roles in passing of property was arguably not on his mind; to use intent and contract interchangeably was just loose talk, and therefore one cannot make very much of it to deny the existence of a separate intent to convey which passes title in the context of sale of goods.

6 A Consensual and Abstract System in Sale of Goods

It is further suggested that an implication can be drawn from the central argument that it is the conceptually separate intent to convey rather than the intent in contract which passes title to goods in cases of sale of goods. This is the possibility of having a system being consensual and abstract. There are two dividing lines that are familiar to European comparative lawyers for dividing systems of transfer in different jurisdictions. The first one is 'consensual versus *traditio*', divided by whether property can only be transferred by the additional step of conveyance (such as delivery). The second one is 'causal versus abstract', divided by whether the validity of conveyance can be affected by the validity of the underlying obligation (usually a contract).[55] By multiplying them we obtain a matrix of

54 Chalmers, 1894, p. 37.

55 See e.g., V. Sagaert, 'Consensual versus Delivery Systems in European Private Law – Consensus about Tradition' and S. Bartels, 'An Abstract or a Causal System' in W. Faber & B. Lurger (Eds.), *Rules for the Transfer of Movables: A Candidate for European Harmonisation or National Reforms?*, Berlin, Sellier, 2008;

four matches. Accordingly, a system could either be, ex hypothesi, (i) *traditio* and causal, or (ii) *traditio* and abstract, or (iii) consensual and causal, or (iv) consensual and abstract. Interestingly, while there are examples of the former three matches among continental European jurisdictions,[56] it is almost impossible to find an example for the last match, i.e. consensual and abstract, in any of these jurisdictions. Yet can we simply reach the conclusion from these real-life examples that the idea of abstraction cannot subsist under a consensual system? It is argued in this section that such a conclusion is erroneous.

Two issues have to be dealt with in order to challenge such a 'real-life' conclusion. The first is a conceptual one, being whether it is conceptually and hypothetically possible for a consensual system to be abstract at the same time. The second is a positive one, being whether there are any real-life examples demonstrating that this has happened at some point in time.

The first issue must be and can be solved based on all the discussions above, the gist of which, as has been said above, is to construe the meaning of 'title passes by intent' that has been rooted in English legal history followed by two sections in the Sale of Goods Acts 1893 and 1979. By distinguishing the intent to convey from the intent in contract, the conclusion is that it is conceptually the intent to convey rather than the intent in contract that passes title, although sometimes they could factually happen simultaneously. Such distinction is of huge importance with respect to the first issue. Suppose the English law of sale of goods is a field of law where contract on its own is the method of conveyance. It could be said that there is no principle of separation in such field of law, and it follows that it is impossible for the principle of abstraction to exist in such field of law;[57] such field of law must follow the principle of causality. The reason is, if the method of conveyance is contract, then there is no conceptual distinction between contract and conveyance; contract is both the underlying basis and the method of conveyance, by which it follows that wherever the contract is void, the conveyance must be void exactly on the same ground, even if there is a subsequent delivery or execution of deed involved.[58] On the contrary, as

L.P.W. van Vliet, *Transfer of Movables in German, French, English and Dutch Law*, Nijmegen, Ars Aequi Libri, 2000, pp. 23-25; S. van Erp & B. Akkermans (Eds.), *Cases, Materials and Text on National, Supranational and International Property Law*, Oxford, Hart Publishing, 2012, ch. 8.

56 Examples of a system being (i) *traditio* and causal can be found in the Netherlands and Austria, a system being (ii) *traditio* and abstract in Germany and Estonia, a system being (iii) consensual and causal in France, Belgium and Italy.

57 The difference between separation and abstraction is briefly clarified as this. Separation means whether the validity of conveyance is determined by its *own* rules (whether in property law or in general provisions) which is separate from the validity of the underlying contract, which is determined by its own rules in contract law. Abstraction means a conveyance which is valid according to its own rules would not be infected by the invalidity of the underlying contract.

58 It is based on such reasoning that some comparative lawyers believed that in English law 'the principle of separation is not recognised': B. Markesinis *et al.*, *The German Law of Contract: A Comparative Treatise*, 2nd ed., Oxford, Hart Publishing, 2006, p. 31. See also U. Mattei, *Basic Principles of Property Law*, Westport, Greenwood, 2000, p. 106; U. Drobnig, 'Transfer of Property' in A. Hartkamp *et al.* (Eds.), *Towards a*

having been argued in previous sections, the English law of sale of goods is a field of law where the intent to convey is the default method of conveyance, then it follows that as long as such intent to convey is valid, the conveyance in question would not be affected by any flaw in the underlying contract of sale. It is therefore conceptually and hypothetically possible for such kind of 'consensual system' in this sense to be simultaneously abstract not causal.

A real-life example for the second issue just lies in the English law of sale of goods as well. It was held in *Belvoir Finance v. Stapleton*[59] that title passes irrespective of the existence of an illegal contract of sale plus the non-existence of delivery as the method of conveyance.[60] The plaintiff, a finance company, bought several cars under a contract of sale from a dealer via consensual transfer between them (without delivery). The plaintiff then sold these cars on to another company, Belgravia, on hire-purchase. The dealer, upon the plaintiff's request, directly delivered the possession of the cars to Belgravia. Afterwards, the defendant, an assistant manager of Belgravia, sold these cars again to some third-party successors. The plaintiff brought a case against the defendant for breaching the bailment and reverting the cars to his own use. Obviously, a prerequisite for the plaintiff to maintain ownership was to assert title to these cars. The defendant forwarded two counter-arguments. First, since the hire-purchase agreement (between Belgravia and the plaintiff) violated the statutory requirement of a down payment above 20 per cent of the entire price required for this kind of hire-purchase agreement,[61] and since the contract of sale (between the plaintiff and the dealer) was tainted with such illegality, both contracts were void. Second, even if *Singh v. Ali*[62] is correct, it only concerns cases where a valid delivery exists to convey a property right, whereas in this case, there is no delivery between the original transferor and the transferee, the plaintiff. Accordingly, title should be deemed to never have passed to the plaintiff under such a void contract without delivery. Both of these counter-arguments

---

European Civil Code, 4th ed., New York, Kluwer, 2011, pp. 1006, 1014. This, based on arguments submitted above, is a misunderstanding of English law.

59 [1971] 1 Q.B. 210.

60 A counter-argument to this example could be: if there is no contract (illegal and void contract means no contract at all), then the rule contained in section 17 of the Sale of Goods Act 1979 cannot logically apply, hence there cannot be an 'intent alone' transfer.

61 Hire-Purchase and Credit Sale Agreements (Control) Order 1964, art. 1(1), sch. 2, pt. 1, para. 3(1).

62 [1960] A.C. 167. The claimant asked the defendant if he could help circumvent certain government requirements for a haulage permit which prevented the claimant from operating a business with a lorry. The defendant agreed. He purchased a lorry and registered it under his own name, and then transferred title to the lorry to the plaintiff secretly by delivery. When the two parties fell out, the defendant dispossessed the lorry from the plaintiff's place. The claimant brought detinue against the defendant, which was successful in the Malaya Supreme Court and the Privy Council, where it was held that although the underlying contract between the claimant and the defendant was illegal and void due to deliberately circumventing administrative prohibitions, title to the lorry was nevertheless passed via delivery 'despite of the illegality of the contract'. Possible administrative punitive consequences on the part of the claimant have nothing to do with the property right validly acquired by him, which cannot be automatically revested to the defendant, or be confiscated by the Court simply due to illegality.

were dismissed by Lord Denning, who explained that firstly, the consequence of illegality had nothing to do with the title transfer so long as the contract had been executed (by completion of conveyance), and secondly, *Singh v. Ali* applied 'even where the transferee has not taken possession of the property, so long as the title to it has passed.'[63] Here, although not explicitly stated, Lord Denning must have been referring to section 17 of the Sale of Goods Act 1893, according to which title to these cars could pass without a change of possession (delivery), but by parties' mere intent to convey. It follows that the reason why the plaintiff successfully maintained conversion in this case is because he acquired title to the cars by consensual transfer (as opposed to *traditio* transfer) which was nevertheless abstract not causal. To put it in another way: so long as there was a separate, valid intent of the transferor to transfer title, no matter whether it had additional methods such as delivery, and no matter whether the underlying basis of such transfer was defective or not, the title in question could effectively pass to the transferee.

7 Conclusion

To say in the English law of sale of goods title passes by virtue of the 'contract' is an erroneous understanding among judges and academics that could be traced back to Holdsworth's analysis of an old case in the fifteenth century. His reasoning based on detinue was flawed due to an oversight of the fluid scope of exigibility in detinue. As reflected by historical material, detinue cannot be seen as a reliable test for determining the belonging of title. The correct way of understanding the rule of passing title in the English law of sale of goods, on the contrary, is that title passes by virtue of the 'intent' to convey, which is what the Sale of Goods Acts 1893 and 1979 literally provided for. Such an intent to convey is conceptually distinguishable from the intent in contract to incur contractual obligations to convey, regardless of the fact that they may coincide with each other. Although it can be found in the words of the draftsman of the 1893 Act that property may pass by contract according to pre-1893 authorities, it should not be taken seriously. This is because the major authority he cited is not in reality a case demonstrating property passing by contract. A further implication of comparative property law could be drawn that the English law of sale of goods is a good example demonstrating that a system of transfer can be both consensual and abstract.

Two additional concluding remarks are made here. First, given that all the discussions above are based on a conceptual approach, what does it mean if a functional approach is taken? For instance, suppose there is a contract of sale between the parties, but no intent to convey can be found, then would the consequence in English law be similar to its

63 *Belvoir Finance v. Stapleton* [1971] 1 Q.B. 210, 217.

European civilian counterparts? The answer could be in the negative from a functional perspective, thanks to the so-called vendor-purchaser constructive trust by which it might loosely be said that property passes in equity by a specifically enforceable contract.[64] Yet an accurate analysis of this notion will open a rather broad topic relating to the nature of such trust, proprietary attributes (especially the immunity from insolvency) of such trust, and the pervasive misconception of split/dual ownership of English law of trusts. Second, it is notable to find that arguments for distinguishing the intent to convey from intent in contract also appeared in French and Belgian law, which are the two most representative countries of the consensual system. Although the traditional and prevailing understanding in French and Belgian law is that property rights pass by virtue of obligation (i.e., the consensus between the parties with regard to the contractual rights and obligations suffices to transfer ownership), it was argued that a correct understanding should be that "a transfer would conceptually not be effected by virtue of party autonomy, but by virtue of a fictitious transfer", and "the concept of real agreement in the sense of a 'property transfer agreement' is also used in the Belgian and French transfer system", which "in principle, coincides with the obligatory agreement".[65] This being the case, then the principle of, or at least the notion of, separation would be a conceptually universal one which not only exists in English law, but also in those jurisdictions with a uniform consensual system.

64 *Holroyd v. Marshall* (1862) H.L.C. 191, 209; 11 E.R. 999, 1006. See also *Rose v. Watson* (1864) H.L.C. 672, 678; 11 E.R. 1187, 1190. Note that the vendor-purchaser constructive trust itself is not unquestionable. For instance, it was argued in W. Swadling, 'The Vendor-Purchaser Constructive Trust' in S. Degeling and J. Edelman (Eds.), *Equity in Commercial Law*, Sydney, Law Book Co, 2005 that such remedy of specific performance should not be masked with the label 'constructive trust' at all.

65 V. Sagaert & J. del Corral, 'Acquisition of Ownership of Goods in the DCFR: A Belgian Perspective' in V. Sagaert *et al.* (Eds.), *The Draft Common Frame of Reference: National and Comparative Perspectives*, Cambridge, Intersentia, 2012.

7 Security Interests in Movable Property: A Need for Reform in Mexico?

Rafael Ibarra Garza[*]

1 Introduction

The first major Mexican reform of our current movable property security law was from the year 2000;[1] so why is there still need for a discussion about reforming our system eighteen years later? There is a movement backed by the Organization of American States to modernize their movable property security law; this is the case of Guatemala,[2] Honduras,[3] Panama,[4] Peru[5] and Colombia.[6] This model consists of the creation of a unique regime for security interests in movable property security, an influence of the American concept of security interests.

Thus, the question has to be asked as to whether or not it is necessary to reform our security law on movable property. This necessarily involves the analysis of our actual law and therefore of our most recent reforms. If the last reforms were successful, there would not be a need to reform existing law; if this was not the case, reforming our movable property security law is necessary. But how are reforms deemed to be successes or failures? To answer the question, a point of reference such as the protection of creditors, the existence of a coherent system, or a system that balances the parties' interests is required.

In this analysis the point of reference is the legal policy behind the reforms of security law in movable property. For the legal policy of the reforms to be a valid reference it must be a correct reference; if not the analysis will be invalid. The policy behind the Mexican reforms is to open the credit market;[7] in other words, access to more and cheaper credit. The question that has to be answered is if that policy is correct or not.

---

* Universidad de Monterrey, Escuela de Derecho y Ciencias Sociales, Dean of the Academic Department of the School of Law; Researcher of the SNI (CONACYT); Of Counsel of Leal-Isla & Horváth, S.C.: Email: rafael.Ibarra@udem.edu and ribagar@hotmail.com. The author would like to thank Cynthia Alejandra Sánchez Torres and Roberto Helio Colyer Ayala for helping in the publication of this paper.

1 *Diario Oficial de la Federación*, Tuesday 23 May 2000.

2 Decreto del Congreso 51-2007 24 October 2007

3 Decreto n° 189-2009, *La Gaceta* Thursday 28 January 2010.

4 *Ley 129 de 31 de diciembre de 2013.*

5 Ley N° 28677, *Diario Oficial* 1 March 2006.

6 Ley 1676 DE 2013, *Diario Oficial*, No. 48.888, 20 August 2013.

7 See Anteproyecto de *Ley Federal de Garantías de Crédito* 7 April 1999; Aprobación de la Miscelánea de Garantías por el H. Congreso de la Unión, 29 April 2003; F. Ciscomani, 'La prenda sin transmisión de

To respond to that question, the first step is to study the relationship between credit and security interests. By credit one can understand confidence: On the honourability of the debtor and on his solvency.[8] In principle, therefore, if a credit is conferred, it is because the creditor trusts that the debtor will want to and will be able to honour his obligation. On the other hand, not only can the creditor err on the honourability and solvency of his debtor, but also over time the morality and solvency of the debtor may change as well. Thus, the confidence in the debtor should not be blind.

In fact, when credit is given, the creditor always assumes the risk of the debtor not paying because, between the creation of the obligation and its performance, the debtor may become insolvent. Furthermore, in the event of insolvency of the debtor, unsecured creditors are most probably not going to be paid.[9]

If the debtor fails to provide a guarantee of payment there are two possibilities: The first is that the creditor does not give credit to the debtor. The second possibility is that the creditor provides credit, but at a higher interest rate; the rate of interest depends upon the risk of being paid.

This demonstrates the relationship between movable property security law and the credit market. Because security devices reduce the risk of default, the constitution of a security in favour of the creditor improves the possibility for a creditor to give credit at a lower rate of interest. Therefore, the role that movable property security law has in the credit market and thus in the economy of a country is vital. It is for this reason that the Mexican government pushed for reforms: To reactivate the credit market and therefore the economy in Mexico that had been paralyzed since the 1994 financial crisis.[10] For these reasons the legal policies behind the reforms are correct.

To achieve that legal policy, legislators had to create legal techniques and legal mechanisms. Therefore, this paper aims to compare those legal techniques with the legal policy that created them; the analytical method will be used to discover if the different elements of the reform are in conformity or not with the objectives of the reforms. In other words: Do the legal techniques created by the reforms help obtain more and cheaper credit?

The question stated above will be answered by studying the successes of the Mexican reforms (3) and its failures (4); but first we must summarize Mexican movable security law (2).

---

posesión en México', *Revista de Derecho Privado*, nueva época, año II, September-December, 2003, pp. 3, 7-9.

8 M. Acosta, 'Crédito', *Nuevo Diccionario Jurídico Mexicano, Tomo A-C*, Editorial Porrúa, 1998, p. 923.

9 This is so because the value of the assets will be distributed proportionately between all the creditors (Art. 222 of the [Commercial Bankruptcy Act] [*Ley de Concursos Mercantiles*]).

10 For an impact of an adequate security law system on the credit market, see B. Kozolchyk, 'Secured Lending and its Poverty Reduction Effect', *Texas International Law Journal*, No. 42, 2007, pp. 727, 728 *et seq.*

2 MEXICAN MOVABLE SECURITY LAW AND THE REFORMS

The analysis starts by explaining the Mexican movable security law (2.1) and will continue with a summary of the reforms (2.2).

2.1 *Mexican Movable Security Law*

Typology of guarantees. – Mexican law has a multiplicity of securities, each with its own regime. In positive law, there is the pledge, the mortgage, the right of retention, and various guarantees that operate around the notion of the right of ownership.

Among the different types of pledges, there is the civil law pledge.[11] In addition to the civil pledge, there are several commercial pledges. As to the commercial pledges, the *Ley General de Títulos y Operaciones de Crédito* (Securities and Credit Operations Act) provides a possessory pledge[12] and a non-possessory pledge.[13]

The same Act establishes other special pledges, such as the *bono de prenda* (warehousing), by which the performance of an obligation is guaranteed by the property indicated in the certificate of deposit.[14] Then there is the *crédito de habilitación o avío* (operating credit), which concerns credit for the acquisition of goods and payment of administration costs which are essential for the business; the credit is secured by the assets acquired with the money lent and with the fruits and products obtained by the loan.[15] Another pledge is the *crédito refaccionario* (equipment credit) which consists of a credit operation where the borrower is obliged to invest in agricultural tools, fertilizers, livestock, machinery, and buildings necessary for the development of the debtor's business.[16] This credit would be secured by the immovable and movable property of the company that was obtained with the money lent.[17] Both the *crédito de habilitación o avío* and the *crédito refaccionario* are pledges that can be with or without dispossession.[18]

---

11 Arts. 2856 *et seq.* of the *Código Civil Federal* (Federal Civil Code). On the subject, see B. Pérez, *Contratos Civiles*, 10th ed., Mexico, Editorial Porrúa, 2004, p. 351 *et seq.*

12 Arts. 334 *et seq.* of the Securities and Credit Operations Act. On the subject, see V. Castrillón, *Contratos Mercantiles*, 2nd ed. Mexico, Editorial Porrúa, 2003, p. 373 *et seq.*

13 Arts. 346 *et seq.* of the Securities and Credit Operations Act. On the subject, see F. de la Mata & R. Garzón, *Derechos Reales de Garantía*, Mexico, Editorial Porrúa, 2005, pp. 412 *et seq.*

14 Arts. 229 *et seq.* of the Securities and Credit Operations Act. On the subject, see R. Guzmán, *Derecho Bancario y Operaciones de Crédito*, 2nd ed., Mexico, Editorial Porrúa, 2004, pp. 19 *et seq.*

15 Arts. 321 *et seq.* of the Securities and Credit Operations Act. On the subject, see Castrillón, 2003, p. 240 *et seq.*

16 Arts. 323 *et seq.* of the Securities and Credit Operations Act. On the subject, see Castrillón, 2003, p. 240 *et seq.*

17 Art. 323 of the Securities and Credit Operations Act.

18 Arts. 329 and 334, VII of the Securities and Credit Operations Act.

As for the mortgage, it is first regulated in the Civil Code.[19] The *Ley de Navegación y Comercio Marítimo* (Navigation and Maritime Trade Act) provides a special regime of maritime mortgages;[20] these types of mortgages are designed for finished vessels or ones that are under construction. Another type of mortgage is the *hipoteca industrial* (industrial mortgage) where the guarantee is constituted on the company as a unit.[21] Thus, the industrial mortgage would be on all movable and immovable property of the company.

Mexican law also allows certain creditors to retain their debtor's movable assets until the debt has been completely repaid. This is the case for example of a custodian (only under a judiciary order),[22] agent, carrier,[23] shareholder,[24] etc. Finally, in Mexican law there are security interests that operate around the notion of the right of ownership. This is the case of retention of title clause,[25] security trust (*fideicomiso de garantía*)[26], and leasing.[27]

When the special pledge regimes provided in the Securities and Credit Operations Act are silent or insufficient on a particular point, the commercial possessory pledge is applicable to fill these legal gaps.[28] If the legal loopholes of the special regimes cannot be met by the rules of the commercial possessory pledge, by rules provided in other special laws, or by commercial customs, the Federal Civil Code would apply.[29] Thus, the rules of the civil pledge may complement the pledges provided in the Securities and Credit Operations Act.

---

19 Arts. 2893 *et seq.* of the Federal Civil Code. On the subject, see Pérez, 2004, p. 359 *et seq.*

20 Art. 101 *et seq.* of Navigation and Maritime Commerce Act. On the subject (but in Spanish Law), see J. Gabaldón & J. Ruíz, *Manual de Derecho de la Navegación Marítima,* 3rd ed., Mexico, Marcial Pons, 2006, p. 325 *et seq.*

21 The *hipoteca industrial* is provided for in Art. 67 of the *Ley de Instituciones de Crédito* (Act of Credit Institutions), art. 50 of the *Ley General de Organizaciones y Actividades Auxiliares de Crédito* (Act of Organizations and Auxiliary Credit Activities) and Art. 28 of the *Ley Federal de Instituciones de Fianzas* (Federal Act on Bond Institutions).

22 Art. 2533 of the Federal Civil Code. On the contract of deposit, see Castrillón, 2003, p. 129 *et seq.*

23 Art. 591, VII of the *Código de Comercio* (Commercial Code).

24 Art. 2708 of the Federal Civil Code.

25 Arts. 2312 *et seq.* of the Federal Civil Code. On the subject, see J. Rosado, 'Consideraciones en torno a las modernas figuras de garantía: las reservas de dominio complejas', *Revista de Derecho Privado,* Jul-Ago, 2003, p. 461; R. Ibarra, 'La Clause de Réserve de Propriété, une Étude de Droit Comparé Franco-Latino-Américain' in C. Larroumet (ed) *L'Évolution des Garanties mobilières dans les Droits Français et Latino-Américains,* Panthéon-Assas, 2016, p. 45.

26 Arts. 395 *et seq.* of the Securities and Credit Operations Act. On the subject, see Castrillón, 2003, p. 339 *et seq.*; M. Alessio, *Temas de Derechos Reales,* 2nd ed., Mexico, Editorial Porrúa, 2006, p. 30 *et seq.*; S. Ortiz, El Fideicomiso Mexicano, 3rd ed., Mexico, Editorial Porrúa, 2006, p. 195 *et seq.*; E. Rocha, 'El fideicomiso de infraestrutura y bienes raíces', *Revista Internacional de Derecho y Ciencias Sociales. Universidad de Monterrey,* No. 10, Primavera 2007, pp. 47-48.

27 Arts. 408 *et seq.* of the Securities and Credit Operations Act. For authors on the subject, see L. Haime, *El Arrendamiento Financiero,* 13th ed., ISEF, 2003.

28 Thus, for example, the second paragraph of Art. 346 of the Securities and Credit Operations Act on non-possessory pledges explicitly states that in the event of shortcomings the non-possessory pledge scheme would apply.

29 Art. 2, IV of the Securities and Credit Operations Act.

Similarly, article 101 of the Navigation and Maritime Trade Act provides that the constitution of the maritime mortgage would be governed by this law and in the event of silence of the law the civil mortgage regime would apply. The same applies to the *hipoteca industrial* since its special regime is limited to only three paragraphs.[30]

The legal sources. – In Mexican law, security interests have a tripartite source: Conventional, legal, and judicial. Conventional security interests are the civil pledge, the commercial pledge, the *crédito de habilitación o avío,* the *crédito refaccionario*, the *bono de prenda*, the voluntary civil mortgage, the *hipoteca industrial*, the maritime mortgage, the security trust, leasing, and the retention of title clause. Legal security interests are those created by the effect of the law, this is the case for example of the right of retention provided for the agent, the carrier, the shareholder and the commercial agent. The custodian's right to withhold property from the owner until payment is provided as a judicial guarantee, since Article 2533 of the Federal Civil Code provides that the depositary cannot retain by his own right the object of deposit, but that he may demand the retention judicially.

The principal effects of the different security interests. – Under Mexican law, the essential effect of security interests on tangible movable property is the right of the owner to be paid in priority to the other creditors.[31] Indeed, the right of preference is mentioned in the definitions of certain guarantees; this is the case, for example, of the civil pledge[32] and the commercial non-possessory pledge.[33]

In the security trust, when the trustee is the creditor, it is technically incorrect to say that the creditor-trustee has a preferential right; they have exclusivity rather than a preferential right. It is because the trustee is the owner of the trust property and under the right of ownership, the creditor-trustee is excluded from competing with other creditors in bankruptcy procedures. In fact, the trustee can separate the trust property from the bankrupt's estate;[34] something that other creditors with security interests cannot do.

Another effect is the right of the creditor to seize the encumbered asset from whichever hand it may be in. Thus, the creditor who is the beneficiary of a pledge has a right to follow.[35] This is the case for example of the commercial non-possessory pledge.[36]

Foreclosure. – Before a creditor can apply for a foreclosure procedure, the debtor has to default payment. If the creditor has a civil pledge, the asset used as collateral will be sold

30 Art. 6, III of the Act of Credit Institutions.

31 For authors on the right of preference, see Mata & Garzón, 2005, p. 403.

32 Art. 2856 of the Federal Civil Code.

33 Art. 346 of the Securities and Credit Operations Act.

34 Art. 71 of the Commercial Bankruptcy Act. On the theory of the right of ownership as a means of security (but in French law), see P. Crocq, *Propriété et Garantie*, LGDJ, 1995.

35 For authors on the right to follow, see Mata & Garzón, 2005, p. 403.

36 Art. 376 of the Securities and Credit Operations Act.

judicially by public auction or by an extrajudicial sale.[37] If no offer reaches the reserve price, the creditor may request that the property be awarded in his favour.[38]

As for commercial pledges, the *bono de prenda* is foreclosed by the sale of the goods indicated in the certificate of the deposit and from the proceedings of the sale the creditor is paid; the sale is extrajudicial and organized in a public auction by the *Almacén General de Depósito* (General warehouse).[39] In the event that the creditor has a possessory commercial pledge, he may apply to the judge for the sale of the property; however, if the debt is greater than the value of the property and the property is not the subject of another security, the creditor may demand that the property be transferred to him.[40] When a pledge is constituted in the *crédito refaccionario* and *habilitación o avío*, nothing is foreseen; thus, the regime of the possessory commercial pledge will apply.

The non-possessory commercial pledge and the security trust have the same foreclosure procedure.[41] The foreclosure procedure is divided into two chapters: The first is on the extrajudicial procedure while the second is on the judicial procedure. Once the possession is in the hands of the creditor, the trustee, or a third party designated by the creditor, the collateral can be sold.[42] If the value of the collateral exceeds the debt, the property must be sold[43] but if the value of the collateral is equal or lower than the amount of the debt then the creditor may freely dispose of the property, with a right of the creditor to be paid for the remainder still due by the debtor.[44] These rules also apply to the judicial foreclosure procedure of the non-possessory commercial pledge and the security trust.[45]

In the event of a maritime mortgage, article 275 of the Navigation and Maritime Trade Act provides for the judicial sale of the vessel. If the purchaser of a sale with a reservation of title clause fails to pay, the seller has the right to apply for legal rescission of the sales contract; if the contract is terminated, the parties must refund the services provided during the validity of the contract and thus the buyer will have to pay a sum for the use of the thing and compensation if the thing has been damaged.[46]

---

37 Arts. 2881 and 2884 of the Federal Civil Code.
38 Art. 2882 of the Federal Civil Code.
39 Arts. 243 and 244 of the Securities and Credit Operations Act.
40 Art. 1414 bis 17, I and II of the Commercial Code.
41 Arts. 1414 bis *et seq.* of the Commercial Code.
42 Art. 1414 bis 4 of the Commercial Code.
43 The extrajudicial procedure provided in art. 1414 bis 4 refers to art. 1414 bis 17. II of the Commercial Code.
44 Art. 1414 bis 17, I and II of the Commercial Code.
45 In fact art. 1414 bis 17 of the Commercial Code is of the judicial proceedings.
46 Arts. 2311 and 2314 of the Federal Civil Code.

2.2 The Reforms

The financial crisis of 1994 and 1995 led to credit rationing. In order to unlock the credit market, the Government proposed the modernization of the real security law, particularly that of movable property.

The modernization of our security rights began with the reform published on 23 May 2000.[47] This reform was only concerned with commercial security interests. In the Securities and Credit Operations Act, two new mechanisms were introduced in Mexican law: The non-possessory pledge[48] and the security trust.[49] The reform also reformed the Commercial Code by adding a new chapter on the procedure of foreclosure of the non-possessory pledge and security trust.[50] In legal practice, the non-possessory pledge was already being used but there was legal insecurity because it was not regulated; the same can be said of the security trust.[51]

Almost a week after the first reform, on 29 May 2000, the reform of the Public Registry of Commerce was published.[52] The main objective of this reform was to modernize and unify the registry in a national system that previously had a register for each federal state.

In 2003, new reforms were issued on 16 June;[53] the reforms were aimed at correcting the errors of the reform of 23 May 2000. The 2003 reform did not significantly change the regime established in 2000 except for the following points:

1. The 2003 reform repealed article 379 of the Securities and Credit Operations Act and amended article 1414 bis 17 of the Commercial Code. Prior to the 2003 reform, the mentioned articles stipulated that if the proceeds of the sale of the collateral subject to the non-possessory pledge or the security trust were insufficient to cover the full amount of the collateral obligations, the debtor would be released from his obligations and no longer needed to pay the outstanding balance. The 2003 reform eliminated this limitation which was not only contrary to the principles of contract law but also contrary to the interests of creditors and therefore negative to the credit market. Thus, thanks to the 2003 reform, the creditor has a right to sue the debtor for the missing balance.
2. The 2003 reform amended article 403 of the Securities and Credit Operations Act; this amendment established the possibility of establishing a non-judicial procedure to foreclose the collateral in a security trust.

47 *Diario Oficial de la Federación*, Tuesday 23 May 2000.
48 Regulated from Arts. 346 to 380.
49 Regulated from Arts. 395 to 414.
50 Regulated from Arts. 1414 bis to 1414 bis 20.
51 The only regulation of a security trust before the reforms of 2000 was the permission of the trustee to be a beneficiary in a security trust (*Diario Oficial de la Federación*, Friday 24 May 1996).
52 *Diario Oficial de la Federación*, Monday 19 May 2000.
53 *Diario Oficial de la Federación*, Monday 16 June 2003.

On 24 October 2003 the new *Reglamento del Registro Público de Comercio* (Regulation of the Public Registry of Commerce) was published and repealed the old regulation from 1979.[54] In this regulation, the way in which the registry works was established. One of the key points of the new regulation was the implementation of the *Sistema Integral de Gestión Registral* (Integral System of Registry Management), which consists of software through which registry information is captured, stored, protected, consulted, reproduced, verified, administered, and transmitted.[55] This system provided the necessary infrastructure for a national registration system.

The latest reforms concerned the creation of a registry of movable security interests, referred to as the *Registro Único de Garantías Mobiliarias* (Sole Registry of Movable Security Interests). On 27 August 2009, the registry was created;[56] any movable security interest must be registered there for it to be effective against third parties.[57] On 23 September 2010, the *Reglamento del Registro Público de Comercio* (Regulation of the Public Registry of Commerce) was reformed by introducing the necessary rules for the Sole Registry of Movable Security Interests to function.[58] On 12 October 2010, the forms to be used for the registry were published.[59] These forms were for registering, modifying, canceling, renewing, transferring a security interest, or correcting an error.

3 THE SUCCESS OF THE REFORMS

These reforms have several positive points: One is the modernization of Mexican security law (3.1), another success is the adoption of techniques that allow the debtor to always have access to new credit (3.2), in addition, a system has been introduced that increases the debtor's chances of having income (3.3) and the Sole Registry of Movable Security Interests is another triumph (3.4).

54 *Diario Oficial de la Federación*, Friday 24 October 2003.

55 Art. 4 of the *Reglamento del Registro Público de Comercio*. For authors on *Sistema Integral de Gestión Registral*, see. P. Labariega, 'La Digitalización del Registro Público de Comercio. ¿La New Age en la Legislación Patria?, *Boletín Mexicano de Derecho Comparado, nueva serie, año XXXVIII*, No. 113, May-August 2005, pp. 763, 798 *et seq*.

56 *Diario Oficial de la Federación*, Thursday 27 August 2009.

57 Art. 32 bis 6 of the Commercial Code.

58 *Diario Oficial de la Federación*, Thursday 23 September 2010.

59 *Diario Oficial de la Federación*, Tuesday 12 October 2010.

3.1 *The Harmonization of Security Law with the Needs of a Modern Economy*

The expression *res mobilis res vilis* (moveable things are without value) explains the anachronism of Mexican security law before the reforms. Before them, the majority of rules dated from 1928 which meant that immovables where the preferred object of security interests. This is explained by the fact that Mexican society was based on agriculture and therefore land formed the backbone of the economy.

With the industrial revolution, the importance of moveable property rose to the point where most of the world's wealth was in these types of property. As a result, it became possible to use movable property as a source of credit if it was used as collateral. Another big difference between ancient and modern economies is the place of intangibles. Currently intangible assets are an important source of wealth and they play a vital role in today's economies.

In these circumstances, it is not surprising that reforms to Mexican law needed to be made. What is surprising is that it took so long for the legislation to be brought in; the industrial revolution began in the eighteenth century and the reforms on security rights under Mexican law began in the year 2000.

For this reason, the modernization of Mexican security law was, in itself, the huge success resulting from the Mexican reforms (independent of the criticisms that can be made). In other words, the over-riding success of the reforms was the synchronization of security law with the realities and economic needs of society by improving the movable property market as a source of collateral, thus of credit.

From the point of view of security law, the object of a security interest should not be important; what is important is its value. Therefore, once an object has monetary value its owners should be able to use it as a security. Because of the reforms, any movable property (tangible and intangible) may be the object of a non-possessory pledge[60] and a security trust.[61]

In addition, the fact that a person may own property in the future implies that those future assets could also be a significant source of credit if future property were to be used as collateral. Fortunately, thanks to the reforms, future property can be the object of a non-possessory pledge.[62]

On the other hand, there is no provision in the security-trust for property that could be owned in the future. This is because future property does not exist in the present and therefore cannot be the object of a security trust; the Mexican trust entails a transfer from

60 Art. 355, I of the Securities and Credit Operations Act.
61 Arts. 386 of the Securities and Credit Operations Act.
62 Art. 355, II, III, IV and V of the Securities and Credit Operations Act.

the settlor to the trustee[63] which necessarily implies the existence of property at the time of transfer. But we must accept the possibility that after the constitution of a security trust, the future property of the trust fund may be the object of the already constituted security-trust.

Thus, the 2000 reform provides that any asset, tangible or intangible, present or future, may be subject to a security interest. This is one of the biggest successes of the reforms because it, in principle, increases the chances of a person being entitled to credit. This is without taking into account the fact that there are a large number of people who do not own real estate and therefore without a modern security law it would be impossible for them to obtain credit.

3.2 *The Perpetual Access to New Credit*

Nowadays it is possible for a person to subject all present and future assets which prevents them from having further access to credit because they have no more assets available as collateral. Thus, it would be difficult to find someone willing to grant a new credit and if they did so, they would probably only agree to it with a higher rate of interest by virtue of risks implied by lack of collateral.

To solve this problem, the reforms provide for the non-possessory pledge that "the debtor may pledge to new creditors [...] the assets acquired with the credit given by those new creditors".[64] Thus, the debtor may still have access to new credit because he can always pledge new assets to be purchased with the new credit.

In line with the reforms outlined, the first creditor retains priority on all the assets of the debtor except for new goods purchased with the credit granted by a second creditor. In this instance the second creditor has priority. In other words, although all the current and future assets of the debtor are already committed, there would be an exception in favour of a new creditor, but only when the resources have been granted to acquire new assets. Thus, the debtor can still have access to more credit because he can always pledge new goods purchased with it.

Regarding the security trust it is possible to use the same trust with the same assets to ensure not only simultaneous but successive obligations.[65] If the debtor pays his debts, the trust can be used to guarantee new debt by simply designating a new trust beneficiary. In other words, when the security trust is *rechargeable* the debtor has the ability to obtain new credit with the same security.

---

63 Arts. 381 of the Securities and Credit Operations Act. In fact the transfer from the settlor to the trustee is considered one of the settlor's main obligations (in that sense, see J. Villagordoa, *Doctrina General del Fideicomiso*, 4th ed., Mexico, Editorial Porrúa, 2003, p. 195).

64 Art. 358 of the Securities and Credit Operations Act.

65 Art. 397 of the Securities and Credit Operations Act.

3.3 The Creation of Capital by the Debtor

A creditor will be more willing to extend credit if voluntary payment options increase. This is the case when the debtor is able to obtain revenues with the security interest. This is, however, only possible if the debtor retains possession and uses the collateral. In fact, using the security interest is normally necessary for the debtor's activities and to generate income that enables him to pay off his debts. A clear example of this is a non-possessory pledge of the machines producing the goods that the debtor sells; if the possession of these machines where in the hands of the creditor, it would be impossible for the debtor to create the product he sells. In order for the debtor to use the goods, it is necessary for him to retain possession of them. For this reason, it must be recognized that the debtor's ability to retain possession and use of the assets object of the non-possessory pledge[66] and the security trust[67] is a great virtue of the Mexican reforms.

However, simply using the property will not always be sufficient; it may be necessary for the debtor to sell the object of the security and for that the collateral must first be transformed into a final product. This is the case, for example, when a credit is requested for the purchase of raw materials that are required for the manufacture of other products. In this case, security interests are created on these raw materials. Sometimes this is essential for the debtor to obtain income and pay his secured debts.

For this reason, the reforms offer the possibility for the debtor to sell and transform the assets object of a security interest.[68] There is a peculiarity in the security-trust; the trustee, and not the debtor, is the owner of the trust property.[69] So technically it is not the debtor who sells; thus, when the debtor wants the assets to be sold, instructions must be given to the trustee in this sense and it is thus provided for in Mexican law.[70]

However, this is still not enough; for the system to work the creditor must continue to be protected and it is for this reason that Mexican law provides that the guarantee will be extended to the transformed property[71] and the price of the sale.[72] Thus, the creditor will

66 Art. 346 of the Securities and Credit Operations Act.

67 Last paragraph of Art. 398 and Art. 400 of the Securities and Credit Operations Act.

68 Art. 356, I and III (non-possessory pledge) and Art. 398, I and III (security trust) of the Securities and Credit Operations Act.

69 Tesis 1a./J. 12/2007, Semanario Judicial de la Federación y su Gaceta, Novena Época, Tomo XXV, Abril de 2007, p. 95; Tesis 3a./J. 42/90, Semanario Judicial de la Federación, Octava Época, Tomo VI, Primera Parte, July-December 1990, p. 197; Tesis 228455, Semanario Judicial de la Federación, Octava Época, Tomo III, Segunda Parte-1, January-June 1989, p. 348.

70 Art. 389, III of the Securities and Credit Operations Act.

71 Art. 356, I and III (non-possessory pledge) and Art. 398, I and III (security trust) of the Securities and Credit Operations Act. For other measures of protection of the creditor with a non-possessory pledge, see Arts. 357 and 362 of the Securities and Credit Operations Act. For other measures of protection of the creditor with a security trust, see Arts. 399, 400 and 401 of the Securities and Credit Operations Act.

72 Art. 355, V and 356, III (non-possessory pledge) and Art. 398, III (security trust) of the Securities and Credit Operations Act.

not lose his security interest and will therefore be protected; that will give him the incentive to allow the debtor to use, transform, and sell the objects of the security interest.

However, it must be taken into account that it is not enough that the debtor has the right to sell the goods, or that the creditor is protected; the buyer also needs to be protected. Therefore, the buyer must receive the assets free from any security interest. This would, in fact, encumber trade as buyers would always have to determine whether the assets they are buying are the object of a security interest or not. Therefore, Mexican law provides that if the purchaser is in good faith he acquires the property free from any security;[73] defining bad faith as having knowledge of two things: The security and that the creditor has prohibited the sale of the property.[74]

3.4 *The Security Registration System*

A problem that may arise from the fact that the creditor does not have possession of the assets subject to a security interest is the creation of a false appearance of the debtor's actual situation vis-à-vis third parties. To protect third parties from this false appearance, movable security interests are unenforceable against them if they are not registered;[75] which leaves the creditor unprotected. To have an efficient security law, security interests have to be binding on third parties. To obtain that, an efficient registry of moveable security interests is necessary.

For the registry to be effective it must be sole and universal. With a sole registry, there is a single registry of security interests which makes sense in a federal country such as Mexico where they might have a register for each state. By universal, we understand that the register is for all types of security.

The security registration system did not exist before the reforms of 2000; its reforms created the sole registration system. However, it was only in 2003 that the Integral System of Registry Management (known in Mexico under the acronym SIGER) was established; by SIGER a sole registration system for non-possessory pledge and for trust-security was created.[76] Before the implementation of the SIGER system, although the Public Registry of Commerce was in theory a sole national register, in practice it was not, as it was administered by each federal state without any coordination between them.

The absence of a national registry hinders credit, as there is no legal certainty for the future creditor, unless the creditor registers the security interest in all thirty-two states, but this would be extremely time consuming and expensive. To get over this problem,

73 This is the case of the non-possessory pledge (Art. 356, III of the Securities and Credit Operations Act).

74 Art. 373 of the Securities and Credit Operations Act.

75 Art. 32 bis 1 of the Securities and Credit Operations Act (*Ley General de Títulos y Operaciones de Créditos*); second paragraph of Art. 365 and Art. 366 of Securities and Credit Operations Act.

76 *Supra* note 55.

SIGER created the necessary infrastructure for a true national system. Now, while there are still special registers, the unit is maintained because the 2010 reform provides that if a security interest is entered in a special register, such a registration is automatically replicated on the registry by SIGER.[77]

The failure of the reforms of 2000 and 2003 consisted in the limited field of application of the registry; it was only possible to register non-possessory pledges and security trusts. In this way the proposed registration system is incomplete as it was not a universal system where all the different types of security interests could be registered. Taking advantage of the fact that with SIGER a national system of registration was created, a universal register was created with the Sole Registry of Movable Security Interests;[78] thus all security interests may be registered. This registry works around the debtor, so if a person wants to know the legal situation of the debtor's assets he can search using the name of his debtor. This is one of the main reasons that the creation of this registry was one of the great successes of the Mexican reforms.

4 The Failures of the Reforms

The failures of the reforms are three: The absence of a unitary concept of security (4.1), the absence of an effective mechanism of foreclosure (4.2) and the absence of a real coordination with the bankruptcy law (4.3).[79]

4.1 *The Multiplicity of Security Techniques*

If the constitution process of security interests is too complicated, it becomes an obstacle to obtain credit. The simplification process should start by having less security techniques or even a unitary concept of security,[80] a system where there is only one type of security, as is the case of *security interest* in American law.

Interestingly, the reform of 2000 had the opposite effect; it added two new types of collateral: The non-possessory pledge and the security trust.[81] As demonstrated in the introduction, Mexican law has a multiplicity of movable securities: First of all, there is the

---

77 Art. 31 bis of the Regulation of the Public Registry of Commerce.

78 See *supra* notes 57, 59 and 60.

79 In addition, it is necessary to say something about the security trust, but it does not deserve a section; the security trust is a very expensive mechanism, which goes against the policy of access to cheap credit.

80 For a discussion of a unitary concept of security interests from a perspective of the Model Inter-American Law, see B. Kozolchyk & J. Wilson, 'The Organization of American States: The New Model Inter-American Law on Secured Transactions', *Uniform Law Review*, No. 7, 2002, p. 69.

81 On the subject, see A. Iturbide, 'Las Nuevas Garantías: Prenda Sin Transmisión de Posesión y el Fideicomiso de Garantía', *Revista Mexicana de Derecho*, No. 3, 2001, p. 101.

pledge; the pledge can be divided in the civil pledge and commercial pledge. The commercial pledge has different types such as: The possessory pledge, *bono prenda, crédito habilitación o avío, crédito refaccionario*, and the non-possessory pledge. There are also mortgages on movables which is the case in ship mortgages (*hipoteca marítima*) and industrial mortgages (*hipoteca industrial*). In addition, there is the right of retention and various guarantees which operate around the notion of ownership such as the sale with retention of title, security trust, and leasing.

As each type of guarantees has its own set of rules, the multiplicity of types of guarantees requires an analysis to be carried out by a lawyer to find out what mechanism is the most appropriate for the needs of a creditor. This can cause delays for the granting of credit which can be harmful to the merchant and it also leads to incurred costs as legal fees must be paid. This cost will, of course, be passed on to the debtor. On the other hand, if there were only one option, one security, there would not be much to discuss which would speed up the credit process and reduce the cost of the transaction.

What is striking about the 2000 reform is that the effects of having a unitary concept were already known; not only did our NAFTA partners (United States of America and Canada) have a unitary concept of security, but it was the Mexican delegation that played a major role in the development of the Inter-American Model Law on Security Interests.

The only reason that is apparent for having a multiplicity of security techniques is the legislator's lack of interest in creating a unique system of movable securities and the importance given in our legal system to legal technique (some techniques become dogmas). It is imperative to remember that it is legal policy that creates legal technique and not vice versa. In fact, "the law is a legal rule issued by a historic legislator to solve a particular social problem";[82] therefore, we can change our laws when social problems demand it and today's demand can be that of having a unitary concept of movable security.

4.2 The Foreclosure of Securities

Securities are designed to protect a creditor in case of default by the debtor; thus, an effective security law requires adequate enforcement. If it is not certain that the creditor can foreclose its security in case of default, the risk of default is not diminished by the fact that the creditor has a guarantee of payment in his favour. Also, if the security cannot be foreclosed promptly, the risk of default is created because the value of the debt may become greater than the value of the object of the security; either because the value of the security has decreased or because the debt has increased. This is why it is extremely important to implement efficient procedures of foreclosure.

82 Massini in R. Sánchez, 'Algunas Consideraciones Sobre el Método Exegético Jurídico', *Anuario Jurídico*, México, No. XVI, 1989, pp. 269, 280.

The reforms were designed to introduce effective foreclosure procedures. The reforms introduced special extra-judicial[83] and judicial[84] foreclosure proceedings but these procedures are only limited to the non-possessory pledge and security trust. Although the intention was there, the technique created by the legislator was not entirely appropriate since neither the extra-judicial nor the judicial proceedings fulfil their mission.

In terms of the extra-judicial procedure, the debtor is over-protected; by reading the reforms it becomes very clear that the legislators do not trust creditors. Even if the debtor has agreed to an extra-judicial foreclosure of the guarantee, there is no legal certainty that he will comply with the agreement. The debtor can easily prevent or stop the extra-judicial procedure simply by establishing a controversy over the credit (such as the amount due or the due date)[85] or if he refuses to transfer the possession to the creditor of the object of a non-possessory pledge or security trust.[86]

Now, imagine that the debtor acts in good faith and agrees to follow the extra-judicial procedure. This procedure must be carried out with the intervention of a Notary Public[87] which adds an additional cost to the credit. Furthermore, a third party must assess the value of the goods, which also adds an extra cost.[88] Thus, if the debtor acts in good faith it is far better to have a dation in payment[89] or novation[90] than to undergo the extra-judicial procedure introduced by the 2000 reform.

The judicial procedure of foreclosure is quite effective in terms of the location of the object of a non-possessory pledge or a security trust. It is, however, ineffective when the creditor does not know where the asset is located and the debtor is not willing to cooperate.

This is because even if, in practice, the debtor may be sanctioned for not delivering the possession of the collateral,[91] these measures are insufficient to obtain the debtor's possession. For this reason, a criminal sanction is provided for.[92] Unfortunately this sanction requires more time, effort, and money on the part of the creditor and it is not worth pursuing for small debts.

When taking all the facts into consideration it is clear that the judicial process is not efficient because it does not allow for prompt possession and thus execution of the security.

83 Art. 1414 bis *et seq.* of the Commercial Code.
84 Art. 1414 bis 7 *et seq.* of the Commercial Code.
85 Art. 1414 bis of the Commercial Code.
86 Art. 1414 bis 2, I of the Commercial Code.
87 Art. 1414 bis 1 of the Commercial Code.
88 Art. 1414 bis of the Commercial Code.
89 Dation in payment is established in Arts. 2095 and 2096 of the Federal Civil Code.
90 Novation is established in Art. 2213 of the Federal Civil Code.
91 Art. 1414 bis 19 provides that in the event that the debtor does not issue possession of the asset, coercive measures may be used against him: fine up to 32,000 euros; the use of law enforcement (this only applies when the location is well known), and arrest for up to thirty-six hours. In addition, the judge can sanction with a fine of 300 euros up to 9,000 euros per day that the debtor does not give the possession.
92 Arts. 380 and 406 of the Securities and Credit Operations Act.

4.3 *The Disharmony of Insolvency Law*

The main legal policy of Mexican insolvency law is "to preserve businesses and prevent a generalized default of obligations which threatens their viability and that of other businesses with which they have a commercial relationship".[93] This obviously implies the prohibition of foreclosure proceedings and payment[94] and further suggests that creditors with security interests cannot exercise their rights. This is because, if it were possible to enforce the creditors' rights during bankruptcy proceedings, the assets of the debtor would be diminished and subsequently it would become impossible for the company to continue its operations.[95]

In addition, there are privileged creditors, such as employees who must be paid even before the creditors with security interests.[96] In light of the above, there is an increased risk for creditors with security interests for not being able to enforce their security. This, of course, is contrary to the interests of creditors and therefore to the credit market as a whole.

The prohibition of individual prosecutions and of enforcement of securities does not, however, apply to the creditor of a security trust. This is because, upon the constitution of the trust, the object of the security trust is transferred from the debtor to the trustee. Thus, these assets no longer belong to the debtor and the secured creditor through the trust has exclusive rights to the trust property.

This is why Mexican insolvency law permits the execution of the security trust,[97] so that the opening of proceedings against the debtor does not affect the creditor. For this reason, Mexican insolvency law can be deemed hypocritical because it essentially aims to save the insolvent company whilst at the same time allowing the realization of the security trust. Also, Mexican insolvency law aims to protect certain creditors such as employees but at the same time permits security trusts to be performed in favour of creditors. This inconsistency is one of the failures of the reforms: As previously demonstrated, there are several techniques based on the property that allow the realization of the guarantee despite the opening of bankruptcy procedures.[98] This of course diminishes the possibilities for creditors secured with traditional securities to be paid.

---

93 Art. 1 of the Commercial Bankruptcy Act. On this legal policy, see R. Ibarra, 'The Reappearance of Ownership as a Means of Security in Mexican and French Law, the Battles Between Legal Technique and Legal Policy in Insolvency Law' *in* D. Gruyaert, E. Ramaekers & L. Rostill (eds), *Property Law Perspectives IV*, Intersentia, 2016, p. 81 *et seq*. For a general bibliography on Mexican bankruptcy law, see L. Sanromán, *Concursos Mercantiles,* 2nd ed., Mexico, Editorial Porrúa, 2016.

94 Art. 65 of the Commercial Bankruptcy Act.

95 In this sense, see case [TA]; 9ª Época; TCC; SJF y su Gaceta; Tomo XI, Enero de 2000; Pág. 1006.

96 See art. 217 *et seq.* of the Commercial Bankruptcy Act.

97 Art. 71, VII, e) of the Commercial Bankruptcy Act. On this subject, see Ibarra, 2016, p. 86 *et seq.*

98 Art. 71, VII, a) of the Commercial Bankruptcy Act.

5 CONCLUSION

What are the successes of the Mexican reforms? The successes consist of: 1) harmonizing Mexican security law in line with the needs of the economy by permitting any asset to be used as collateral and therefore as a source of credit; 2) the introduction of techniques that allow the debtor to always have access to new credit; 3) the introduction of techniques that increase the possibilities of obtaining income from the collateral and therefore increase the possibilities of voluntary payment; and 4) the creation of a Sole Registry of Movable Security Interests.

Now, what are the failures of the Mexican reforms? The failures consist of: 1) the multiplicity of security techniques; 2) the lack of efficient means of execution of securities in case of default by the debtor; and 3) the disharmony of insolvency law.

Therefore, reforms still need to be made to improve security law and this will probably come about at some point in the future. The question and biggest concern is when? It has already been sixteen years since the first reform and glaring errors still exist and need correcting.

BIBLIOGRAPHY

Acosta, M., 'Crédito', *in Nuevo Diccionario Jurídico Mexicano, Tomo A-C*, Mexico, Editorial Porrúa, 1998.

Alessio, M., *Temas de Derechos Reales* (2nd ed.), Mexico: Editorial Porrúa, 2006.

Castrillón, V., *Contratos Mercantiles* (2nd ed.), Mexico: Editorial Porrúa, 2003.

Ciscomani, F., 'La prenda sin transmisión de posesión en México', *Revista de Derecho Privado*, nueva época, año II, September-December, 2003, p. 3.

Crocq, P., *Propriété et Garantie*, LGDJ, 1995.

Gabaldón, J. & Ruíz, J., *Manual de Derecho de la Navegación Marítima* (3rd ed.), Marcial Pons, 2006.

Guzmán, R., *Derecho Bancario y Operaciones de Crédito* (2nd ed.), Mexico: Editorial Porrúa, 2004.

Haime, L., *El Arrendamiento Financiero* (13th ed.), ISEF, 2003.

Ibarra, R., 'The Reappearance of Ownership as a Means of Security in Mexican and French Law, the Battles Between Legal Technique and Legal Policy in Insolvency Law" *in* Gruyaert, D., Ramaekers, E. & Rostill, L. (eds.), *Property Law Perspectives IV*, Intersentia, 2016.

Ibarra, R., 'La Clause de Réserve de Propriété, une Étude de Droit Comparé Franco-Latino-Américain' *in* Larroumet, C. (ed.) *L'Évolution des Garanties mobilières dans les Droits Français et Latino-Américains*, Paris: Panthéon-Assas, 2016.

Iturbide, A., 'Las Nuevas Garantías: Prenda Sin Transmisión de Posesión y el Fideicomiso de Garantía', *Revista Mexicana de Derecho*, No. 3, Mexico, 2001, p. 101.

Kozolchyk, B., 'Secured Lending and its Poverty Reduction Effect', *Texas International Law Journal*, No. 42, 2007, p. 727.

Kozolchyk, B. & Wilson, J., 'The Organization of American States: The New Model Inter-American Law on Secured Transactions', *Uniform Law Review*, No. 69, 2002, p. 69.

Labariega, P., 'La Digitalización del Registro Público de Comercio. ¿La New Age en la Legislación Patria?', *Boletín Mexicano de Derecho Comparado*, nueva serie, año XXXVIII, No. 113, May-August 2005, p. 763.

Martínez, J., 'Consideraciones en torno a las modernas figuras de garantía: las reservas de dominio complejas', *Revista de Derecho Privado*, July-August 2003, p. 461.

De la Mata, F. & Garzón, R., *Derechos Reales de Garantía*, Mexico: Editorial Porrúa, 2005.

Ortiz, S., *El Fideicomiso Mexicano* (3rd ed.), Mexico: Editorial Porrúa, 2006.

Pérez, B., *Contratos Civiles* (10th ed.), Mexico: Editorial Porrúa, 2004.

Rocha, E., 'El fideicomiso de infraestructura y bienes raíces', *Revista Internacional de Derecho y Ciencias Sociales*, Universidad de Monterrey, No. 10, Spring 2007, pp. 47-48.

Sánchez, R., 'Algunas Consideraciones Sobre el Método Exegético Jurídico', *Anuario jurídico*, México, No. XVI, 1989, p. 269.

Sanromán, L., *Concursos Mercantiles* (2nd ed.), Mexico: Editorial Porrúa, 2016.

Villagordoa, J., *Doctrina General del Fideicomiso* (4th ed.), Mexico: Editorial Porrúa, 2003.

8 The Interaction between Preemption Rights and Security Trusts

*Rafael Ibarra Garza** *and Eduardo Javier Odriozola Garza***

1 Introduction

Article 381 of the *Ley General de Títulos y Operaciones de Crédito* (Securities and Credit Operations Act) describes the *fideicomiso* (from now on: the trust) as an agreement by means of which one of the parties, called the settlor, transfers rights to a second party, called the trustee, so that such rights are destined to serve a particular and legal purpose.[1] Such purpose may be for the benefit of another called beneficiary.[2] This would be the case for example if person A (the settlor) transferred land and money to person B (the trustee) for the construction of a house (the purpose of the trust); once the house has been constructed, person C (the beneficiary) would have the right to use the house until his death.

If a Mexican trust entails a transfer of rights, this means that the right of ownership is amongst the various different rights that the settlor can transfer to the trustee.[3] Therefore a problem arises if the settlor's freedom to transfer his right of ownership is limited. This would be the case where someone has a right of preemption on the right of ownership that the settlor intends to transfer to the trustee. The most common examples of assets that

* Universidad de Monterrey, Escuela de Derecho y Ciencias Sociales, Dean of the Academic Department of the School of Law; Researcher of the SNI (CONACYT); Of Counsel of Leal-Isla & Horváth, S.C.: Email: rafael.ibarra@udem.edu and ribagar@hotmail.com. The authors would like to thank Cynthia Alejandra Sánchez Torres and Roberto Helio Colyer Ayala for helping in the publication of this paper.

** Associate at Creel, García-Cuéllar, Aiza y Enríquez S.C.

1 For a general analysis of the Mexican trust, see, M. Retteg, 'The Mexican Fideicomiso: Theoretical and Practical Approach', Unil| Université de Lausanne, 2009. Available at www.unige.ch/droit/mbl/upload/pdf/M_moire_RETTEG.pdf. (accessed 4 March 2018); R. Batiza, *El Fideicomiso. Teoría y Práctica*, 8th ed., Mexico, Editorial Jus, 2001; S. Rodríguez, *Negocios Fiduciarios*, 1st ed., Colombia, Legis Editores, 2005; J. Villagordoa, *Doctrina General del Fideicomiso*, 4th ed., Mexico, Editorial Porrúa, 2003; and N. Malumian, *Trusts in Latin America*, New York, Oxford University Press, 2009

2 Securities and Credit Operations Act 1932, Art. 382. For bibliography on the Mexican beneficiary, see S. Ortiz, *El Fideicomiso Mexicano*, 3rd ed., Mexico, Editorial Porrúa, 2006, pp. 140-148; M. Acosta & P. Almazán, *Tratado Teórico Práctico de Fideicomiso*, 3rd ed., Mexico, Editorial Porrúa, 1999, pp. 254-266 and Villagordoa, 2003, p. 201.

3 Ortiz, 2006, p. 103.

have preferential rights attached to them are partnership interests,[4] rural land on its first transfer,[5] assets under co-ownership,[6] and leased property.[7]

Rights of preemption limit the owner's freedom to dispose because this right, in a broad sense, grants its holder the possibility or opportunity to acquire an asset before a third party does upon seller's intent to convey it.[8] Article 973 of the *Código Civil Federal* (Federal Civil Code) states that in virtue of the preemption right, the owner of an undivided asset who intends to sell must first notify the preferential right holders of the terms and conditions of sale; therefore, the preemption right holders may acquire the asset preferentially under the same terms, or waive their right to purchase.[9] It is worth mentioning, as well, that subsequent to the notice given to the right holders, any substantial change to the offer, terms, and/or conditions of sale triggers the need for a new notification to the right holders.[10] Only if the preemption right holder decides to waive his rights then the owner can have the right to sell to another person. In other words, *ab initio* the owner cannot freely choose the potential purchaser.

Under Mexican civil law there are two variations of the right of preemption: *derecho del tanto*[11] and *derecho de preferencia por el tanto*. The *derecho del tanto* is the one conferred by law to co-owners,[12] to heirs,[13] to a usufructuary,[14] and to partners of a civil legal entity.[15] The *derecho de preferencia por el tanto*, on the other hand, is equally a right that binds the owner to offer the right holders the opportunity to purchase before third parties; for example, it is a right conferred to tenants under a lease agreement,[16] but it may also be agreed upon in any contract.

The difference between the *derecho del tanto* and the *derecho de preferencia por el tanto* was established by a ruling of the Supreme Court in 1985; the difference lay in the consequence of the breach of these rights. The breach of the *derecho del tanto* could entail the nullity of the contract by which the right was breached; the breach of the *derecho de pref-*

4 *Ley General de Sociedades Mercantiles* (Commercial Companies Act 1934), Art. 66.

5 *Ley Agraria* (Agrarian Act 1992), Art. 84.

6 Federal Civil Code 1928, Art. 950 and Art. 973.

7 Federal Civil Code 1928, Art. 2448-J.

8 M. Zamora, 'El Derecho del Tanto de los Arrendatarios de Casa Habitación y la Intervención Notarial', *Revista de Derecho Notarial Mexicano*, No. 96, 1987, p. 17, 35.

9 J. Arce, 'El Derecho del Tanto de los Copropietarios', *Revista de Derecho Notarial Mexicano*, No. 33, 1968, p. 21, 40.

10 B. Castillo, *Fideicomiso Inmobiliario en México*, 2nd ed., Mexico, Editorial Porrúa, 2014, p. 21.

11 J. Ponce de León, *Glosa a los Contratos Civiles (Primera Parte). De los Contratos Preparatorios, Traslativos de Dominio y Traslativos de Uso*, Mexico, Tirant lo Blanch, 2015 p. 196; UNAM, *Nuevo Diccionario Jurídico Mexicano*, 1st ed., Mexico, Editorial Porrúa, 2001, pp. 1167-117.

12 Federal Civil Code 1928, Art. 950 and Art. 973.

13 Federal Civil Code 1928, Art. 1292.

14 Federal Civil Code 1928, Art. 1005.

15 Federal Civil Code 1928, Art. 2706.

16 Federal Civil Code 1928, Art. 2448-J.

erencia por el tanto could generate the obligation of the seller to pay for damages caused to the preemption right holder, but the sale would be valid and would continue to exist.[17] Given that the two variations of preemption rights are essentially similar, from here on after they will be referred to as preemption rights or rights of preemption.

If the settlor is legally bound by preemption rights a problem arises at the moment of the constitution of the trust. A scenario can also be imagined where, despite the existence of preemption rights, the settlor transfers ownership to a trustee. This gives rise to another problem as it is possible for the trustee to further transfer ownership in breach of such preemption rights. In both cases a conflict ensues between the settlor, the trustee, and the preemption right holders. Therefore, a study of the interaction between trust law and preemption rights becomes relevant.

The study of this interaction will be limited to security trusts, which can be described as a trust that guarantees the payment of a debt.[18] This would be the case for example where A (the settlor-debtor) transfers ownership of a house to B (the trustee) to secure payment for C (the beneficiary-creditor). If A does not pay C, the security trust would be foreclosed or enforced in favor of C; the foreclosure, for example, would take place by B selling the house and paying C with the price of sale.[19] Thus, the foreclosure or enforcement of the security trust entails the transfer of the trust property from the trustee to another person.[20] Now, if A paid C, then B would transfer the ownership of the house back to A.

Therefore, in a security trust there may be two distinct transfers of ownership: The first one being the transfer from the settlor to the trustee upon the constitution of the security trust, and the second one upon its foreclosure or enforcement, where the trustee will transfer the ownership for the payment of the debt.

For this reason, the analysis of the interaction between the preemption rights and the security trust can be divided into two different moments: Firstly the moment of transfer of the right of ownership on the constitution of the trust (2) and secondly the transfer as a result of foreclosure or enforcement of the security trust (3).

---

17 *Semanario Judicial de la Federación*, 1985, Séptima Época, Tercera Sala, Volumen 199-204, cuarta parte, septiembre, pág. 17, (Registro IUS: 240073), [T.A.].

18 Securities and Credit Operations Act 1932, Art. 395. On security trusts, see J. Suayfeta, 'Las Reformas a la Ley General de Títulos y Operaciones de Crédito. Nuevo e Irresponsable Atentando a la Institución Jurídica de Fideicomiso', *Revista de Derecho Privado*. Biblioteca Jurídica Virtual del Instituto de Investigaciones Jurídicas de la Universidad Nacional Autónoma de México, No. 2, 2002. For other uses of trusts, see: J. Malagón, *Fideicomiso y Concesión. Ensayo sobre Estructuras Financiables para Obras y Servicios Públicos en Latinoamérica*, 1st ed., Mexico, Editorial Porrúa, 2002; O. Mendoza, *El Fideicomiso Público*, 1st ed., Mexico, Editorial Porrúa, 2010, p., and Acosta & Almazán, 1999, p. 389.

19 Securities and Credit Operations Act 1932, Art. 403.

20 J. Domínguez, *Dos Aspectos de la Esencia del Fideicomiso Mexicano*, 2nd ed., Mexico, Editorial Porrúa, 1996, pp. 159-160.

2 The Interaction between Preemption Rights and the Constitution of the Security Trust

Upon the constitution of a security trust, the legal dilemma arises: May the settlor convey property to the trustee without being bound by preemption rights related to the trust property? In other words, is the settlor obliged to offer a property to the preemption right holders before it conveys it to the trustee? It will be demonstrated that despite the fact that the constitution of a trust (in our case a security trust) implies a transfer of the right of ownership from the settlor to the trustee[21] (2.1), such a transfer cannot be considered a definitive transfer and thus the settlor should not be bound by the preemption rights attached to the trust property (2.2).

2.1 The Existence of a Transfer of the Right of Ownership from the Settlor to the Trustee

Before the existence of the description of the trust of article 381 of the Securities and Credit Operations Act, article 346 of the same Act described the trust as an agreement by means of which the settlor would only use assets for the fulfilment of a purpose, and the trustee would only have the responsibility to carry out the acts necessary for such an end. There was no mention of a transfer from the settlor to the trustee. The law also provided for the possibility of constituting a trust without appointing a trustee. Several authors therefore denied that the constitution of the trust entailed a transfer of rights from the settlor to the trustee. Thus the questions surrounding the transfer of ownership from the settlor to the trustee became a controversial aspect of the Mexican trust.

One of the most fervent defenders of the theory that the Mexican trust did not imply a transfer was Jorge Alfredo Domínguez Martínez; he wrote that the Mexican trust did not involve a transfer of ownership from the settlor to the trustee but that the trust merely affected the trust property to a certain purpose.[22] Before Domínguez Martínez, other Mexican authors (which were influenced by Pierre Leppaulle) wrote that the trust created an additional patrimony, and that from an economical and legal standpoint, it was plausible for this new patrimony to lack a holder or owner and only needed the intervention of a body to fulfil the purposes of the trust.[23] In this logic, Raúl Cervantes Ahumada stated that even though the trustee held an autonomous patrimony (the trust patrimony), this did

21 R. De Pina, *Elementos de derecho mercantil*, 18th ed., Mexico, Editorial Porrúa, 1985.

22 Domínguez, 1996.

23 J. Landerreche, 'Naturaleza Jurídica del Fideicomiso en el Derecho Mexicano', No. 50 *Revista Jus*, 1942.

not mean that the trustee was the owner *per se* of the trust estate, but only its holder, as would be provided for in the trust agreement itself.[24]

Other jurists did not share this theory. Some conceptualized the trust as an agreement entailing a transfer of ownership from the settlor to the trustee;[25] they considered that the trustee's right of ownership was not of the same nature as an ordinary ownership, but rather a special ownership (*propiedad fiduciaria*).[26] Other authors thought that there was an absolute transfer of ownership to the trustee.[27]

This doctrinal discussion was settled with the new article 381 of the Securities and Credit Operations Act, which is current as of this date. Such reform left no room for interpretation, as it clearly states that the right of ownership is transferred to the trustee by the settlor.[28] And even before article 381 was redacted in that way, there were court rulings considering the trustee as the owner of the trust property,[29] which meant that the constitution of trusts entailed a transfer from the settlor to the trustee.

With this taken into consideration, there is no doubt that the trust entails a transfer of ownership of the assets that the trust estate is comprised of, but is that transfer of ownership sufficient for the preemption rights to be triggered? This question will be answered in the next section.

2.2 *A Non-Definitive Transfer of the Right of Ownership from the Settlor to the Trustee: The Non-Enforceability of Preemption Rights*

If a transfer of the right of ownership occurs upon the constitution of the trust (in our case a security trust), at first glance it has to be concluded that the preemption rights attached

24 R. Cervantes, 'Naturaleza Jurídica del Fideicomiso en el Derecho Mexicano', No. 50 *Revista Jus*, 1942. In this sense also see, M. Carreras, 'Naturaleza Jurídica del Fideicomiso en el Derecho Mexicano', No. 50 *Revista Jus*, 1942.

25 See in Domínguez, 1996.

26 *Ibid.*

27 Jorge Barrera Graf as cited in Domínguez, 1996.

28 J. Suayfeta, 'Reformas Vs. Reformas. Hacia una Restauración del Fideicomiso', *Revista de Derecho Privado*. Biblioteca Jurídica Virtual del Instituto de Investigaciones Jurídicas de la Universidad Nacional Autónoma de México, No. 4, 2003.

29 *Semanario Judicial de la Federación*, 1990, Octava Época, Tercera Sala, Tomo VI, Primera Parte, Julio-diciembre, pág. 197, (Registro IUS: 207125), [T.J.]. There is a doctrinal discussion on the nature of the trustee's (in civil law trusts) right of ownership. This is so because the trustee may only act in accordance with the indications of the trust agreement and with the trust purpose and his right of ownership is limited in time because at the extinction of the trust he must transfer it to the beneficiaries. For these reasons his rights on the trust property are not considered a right of ownership. Even though there is some logic in that reasoning, ownership coexists with limitations and modalities, therefore the trustee's rights on the trust property can be considered a right of ownership. On the discussion of the nature of the trustee's right of ownership see: Rafael Ibarra Garza, *La Protection du Patrimoine Fiduciaire-Trust Fund (Étude du Droit Comparée: Droit Français-Droit Anglais*, LGDJ, 2014, para 391ff (even though this discussion is on French law, the logic behind it can also be used for Mexican law).

to the future trust property are triggered. This implies then that the settlor will first offer the property to the holders of preemption rights; only when and if they refuse to acquire the property can the settlor constitute a trust and transfer the property to the trustee. Even if this conclusion is logically correct, it is legally flawed and over simplistic. To answer the questions established above, it is necessary to not lose sight of how Mexican trusts work (thus security trusts) and the nature of the transfer of ownership from the settlor to the trustee. As will be seen, there are elements that indicate that the mentioned transfer of ownership does not trigger the enforceability of preemption rights.

Article 381 of the Securities and Credit Operations Act establishes that the trust property will be transferred for it to be destined to a specific purpose (the trust purpose) and that the trustee will be the person who accomplishes that purpose. For this reason, the trustee will have all the rights and actions that are required to accomplish the trust purpose.[30] Thus, the core of the Mexican trust is the specific purpose for which it was created[31] and the trustee may only act in accordance with such purpose.[32] Once this purpose has been attained or if it becomes impossible to attain, the trust is extinguished and therefore the trustee must retransfer the trust property to the beneficiaries.[33] In other words the trustee, as trustee, will not keep the trust property indefinitely.[34]

If the transfer to the trustee is for the accomplishment of a specific purpose and does not keep the trust property indefinitely, this means that the transfer of ownership from the settlor to the trustee is provisional. This is because the transfer to the trustee is a means and not an end.[35] Therefore, in the case of security trusts, the transfer of ownership is only carried out with the purpose of guaranteeing payment of one or more obligations and not for the purpose of having the trustee become the ultimate owner of the trust property.

So if the creditor is duly paid, the guaranteed obligation ceases to exist and the security trust will terminate (unless otherwise provided in the trust instrument).[36] In this case the trustee's ownership will also terminate because it must retransfer the trust property to the settlor;[37] the transfer therefore in a security trust is provisional. In other words, where A (the settlor) transfers ownership of a house to B (the trustee) to guarantee the payment of a debt owed to C (the beneficiary) and A voluntarily pays the debt to C, B is obliged to transfer back the ownership of the house to A. This demonstrates that the transfer of

30 Securities and Credit Operations Act 1932, Art. 391. On the powers of the trustee see: L. Muñoz, *El Fideicomiso*, 2nd ed., Mexico, Cardenas Editor y Distribuidor, 2001, p. 332.

31 A. Iturbe, 'Las Nuevas Garantías; Prenda sin Transmisión de Posesión y el Fideicomiso de Garantía', No. 3, *Revista Mexicana de Derecho*, 2001, p. 124.

32 If it does not, then it will be in breach of trust and liable for any loss occurred to the trust fund (Securities and Credit Operations Act 1932, Art. 391).

33 Securities and Credit Operations Act 1932, Art. 385, fraction I and fraction II.

34 Castillo, 2014, p. 96.

35 Ortiz, 2006, p. 104.

36 Securities and Credit Operations Act 1932, Art. 392.

37 Securities and Credit Operations Act 1932, Art. 393.

ownership on the constitution of the security trust is not a definitive transfer, thus the enforceability of the referred preemption rights should not be triggered.

Also, the retransfer from the trustee to the settlor should not trigger the preemption rights either, as the trust property is returning to its original owner, hence the party bound to abide by the preemption rights is once more the owner.

There is another reason that justifies the settlor not being bound by preemption rights. The owner that intends to transfer the asset with a preemption right attached to it must offer the asset to the preferential right holders with the same terms and conditions. However, in the case of the constitution of a security trust it will not be possible to offer the property in the same circumstances because the preemption right holders are not allowed to be trustees. In fact, the quality of the trustee is limited generally to financial institutions.[38] Thus, if the preemption right holders cannot hold property as trustees it is impossible for the settlor to offer them the property as trustees.

As already shown, the transfer that entails the constitution of the security trust does not trigger preemption rights attached to the trust property. This begs the question: Does the enforcement of the security trust trigger those preemption rights? This will be analyzed in the next section.

3 The Interaction between Preemption Rights and the Enforcement of the Security Trust

To be able to analyze whether preemption rights attached to a trust property are triggered by the enforcement of the security trust (3.2), how the security trust is enforced in Mexican law must first be analyzed (3.1). This is necessary because the fact that the enforcement of the security trust entails a transfer of ownership from the trustee to another person must be demonstrated.

3.1 The Enforcement of the Security Trust

The security trust is designed to guarantee payment;[39] therefore the trust property may be disposed of if the debtor fails to carry out its obligations.[40] In other words, the security trust will be enforced in case of non-payment.

38 Securities and Credit Operations Act 1932, Art. 385. On who can be a trustee in Mexican law, see: Mendoza, 2010, p. 55.

39 Securities and Credit Operations Act 1932, Art. 395. For a critical analysis of the Mexican security trust, see Domínguez, 1996, p. 339.

40 On the enforcement of the security trust, see: L. Camp, *Fideicomisos en México*, Mexico, Editorial Porrúa, 2008.

The enforcement of a security trust is enforced *in rem*, that is because it is enforced upon the trust property[41] and it consists of a series of legal procedural actions as a result of a default by the debtor.[42] These actions consist of the disposal of a trust property and the payment of the creditor (beneficiary of the security trust). The debtor is given a last opportunity to pay before the security trust will be enforced.[43]

Under Mexican law there are two means by which the enforcement of a security trust may take place. The first consists in awarding the trust property to a creditor/beneficiary in which case the debt will be considered as paid; in this scenario the trustee will transfer the trust property to a creditor/beneficiary who will thereafter become the owner of the assets. In Mexican trust law this is only possible if the value of the trust property is equal or inferior to the debt, and the creditor will have a right to demand payment of what's left of the debt.[44]

The second means of enforcement consists in the trustee selling a trust property to a third party so that the proceeds of the sale are allocated to the payment of the debt in favor of the creditor/beneficiary.[45] Thus the trust property will be transferred to a third party. This will always take place when the value of the trust property is superior to the value of the debt.[46]

The sale of a trust property as a result of the enforcement of a security trust must be done through a public auction[47] in order to ensure the lawfulness of the transaction and protect the debtor's interests.[48] If the trust property is not sold at the first auction, a second auction will take place but with an inferior reserve price and so on;[49] if the reserve price of future auctions becomes equal or inferior to the value of the debt the enforcement by adjudication will be possible.[50]

Either one of these options may be carried out either judicially[51] or extra-judicially,[52] nevertheless, an analysis of the specifics of the enforcement procedures was not undertaken because it did not add value to this study. In fact, what is important to retain from the enforcement of the security trust is the fact that a trust property will be transferred to the

41 E. Couture, *Vocabulario Jurídico*, Depalma. 1976, p. 464-465.
42 L. Palacio, *Derecho Procesal Civil*, 17th ed., Abeledo Perrot, 1999.
43 *Código Federal de Procedimientos Civiles* (Federal Code of Civil Procedures 1943), Art. 493.
44 Commercial Code 1889, Art. 1414 bis 17, fraction I and fraction II.
45 G. Moreno, 'El Impuesto sobre la Renta en el Régimen del Fideicomiso', *Revista de Derecho Notarial Mexicano*. Biblioteca Jurídica Virtual del Instituto de Investigaciones Jurídicas de la Universidad Nacional Autónoma de México. núm. 42, 1971.
46 Commercial Code 1889, Art. 1414 bis 17, fraction III.
47 Commercial Code 1889, Art. 1414 bis 17, fraction III, indent a) and indent b).
48 A. Pérez, 'Adjudicaciones y Ventas Judiciales', No. 4, Biblioteca Jurídica Virtual del Instituto de Investigaciones Jurídicas de la Universidad Nacional Autónoma de México, 2002, p. 13, 25.
49 Commercial Code 1889, Art. 1414 bis 17, fraction III, indent b).
50 Commercial Code 1889, Art. 1414 bis 17, fraction III, indent b), second paragraph.
51 Commercial Code 1889, Arts. 1414 bis ff.
52 Commercial Code 1889, Arts. 1414 bis 7ff.

creditor/beneficiary in the case of adjudication or to a third party by virtue of a purchase and sales agreement.

In consideration of the foregoing, the following question arises: Does the enforcement of a security trust bind the trustee to comply with the preemption rights attached to a trust property in these scenarios? In other words, are the preferential rights enforceable by their holders on the enforcement of a security trust? This question will be answered in the next section.

3.2 *A Definitive Transfer on the Enforcement of a Security Trust: The Enforceability of Preemption Rights*

In the first chapter, it was concluded that the settlor was not bound by preemption rights because the transfer to the trustee was only provisional. Therefore the compliance of preemption rights attached to the trust property will depend on whether the transfer, upon the enforcement of a security trust, is considered as a provisional or a definitive transfer. This implies the question of whether or not the transfer of ownership resulting from the enforcement of a security trust is provisional or definitive.

In the context of the enforcement of a security trust, the situation is very different to the context of the constitution of the trust. This is because the transfer of the right of ownership shifts from being a means to being an end. Enforcement of a security trust will result in a trust property being transferred from the trustee to another person who cannot be the settlor, therefore the settlor will lose any possibility of reacquiring the trust property and will not be able to comply with the preemption rights attached to the trust property.

In awarding the trust property to the creditor/beneficiary there is a transfer of ownership from the trustee to the creditor/beneficiary, and in the sale of the trust property there is a transfer of property from the trustee to a third party.[53] In these two scenarios the transfer of property is permanent and not provisional; the settlor will not be able to recover the trust property. It is by virtue of the aforementioned that it can be concluded that the enforcement of the security trust entails a permanent and definitive transfer of ownership; hence, the preemption right holders have the right to be offered to acquire the trust property before anybody else.

In light of the above, the next and last question that arises is: In what ways shall the preemptive rights be abided by enforcement of a security trust? This answer is a doctrinal one because nothing in Mexican law mentions a case involving a security trust. The answer to this question will depend on whether the trust property is awarded to the creditor/beneficiary or if it is sold at auction. The procedures that can be followed to carry out an

53 Moreno, 1971.

enforcement of a security trust are established in Title Three Bis, Book Five of the *Código de Comercio* (Commercial Code).

In awarding the trust property to the beneficiary there are two different scenarios that may take place: One is when it is directly awarded (without any previous attempts to auction);[54] the second is when the auctions have failed (which we will call an indirect award), and subsequently the assets are awarded.[55]

Pursuant to article 1414 Bis 17 of the Commercial Code, a beneficiary will have the right to be awarded a trust property (or to freely dispose of it) if and only if the value of such trust property is equal or inferior to the value of the debt. This is because where the value of the assets is superior to the amount owed it would not be fair for the settlor if a beneficiary obtained more than the amount of any outstanding debt. Of course, if the value of the assets is inferior to the debt, then the beneficiary would still hold an action against the debtor for the payment of the rest of the debt.

On the other hand, in the event that the value of a trust property is superior to the debt, then the trust property must be sold at auction and the proceeds of the sale first allocated to the payment of the debt; secondly any amount obtained in excess of the debt would be transferred to the settlor (this, of course, in the understanding that all of the trustee's fees and other fees payable as a result of the enforcement of the trust are fully paid).[56]

If a trust property is not sold in the first auction, a second auction would be called upon but the initial selling price would be 10% lower than the price set forth in the first auction.[57] Upon failure to sell, subsequent auctions would be held and the initial selling price would continue to decrease until the trust property is sold or, as mentioned above, until the initial selling price is equal to or lower than the value of the debt, in which case the trust property may be awarded to a creditor-beneficiary.

In these adjudication scenarios (regardless of whether such is to be carried out judicially or extra-judicially), the means by which the preemption rights must be complied with first starts with the notification by the settlor of the existence of current preferential rights holders. This notice must contain the full names of all the right holders, addresses, and contact information (to the fullest extent possible), as well as a description of the circumstances or copy of the document(s) that give rise to the right of each holder. The notification must be made after the debt is due and it must remain unpaid. Before that moment information on the preemption right holders is not necessary.

Once the notice is provided by the settlor, then the execution of the security trust should continue its natural course. In the case of a direct award, the creditor/beneficiary would be awarded the trust property at a value that results from the appraisal of the trust property.

---

54 See note 36.

55 See note 41.

56 *Commercial Code* 1889, Art. 1414 bis 17, fraction III, indent c).

57 See note 40.

Therefore, the means of abiding by the preemption rights is by offering its holders the trust property at the same value at which the beneficiary would acquire those assets. On the other hand, in the case of an indirect award, the offer to preemption right holders would be made at the value at which it would have been awarded to a creditor/beneficiary, which is, naturally, inferior to the one set out in an appraisal.

In the case of a sale via auction, the first sale attempt would be publicly called with express mention of the existence of preferential right holders, and the bidding process would begin. The first attempt would be to sell a trust property for a price equal to the appraisal value, and once a highest bidder had come forward, the process would be suspended. The preemption right holders would then be notified by a competent authority or the trustee of the conditions of the sale so that they were in position to exercise their rights regarding the assets subject to the sale. This formal notification has to be done within the same eight day period as the notice, which is consistent with the period provided in article 973 of the Federal Civil Code. On conclusion of such a term, the preemption right would cease to be enforceable. Needless to say, given the nature of the auction, the price may increase if higher bids are placed. For practical reasons, it does not make sense to notify the preemption right holders of each bid and therefore the only offer that needs to be taken into account is the one made by the final highest bidder.

Should the first auction attempt come to an end with no sale, then the second auction would be called for with the reduced initial selling price, as stated above, and the same process followed.

Should the settlor fail to promptly inform of the existence of preferential right holders in bad faith, then, (i) if the holders appear before the competent authority or trustee, as the case may be, and become legally involved in the foreclosure procedure, during such lawfully evidencing their right, then, (a) such person or entity should be taken into consideration for the procedure mentioned above, and (b) the settlor shall be sanctioned under the claim of willfully giving false testimony; and (ii) if the holders appear subsequent to the conveyance of the assets, lawfully asking for their rights, then the settlor should be bound to pay damages and losses caused to the right holders that effectively appeared before the competent authority or trustee, and the sanction for false testimony shall be equally applicable.

4 Conclusion

The main question that was asked in this paper was if preemption rights were to be complied with in the context of a security trust. This of course has two sub-questions: The first is if the settlor must comply with preemption rights upon the transfer of property to the trustee on the constitution of the security trust; the second sub-question is if the trustee must abide by the preemption rights upon the disposition of trust property on the enforcement of the security trust.

The answer to the first sub-question is that even if the constitution of a security trust implies a transfer from the settlor to the trustee, this does not entail the trigger of preemption rights because the transfer to the trustee is only provisional, with the possibility for the settlor to regain ownership of the trust property if a debtor pays its debt.

The answer to the second sub-question is that because the transfer of property that results from the enforcement or foreclosure of a security trust, whether by sale or award, is a permanent transfer (excluding the possibility for the settlor to regain ownership of that property), the trustee must comply with the preemption rights attached to the trust property.

Because Mexican law is silent on the relationship between preemption rights and the security trust, it cannot be foreseen how preemption rights are to be complied with in the enforcement of a security trust. In any case where a trust property is to be awarded to a creditor, the preemption right will be complied with if its holders are offered the assets at the same price as they are to be awarded to a creditor. If a trust property is to be sold to a third party at auction, then the preemption rights are said to be complied with if its holders are offered the trust property at the same price as the highest bidder.

Part III
New Avenues in Property Law Research

9 E-Books, Music and Film Files

Things as Defined by Section 90 BGB?

Stefan Bucher[*]

1 Introduction

This article covers an excerpt of the issues that I have examined in my PhD thesis. In case the presentation of the questions addressed in this paper may appear a little too concise in some cases, those questions are discussed in more detail in my thesis.

In consequence of the linkage to my PhD thesis, most of the questions discussed in this contribution are rooted in the specific wording of a legal rule of the German civil code (BGB). Clearly, the best suited language for an in-depth discussion about these problems is German. However, trying to translate every single relevant detail of the German code into English would not truly reflect the difficulty of each problem. Thus, a certain language barrier cannot be avoided. In order to keep this barrier as small as possible, I shall try to keep the remarks as simple as possible and give a general idea of the questions that have to be answered when German property law becomes digital.

1.1 The Concept of the Thing: The Heart of Property Law

For a better understanding of the following investigation, it is essential to know that the whole property law system of the German Civil Code hinges on the concept of the *thing*. Therefore, only objects that can be subsumed under the concept of the *thing* in Section 90 BGB may be subject of rights in rem, in particular ownership in the sense of Section 903 BGB as well as possession pursuant to Section 854 BGB.[1] Where pieces of digital media do not qualify as *things* in a legal sense, property law cannot be applied and only relative rights will exist in respect of pieces of digital media. Thus, the question of whether pieces

* PhD, University of Würzburg (Germany).

1 Hk-BGB/*Dörner*, § 90 recital 4; BeckOK-BGB/*Fritzsche*, § 90 recital 1; Jauernig/*Mansel*, § 90 recital 2; Erman/*Schmidt*, § 90 recital 1; M. Wolf & J. Neuner, *Allgemeiner Teil des Bürgerlichen Rechts*, 10th ed., Munich, Beck, 2012, § 20 recital 17; *cf.* also Mot. III, p. 33 = *Mugdan* III, p. 18.

of digital media are *things* as defined by Section 90 BGB has central meaning with effect on the rest of the analysis.[2]

Despite the focus on property law in this paper, the concept of the *thing* that is ruled on in the General Part of the German Civil Code should be taken into account. Therefore, the concept of the *thing* does not only apply to Book 3, the Law of Property, but as well to the other books of the BGB.[3] It therefore has to not merely fit property law purposes, but rather fit all cases of application. This requires an overall "broader" concept of the *thing* than it is demanded by its application to property law cases.[4] It should therefore be pointed out that, for subsequent investigations, the concept of the *thing* is always considered from the perspective of property law which is most relevant to the given problem.

1.2 Classical and Modern Channels of Distribution for Media Content

The continuously extending ways of using the internet constantly causes new problems for the law. Hence it cannot be avoided that the law is always lagging behind the new technological circumstances a certain bit.[5]

These technological developments also apply to the trade with digital media content. Not too long ago, it was common to purchase literature, music or film products in a suitable shop as there was no alternative option. Therefore, a shop had to be visited, the desired product in form of an analogue object had to be taken off the shelf, paid for and taken home. The next step in technological development was the opportunity to purchase a product via distance selling. The product was ordered via the Internet and was delivered a few days later. Concerning the legal assessment in terms of Property Law, the option of distance selling via the Internet does not differ from the first method. What these ways of purchasing goods have in common is that ownership in the sense of Section 903 BGB of the particular analogue object is transferred to the purchaser according to Section 929 ff BGB and he or she eventually holds a tangible version of the product in his or her hands.[6]

---

2 *Cf.* at least for software contained on a data carrier e.g. BGH case VIII ZR 314/86, BGHZ 102, 135, 144; also BGH case I ZB 8/84, NJW-RR 1986, 2190.

3 Staudinger/*Stieper*, Vorbem. zu §§ 90-103 recital 1, § 90 recital 5; to other affected areas of law *see* P. Bydlinski, 'Der Sachbegriff im elektronischen Zeitalter: zeitlos oder anpassungsbedürftig?', *AcP*, Vol. 198, 1998, pp. 287 *et seq.*, at 298; regarding criminal law aspects, e.g. G. Haß, 'Der strafrechtliche Schutz von Computerprogrammen' *in* M. Lehmann (Ed.), *Rechtsschutz und Verwertung von Computerprogrammen*, Cologne, Schmidt, 1993, pp. 467 *et seq.*; T. Hoeren, *in* I. Conrad & M. Grützmacher (Eds.), *Recht der Daten und Datenbanken im Unternehmen*, Cologne, Schmidt, 2014, § 23.

4 BeckOK-BGB/*Fritzsche*, § 90 recital 2; Staudinger/*Stieper*, § 90 recital 5; Palandt/*Ellenberger*, Überblick v § 90 recital 1.

5 M. Berberich, *Virtuelles Eigentum*, Tübingen, Mohr Siebeck, 2010, p. 1.

6 *Cf.* M. Ganzhorn, *Rechtliche Betrachtung des Vertriebs und der Weitergabe digitaler Güter*, Frankfurt am Main, Fachmedien Recht und Wirtschaft, 2015, p. 66.

Today, books, music and films are also offered as files that can be downloaded. Sometimes this is even the only possible option. Buying the product in form of an only digital version as an alternative to the traditional way of purchase became more and more popular, as the digital versions fulfil the same function as their analogue counterparts.[7] Literature is no longer purchased and consumed in printed form, music and film are no longer consumed as vinyl-records or CDs, DVDs or Blu-Rays. They are simply purchased and consumed as e-books, music or film files. The use of modern channels of distribution corresponds to the spirit of today's time and poses a pleasant, fast and comfortable extension of the consumer's options to enjoy those works.[8] For this reason the trade with media in file form via electronic channels of distribution has become more and more important.[9] This on-going process related to consumer behaviour has to be retraced by the law in the shortest possible period of time in order to avoid regulatory gaps and thus possibilities of abuse.

Hence the question arises whether someone who purchases a digital version of a book, a song or a film can – in a legally correct sense – be called the "owner" just as if he or she had bought the product in a classical and tangible form. Put differently: Do buyers of digital versions of a product have the same legal status as buyers of the identical media in classical form?

Indeed, the process of dematerialization has not been completely disregarded in the legal world: the density of judicial decisions regarding the digital world has increased in recent years[10] and the German Jurists' Conference (Deutscher Juristentag) has dealt with questions concerning the digitisation of media during the last conferences.[11]

---

7 In the music sector, online offers accounted for 20.5% of the industries total sales in 2012, in 2013 it was 22.6%, in 2014 25.1%, in 2015 31.4%, in 2016 37.9% and in 2017 already 46,6 %, *cf.* annual reports of the Bundesverband Musikindustrie (BVMI), Musikindustrie in Zahlen 2012, 2013, 2014, 2015, 2016 and 2017, pp. 10, 13, 13, 13, 6 resp. 7, http://www.musikindustrie.de/download-jahrbuch (accessed 4 May 2018).

8 Similarly G. Spindler & L. Klöhn, 'Neue Qualifikationsprobleme im E-Commerce', *CR*, 2003, pp. 81 *et seq.*, at 82, 84.

9 *See supra* note 7.

10 Eg. fundamentally judgement of 3 July 2012 in *Case C-128/11, UsedSoft GmbH v. Oracle International Corp. (UsedSoft)*, ECLI:EU:C:2012:407; recently judgement of 10th November 2016 in *Case C-174/15, Vereniging Openbare Bibliotheken v. Stichting Leenrecht (VOB/Stichting)*, ECLI:EU:C:2016:856, judgment of 12 October 2016 in *Case C-166/15, Ranks and Vasiļevičs v. Finanšu un ekonomisko noziegumu izmeklēšanas prokoratūra and Microsoft Corp. (Ranks)*, ECLI:EU:C:2016:762; BGH case I ZR 4/14 (*Green-IT*), NJW 2015, 3576 *et seq.*; BGH case I ZR 8/13 (*UsedSoft III*), GRUR 2015, 772 *et seq.*; BGH case I ZR 129/08 (*UsedSoft II*), GRUR 2014, 264 *et seq.*; OLG Hamburg case 10 U 5/11, CR 2015, 534 *et seq.*; OLG Hamm case 22 U 60/13, NJW 2014, 3659 *et seq.*; OLG Stuttgart case 2 U 49/11, ZUM 2012, 811 *et seq.*; LG Bielefeld case 4 O 191/11, CR 2013, 812 *et seq.*

11 *See* http://www.djt.de/die-tagungen/70-deutscher-juristentag/ and http://www.djt.de/die-tagungen/71-deutscher-juristentag/ (accessed 4 May 2018).

1.3 *Analysis of the Neglected Aspects of Property Law of the Problematic*

The discussion is, however, characterised to a large extent by copyright law. Copyright law is indeed an essential pillar of the legal treatment of the trade with digital media. It has to be noted though, that legal questions concerning objects used in our normal day to day lives, which online trading with digital media certainly is, have to be primarily an issue of general civil law. Accordingly, in addition to copyright problems, there is a need for the protection of files in terms of tort law.[12] One may think of cases where unauthorized remote access, for example deletion, is acquired to files that are stored on a hard disk which does not belong to the property or domain of the owner of the files and which is accessed by the owner of the files via cloud services.[13,14] In these cases the holder of the files has no claim derived from the ownership or possession of the hard disk.[15] He can neither claim damages according to the principles of third-party liquidation due to a lack of a(n) (accidental) damage shift.[16] There is, therefore, a need to grant tort protection in respect of files themselves. In this respect the law of property can add an important facet to the discussion primarily characterised by copyright law, especially since the prerequisite for tort protection is the existence of absolute rights.[17]

2 The Legal Nature of Pieces of Digital Media

Before analysing the legal situation concerning media distributed via internet and downloading e-books, music or film files, it must be determined whether pieces of digital media are to be considered *things,* since the existing rights relating to these media hinge on their

12 Regarding tort protection of data, *cf.* A. Spickhoff, 'Der Schutz von Daten durch das Deliktsrecht' *in* S. Leible, M. Lehmann & H. Zech (Eds.), *Unkörperliche Güter im Zivilrecht*, Tübingen, Mohr Siebeck, 2011, pp. 233 *et seq.*; regarding tort protection of software *cf.* M.Bartsch, 'Software als Schutzgegenstand absoluter Rechte', ibid., pp. 247 *et seq.*

13 *See* generally for the operating principle of a cloud J. Lenzer, *in* Conrad & Grützmacher, 2014, § 9 and M. Bisges, 'Urheberrechtliche Aspekte des Cloud Computing', *MMR*, 2012, p. 574.

14 *Cf.* the examples from M. Bartsch, *in* Conrad & Grützmacher (Eds.), 2014, § 22 recital 10 *et seq.*; *see* also B. Kian, *Cloud Computing*, Baden-Baden, Nomos, 2016, pp. 68 *et seq.*

15 F. Faust, *in Verhandlungen des 71. DJT*, Vol. I, Munich, Beck, 2016, p. A 72 f.; Bartsch, 2014, § 22 recital 3; M. Grützmacher, 'Dateneigentum – ein Flickenteppich', *CR*, 2016, pp. 485 *et seq.*, at 489; M. Dorner, 'Big Data und „Dateneigentum"', *CR*, 2014, pp. 617 *et seq.*, at 619.

16 The owner of the disk regularly suffers damage himself as a result of being unable to fulfil his contractual obligation to keep the data in the cloud, *cf.* F. Faust, 2016, p. A 73; M. Beurskens, 'Vom Sacheigentum zum „virtuellen Eigentum"?' *in* T. Domej *et al.* (Eds.), *Einheit des Privatrechts*, Stuttgart, Boorberg, 2009, pp. 443 *et seq.*, at 470 at and in n. 126.

17 The so far little attention to the law of property is also noticed by J. Druschel & M. Oehmichen, 'Digitaler Wandel 3.0?', *CR*, 2015, pp. 173 *et seq.*, at 177.

legal nature.[18] Often pieces of digital media are not considered *things* by the – without further discussion of the problems behind it – rather feeble argument, data as such would lack the necessary corporeality.[19] This argument is based on a synonymous understanding of the terms "corporeal object" and "thing" and consequently the same assessment criterion is used to determine the respective meaning. This assessment criterion is the perspective of an ordinary and reasonable person. In England this person is also known as the *man on the Clapham omnibus.*[20,21]

This idiom dates back to the 19th century, when Clapham, a southwest suburb of London, became increasingly associated with the city. Clapham was connected to London by a road on which commuters working in London used a horse-drawn wagon known as the "omnibus" to get into town for work. Therefore, everyone who used the Clapham omnibus was considered the personification of a well-to-do and educated man, belonging neither to the working class, nor to the aristocracy.[22] From that moment on, the *man on the Clapham omnibus*' career as the descriptive embodiment of an ordinary and reasonable person began. His hypothetical thoughts shall therefore be the measuring scale throughout the forthcoming remarks.

However, since the man on the Clapham omnibus' hypothetical understanding of corporeal objects and *things* is not always identical, the results obtained on the basis of the synonymous understanding of "corporeality" and "thingness" are not in every case free from inconsistencies. The aim of this chapter is to demonstrate the inadequacies of the prevailing opinions which are the result of these inconsistencies, and to provide an understanding of the concept of the *thing* and its prerequisites which leads to coherent results. In particular, the meaning of the term "corporeal object" is to be questioned and re-assessed.[23] In this regard, according to the approach presented here, the concepts of the corporeal object and the *thing* are to be seen in a hierarchical relationship, in order to be able to apply different criteria to the respective subsumption and thus to achieve consistent results.[24] Subsequently, the concept of the *thing* is examined and it is worked out on the

18 *See* above 1.1 The concept of the thing: The heart of property law, and below 5. Existing rights regarding e-books, music and film files.

19 E.g. MünchKomm/*Stresemann*, § 90 recital 25; Staudinger/*Stieper*, § 90 recital 12; LG Konstanz case 1 S 292/95, NJW 1996, 2662; B. Wemmer & K. Bodensick, 'Virtueller Handel – Geld und Spiele', *K&R*, 2004, pp. 432 *et seq.*, at 436; F. Boehm, 'Herausforderungen von Cloud Computing: Vertragstypologische Einordnung, Haftung und Eigentum an Daten', *ZEuP*, 2016, pp. 358 *et seq.*, at 379 *et seq.*, 381; recently F. Faust, 2016, p. A 72 with further references.

20 McQuire v Western Morning News Co., Ltd., [1903] 2 KB 100 (CA), 109, per Collins MR; thereon worth reading R. Zimmermann, 'Der Hund im Clapham Omnibus – von verständigen Menschen und Tieren', *ZEuP*, 1994, pp. 733 *et seq.*, and based on this A. McPherson & R. Zimmermann, 'The Clapham Omnibus – Revisited', *ZEuP*, 2015, p. 685.

21 References for this relevant perspective in *infra* note 30.

22 *See* thereon in detail McPherson & Zimmermann, 2015, p. 685.

23 Thereon below, 2.4 Own Approach.

24 *See* below, 2.4.2 Things as a subset of corporeal objects.

basis of which criteria it can undoubtedly be checked whether a random object can be subsumed under Section 90 BGB.[25]

2.1 *The External Structure of Section 90 BGB as the Starting Point of the Investigation*

At a first glance the wording of Section 90 BGB is already apparent. Section 90 BGB states: "Only corporeal objects are things [...]." By the use of the term "corporeal objects", the law, on the one hand, specifies the necessary distinction between corporeal and non-corporeal objects, and presupposes, on the other hand, the generic term of the object.[26] However, the concept of the object is not defined in the code and is used with different meanings.[27] In terms of content, it generally encompasses all individualisable assets of the natural world, over which legal power can be exercised.[28] An "object" in the sense of the law is, therefore, everything to which rights can refer.[29]

Before understanding precisely the concept of the *thing* conceived in Section 90 BGB, it is important to look at this in more detail.

2.2 *The Opinion in the Literature on the Concept of the Thing Pursuant to Section 90 BGB*

In order to find general characteristics for the objects which can be subsumed under the concept of the *thing*, and thus define the requirements of a *thing*, various criteria are proposed in the literature, which all shall be considered from the natural perspective of the

25 Thereon below, 3. The concept of the thing as defined by the BGB.

26 M. Schneider, *Virtuelle Werte*, Baden-Baden, Nomos, 2010, p. 88; Staudinger/*Stieper*, Vorbem. zu §§ 90-103 recital 4; BeckOK-BGB/*Fritzsche*, § 90 recital 3; MünchKomm/*Stresemann*, § 90 recital 4; K. Vieweg & A. Werner, *Sachenrecht*, 7th ed., Munich, Vahlen, 2015, § 1 recital 12; J. Wilhelm, *Sachenrecht*, 5th ed., Berlin, De Gruyter, 2016, p. 37, recital 58; fundamentally on the concept of the thing F. Wieacker, 'Sachbegriff, Sacheinheit und Sachzuordnung', *AcP*, Vol. 148, 1943, pp. 57 *et seq.*; thereon also Mot. III, p. 33 = *Mugdan* III, p. 18; on the historical development of the concept of the thing HKK/*Rüfner*, §§ 90-103 recital 3 *et seq.*

27 Staudinger/*Stieper*, Vorbem. zu §§ 90-103 recital 4; jurisPK-BGB/*Vieweg*, § 90 recital 1, 6 *et seq.*; MünchKomm/*Stresemann*, § 90 recital 1; BeckOK-BGB/*Fritzsche*, § 90 recital 3; Palandt/*Ellenberger*, Überbl. v § 90 recital 2.

28 Wieacker, 1943, p. 65; MünchKomm/*Stresemann*, § 90 recital 1; Soergel/*Marly*, Vor § 90 recital 2; BeckOK-BGB/*Fritzsche*, § 90 recital 4; against the financial asset as a characteristic feature R. Sohm, *Der Gegenstand*, Leipzig, Duncker & Humblot, 1905, pp. 7, 22; thereon critical J.W. Hedemann, 'Zivilistische Rundschau 1906-1907', *ArchBürgR*, 1908, pp. 287 *et seq.*, at 322 *et seq.*; thereon HKK/*Rüfner*, §§ 90-103 recital 10; *see*, moreover, the detailed presentation of different definitions approaches by Staudinger/*Stieper*, Vorbem. zu §§ 90-103 recital 4 *et seq.*

29 H.J. Wieling, *Sachenrecht*, 5th ed., Vol. I, Berlin, Springer, 2007, § 2 I 1 a with reference to Wieacker, 1943, pp. 65 *et seq.*; jurisPK-BGB/*Vieweg*, § 90 recital 6; Palandt/*Ellenberger*, Überbl. v § 90 recital 2; BeckOK-BGB/*Fritzsche*, § 90 recital 4; Vieweg & Werner, 2015, § 1 recital 12.

man on the Clapham omnibus, the stereotype of an ordinary and reasonable person.[30] The one criterion which is always referred to is *corporeality* as mentioned in Section 90 BGB.[31] With regard to the wording of Section 90 BGB, it is mostly equated with the concept of the *thing* and thus considered a generic term of the criteria which define the concept of the *thing*.[32] There is almost a consensus in Germany on three further requirements that objects have to exhibit to be considered corporeal and – as a consequence – a *thing*: They have to be *controllable, physically defined* and *sensuously noticeable*.[33]

2.3 *Criticism of the Present Approach*

2.3.1 Inconsistencies of the Results of the Prevailing Opinion

The synonymous understanding of the terms “thing” and “corporeal object” produces peculiar results on the basis of the perspective of an ordinary and reasonable person, the man on the Clapham omnibus:

The open sea is undoubtedly corporeal for the average user of law, as it is at least visually and haptically perceptible, however it is by no means a *thing*, for the reason alone that it cannot be purchased as a whole.[34] The other way around, an inconsistent assessment of *thingness* and corporeality can be discerned, too. An average reasonable person would perceive free gas, for example, as neither corporeal nor as a *thing*. But when gas is put into a container, it is generally considered a *thing*. Consequently, it would have to be a(n) (individual) corporeal object then.[35] In this respect, it is striking that, according to the

30 *Cf.* Staudinger/*Stieper*, Vorbem. zu §§ 90-103 recital 9; Staudinger/*Stieper*, § 90 recital 63; Vieweg & Werner, 2015, § 1 recital 13; J-P. Pszolla, ‘Virtuelle Gegenstände als Objekte der Rechtsordnung’, *JurPC Web-Dok.* Vol. 17, 2009, para. 5, 8; on the relation of the assessment criterion of a fictitious ordinary and reasonable person on the one hand and detailed criteria on the other, *see* M. Schenk, *Die Verkehrsauffassung in BGB und UWG*, Frankfurt am Main, Lang, 2010, pp. 80 *et seq.*

31 *Cf.* eg. Staudinger/*Stieper*, § 90 recital 1; MünchKomm/*Stresemann*, § 90 recital 8; BeckOK-BGB/*Fritzsche*, § 90 recital 5; J.F. Baur & R. Stürner, *Sachenrecht*, 18th ed., Munich, Beck, 2009, § 3 recital 2; Vieweg & Werner, 2015, § 1 recital 12; Wilhelm, 2016, recital 58; M. Wolf & M. Wellenhofer, *Sachenrecht*, 32nd ed., Munich, Beck, 2017, § 1 recital 16.

32 Likewise eg. BeckOK-BGB/*Fritzsche*, § 90 recital 5; jurisPK-BGB/*Vieweg*, § 90 recital 1, 5; MünchKomm/*Stresemann*, § 90 recital 8; Wolf & Neuner, 2012, § 20 recital 17; J. Striezel, *Der Handel mit virtuellen Gegenständen aus Onlinewelten*, Stuttgart, Boorberg, 2010, p. 71.

33 Staudinger/*Stieper*, Vorbem. zu §§ 90-103 recital 9; BeckOK-BGB/*Fritzsche*, § 90 recital 5.

34 Similarly jurisPK-BGB/*Vieweg*, § 90 recital 11; Jauernig/*Mansel*, Vorbem. zu §§ 90-103 recital 4, who rejects the corporeality of ocean waves; Soergel/*Marly*, Vor § 90 recital 33; Wolf & Neuner, 2012, § 25 recital 4; H. Hübner, *Allgemeiner Teil des Bürgerlichen Gesetzbuches*, 2nd ed., Berlin, De Gruyter, 1996, recital 291; regarding groundwater MünchKomm/*Stresemann*, § 90 recital 9 with reference to § 4 Abs. 2 WHG.

35 *Cf.* hereto Staudinger/*Stieper*, § 90 recital 3; BeckOK-BGB/*Fritzsche*, § 90 recital 7; Hk-BGB/*Dörner*, § 90 recital 2; K. Larenz and M. Wolf, *Allgemeiner Teil des Bürgerlichen Rechts*, 9th ed., Munich, Beck, 2004, § 20 recital 13; on electrical energy also Bydlinski, 1998, p. 304; Wieling, 2007, § 2 I c; note also the difference between drink price and bottle deposit, thereon BGH case I ZR 218/91, NJW-RR 1994, 301 *et seq.*; different

assessment of ordinary and reasonable people, physical definition would have to have an effect on the perception of corporeality, for not as a *thing*, and thus as non-corporeal perceived gas becomes a corporeal object as soon as it is physically defined. This is odd. Neither from a natural nor a scientific perspective the physical definition of an object is connected with its material composition. So, does physical definition lead to corporeality, or not? If these two criteria are put into practice, corporeality seems to be a prerequisite for physical definition, since boundaries can only be drawn for corporeal objects. Accordingly, everything that is physically defined is necessarily also corporeal. However, if the starting point is a (factually[36]) non-corporeal object, it is logically not physically definable. This result, however, is contradicted by the assessment of the fictitious ordinary and reasonable person, that gas, which is actually perceived as immaterial, by putting it into a container suddenly becomes a *thing* in the sense of Section 90 BGB and thus a corporeal object. The fact that the same object is once judged as corporeal and once as non-corporeal reveals the low value of the criterion of corporeality for the assessment of *thingness* according to the perspective of the *man on the Clapham omnibus*, and the resulting inconsistency of the results of the present approach of the prevailing opinion.

2.3.2 Background and Consequence of the Prevailing Opinion

These inconsistencies in the finding of results on the basis of the prevailing opinion are due to the apparently widespread assumption that the concepts of "corporeal object" and "thing" are to be understood as synonymous, that is, all corporeal objects are simultaneously *things* and vice versa.[37] It should be noted that, in the case of understanding two or more terms as identical in content, a judgment must necessarily be made on the same scale. However, it is evident that this approach leads to unresolvable contradictions, in view of the unanimous opinion of the literature that the perspective of an ordinary and reasonable person is the relevant perspective of consideration.[38] Prerequisite to a consistent synonymous understanding would be that the assessments of the fictitious ordinary and reasonable person regarding the corporeality and the *thingness* of a particular object always correspond. The fact that this is not always the case, however, has just been shown by the examples of the open sea and of gas considered from the perspective of an ordinary and reasonable person in relation to the respective corporeality and *thingness*. The aim of an appraisal on

---

view for electrical energy stored in a battery jurisPK-BGB/*Vieweg*, § 90 recital 11; contrarily also B. Adler, *Rechtsfragen der Softwareüberlassung*, Berlin, LIT, 2004, p. 35.

36 Regarding the significance of a scientific assessment, *cf.* 2.4.2.2 Upper level: "Corporeal object" and the scientific point of view.

37 Like this Striezel, 2010, p. 71; jurisPK-BGB/*Vieweg*, § 90 recital 1; MünchKomm/*Stresemann*, § 90 recital 8; Jauernig/*Mansel*, Vorbem. zu §§ 90-103 recital 1; on the criterion of corporeality in the context of the concept of the thing in general BeckOK-BGB/*Fritzsche*, § 90 recital 5; MünchKomm/*Stresemann*, § 90 recital 1, 8; Staudinger/*Stieper*, § 90 recital 1 *et seq.*

38 2.2 The Opinion in the literature on the concept of the *thing* pursuant to Section 90 BGB at *supra* note 30.

the basis of the opinion of a fictitious ordinary and reasonable person is always to achieve reasonable results of the subsumption under the concept of the *thing*, and not under that of the corporeal object. However, this aim is not achieved when the evaluations of *thingness* and corporeality mismatch in relation to the same object.

2.4 *Own Approach*

In the following, an understanding of the concept of the *thing* will be presented, according to which subsumptions within the scope of Section 90 BGB succeed without contradiction. The starting point is the wording of the provision. The formulation that "*only* corporeal objects"[39] are *things* as defined by law raises questions, which are either not at all or at least inadequately treated by the prevailing opinion: Which objects are corporeal, and in what relation to the expression of the "corporeal object" does the concept of "thing" stand? From the wording of the provision *a contrario* undoubtedly arises that incorporeal objects can never exhibit *thingness* as defined by law.[40] On the other hand, it cannot be inferred from their formulation that the concepts of the corporeal object and the *thing* are necessarily synonymous. As shown, however, this assumption is the basis of the prevailing opinion. Such an interpretation, which, in conjunction with the uniformly used assessment criterion of the fictitious ordinary and reasonable person's perspective, results in the contradictions shown, is indeed covered by the wording of Section 90 BGB, but is by no means the only possibility.

The contradictions shown on the basis of the prevailing opinion can, however, be resolved if at least one of the two concepts, that of the corporeal object or the *thing*, can no longer be judged from the perspective of a random person on a London bus. This is possible in two ways:

Firstly, a uniform assessment criterion different from the perspective of an ordinary and reasonable person could be applied to the content determination of the two concepts, which leads to a consistency of the results in the subsumptions.

Secondly, corporeality and *thingness* could be judged on different scales. For this purpose, it is necessary to see these two concepts systematically not on the same level as synonyms, but in a hierarchical relationship. If, therefore, Section 90 BGB is understood in a way that the concept of the corporeal object is the generic concept, all *things* would be necessarily corporeal objects, but not all corporeal objects are also *things*. To this extent, some corporeal objects could be denied their *thingness*, with the result that *things* represent a subset of the corporeal objects. Thereby, the corporeality of an object would continue to be a direct prerequisite for the concept of the *thing*. However, since it is to be seen hierar-

39 Emphasis by the author.
40 jurisPK-BGB/*Vieweg*, § 90 recital 6; BeckOK-BGB/*Fritzsche*, § 90 recital 4.

chically "above" the concept of the *thing*, it would not need to be assessed according to the perspective which is relevant to the latter. Therefore, the assessment of the concepts of the *thing* and of the corporeal object could be different in content, without any logical contradictions arising.

2.4.1 Uniform Assessment According to Current State of Natural Science

With regard to the first of the two approaches, the only possible alternative is the current state of natural science. According to this, both the concept of the corporeal object and that of the *thing* would have to be judged from a scientific point of view. Therefore, all those objects would have to be considered a *thing* which have a molecular structure according to the current state of science. This would result in the fact that ultimately every object which consists in its chemical composition of matter, that is, everything that is not merely present in imagination, would be a *thing* as defined by law.[41]

This approach has the advantage that it always delivers *factually correct* results.[42] For this reason, it leads to increased legal certainty, since the results would be based on verifiable rules of science and thus provide optimal conditions for clear subsumptions.

However, there are a number of disadvantages to a science-based point of view. In this respect, the latest state of scientific research is argued as a criterion of assessment, that science as such is very abstract and therefore has not yet had a significant influence on the general view of life.[43] This argument cannot be accepted for two reasons. Firstly, it is dogmatically lacking, since, on the one hand, it attempts to simultaneously apply the assessment perspectives of natural science facts and, on the other, the view of a fictitious reasonable person on the same level and mix them together. Apart from that, it is simply incorrect. It is to be accepted in so far as, for example, light from laity is incorporeal, and the scientifically proven particle character has so far not been taken into account by the general view of life. Air, although this mixture of gases consists scientifically of the smallest particles, is as well not seen as corporeal in the layman's sphere, and therefore not as a *thing* in the sense of Section 90 BGB.[44] Other examples of objects, which, despite their actual corporeality are yet considered incorporeal, are easy to come up with. But then examples of an existing impact of an advancing scientific research on the general view of life are also to be found. It is here, for example, that we can once again come back to the gas, which, considered individually, is perceived as incorporeal and therefore not perceived as a *thing*. Since, however, bottling in special gas bottles has become technically possible, and thereafter an ordinary circumstance of the general view of life, gas in this portioned state is – justifiably

41 *Cf.* Mot. III, p. 32 = *Mugdan* III, p. 18.
42 *See* thereon, 2.4.2.1 Lower level: "Thing" and the perspective of an ordinary and reasonable person.
43 jurisPK-BGB/*Vieweg*, § 90 recital 8.
44 *Cf.* only Palandt/*Ellenberger*, § 90 recital 1; Wolf & Neuner, 2012, § 25 recital 4.

– a *thing*.[45] Another example is electrical energy, which can now be stored in units of different sizes in batteries and therefore is in layman's sphere conceived as a *thing*.[46] These examples show that the assumption that science has not yet shaped the general view of life is by no means true in general terms.

Against a purely scientifically determined assessment of corporeality and *thingness*, however, it is argued that the statutory provisions should primarily be comprehensible for those at whom the law is directed, and not just for natural scientists.[47] This does not mean that every legal layman has to comprehend the legal situation just by reading the code. Such a request would, of course, be unrealistic because of the complexity of many regulatory areas. Rather, the legal situation to be determined by legal work is intended to meet the expectations of the addressed people. However, if only scientific scales were used to determine the quality of the *thingness* of an object, the results obtained would lead to an unduly wide understanding of *thingness* and, consequently, would not coincide with the expectations and the understanding of the users of the law who are regularly scientific laymen. This would lead to the fact that the actual legal situation for laymen would often be surprising and, in the absence of appropriate specialist knowledge, would be incomprehensible. One can think of tiny or enormously large things, such as individual bacteria or whole planets, which are certainly corporeal objects, according to a scientific understanding. It is probable that the vast majority of the users of the law would not consider these objects as *things* in the legal sense; that is, not something on which "private" rights can be acquired. For this reason, such objects sensibly should not be covered by the concept of the *thing* as defined by the BGB.

The fact that it is possible to make certain "stuff" visible today by means of modern technology, which exist only in peoples' imaginations, such as ideas, should also be taken into account. Thus, from a purely scientific point of view, certain elements of *thingness* are attributed to these things. This makes the scope of this erroneous approach, according to which the existence of *thingness* is to be judged solely by natural science, even more clear.

2.4.2 Things as a Subset of Corporeal Objects

These problems do not exist when one takes the second approach suggested above and sees the terms "corporeal object" and "thing" in a hierarchical relationship and judges them based on different scales.

45 *Cf. infra* note 57.
46 So before Bydlinski, 1998, p. 304.
47 Likewise Staudinger/*Stieper*, Vorbem. zu §§ 90-103 recital 9.

2.4.2.1 Lower level: "Thing" and the Perspective of an Ordinary and Reasonable Person
The reflections on a uniform scientific evaluation of corporeality and *thingness* have shown that, in relation to the latter, the average understanding of the addressees of the law must be taken into account, therefore the concept of the *thing* is to be assessed from the perspective of an ordinary and reasonable person.[48]

This perspective of evaluation has the advantage of being adaptable, changeable and dynamic. With regard to the problem in question here, the changeability of the opinion of a fictitious ordinary and reasonable person allows for the possibility of considering certain objects, which have initially been classified as incorporeal, later as corporeal and thus as well as *things* as defined by Section 90 BGB. The change of the ordinary and reasonable person's hypothetical judgement thus means that the general view of life adapts to the intervening technological progress and so "grows" with it.[49] This "growing-with" of the general view of life, and thus also of the concept of the *thing* assessed by it, demonstrates that the concept of the *thing* is not rigid and threatens to become obsolete sooner or later, unless it is amended by law. Through its ability to change and adapt, the hypothetical opinion of a fictitious ordinary and reasonable person as the criterion of assessment always corresponds to the Zeitgeist. This results in a welcome flexibility of the concept of the *thing*. This is the cause for the above-mentioned phenomenon that an object, through a changed perception of its *thingness* can, from today's point of view, be a *thing* in the sense of Section 90 BGB, even if it was previously not regarded as such. Through this adaptability of the concept of the *thing*, the legal system is given a dynamic and timelessness, which leads to the fact that issues remain subsumable despite developments in the non-legal world without a need for change and adaptation of the law.[50] It therefore contributes to a high stability of the BGB.

2.4.2.2 Upper Level: "Corporeal Object" and the Scientific Point of View
Above the level of *things* is that of the corporeal objects. The function of this "upper" level is to define the set of objects, some of which are emphasised as *things* by reference to the scale of the ordinary and reasonable person. The assessment as to whether an object is corporeal in a legal sense, and thus is accessible to subsumption under the concept of the *thing*, is, as shown, to be made from a different perspective than the ordinary and reasonable person.[51] In order to ensure that, according to the wording of Section 90 BGB, "only corporeal objects" are treated as *things* as defined by law, it is necessary to limit the evaluation

48 *Cf.* Mot. III, p. 32 = *Mugdan* III, p. 18; RG case V 19/15, RGZ 87, 43 (45); Staudinger/*Stieper*, Vorbem. zu §§ 90-103 recital 9; Staudinger/*Stieper*, § 90 recital 63; jurisPK-BGB/*Vieweg*, § 90 recital 8; Palandt/*Ellenberger*, § 90 recital 1; Jauernig/*Mansel*, Vorbem. zu §§ 90-103 recital 4; Vieweg & Werner, 2015, § 1 recital 13; restrictive Bydlinski, 1998, p. 302.

49 *Ibid.* p. 304; this also constitute Wemmer & Bodensick, 2004, p. 435.

50 *Cf.* Bydlinski, 1998, p. 304.

51 *See* 2.3 Criticism of the present approach.

of *thingness* to factual corporeal, i.e. physical objects. The judgement criterion for the "upper level" can therefore only be natural science. This is the only way to prevent the dogmatically compelling distinction between rights and *things* being thwarted and factually incorporeal objects, such as rights, contrary to the unambiguous wording of Section 90 BGB, being classified as *things*.

The fact that the concept of the corporeal object is to be assessed according to scientific criteria can also be inferred from the "motives of the BGB":[52] There, incorporeal objects are described as "existing only in imagination (*res, quae in jure consistunt*)".[53] This leads to the conclusion that everything that does not only exist in the imagination has to be corporeal. Those objects existing only in the imagination do not exist materially, e.g. an idea or a right. According to the idea of the authors of the BGB, corporeal things are, therefore, all objects made of matter. This distinction corresponds, from today's point of view, to a natural scientific demarcation, according to which everything that has a corpus is corporeal, that is, every spatially revealed matter.[54]

2.4.3 Interim Result

Overall, the following two-step systematic structure results within Section 90 BGB: The concept of the corporeal object stands on the upper level together with "incorporeal objects" and is to be assessed scientifically.[55] It then is divided on a lower level into "things" and "other corporeal objects". As seen, this distinction is based on the hypothetical view of a fictitious ordinary and reasonable person. An assessment of the *thingness* of an object from this perspective, can, and should, only lead to a positive or a negative evaluation of the *thingness* of, either way, actually corporeal objects.

Once more, the problematic example "gas" shows how this works: If the corporeality of gas is judged scientifically, it has a molecular structure and as such consists not only in the imagination but of matter, and is a corporeal object. This makes it accessible to the assessment of the fictitious ordinary and reasonable person, whether it is also a *thing* within the meaning of Section 90 BGB. In this respect one will have to distinguish: As long as gas is not enclosed and "floats" freely within space, it is, according to an ordinary and reasonable person's opinion, no *thing*. This changes as soon as the gas is put into an enclosing container, for example into a gas bottle.[56] From the general view of life, the gas bottle and the gas contained therein are two different *things*.[57]

52 *I.e.* a full compilation of the motives of the BGB's founding fathers.

53 Mot. III, p. 32 – *Mugdan* III, p. 18.

54 Soergel/*Marly*, § 90 recital 1; jurisPK-BGB/*Vieweg*, § 90 recital 8; Erman/*Schmidt*, § 90 recital 1.

55 Different view explicitly regarding corporeality jurisPK-BGB/*Vieweg*, § 90 recital 8.

56 Staudinger/*Stieper*, § 90 recital 3; BeckOK-BGB/*Fritzsche*, § 90 recital 7; jurisPK-BGB/*Vieweg*, § 90 recital 11; Larenz & Wolf, 2004, § 20 recital 13; T. Korenke, *Bürgerliches Recht, Eine systematische Darstellung der Grundlagen mit Fällen und Fragen*, München, Oldenbourg, 2006, p. 79.

57 *Cf. supra* note 35.

3 The Concept of the Thing as Defined by the BGB

In this section, it will be considered which objects are referred to as *things* as defined by law, i.e. what characterises a *thing*.[58] Because of the above-mentioned hierarchical relationship, the corporeality is, with regards to the wording of the code, a constituent element of *thingness*. However, since corporeality is already a prerequisite for the investigation of the *thingness* of a particular object in general ("upper level"), it is not relevant in the delineation of which (factually corporeal) objects are regarded as *things* and which are not ("lower level") from the perspective of the fictitious ordinary and reasonable person.

3.1 *Presently Demanded Criteria of the Concept of the Thing*

As mentioned above, the criteria proposed in the literature for the examination of *thingness* are *controllability, physical definition* and *sensuous noticeability*.

Although these criteria are undoubtedly useful according to the view expressed here, they are not, however, sufficient to ensure a coherent subsumption.

3.2 *Marketability*

In addition, attention must be drawn to the criterion of marketability. Against the background of the fact that the concept of the *thing* fulfils above all the function of defining what can be the subject of the provisions of property law,[59] the question arises as to the importance of the marketability of corporeal objects for the concept of the *thing*.[60]

In order to understand the role of marketability in terms of the *thingness*, the focus must first be directed to the ratio legis of the provisions on the transfer of ownership and their economic significance.[61]

People have the need to legally document actual trade processes, that is, to be able to gain and transfer ownership of objects, for example, in order not only to be able to oppose the influence of third parties on these objects, but also to be allowed to defend themselves.[62]

58 *Cf.* the detailed comparative account of the historical development of the concept of the thing by G.L. Gretton, 'Ownership and its Objects' *RabelsZ*, 2007, pp. 802, *et seq*, at 807 *et seq.*

59 *Cf., e.g.* Korenke, 2006, p. 79; Hübner, 1996, recital 300.

60 On the marketability of virtual objects and the resulting consequences Schneider, 2010, pp. 90 et seq.

61 On the economical function of contract law H.-B. Schäfer & C. Ott, *Lehrbuch der ökonomischen Analyse des Zivilrechts*, 5th ed., Berlin, Springer Gabler, 2012, pp. 427 *et seq.*; in general on the so called "institutional economics" E.-M. Kieninger, *Wettbewerb der Privatrechtsordnungen im Europäischen Binnenmarkt*, Tübingen, Mohr Siebeck, 2002, p. 16, with further references.

62 *Cf., e.g.* BeckOK-BGB/*Fritzsche*, § 903 recital 20; Jauernig/*Berger*, § 903 recital 3; Schulze/Grziwotz/Lauda/*Siede*, § 903 recital 3; MünchKomm/*Joost*, § 859 recital 1 *et seq.*; Staudinger/*Gutzeit*, § 859

The law provides for these legal consequences in the provisions of property law in connection with the rules on the purchase of goods, cf. Sections 929 ff. and Sections 433 ff. BGB. The prerequisite for the application of these two regulatory areas and the corresponding legal consequences, in particular those of property law,[63] is always the existence of a *thing* as defined by Section 90 BGB.[64] The concept of the *thing* thus constitutes the 'legal link' between the endeavour to legally manifest the trading process and the corresponding codification in Sections 929 ff. BGB. It is certain that the subsumption under the concept of the *thing* should indicate whether an object can be transferred according to the provisions on the transfer of ownership. At the same time, however, there is an interaction between the concept of the *thing* and the law of property. Therefore there is also in the opposite direction the need to define all those objects as *things* which can be transferred according to Sections 929 ff. BGB.[65] Not to regard an (actually corporeal) object which is a suitable object of trade as a *thing* as defined by law, with the consequence of withdrawing it from the legal manifestation of trade which nevertheless takes place, would be contrary to the fundamental idea of a civil code. Against this background, the different results of the perspective of an ordinary and reasonable person are also clear when assessing the *thingness* of not enclosed and enclosed gas: By filling a vessel with gas, the gas can be sold in portions and the possessor can change. In this way, the practical need is met to apply the provisions of property law to a raw material, which is actively traded despite its supposed lack of corporeality. The same applies to liquids. Here filling containers with a liquid leads to the fact that water or petroleum, for example, become marketable and are therefore regarded as *things* in legal terms.

Thus, the idea behind important parts of the law of property is the tradability or the marketability of objects.

3.3 *Function of the Determined Criteria and the Relationship between Them*

It is now necessary to clarify in which function the examined criteria are to be seen in relation to the concept of the *thing*, and how they are interrelated.

---

recital 1 *et seq.*; Wolf & Wellenhofer, 2017, § 2 recital 4; W. Lüke, Sachenrecht, 4th ed., Munich, Beck, 2018, § 3 recital 124; Wilhelm, 2016, recital 740, Baur & Stürner, 2009, § 24 recital 5.

63 For other affected areas of law: Bydlinski, 1998, p. 298.

64 Regarding sales law, however, the purchase of rights is meanwhile equal to the purchase of goods, *cf.* Section 453 BGB.

65 *Cf.* BeckOK-BGB/*Fritzsche*, § 90 recital 9; *cf.* thereon also MünchKomm/*Wendehorst*, Art. 43 EGBGB recital 14, who states as a condition for a subsumption under Section 90 BGB that the objects would have to be "accessible to the property law institutes (possession, ownership, pledge etc.)".

3.3.1 Present Approach

According to the prevailing opinion expressed above, the criteria discussed are cumulative prerequisites for the existence of *thingness*.[66] However, it is not necessary, on the grounds set out below, to define the concept of the *thing* by formulating mandatory criteria.

3.3.1.1 Criteria of the Concept of the Thing Shift the Subsumption

The well-known function of a definition is to specify a condition whose content cannot be determined without difficulty, in order to allow a clear subsumption. Regarding the concept of the *thing*, this purpose is addressed by the described discussion about its definitive prerequisites, but is only partly achieved, since the proposed criteria per se and their relationship to one another do not lead to a clear definition of *things*. Whether the decision that an object is a *thing* or not ultimately has to be made according to the criteria of corporeality, controllability, physical definition and sensuous noticeability does not contribute to the solution, but merely shifts the problem. It would be equally possible to judge the concept of the *thing* per se on the basis of the hypothetical opinion of an ordinary and reasonable person, without resorting to the supposed criteria which ultimately complicate the subsumption. In the end, and at some point, the very same decision must always be made: Is object X a *thing* in a legal sense or not?

3.3.1.2 Incompatibility of the Perspective of a Fictitious Ordinary and Reasonable Person on the One Hand and Mandatory Criteria on the Other

The normative assessment of a situation in which the hypothetical opinion of an ordinary and reasonable person is to be taken into account is not possible in the form of an examination of several compelling criteria. The uncertainty of his judgment, which is typical of the fictitious ordinary and reasonable person, is further reinforced by the fact that, with regard to controllability, physical definition and sensuous noticeability, a total of up to three criteria based on natural sciences are to be judged according to the hypothetical opinion of the fictitious ordinary and reasonable person – plus according to the view expressed here, the economic aspect of marketability. The reason for the existing incompatibility is that the ordinary and reasonable person, the man on the Clapham omnibus, does not "think" in the rigid categories mentioned. An average consumer will never concretely ask the question as to whether object X is physically defined, controllable, sensuously noticeable, or marketable, in the intuitive consideration of whether the object is a *thing* as defined by law.

In this respect, it is in principle impossible to describe in a legally comprehensible manner, by means of compelling criteria, the ideas of average people when they ask

66 *See* the statement in 2.2 The Opinion in the literature on the concept of the *thing* pursuant to Section 90 BGB.

themselves whether a particular object is a *thing* as defined by law. The considerations made can be so diverse, varied and – at least from the legal point of view – unstructured, that they cannot be covered by scientific considerations such as specifically named terms. Without an empirical survey or judicial judgement, there is therefore no way of actually determining or defining the hypothetical judgement of the fictitious ordinary and reasonable person. The selection of the criteria considered for the purpose of the definition of the concept of the *thing* can therefore never be too meticulous: The consideration of a number of interconnected, compulsive prerequisites from the perspective of a fictitious ordinary and reasonable person does not ultimately contribute to a precise definition of the concept of the *thing*.

3.3.2 Own Approach: Criteria as Indices Rather Than Mandatory Requirements

If the mentioned criteria are not regarded as cumulative and constitutive prerequisites, but are merely seen as indications for the existence of *thingness*, the contradictions are eliminated at once. At the same time no selectivity of the concept of the *thing* is lost. Moreover, there is no longer a basis for the problem of the confusing relationship between the different criteria, since not all criteria have to be met and the determination of a distinctive meaning of each criterion is not necessary. A general statement, the combination of which criteria doubtlessly indicate the *thingness* of an object from the point of view of an ordinary and reasonable person, cannot be made. A certain residual risk, in spite of a diligent assessment and weighting of the indices mentioned, of not finding a result that corresponds with the ordinary and reasonable person's view, is not completely unavoidable and is therefore to be accepted.

3.4 Interim Result

Which objects are *things* as defined by Section 90 BGB is to be assessed normatively, in particular taking the hypothetical opinion of a fictitious ordinary and reasonable person into account. Which objects are actually considered *things* by the fictitious ordinary and reasonable person, can in the end only be answered with certainty either by empirical determination of the actual average national opinion, or by a judicial decision (by a supreme court). Since both cannot be implemented practically in legal practice, an alternative solution has to be found. The goal, as we have seen, can therefore merely be to identify indices which describe in a verifiable manner what the fictitious ordinary and reasonable person refers to as a *thing* which is different in the individual case and therefore not generally comprehensible.

In this respect, in addition to the controllability, physical definition and sensuous noticeability, the marketability of objects has proved to be suitable for the ordinary and reasonable person's hypothetical opinion.

4 SUBSUMPTION

In this section, whether e-books, music and film files can be subsumed under the previously examined concept of the *thing* will be investigated.

In order to do this it is necessary to step into the shoes of the *man on the Clapham omnibus*, the fictitious ordinary and reasonable person, and look at digital files in respect of controllability, physical definition, sensuous noticeability and marketability from this perspective. If this is done, a clear picture emerges:

4.1 Physical Definition

According to the view of an ordinary and reasonable person, e-books, music and film files are not limitless in the way of open sea or gas, but rather clearly limited objects. This results from the fact that a file must always be stored on a data carrier, which itself is undoubtedly a delimited object. In consequence, if the data carrier of a file is delimited, from a normative perspective[67] the file stored on it cannot be unlimited. Apart from that, when looking at the files themselves, their physical definition results, too. In contrast to data as such, these data-packages unambiguously represent a unit which is perceivable as a group.[68] For example, files can be "selected", i.e., by clicking on a screen and an input device such as a computer mouse. This makes the outer boundaries of files visible on a screen. This is different for virtual objects or goods. The part of a data set on which, for example, the graphical representation of a virtual sword in a computer game is based, is, as opposed to files of electronic media, regularly not recognizable as such or separated from other parts "clickable".[69] Virtual goods can therefore not be perceived as physically defined objects in the form of a file, but can only be consumed as a finished product by graphical representa-

67 This – *a fortiori* – is true for a scientific point of view, as well.

68 In this direction also H. Zech, 'Daten als Wirtschaftsgut – Überlegungen zu einem Recht des Datenerzeugers', *CR*, 2015 pp. 137 *et seq.*, at 138; *cf.* thereon also T. Büchner, *Die rechtlichen Grundlagen der Übertragung virtueller Güter*, Baden-Baden, Nomos, 2011, pp. 47 *et seq.*, whose comments on virtual goods allow inference as here in relation to files.

69 In any case, not as a file, at most its graphic representation on the screen, which, however, cannot be copied and moved in a comparable manner, but can only be perceived as a virtual object within the game, *cf.* Büchner, 2011, pp. 47 *et seq.*

tion.[70] The process of "clicking" on either one or numerous files is comparable to touching or grabbing a traditional book, a music CD or a DVD. In this respect, pieces of media in file format can therefore be treated as their analogous counterparts. Files must therefore be designated as physically defined.[71]

4.2 *Controllability*

Furthermore, files are easily controllable for humans. They may be opened, closed, deleted, copied or sent upon request and without special effort by means of input devices such as a computer mouse, and are thus suitable for possession according to Section 854 BGB.

4.3 *Sensuous Noticeability*

Sometimes files are not considered *things* by the argument that they are not sensuously noticeable.[72] It is argued that files could be displayed only with the help of a carrier medium or by light pulses, but not without these tools, sensuous noticeability is therefore to be rejected.[73] This approach, however, is wrong in the premise, since technical aid for the perception of objects is to be considered permissible. Otherwise, the sensuous noticeability and thus also the *thingness* of the individual objects also depend, for example, on whether the respective viewer may or may not wear and need glasses (i.e. a technical aid) due to poor eyesight.

Moreover, the argumentation is also wrong in content: Files can be perceived not only on a display, but sometimes also as such.[74] For example, the part of a CD or DVD where files are written on is visually recognizable by looking at the underside of the data carrier, since it has a slightly different colour compared to the blank part. It is certain that in this way only the existence of files but not their decrypted content can be perceived in an abstract form. However, comparisons with a text that is too small for the human eye and can only be read by means of a magnifying glass, a text written in sufficient text size, but written in a foreign font, or simply the example of a folded book[75] prove the fact that the

70 Like this also Berberich, 2010, p. 87, references in n. 11; Büchner, 2011, pp. 47 *et seq.*; A. Lober & O. Weber, 'Money for Nothing? Der Handel mit virtuellen Gegenständen und Charakteren', *MMR*, 2005, pp. 653 *et seq.*, at 655.

71 *Cf.* also Zech, 2015, p. 138.

72 Eg. Striezel, 2010, p. 72; I. Hantschel, *Softwarekauf und -weiterverkauf, Zur Vertragsnatur und Erschöpfungswirkung körperlicher und unkörperlicher Übertragungsformen von Software*, Berlin, Duncker & Humblot, 2011, p. 59.

73 Striezel, 2010, p. 72.

74 In contrast Striezel, 2010, p. 72; this also seems to be mistaken by J. Druschel, 'Die Regelung digitaler Inhalte im Gemeinsamen Europäischen Kaufrecht (GEKR)', *GRUR Int.*, 2015, pp. 125 *et seq.*, at 126 at n. 17.

75 *Cf.* Bydlinski, 1998, p. 306, however, in a different context.

actual perception of the content is not necessary.[76] If, however, files on a CD are sensuously noticeable, this must also apply to files stored on a hard disk, even though no optically perceptible boundary can be seen between used and free parts. Otherwise, there would be an unjustifiable difference between files on a CD and files on a hard disk, and therefore a dependency of the *thingness* of an object on the respective carrier media. A direct perception of data as such is therefore not necessary within the concept of the *thing*.[77]

However, because files are depicted at least by means of technical devices independent of the medium on which they are stored, the indication of sensuous noticeability is fulfilled.[78]

4.4 *Marketability*

The question of marketability is the last and most important indication of a possible *thingness* of an object.[79] At this point it should again be pointed out that not every marketable object is to be regarded as a *thing*. Otherwise – contrary to the system – rights could also be *things*. The decisive point, as with all other indices of *thingness*, is the starting point of a corporeal object.[80] From the set of (actual) corporeal objects, those objects are *things* in the sense of Section 90 BGB, which represent an independent object of trade.

The fact that pieces of electronic media are subjects of trade is evident through the lively online trade.[81] There is a difference to streaming here. In the case of the latter, the user pays a fee for the time-limited provision of the possibility of consumption of a piece of music or a film, i.e. for a service. On the other hand, when purchasing an e-book, a music or a film file, the purchase price is paid for the possibility of storing a permanent copy of the file embodying the art piece on the own hard disk by means of a download. Thus, the object of trade is the file itself. There is therefore no doubt as to the marketability of pieces of media in file form.

---

76 Again, the example of a person who, unlike another, relies on glasses shows that the perception of the actual content cannot be relevant, otherwise small printed text would be perceivable to people with better visual acuity, while this would maybe not apply to humans with poor eyesight.

77 In contrast Striezel, 2010, p. 72 *et seq.* who, astonishingly, does not consider a burning light bulb electronic energy that has become visible, but only the "active power" of the same; where insofar, from the point of view of an ordinary and reasonable person, should be the difference, remains questionable.

78 Like this also Berberich, 2010, p. 92 with further references in n. 44.

79 *Cf.* 3.2 Marketability.

80 2.4.2.2 Upper level: "Corporeal object" and the scientific point of view.

81 Hantschel, 2011, p. 63; J. Preuß, *Rechtlich geschützte Interessen an virtuellen Gütern*, Berlin, Duncker & Humblot, 2009 p. 43; J. Marly & A.-L. Wirz, 'Die Weiterverbreitung digitaler Güter' *EuZW*, 2017, p. 16; R. Hauck, 'Gebrauchthandel mit digitalen Gütern', *NJW*, 2014, p. 3616; *cf.* also the references regarding the increasing popularity of the online trade in *supra* note 7; for quality as an asset of virtual objects Wemmer & Bodensick, 2004, pp. 434 *et seq.*; for the independent role of the work as a commodity in economic life in relation to the person of the creator M. Rehbinder & A. Peukert, *Urheberrecht*, 17th ed., Munich, Beck, 2015, recital 46.

5 Existing Rights Regarding E-Books, Music and Film Files

The next step is to ask what rights exist in e-books, music and film files. Here, as for all *things*, the two most important rights are possession pursuant to Section 854 BGB and ownership pursuant to Section 903 BGB.

5.1 *Possession*

Possession means the question as to whether there is in principle the possibility of exercising actual control over e-books, music and film files. This assessment is also to be made from the perspective of a fictitious ordinary and reasonable person.[82] Insofar, the possibility to influence the *thing* itself and to exclude others from it is always considered necessary.[83]

If one attempts to subsume e-books, music and film files under these conditions which characterise possession, there is no major difficulty in accepting the necessary controllability from a normative point of view: The person who has stored electronic media on his hard drive is free to access these files. At the same time, it is also easy for him to ensure that no one reads his books, listens to his music, or watches his films by either controlling access to the data carrier containing the files or password-protecting the files. Thus, there are no differences between books, music and films in analogue and digital form.

Hence the following statement can be made: E-books, music or film files can be controlled as required by law without distinction to their analogous correlates. As a result, regarding electronic media, in particular in the form of files, possession in the sense of Section 854 BGB can be gained.[84]

5.2 *Ownership*

The conclusion can be drawn that the creation of ownership as defined by Section 903 BGB concerning files is not less than the logical consequence of the view expressed here, i.e. pieces of electronic media are *things* pursuant to Section 90 BGB, since ownership can only be gained of *things* as defined by Section 90 BGB.[85] The reference of Section 903 BGB to Section 90 BGB allows a conclusion in the other direction, i.e. from Section 90 BGB to

---

82 Palandt/*Bassenge*, § 854 recital 3; Hk-BGB/*Schulte-Nölke*, § 854 recital 3; jurisPK-BGB/*Diep*, § 854 recital 3.

83 Hk-BGB/*Schulte-Nölke*, § 854 recital 3; jurisPK-BGB/*Diep*, § 854 recital 3; Soergel/*Stadler*, § 854 recital 4; *cf.* already F.C. von Savigny, *Das Recht des Besitzes*, Baden Baden, Nomos, 2011 (first published 1803), § 14, p. 125.

84 Different for software, based on its alleged lack of corporeality, C. Cichon, *Internet-Verträge, Verträge über Internet-Leistungen und E-Commerce*, 2nd ed., Cologne, Schmidt, 2005, § 8 recital 982.

85 jurisPK-BGB/*Rösch*, § 903 recital 13; Jauernig/*Berger*, § 903 recital 1.

Section 903 BGB.[86] If therefore a *thing* pursuant to Section 90 BGB exists, apart from the exception of ownerlessness, the legal power over this *thing* is always exercised by someone. Against the fundamental compatibility of ownership with electronic media, there is therefore not only no concern, it is even a direct result of the *thingness* of such files.[87] In addition to the creation of possession, the creation of ownership in the sense of Section 903 BGB of e-books, music and film files is also possible.[88]

6 Summary and Result

The prerequisites of the concept of the *thing* according to Section 90 BGB are not readily apparent. Only a detailed analysis provides the necessary insight.[89] In particular, the assessment of the *thingness* of goods on the basis of the hypothetical opinion of a fictitious ordinary and reasonable person poses problems in finding a clear definition which can be used for the legal subsumption. Here the relationship between corporeality and *thingness* is particularly problematic. In order to avoid indissoluble contradictions, both concepts must not be equated in content. Instead, *things* are to be seen as a subset of all corporeal objects.[90] Since the hypothetical opinion of a fictitious ordinary and reasonable person cannot be described in terms of legal work, an alternative, scientifically comprehensible definition is to be developed in which the criterion of marketability is of particular importance. After all it can be stated that electronic media such as e-books, music and film files fulfil the requirements of Section 90 BGB and are therefore *things* as defined by law.

Due to the fact that the creation and exercise of both possession and ownership, i.e. absolute rights, of e-books, music and film files has been concluded to be possible, it can also be said that the need for a protection of files in terms of tort law should be taken into account.

86 Thereon B. Windscheid & T. Kipp, *Lehrbuch des Pandektenrechts*, 8th ed., Vol. 1, Goldbach, Keip, 1900, p. 759 ("A corporeal thing has been called to object of ownership.").

87 Consistently, due to rejected *thingness*, negating Wemmer & Bodensick, 2004, p. 436.

88 So also with reference to the UsedSoft decision of the ECJ M. Neuber, 'Online-Erschöpfung doch nur für Software?' *WRP*, 2014 1274 *et seq.*, at 1277.

89 *Cf.* 3. The concept of the *thing* as defined by the BGB.

90 *Cf.* 2.3 Criticism of the present approach.

10 3D Printing as a Challenge for Patent Law in Europe

Legal and Practical Limits, and Practical Chances for Rights Holders

Constantin Blanke-Roeser[*]

1 Introduction[1]

3D printing is one of the most significant technical developments of the recent past. The falling cost of printers and materials have made 3D printing more accessible to a growing number of private users.[2] This imposes challenges to Intellectual Property Law, as does digitalization in general.[3] By means of 3D printing, more and more users are able to manufacture products which are protected by IP laws.[4] In many industries, the distribution of 3D printing will change the entire traditional chain of production, from design and manufacture of the product and its distribution to the consumption by customers.[5] Following that, many consumers will manufacture products themselves at home or have them produced by 3D printing shops or services.[6] This paper focuses on the challenges to patent law. The first section introduces the technical background of 3D printing. The following section will discuss its relevance under the current patent law regime and, on that basis, the limits of the current legal framework will be analyzed, with a subsequent discussion of conceivable solutions.

---

* Dr. med. Constantin Blanke-Roeser, LL.B., Research assistant, Center for Transnational IP, Media and Technology Law and Policy, Bucerius Law School, Jungiusstraße 6, 20355 Hamburg; PhD student, Humboldt University of Berlin.

1 The original, more detailed German version of this paper was published in (2017) 119 GRUR 467-475 (see bibliography below). A shorter version which is similar but consistent with this will be published in J. Wulfsberg, T. Redlich & M. Moritz (Eds.), *Vernetzt – Dezentral – Kollaborativ – Interdisziplinäre Perspektiven zur Zukunft der Wertschöpfung* (German, Springer Gabler 2018) and in J. Wulfsberg, T. Redlich & M. Moritz (Eds.), (English, Springer 2018).

2 J.B. Nordemann, M. Rüberg & M. Schaefer, '3D-Druck als Herausforderung für die Immaterialgüterrechte', *NJW*, Vol. 68, 2015, p. 1265.

3 S. Bechtold, '3D Printing, Intellectual Property and Innovation Policy', *IIC*, Vol. 47, 2016, p. 517; R. Schulze & D. Staudenmeier, 'Digital Revolution: Challenges for Contract Law in Practice', EuCML, Vol. 4, 2015, p. 215.

4 Nordemann, Rüberg & Schaefer, 2015, p. 1265; M. Mengden, '3D-Druck – Droht eine „Urheberrechtskrise 2.0"? Schutzumfang und drohende Rechtsverletzungen auf dem Prüfstand', *MMR*, Vol. 17, 2014, p. 80.

5 Bechtold, 2016, p. 518.

6 Schulze & Staudenmeier, 2015, p. 216.

2 Technical Background of 3D Printing

3D Printing is a general term used to describe the range of processes encompassing the production of three dimensional objects. These objects are produced from specific materials which are applied layer by layer to a platform, until a solid object is formed.[7] A more precise term is *additive manufacturing*.[8] The template for the printing process is the so-called *Computer-Aided Design* (CAD) file which contains all the required information. These files can be newly designed by users, either with the help of specific software or by 3D scanning an existing object.[9] Moreover, CAD files can be downloaded from the internet, especially from specialized online platforms.[10] Food or living cells can also be used as materials in production, in addition to the more traditional materials such as industrial metal.[11] A recent highlight was the production of chocolate which could be designed by customers online, according to their individual taste.[12] As a matter of fact, more complex 3D printers have already been in use in several industries for decades. Meanwhile, more versatile and inexpensive printers are finding their way to private households.[13] Professional 3D printing shops and services are cropping up with increasing frequency, offering their services to customers.

3 Relevance of 3D Printing for the Current Patent Law

3.1 Overview: The Three Types of Patents

The current legal framework allows for technical inventions to be protected by two types of patents in Germany: the traditional *national patent* under the German Patent Act (Patentgesetz, PatG) and the *European patent* on the basis of the European Patent Convention (EPC). Despite appearances to the contrary, the European patent only grants protection for particular states, which are chosen in the application (thus, it is often referred to as a

7 V. Zukas & V.A. Zukas, *An Introduction to 3D Printing*, Sarasota (FL), 1st ed., Design Publishing, 2015, 1.1.

8 Nordemann, Rüberg & Schaefer, 2015, p. 1265.

9 Nordemann, Rüberg & Schaefer, 2015.

10 A. Schmoll *et al.*, 'Dreidimensionales Drucken und die vier Dimensionen des Immaterialgüterrechts. Ein Überblick über Fragestellungen des Urheber-, Design-, Patent- und Markenrechts beim 3D-Druck', *GRUR*, Vol. 117, 2015, p. 1042.

11 Bechtold, 2016, p. 519; S. Bose, S. Vahabzadeh & A. Bandyopadhyay, 'Bone tissue engineering using 3D printing', *Materials Today*, Vol. 16, 2013, p. 497.

12 P. Li *et al.*, 'Intellectual Property and 3D Printing: a Case Study on 3D Chocolate Printing', *GRUR Int*, Vol. 64, (2014), p. 98.

13 Bechtold, 2016, p. 517.

bundle of national patents).[14] However, a third type of patent will become available in the near future which will be known as the European patent with unitary effect (also known as *Unitary patent*). It is designed to protect inventions within the entire territory of those EU Member States participating in the new system.[15] The legal basis of the new patent is the so-called patent package, consisting of two EU regulations (Regulation (EU) No 1257/2012 of 17 December 2012 implementing enhanced cooperation in the area of the creation of unitary patent protection (EPUE-Reg)) and Regulation (EU) No 1260/2012 of 17 December 2012 implementing enhanced cooperation in the area of the creation of unitary patent protection with regard to the applicable translation agreements (EPUET-Reg)) and the international Agreement on a Unified Patent Court (UPCA). The latter still needs to be ratified by a minimum number of Member States, which is required to set the whole system into force.[16] Even if Brexit goes ahead resulting in the withdrawal of Great Britain from the EU, it is expected that the Unitary patent system will come into force within the course of the next few years.

3.2 *National Patent, Using the Example of the German Patent*

In the context of 3D printing, direct infringement falls under § 9 s. 2 no. 1 PatG which refers to objects. According to this provision, only the patent holder is allowed to use the patented invention, meaning that third parties are prohibited from manufacturing a product covered by the patent, and are forbidden from launching any such product onto the market. Any indirect infringement falls under § 10 PatG, which will be presented later in the context of CAD files. In the context of 3D printing, several acts take place. The most important ones will be examined in the following sections.

3.2.1 Manufacture and Distribution of an Object

The reproduction of a patented object which is the subject-matter of a patent by means of 3D printing is a manufacture of that product in the sense of § 9 s. 2 no. 1 PatG and therefore a direct use of that patent, unless the end product differs from the original product technically to a relevant extent.[17] If this is not allowed but is carried out, a direct patent infringement can be said to have been committed. However, if the production takes place in a private environment for non-commercial use, it is legal (§ 11 no. 1 PatG). This

14 U. Fitzner, R. Lutz & T. Bodewig, *Patentrechtskommentar*, 4th ed., Munich, Beck, 2012, Einl. recital 57.

15 R. Teschemacher, 'Das Einheitspatent – Zu Risiken und Nebenwirkungen fragen Sie Ihren Anwalt', *Mitt.*, Vol. 104, 2013, p. 153.

16 K. Grabinski, 'Der Entwurf der Verfahrensordnung für das Einheitliche Patentgericht im Überblick', *GRUR Int*, Vol. 62, 2013, p. 310.

17 Nordemann, Rüberg & Schaefer, 2015, p. 1269.

exception theoretically allows for the production of an unlimited number of specimens,[18] which can be relevant in case of worn parts. Both prerequirements need to be fulfilled.[19] The *private* area is limited to the personal surrounding and the personal need of the acting person or related persons,[20] e.g. in the home environment or during leisure activities.[21] This means that, if it serves the personal need, users can even be allowed under § 11 no. 1 PatG to have patented products manufactured by a third party.[22]

The prerequisite of *non-commercial use* excludes uses that aim at making any kind of profit.[23] Generally speaking, a product remains non-commercial even if it is handed over to a second party after a period of private use without consideration. In contrast, exchanging the product in return for payment is more problematic. Some scholars consider this as a commercial use.[24] However, given that after a period of private use the product is a used product, one must consider the additional circumstances of the individual case,[25] e.g. whether such products are forwarded in a similar manner repeatedly.[26]

However, professional printers that manufacture patented products for other persons ("manufacturing on demand") may directly infringe patents by this behavior.[27]

3.2.2 Actions in Relation to CAD Files

Actions in relation to CAD files fall into two categories. On the one hand, there is the creation of a CAD file and its distribution. On the other hand, there is the download of an existing CAD file.

The *creation* of a CAD file and its distribution need to be different, e.g. uploading it to an online platform or forwarding it to individual persons, e.g. by email. The creation is a mere preparatory action which is irrelevant under patent law,[28] however the distribution may infringe patents. It is not a direct infringement in the sense of § 9 s. 2 no. 1 PatG, as this rule does not cover the spread of information, according to the general principle that patent law does not aim at preventing the exchange of information.[29] That means that also providers of online platforms do not directly infringe patents.[30]

18 Schmoll *et al.*, 2015, p. 1046.
19 Benkard, *Patentgesetz*, 11th ed., Munich, Beck, 2015, § 11 recital 3.
20 M. Haedicke & H. Zech, 'Technische Erfindungen in einer vernetzten Welt. Das Internet als Herausforderung für das Patentrecht', GRUR-Beil., 2014, p. 56.
21 Schmoll *et al.*, 2015.
22 Schmoll *et al.*, 2015.
23 Schmoll *et al.*, 2015.
24 Benkard, 2015, § 11 recital 5.
25 See also R. Kraßer & C. Ann, *Patentrecht*, 7th ed., Munich, Beck, § 33 recital 245.
26 Benkard, 2015, § 11 recital 5.
27 See [2010] Düsseldorf Higher Regional Court, InstGE 7, 258 – Loom-Möbel.
28 Mengden, 2014, p. 80.
29 Haedicke & Zech, 2014, p. 56.
30 Similar Li *et al.*, 2014, p. 98.

However, the *distribution* of the CAD file may be an *indirect* infringement under § h10(1) PatG.[31] According to § 10(1) PatG, the patent shall further have the effect that in the absence of the patent proprietor's consent, any third party shall be prohibited from supplying or offering to supply, within the territorial scope of the PatG, persons other than those entitled to exploit the patented invention. This refers to means relating to an essential element of the invention, for use within the territorial scope of the PatG if the third party knows or if it is obvious from the circumstances that those means are suitable and intended for using that invention. Uploading a CAD file is *offering to supply*,[32] while forwarding it to specific recipients falls under the alternative term *supplying*. The most difficult issue is whether a CAD file is a means within the meaning of § 10(1) PatG. Traditionally, the term was interpreted as being limited to material things, such as hard copy versions of descriptions or construction plans.[33] The issue arises whether the term also covers the immaterial, *digital* CAD files. The mere wording speaks in favor of limiting the term to material things, as it has a material connotation, especially in the context of the prerequisite of supplying it and of the official heading of § 10 PatG ("prohibited *use* of means"). Furthermore, instead of opting for the term 'use', the legislator could have chosen the mere description that the use of the patented invention is facilitated or made possible. However, a teleological interpretation argues against limiting the scope of application to physical objects. With increasing digitalization, the classical concept of forwarding or sending construction plans etc. in printed format will increasingly be replaced by digital distribution as files. This allows for a more efficient checking of plans and even the simultaneous collaboration on a draft, e.g. by using cloud computing. With regard to 3D printing in particular, a virtual file is much more practical and dangerous from the rights holder's point of view than a hard copy whose transformation to the corresponding material object would be more complex.[34] CAD files may be forwarded to many other persons at the same time and therefore enable simultaneous mass infringements of IP rights, making it even more difficult to identify each direct infringer.[35] This makes claims (e.g. the cease and desist claim, § 139(1) s. 1 PatG) practically useless in many cases. But the rationale of § 10(1) PatG is to close protection gaps of § 9 PatG.[36] It is often easier and more cost-effective to trace indirect infringers.[37] Accordingly, § 10 PatG extends the protection to earlier stages, before a direct

31 Schmoll *et al.*, 2015, p. 1046.
32 Nordemann, Rüberg & Schaefer, 2015, p. 1269.
33 Schmoll *et al.*, 2015.
34 Nordemann, Rüberg & Schaefer, 2015, p. 1269.
35 Haedicke & Zech, 2014, p. 54.
36 C. Solmecke & S. Kocatepe, 'Der 3D-Druck – Ein neuer juristischer Zankapfel? Rechtliche Aspekte des 3D-Drucks mit besonderem Blick auf die Rechte am geistigen Eigentum und das Wettbewerbsrecht', *K&R*, Vol. 11, 2014, p. 780.
37 Benkard, 2015, § 10 recital 2.

infringement actually has taken place.[38] This is also relevant for files, leaving no room for privileging their digital distribution,[39] especially in times of rapidly advancing technologies.[40] Therefore, the term "means" in § 10(1) PatG should be interpreted in a contemporary understanding which covers files in general and CAD files in particular.[41] It remains to be seen whether jurisdiction will follow this understanding.[42]

Other prerequisites are also satisfied in cases of uploading or forwarding CAD files. The file *relates to an essential element of the invention*, as the means does not need to become an element of the produced object itself, to have a technical function in it nor to even be capable of having such a function.[43] This interpretation is not only supported by the wording which requires a *relationship with* the invention, but once again by teleological considerations. A contemporary interpretation requires a broad understanding which actually corresponds with the term measure, as files can (following their digital nature) never be an element of, nor have a technical function *in* a material object. Following this interpretation, a CAD file relates to an essential element of the specific invention, since it contains all parameters of the object and is the basis for the production of the latter, making it one necessary condition for the material existence of the object.[44]

Moreover, the third party *knows* that the CAD file is suitable and intended for the use of that invention if the potential use for the manufacture of the product in question by means of 3D printing is advertised,[45] e.g. by naming it accordingly. But regardless of this, it is sufficient if it is *obvious from the circumstances* that those means are suitable and intended for the use of the invention. As a CAD file allows for the reproduction of one specific product, it is a sufficient circumstance if the product in question is patented.[46]

However, if the CAD file is forwarded gratuitously and to related persons only, this may be allowed by § 11 no. 1 PatG.[47] In contrast, uploading it to the internet never falls under § 11 no. 1, as it leaves the private sphere.[48]

The *download* of an existing CAD file from the internet, e.g. from an online platform, is a mere preparatory action for the reproduction of a given product. However, if the

38 Benkard, 2015.
39 Mengden, 2014, p. 81.
40 Schmoll *et al.*, 2015, p. 1047.
41 P. Mes, *Patentgesetz*, 4th ed., Munich, Beck, 2015, § 10 recital 11.
42 Haedicke & Zech, 2014, p. 56.
43 Haedicke & Zech, 2014.
44 Schmoll *et al.*, 2015, p. 1047.
45 Schmoll *et al.*, 2015.
46 Schmoll *et al.*, 2015.
47 Nordemann, Rüberg & Schaefer, 2015, p. 1269.
48 Haedicke & Zech, 2014, p. 56.

download is followed by further dissemination of the file, this needs to be treated as the distribution of a self-made CAD file on a patented invention (see above).[49]

Providing an online platform for CAD files is not even an indirect infringement.[50] Even with a contemporary interpretation, a platform – as a mere infrastructure for the distribution of CAD files by others – is no means in the sense of § 10(1) PatG. Moreover, the platform itself does not relate to an essential element of the invention.[51] Also, it cannot usually be stated that the third party knows, nor that it is obvious from the circumstances, that the platform is suitable and intended for using that invention. There is an exception for platforms which are explicitly specialized in CAD files referring to products which fall under the subject-matter of patents and do not aim at distributing neutral CAD files.

3.3 *European Patent*

While the EPC contains some material rules on the European patent, its specific properties follow the national laws of the different states that the European patent was granted for (Art. 2(2) EPC).[52] Thus, the German part of a European patent is treated under German national law, making the results from above also valuable for it. However, other national laws differ from German law in some aspects, e.g. some do not have an exclusion which compares to § 11 no. 1 PatG,[53] which would potentially lead to different results for these parts.

3.4 *Unitary Patent*

According to Art. 5(3) EPUE-Reg, the scope of protection of a unitary patent and its exceptions follow law applied to Unitary patents in a participating Member State whose *national* law is applicable to a Unitary patent as an object of property in accordance with Art. 7 EPUE-Reg. This complicated referral includes, inter alia, Art. 25 et seq. UPCA which will be implemented into national law by a Member State participating in the Unitary patent system (see Art. 84(2) UPCA).[54] Art. 25 UPCA regulates the direct use of the patent,

49 Disagreeing T.R. Holbrook & L.S. Osborn, 'Digital Patent Infringement in an Era of 3D Printing', *Univ. of California, Davis*, Vol. 48, 2015, p. 1332.
50 Disagreeing D. Holznagel, 'Die Urteile in Tiffany v. eBay (USA) – zugleich zu aktuellen Problemen der europäischen Providerhaftung', *GRUR Int*, Vol. 59, 2010, p. 659.
51 Disagreeing Holbrook & Osborn, 2015.
52 Fitzner, Lutz & Bodewig, 2012, Einl. recital 57.
53 C. Blanke-Roeser, '3D-Druck und das Patentrecht in Europa – Die Grenzen des geltenden Rechts und des zukünftigen Einheitspatents sowie alternative Lösungsansätze', *GRUR*, Vol. 119, 2017, p. 472; Bechtold, 2016, p. 530.
54 M. Haedicke, 'Rechtsfindung, Rechtsfortbildung und Rechtskontrolle im Einheitlichen Patentsystem', *GRUR Int*, Vol. 62, 2013, p. 610.

whereas Art. 26 regulates the indirect use. Art. 27 UPCA defines exceptions from patent protection. These provisions are consistent with the German §§ 9, 10 and 11 PatG.[55] For instance, Art. 27 lit. a UPCA almost conforms with § 11 no. 1 PatG to the letter. At first glance, the previous results on German law could be directly applied to a Unitary patent. However, the new *Unified Patent Court* (UPC) will be responsible for the Unitary patent. The UPC will be a court common to the Contracting Member States (Art. 1 UPCA), with multinational instances (cf. Art. 8 et seq. UPCA), ensuring an autonomous interpretation of the provisions independent from national legal traditions of single Member States. Furthermore, as Art. 5(3) EPUE-Reg is an incorporating referral, Art. 25 et seq. UPCA needs to be interpreted in accordance with European Union law as mere international treaty,[56] even though it stands outside EU law itself. Therefore, decisions of the European Court of Justice (CJEU) that touch on specific terms must be respected.[57] Thus, on one hand, it is possible that the UPC will interpret Art. 25 et seq. UPCA as proposed above for German law. On the other hand, completely different interpretations are possible as well.[58]

4 LIMITS OF THE CURRENT LEGAL FRAMEWORK

The increasing distribution of 3D printing, especially among consumers, challenges patent law and illustrates its limits.[59] Firstly, the legal framework is limited due to many inventions not being protected by patent law at all, either due to the high prerequisites for patentability or because of the expiry of the term of the patent (20 years, see e.g. § 16 PatG).[60] The latter is of course no specific phenomenon of 3D printing. But as discussed above, even the use of a patented invention is often irrelevant under patent law. The underlying reason is that infringing actions are split up into several partial acts that are of no use to the patent and therefore not an infringement.[61] This is due to the complexity of the 3D printing "society" with its many participants, e.g. creators of CAD files, online platform providers or private households with 3D printers. But even the enforcement of existing legal claims (cf. § 139 PatG, resp. Art. 63(1) and Art. 68(1) UPCA) is hampered by *practical* factors:[62] First, tracing direct infringers in the digital world is difficult and

55 R. Romandini, R.M. Hilty & M. Lamping, 'Stellungnahme zum Referentenentwurf eines Gesetzes zur Anpassung patentrechtlicher Vorschriften auf Grund der europäischen Patentreform', *GRUR Int*, Vol. 65, 2016, p. 560.

56 Haedicke, 2013.

57 Haedicke, 2013.

58 Cf. Romandini, Hilty & Lamping, 2016, p. 560.

59 Similar Bechtold, 2016, p. 527.

60 F. Letzelter, 'Berührungspunkte der 3D-Druck-Technologie mit den IP-Rechten', 2016, available at: www.patente-stuttgart.de/downloads/tgs/2014/Letzelter_3DDruck.pdf (accessed 17 May 2018).

61 Haedicke & Zech, 2014, p. 54.

62 Bechtold, 2016, p. 528.

expensive,[63] especially given the rapid and cheap distribution of CAD files.[64] Secondly, many potentially relevant acts happen in the private area which is not observable.[65] Inspection proceedings in private households would be too complex, its legal possibilities limited.[66] Thirdly, even after having traced a single infringer, the legal enforcement is difficult, especially in case of European patents, as parallel lawsuits in different states may be necessary.[67]

With regard to patent law, 3D printing has had a revolutionary effect: it levels the threshold between the digital and material worlds which had been a protective factor for patents for a long time, even in times of increasing digitalization which have already confronted copyright law with mass infringements for around two decades.[68]

5 Possible Solutions

5.1 *Legal Solutions*

In order to meet the challenges imposed by the digital world, only supranational legal solutions, e.g. on the European level, make reasonable sense.[69] Two of them are discussed here.

One possible solution is the introduction of a *numerical limitation* to the provision in § 11 no. 1 PatG, resp. Art. 27 lit. a UPCA, following the example of § 53(1) s. 1 of the German Act on Copyright and Related Rights (Urheberrechtsgesetz, UrhG), which allows for "single copies of a work" only. This could be complemented by a temporal component in order to take the specifications of worn parts into account. The development of concrete numbers and case groups could be left to a judicial decision. However, tightening up the legal framework is not a sufficient answer to the already existent *practical* difficulties of § 11 no. 1 PatG, resp. Art. 27 lit. a UPCA.[70] Finally, general considerations speak against such an approach:[71] especially in case of worn parts, consumers may indeed frequently reproduce the product in question. However, this does not change the private and non-commercial nature of this use. If the existent prerequisites of § 11 no. 1 PatG, resp. Art.

63 Holznagel, 2010, p. 659.
64 Davis Doherty, 'Downloading Infringement: Patent Law as a Roadblock to the 3D Printing Revolution', *Harv. J.L. & Tech.*, Vol. 26, 2012, p. 354.
65 Haedicke & Zech, 2014, p. 57.
66 Haedicke & Zech, 2014.
67 Bechtold, 2016, p. 527.
68 B. Depoorter, 'Intellectual Property Infringements & 3D Printing: Decentralized Piracy', *Hastings L.J.*, Vol. 65, 2014, p. 1497.
69 Schulze & Staudenmeier, 2015, p. 216.
70 Haedicke & Zech, 2014, p. 57.
71 Haedicke & Zech, 2014.

27 lit. a UPCA are interpreted contemporarily, the rule can sufficiently balance the interests of rights holders and the public, which is the legislator's initial position that must be respected.[72] Thus, this provision is an example of this general objective of patent law. Patents, as industrial property rights, aim at protecting technical inventions in commercial environments, not at constraining the private, non-commercial area.[73]

Several scholars have discussed an *extension of the liability of providers* of online platforms for CAD files.[74] Specific jurisdiction on that matter is still lacking[75] but the issue compares to the liability of providers of file sharing services which has been relevant, inter alia, under copyright and trademark law for many years.[76] Under German law, provider liability derives from the general § 1004 of German Civil Code (Bürgerliches Gesetzbuch, BGB) or the universal safety obligation.[77] The results of that discussion can be transferred to this context.[78] A patent infringement by a third party is a predicate offence which can form the basis of liability of the provider of the online platform where the CAD file was downloaded from.[79] Provider liability lies in an area of tension between the Directive 2004/48/EC on the enforcement of intellectual property rights (Enforcement Directive) and the Directive 2000/31/EC on certain legal aspects of information society services, particularly electronic commerce, in the Internal Market (E-Commerce Directive).[80] While the Enforcement Directive aims at facilitating the direct enforcement of claims against intermediaries, the E-Commerce Directive privileges new business models in the internet.[81] According to that, Art. 14 et seq. of the E-Commerce Directive restricts liability of platform providers.[82] Art. 14 of the E-Commerce Directive was passed into German law by § 10 of the German Telemedia Act (Telemediengesetz, TMG).[83] Providers of online platforms fall under the scope of application of this provision, as they store content for others. According to § 10 s. 1 TMG, service providers shall not be responsible for the information of third parties which they store for a recipient of a service, as long as they have no knowledge of illegal activity or information and, with regards to claims for damages, are not aware of any facts or circumstances from which illegal activity or information is apparent (no. 1). Service providers will not be held responsible if, upon obtaining such knowledge, they

72 Haedicke & Zech, 2014.
73 Benkard, 2015, § 11 recital 2.
74 M. Leistner, 'Störerhaftung und mittelbare Schutzrechtsverletzung', *GRUR-Beil.*, 2010, p. 14.
75 Solmecke & Kocatepe, 2014, p. 783.
76 Haedicke & Zech, 2014.
77 Haedicke & Zech, 2014.
78 Haedicke & Zech, 2014, p. 57.
79 Haedicke & Zech, 2014.
80 Ansgar Ohly, 'Die Verantwortlichkeit von Intermediären', *ZUM*, Vol. 59, 2015, p. 310.
81 Ohly, 2015, p. 310.
82 Ohly, 2015.
83 W. Joecks & K. Miebach (eds), *Münchener Kommentar zum Strafgesetzbuch II*, 2nd ed., Munich, Beck, TMG, § 10 recital 2.

have acted expeditiously to remove the information or to disable access to it (no. 2). Service providers shall not be responsible for their own information which they keep ready for use, in accordance with general legislation, and are not required to monitor the information stored by them or to search for circumstances indicating illegal activity (§ 7(1), (2) s. 1 TMG). But, once rights holders have *made them aware* of a patent infringing file that was uploaded to their platform, providers need to remove it or to disable access to it if they want to avoid liability, as stated in the above-mentioned § 10 s. 1 no. 2 TMG.[84] Uploading infringing CAD files as an indirect patent infringement is sufficient on the basis of a contemporary interpretation, since § 10 s. 1 TMG requires only "illegal activity". § 10 s. 1 TMG follows the example of the *notice and take down* model under US law.[85] However, neither the E-Commerce Directive nor the TMG provide details on the necessary form and content of such a notice to the provider – unlike the copyright-specific § 512(c) U.S. Copyright Act.[86] Furthermore, the exact relationship between provider liability and §§ 7 to 10 TMG (resp. the underlying Arts. 12 to 15 of E-Commerce Directive) is unclear, as is the question of which claims shall be covered (e.g. only claims for damages or also injunctive relief[87]).[88] This should generally be decided by the national or EU legislator, as it has already been discussed for other fields of IP law,[89] in order to increase legal certainty.[90] However, provider liability should not be extended.[91] In an increasingly digitalized environment, intermediaries such as online platform providers play an important role in the development of new ways to manufacture and distribute.[92] Society, as well as rights holders, may benefit from this in the future,[93] and as a result, they should not be hampered. Therefore, the classical conflict of interests which underlies patent law in particular, and IP law in general, should not be unilaterally unbalanced to the benefit of rights owners.[94]

3D printing overcomes traditional borders between the digital and the material worlds.[95] This confronts patent law with problems that have already been well-known to other fields of IP law such as copyright law, for many years.[96] Nevertheless, the current legal framework

84 Solmecke & Kocatepe, 2014, p. 783.

85 Ohly, 2015.

86 D. Holznagel, 'Melde- und Abhilfeverfahren zur Beanstandung rechtswidrig gehosteter Inhalte nach europäischem und deutschem Recht im Vergleich zu gesetzlich geregelten notice and take-down-Verfahren', *GRUR Int*, Vol. 63, 2014, p. 106.

87 G. Nolte & J. Wimmers, 'Wer stört? Gedanken zur Haftung von Intermediären im Internet. Von praktischer Konkordanz, richtigen Antworten und offenen Fragen', *GRUR-Beil.*, 2014, p. 60.

88 Ohly, 2015, p. 312.

89 Holznagel, 2014.

90 Ohly, 2015, p. 313.

91 Holznagel, 2010, p. 659.

92 Bechtold, 2016, p. 530.

93 Ohly, 2015, p. 319.

94 Bechtold, 2016, p. 530.

95 Haedicke & Zech, 2014, p. 52.

96 Bechtold, 2016.

is sufficient to meet these challenges appropriately.[97] Tightening the legal framework is therefore not necessary and should be avoided.[98] Alternatively, a contemporary interpretation of the current provisions is recommended.[99]

5.2 *Practical Measures for Rights Holders*

Rights holders should take more responsibility for the enforcement of their own interests and also think outside the box of (patent) law.

Patent holders should endeavor to have their products and construction plans additionally protected by other IP laws, such as trademark, design and copyright laws[100] whose differing properties may be advantageous in the individual case. For instance, if a construction plan is protected by copyright law, the reproduction and distribution of it in the form of CAD files is prohibited to others without permission.[101] However, also for other IP laws, protection is limited by legal exceptions (e.g. the above-mentioned § 53(1) s. 1 UrhG) and by similar practical factors that hamper enforcement in times of digitalization.[102]

Rights holders should therefore use extra-legal, practical measures, ranging from technical protection measures to a radical change of perspective towards a collaboration with private users.[103] The main example for technical protection measures are digital rights management (DRM) systems, which are common in copyright law.[104] Several methods have already been developed, e.g. one which checks whether the user is entitled to produce the object before the 3D printing process starts.[105] But experience has proven technical protective measures inefficient, as most of them can be bypassed.[106] Generally speaking, using these measures, like tightening the legal framework, is another attempt at fighting the technical developments which will ultimately fail.

Instead, a change of perspective is the preferable answer to the challenges of 3D printing. Rights owners should embrace the technical developments and the increasing participation of third parties in the manufacture of their products as a chance. This would also be a welcome development from a customers' point of view. *Bechtold* proposed some measures

97 Blanke-Roeser, 2017, p. 474; Haedicke & Zech, 2014, p. 57.
98 Haedicke & Zech, 2014, p. 57.
99 Solmecke & Kocatepe, 2014, p. 783.
100 Bechtold, 2016, p. 528.
101 See also Mengden, 2014, p. 83.
102 Blanke-Roeser, 2017, p. 473; Bechtold, 2016, p. 532.
103 Bechtold, 2016, p. 532.
104 Bechtold, 2016, p. 528.
105 S. Krempl, 'US-Patent schützt DRM-System für 3D-Druck', 2014, available at: www.heise.de/newsticker/meldung/US-Patent-schuetzt-DRM-System-fuer-3D-Druck-1729236.html (accessed 17 May 2018).
106 D.R. Desai & G.N. Magliocca, 'Patents, Meet Napster: 3D Printing and the Digitization of Things', *Georgetown L.J.*, Vol. 102, 2014, p. 1719.

recently, three of which shall be named here, as being fruitful concepts.[107] Firstly, patent holders could become more active in selling raw material for printing to customers or 3D printing shops, e.g. powder for specific products.[108] Secondly, they should even outsource a part of their production to professional 3D printing shops or services in the particular customer's neighborhood.[109] Finally, this could even be connected with embracing the creativity of end users. They could participate in the design of the end product which would benefit both sides and even increase customer loyalty towards particular companies.[110] In the long run, it is likely that *flat rate* models will spread. In such models, customers legally download CAD files from databases run by providers who cooperate with rights holders.[111] If the price is moderate, users may be less incited to illegal downloads of CAD files, as this is always connected with the risks of both getting caught, and of accidentally downloading malware.[112] Legal suppliers may exist side by side with patent infringing suppliers.[113]

6 Conclusion

The distribution of 3D printing provides a challenge for patent law. However, this does not question the justification for its existence.[114] Contrarily, rights owners must embrace technical developments. An interaction of patent protection and new business models has the potential to balance the conflicting interests of rights owners and society and lead to new cooperations,[115] and is therefore a great opportunity for innovation in the future. On that basis, 3D printing is also an interesting tool for future collaborations even in the social and medical sectors, given the various possibilities for sharing. However, it remains to be seen in which technologies 3D printing will really be established and to which extent it will be used for production of patent-relevant products in private households.

107 See Bechtold, 2016, p. 531 (in case of 3D printers as products).
108 Bechtold, 2016.
109 Schulze & Staudenmeier, 2015, p. 216.
110 Bechtold, 2016, p. 531.
111 See e.g. D. Sher, 'Authentise Gives Computer Vision to 3D Printers', 2016, available at: https://3dprintingindustry.com/news/authentise-to-deliver-better-computer-vision-3d-printer-39215 (accessed 17 May 2018).
112 Desai & Magliocca, 2014, p. 1719.
113 M.A. Lemley, 'IP in a World Without Scarcity', *NYU L.J.*, Vol. 90, 2015, p. 489.
114 Lemley, 2015, p. 465.
115 Blanke-Roeser, 2017, p. 475; Bechtold, 2016, p. 534.

Bibliography

Bechtold, S., '3D Printing, Intellectual Property and Innovation Policy', *IIC*, Vol. 47, 2016, pp. 517-536.

Blanke-Roeser, C., '3D-Druck und das Patentrecht in Europa – Die Grenzen des geltenden Rechts und des zukünftigen Einheitspatents sowie alternative Lösungsansätze', *GRUR*, Vol. 119, pp. 467-475.

Bose, S., Vahabzadeh, S. & Bandyopadhyay, A., 'Bone Tissue Engineering Using 3D Printing', *Materials Today*, Vol. 16, 2013, pp. 496-504.

Depoorter, B., 'Intellectual Property Infringements & 3D Printing: Decentralized Piracy', *Hastings L.J.*, Vol. 65, 2014, pp. 1483-1504.

Desai, D.R. & Magliocca, G.N., 'Patents, Meet Napster: 3D Printing and the Digitization of Things', *Georgetown L.J.*, Vol. 102, 2014, pp. 1690-1720.

Doherty, D., 'Downloading Infringement: Patent Law as a Roadblock to the 3D Printing Revolution', *Harv J.L. & Tech.*, Vol. 26, 2012, pp. 353-373.

Fitzner, U., R. Lutz & T. Bodewig, *Patentrechtskommentar. PatG, GebrMG, IntPatÜG, PCT und EPÜ mit Nebenvorschriften*, 4th ed., Munich, Beck, 2012.

Haedicke, M. & Zech, H., 'Technische Erfindungen in einer vernetzten Welt. Das Internet als Herausforderung für das Patentrecht', *GRUR-Beil.*, 2014, pp. 52-57.

Haedicke, M., 'Rechtsfindung, Rechtsfortbildung und Rechtskontrolle im Einheitlichen Patentsystem', *GRUR Int*, Vol. 62, 2013, pp. 609-617.

Holbrook, T.R. & Osborn, L.S., 'Digital Patent Infringement in an Era of 3D Printing', *Univ of California, Davis*, Vol. 48, 2015, pp. 1319-1385.

Holznagel, D., 'Melde- und Abhilfeverfahren zur Beanstandung rechtswidrig gehosteter Inhalte nach europäischem und deutschem Recht im Vergleich zu gesetzlich geregelten notice and take-down-Verfahren', *GRUR Int*, Vol. 63, 2014, pp. 105-113.

Holznagel, D., 'Die Urteile in Tiffany v. eBay (USA) – zugleich zu aktuellen Problemen der europäischen Providerhaftung', *GRUR Int*, Vol. 59, 2010, pp. 654-663.

Joecks, W. & Miebach, K., (eds), *Münchener Kommentar zum Strafgesetzbuch: StGB, Band 7: Nebenstrafrecht II. Strafvorschriften aus: MarkenG, UrhG, UWG, AO, SchwarzArbG, AÜG, BetrVG, AktG, AWG, BauFordSiG, BörsG, DepotG, GenG, GewO, GmbHG, HGB, InsO, KWG, WpHG, TKG, TMG*, 2nd ed., Munich, Beck, 2015.

Kraßer, R. & Ann, C., *Patentrecht. Ein Lehr- und Handbuch zum deutschen Patent- und Gebrauchsmusterrecht, Europäischen und Internationalen Patentrecht*, 7th ed., Munich, Beck, 2016.

Krempl, S., 'US-Patent schützt DRM-System für 3D-Druck', 2014, available at: www.heise.de/newsticker/meldung/US-Patent-schuetzt-DRM-System-fuer-3D-Druck-1729236.html (accessed 17 May 2018).

Leistner, M., 'Störerhaftung und mittelbare Schutzrechtsverletzung', *GRUR-Beil.*, 2010, pp. 1-32.

Lemley, M.A., 'IP in a World Without Scarcity', *NYU L.J.*, Vol. 90, 2015, pp. 460-515.

Letzelter, F., 'Berührungspunkte der 3D-Druck-Technologie mit den IP-Rechten', 2016, available at: www.patente-stuttgart.de/downloads/tgs/2014/Letzelter_3DDruck.pdf (accessed 17 May 2018).

Li, P. *et al.*, 'Intellectual Property and 3D Printing: a Case Study on 3D Chocolate Printing', *GRUR Int*, Vol. 64, 2014, pp. 97-104.

Mengden, M., '3D-Druck – Droht eine „Urheberrechtskrise 2.0"? Schutzumfang und drohende Rechtsverletzungen auf dem Prüfstand', *MMR*, Vol. 17, 2014, pp. 79-85.

Mes, P., *Patentgesetz, Gebrauchsmustergesetz: PatG, GebrMG. Kommentar*, 4th ed., Munich, Beck, 2015.

Nolte, G. & Wimmers, J., 'Wer stört? Gedanken zur Haftung von Intermediären im Internet. Von praktischer Konkordanz, richtigen Antworten und offenen Fragen', *GRUR-Beil.*, 2014, pp. 58-69.

Nordemann, J.B., Rüberg, M. & Schaefer, M., '3D-Druck als Herausforderung für die Immaterialgüterrechte', *NJW*, Vol. 68, 2015, pp. 1265-1271.

Ohly, 'Die Verantwortlichkeit von Intermediären', *ZUM*, Vol. 59, 2015, pp. 308-318.

Romandini, R., Hilty R.M., & Lamping, M., 'Stellungnahme zum Referentenentwurf eines Gesetzes zur Anpassung patentrechtlicher Vorschriften auf Grund der europäischen Patentreform', *GRUR Int*, Vol. 65, 2016, pp. 554-560.

Schmoll *et al.*, 'Dreidimensionales Drucken und die vier Dimensionen des Immaterialgüterrechts. Ein Überblick über Fragestellungen des Urheber-, Design-, Patent- und Markenrechts beim 3D-Druck', *GRUR*, Vol. 117, 2015, pp. 1041-1050.

Schulze, R. & Staudenmeier, D., 'Digital Revolution: Challenges for Contract Law in Practice', *EuCML*, Vol. 4, 2015, pp. 215-216.

Sher, D., 'Authentise Gives Computer Vision to 3D Printers', 2016, available at: https://3dprintingindustry.com/news/authentise-to-deliver-better-computer-vision-3d-printer-39215 (accessed 17 May 2018).

Solmecke C. & Kocatepe S., 'Der 3D-Druck – Ein neuer juristischer Zankapfel? Rechtliche Aspekte des 3D-Drucks mit besonderem Blick auf die Rechte am geistigen Eigentum und das Wettbewerbsrecht', K&R, Vol. 11, 2014, pp. 778-783.

Teschemacher, R., 'Das Einheitspatent – Zu Risiken und Nebenwirkungen fragen Sie Ihren Anwalt', *Mitt.*, Vol. 104, 2013, pp. 153-161.

Zukas, V. & Zukas, V.A., *An Introduction to 3D Printing*, Sarasota (FL), First Edition Design Publishing, 2015.

11 Whose Freedom Is It Anyway?

Restrictions on In Rem Security as Obstacles to the Internal Market

Flavius Alexandru Boar[*]

1 Negative Harmonization of In Rem Securities

European market integration is frequently invoked in support of prospective common regulations aimed at approximating internal law. These imperatives however also express themselves through what is considered 'negative harmonization' of national legislations.[1] This concept outlines a rather abstract duty pending upon the Member States of the former Communities and actual European Union ('EU'). Its content is drawn from a number of principles including mutual recognition or country of origin inspired by the *Cassis de Dijon* ruling.[2] All of these rely upon the economic freedoms enshrined in the Treaty on the Functioning of the European Union ('TFEU').[3] Negative harmonization through direct effect of the relevant prescriptions indeed requires Member States to modify by themselves their legislation or behaviour accordingly, without further European intervention.[4] The economic impact of any internal regulation provides legal arguments for how and when to apply the principles of the internal market. Interestingly, this has spurred steady academic inquiries into the impact of these principles and duties on the seemingly sheltered legal framework of *in rem* security.[5] These comprehensively argued ideas refer to the dogmatic

---

* PhD Researcher at Collège Juridique Franco-Roumain in Bucarest.

1 B. Akkermans, 'Property Law and the Internal Market', *in* S. van Erp, A. Salomons & B. Akkermans (Eds.), *The Future of European Property Law*, München, SELP, 2012, p. 202; H. Spamann, 'Choice of Law in a Federal System and an Internal Market' (October 2001) Jean Monnet Working Paper No. 8/01, retrieved from: https://ssrn.com/abstract=729623 (last accessed 19 October 2017), p. 24.

2 Judgment of 20 February 1979 in *Case 120/78, Rewe-Zentral AG v. Bundesmonopolverwaltung für Branntwein* [1979] ECR-00649, Rec. 14. The principle of mutual recognition was only somewhat recently designated as such by the ECJ. *See, e.g.*, Judgment of 10 February 2009 in *Case C-110/05, Commission v. Italian Republic* [2009] ECR I-00519, Rec. 34.

3 B. Akkermans & E. Ramaekers, 'Free Movement of Goods and Property Law' (May 28, 2011) Maastricht European Private Law Institute Working Paper No. 2011/26, retrieved from: https://ssrn.com/abstract=1617182 (last accessed 20 October 2017), pp. 17-18.

4 M. Blanquet, 'Effet direct du droit communautaire', *in Répertoire de droit européen Dalloz*, § 37; F. Picod, 'Libre circulation des capitaux et des moyens de paiement', *in J. Cl. Europe Traité fasc. 890*, § 11; L. Idot, 'L'incidence de l'ordre communautaire sur le droit international privé', *LPA*, No. 248, 2002, p. 27, § 19.

5 *See, e.g.*, B. Akkermans, *The Principle of Numerus Clausus in European Property Law*, Cambridge, Intersentia, 2008, retrieved from: http://digitalarchive.maastrichtuniversity.nl/fedora/get/guid:9388e80c-c577-4c74-a99b-0e27439bd792/ASSET1 (last accessed 22 October 2017), pp. 542-546; P. von Wilmowsky, *Europäisches*

approach to market integration and thus exceed comparative perspectives on different legal systems. As such, they themselves are worth looking at in more detail.

Still, some have partially denied applying principles of market integration in private law.[6] But European imperatives do not differentiate following such flexible and diverse internal classifications as those setting apart public and private law.[7] It became obvious with the case law deemed to have approached mutual recognition of names acquired and companies established in other Member States.[8] Additionally, *in rem* securities became concerned by such inquiries because of their mainly imperative regulatory environment. The consequence would be that, save for adequate justifications, members states not recognizing security rights stemming from another country violate European law in manners equivalent to quantitative restrictions.[9] Contract law, in contrast to this, offers more freedom of choice as it already allows parties to shape agreements according to their needs. Hence, the need to rely on supranational principles for adapting transaction structures is considerably diminished.[10]

It is not simply a question of adapting foreign security instruments in order to fit them within the regulatory environment of another country. This only transforms them into

---

Kreditsicherungsrecht. Sachenrecht und Insolvenzrecht unter dem EG-Vertrag, Tübingen, BtrIPR 60, Mohr Siebeck, 1996, pp. 77-93; Akkermans & Ramaekers, 2011; E.-M. Kieninger, *Mobiliarsicherheiten im Europäischen Binnenmarkt - Zum Einfluss der Warenverkehrsfreiheit auf das nationale internationale Sachenrecht der Mitgliedstaaten*, Baden-Baden, Nomos, 1996, pp. 95-104; E.-M. Kieninger, 'European Regulation of Security Rights', *in* U. Drobnig, H.J. Snijders & E.-J. Zippro (Eds.), *Divergences in Property Law. An Obstacle to the Internal Market?*, München, Sellier, 2006, pp. 165-174; J. W. Rutgers, *International Reservation of Title Clauses - A Study of Dutch, French and German Private International Law in the Light of European Law*, The Hague/Cambridge, TMC Asser Press/Kluwer Law International, 1999, pp. 167-206; P. Sparkes, *European Land Law*, Oxford, Hart Publishing, 2007, pp. 95-103.

6 V. Heuzé, 'De la compétence de la loi du pays d'origine en matière contractuelle ou l'anti-droit européen', *in Le droit international privé: esprit et méthodes. Mélanges en l'honneur de Paul Lagarde*, Paris, Dalloz, 2005, pp. 412-414; H. M. Watt, 'Integration and Diversity: The Conflict of Laws as a Regulatory Tool', *in* F. Cafaggi (Ed.), *The Institutional Framework of European Private Law*, Oxford, OUP, 2006, pp. 108-109.

7 Idot, 2002, § 11; M. Audit, 'Régulation du marché intérieur et libre circulation des lois', *JDI*, No. 4, 2006, doctr. 15, § 36.

8 C. Kohler, 'La reconnaissance de situations juridiques dans l'Union Européenne: le cas du nom patronymique', *in* P. Lagarde (Ed.), *La reconnaissance des situations en droit international privé. Actes du colloque international de la Haye du 18 janvier 2013*, Paris, A. Pedone, 2013, p. 69; M. Fallon, 'Libertés communautaires et règles de conflit de lois', *in* A. Fuchs, H. M. Watt & E. Pataut (Eds.), *Les conflits de lois et le système juridique communautaire*, Paris, Dalloz, 2004, § 14; Ch. Schmid, 'Options under EU Law for the Implementation of a Eurohypothec', *in* A. Drewicz-Tułodziecka (Ed.), *Basic Guidelines for a Eurohypothek. Outcome of the Eurohypothec workshop*, Warsaw, Mortgage Credit Foundation, 2005, pp. 61-62; L. Vogel, *Droit européen des affaires*, Paris, Dalloz, 2013, § 79; T. Ballarino, 'Les règles de conflit sur les sociétés commerciales à l'épreuve du droit communautaire d'établissement. Remarques sur deux arrêts récents de la Cour de justice des Communautés européennes', *Rev. Crit. DIP*, 2003, p. 373.

9 *See, e.g.*, J. Basedow, 'Das kollisionsrechtliche Gehalt der Produktfreiheiten im europäischen Binnenmarkt: favor offerentis', *RabelsZ*, No. 59, 1995, p. 45; L. Radicati di Brozolo, 'L'influence sur les conflits de lois des principes de droit communautaire en matière de liberté de circulation', *Rev. Crit. DIP*, 1993, p. 401, § 6.

10 M. Wolf, 'Privates Bankvertragsrecht im EG-Binnenmarkt. Auswirkungen der II. EG-Bankrechts-Richtlinie auf privatrechtliche Bankgeschäfte', *WM Wirtschafts- und Bankrecht*, 1990, p. 1945.

their closest local equivalent.[11] In addition, mutual reconnaissance in European law boldly requires not applying national laws that annul or deprive such foreign techniques of their initial effectiveness and intended functioning.[12] Generally speaking, it amounts indeed to recognition of norms.[13] More precisely, it concerns the recognition of the internal legal framework for goods, services and capital.[14] So by the beginning of the 1990s, scholars actually deduced similar duties for just about any instrument of private law needed in intracommunity economic activities.[15] As to security techniques, mutual reconnaissance came to be considered particularly inevitable for the uniform supply of financial services within the Union.[16] In term, this was thought to entail some kind of '*Delaware effect*', as with companies nowadays registered in Member States where the conditions are most flexible.[17] Internal operators may subsequently be inclined to invoke reverse discrimination and ask their respective legislators for the benefit of an identical regime.[18] Such process is then bound to repeat itself unabated until the EU eventually steps in with uniform regulations.[19] This paper aims to verify that any conclusion in this respect assumes complex long-term economic predictions.

Research in this field was mainly aimed at movable *in rem* security rights, that is, established on circulating assets.[20] Indeed, the more traditional freedoms of movement come into play here.[21] And it is worth noting that although European Court of Justice ('ECJ') case law has been rather reserved on this matter, a handful of texts in recent direc-

11 Y. Flour, *L'effet des contrats à l'égard des tiers en droit international privé* (Ph. D. thesis at Université Paris 2 Panthéon-Assas), 1977, § 127-128; U. Drobnig, 'Recognition and Adaptation of Foreign Security Rights', *in* U. Drobnig, H.J. Snijders & E.-J. Zippro (Eds.), *Divergences in Property Law. An Obstacle to the Internal Market?*, München, Sellier, 2006, pp. 106-112; Akkermans & Ramaekers, 2011, pp. 20-21.

12 M. Polak, 'Recognition, Enforcement and Transformation of Foreign Proprietary Rights – a handful of observations and suggestions', *in* U. Drobnig, H.J. Snijders & E.-J. Zippro (Eds.), *Divergences in Property Law. An Obstacle to the Internal Market?*, München, Sellier, 2006, p. 128; Sergio Nasarre-Aznar, 'The need for the integration of the mortgage market in Europe', *in* S. van Erp, A. Salomons & B. Akkermans (Eds.), *The Future of European Property Law*, München, SELP, 2012, p. 92; Schmid, 2005, pp. 63-64.

13 P. Mayer, 'La reconnaissance: notions et méthodes', *in* P. Lagarde (Ed.), *La reconnaissance des situations en droit international privé. Actes du colloque international de la Haye du 18 janvier 2013*, Paris, A. Pedone, 2013, pp. 27-28.

14 Akkermans & Ramaekers, 2011, pp. 17-18; Audit, 2006, § 11-12 thus considers mutual recognition to bring about a "free movement of national laws".

15 "Anerkennung der dienstleistungsspezifischen zivilrechtlichen Institute": Wolf, 1990, p. 1944; B. Sousi-Roubi, 'La Convention de Rome et la loi applicable aux contrats bancaires', *D.*, 1993, p. 183.

16 Radicati di Brozolo, 1993, § 3; Wolf, 1990, p. 1943.

17 H.J. Sonnenberger, 'Etat de droit, construction européenne et droit des sociétés', *Rev. Crit. DIP*, 2013, p. 101.

18 Schmid, 2005, pp. 61-62; Heuzé, 2005, p. 401; Spamann, 2001, p. 12; Mayer, 2013, p. 564; Radicati di Brozolo, 1993, § 7; P. C. de Sousa, *The European Fundamental Freedoms. A contextual approach*, Oxford, OUP, 2015, p. 121.

19 Sonnenberger, 2005; Polak, 2006, pp. 117-130; O. Cachard, *Droit international privé*, 4th ed., Bruxelles, Larcier, 2015, § 356.

20 Kieninger, 1996, pp. 95-104.

21 Akkermans, 2012, pp. 218-222.

tives actually contain provisions relevant to movable securities. Duties of principle were indeed imposed to validate the retention of ownership or title transfer financial collateral agreements for security purposes.[22] Additionally however, there is no conclusive argument against an identical reasoning for immovables, as the same principles of market integration apply to both scenarios. Besides cases pertaining to the provision of financial services by the secured party, investments in real estate are generally taken into consideration here as expressions of capital movements.[23] This was explored in detail with the 'euro mortgage' project, a prospective instrument based on the German *Grundschuld*.[24] And it has to be said that any security bestowed upon movables is just as incorporeal and incapable of physical border crossing as their immovable counterparts. The Commission itself once had mutual recognition in mind for a bank "operating mortgage credit [...] in accordance with techniques specifically authorized within its home Member State".[25] Some have actually considered this a means for implementing the 'euro mortgage'.[26] Others at least came to question the legitimacy of internal norms opposing mutual recognition in this respect.[27] It is true that mobile conflict of laws remains objectively impossible for matters concerning real estate. Moreover, some Member States require local notaries to authenticate agreements relative to rights on immovables placed within their territories.[28] As such, it

22 Art. 9 of EP and Council Directive 2011/7 of 16 February 2011 on combating late payment in commercial transactions, OJ 2011 L 48/1 and Art. 6 of EP and Council Directive 2002/47 of 6 June 2002 on financial collateral agreements OJ 2002 L 168/43.

23 Judgment of 16 March 1999 in *Case C-222/97, Manfred Trummer and Peter Mayer* [1999] ECR I-01661, Rec. 24 and Judgment of 11 January 2001 in *Case C-464/98, Westdeutsche Landesbank Girozentrale v. Friedrich Stefan* [2001] ECR I-00173, Rec. 19; Von Wilmowsky, 1996, pp. 82-86; Akkermans, 2008, p. 537; Akkermans, 2012, p. 222; Sjef van Erp, 'European and National Property Law: Osmosis or Growing Antagonism?' (June 23, 2007) Maastricht University Faculty of Law Working Paper, retrieved from: https://ssrn.com/abstract=995979 (last accessed 26 January 2018), pp. 7-8.

24 O. Stöcker, 'The Eurohypothec', *in* S. van Erp, A. Salomons & B. Akkermans (Eds.), *The Future of European Property Law*, München, SELP, 2012, pp. 65-78; H. G. Wehrens, 'Real security regarding immovable objects – Reflections on a Euro-Mortgage', *in* A. Hartkamp *et al.* (Eds.), *Towards a European Civil Code*, 3rd ed., Nijmegen, Kluwer Law International, 2004, pp. 769-783; Nasarre-Aznar, 2012, pp. 79-122; Schmid, 2005, pp. 61-68.

25 Art. 4 of the Proposal for a Council Directive COM (84) 730 final on the freedom of establishment and the free supply of services in the field of mortgage credit.

26 Wolf, 1990, p. 1942; Stöcker, 2012, p. 72; Nasarre-Aznar, 2012, p. 92; Schmid, 2005, pp. 61-62.

27 *See, e.g.*, Akkermans, 2008, pp. 536-537; G. Wunsch, *Möglichkeiten und Grenzen eines europäischen Hypothekarkredits. Problemanalyse und Lösungswege für die Schaffung eines Binnenmarktes für Grundpfandrechte unter Berücksichtigung des deutschen, englischen, schwedischen und spanischen Rechts*, Bielefeld, Gieseking, 2009, pp. 351-352; Akkermans, 2012, p. 33: "an interesting question can therefore be why a financial service provider should be forced to create a, from its perspective, foreign security right in order to grant a loan to a national, just because the immovable object is situated in another Member State?"; J. Basedow, 'La reconnaissance des situations juridiques en droit des affaires (sociétés et sûretés)', *in* P. Lagarde (Ed.), *La reconnaissance des situations en droit international privé. Actes du colloque international de la Haye du 18 janvier 2013*, Paris, A. Pedone, 2013, p. 226 denies however mutual recognition in the field of immovables.

28 *See, e.g.*, Arts. 710-1 al. 1 and 2.417 of the French Civil Code. Such regulations are often accused of infringing by themselves upon market integration: Commission, *The Integration of the EU Mortgage Credit*

is hard to imagine the notary would gamble on the imperatives of market integration and ignore prohibitions imposed by the relevant substantive law. But all this doesn't intrinsically contradict mutual recognition. It only requires precisely defining the interplay between mutual recognition and private international law in this field.

2 Requirement of Trade Restrictions within Security Law

Mutual recognition of *in rem* security is sometimes inferred from a generic duty to limit the *lex rei sitae* conflict rule, where its consequences are hindering trade.[29] Clearly, this covers both movable and immovable assets. But conflict rules by themselves can hardly be held responsible for the substantive outcome of a given case.[30] Any abstract connecting factor in their structure could in theory pinpoint to every other country. Its particular impact over economic relations thus becomes totally unpredictable. In any case, the freedoms of circulation certainly do not imply a country of origin principle, designating the laws of any Member State from which specific goods, products or services come. Clearly, locating the country of origin for capital movements or service supply can sometimes prove rather difficult.[31] And substantive laws of the home Member State have occasionally

Markets (Report by the Forum Group on Mortgage Credit), retrieved from: http://ec.europa.eu/internal_market/finservices-retail/docs/home-loans/2004-report-integration_en.pdf (last accessed 20 October 2017), recommendation No. 34; P. Callé *et al.*, 'Pour la reconnaissance des actes authentiques au sein de l'espace de liberté, de sécurité et de justice', *LPA*, No. 68, 2012, p. 6; E. Pataut, 'La reconnaissance des actes publics dans les règlements européens en droit international privé', *in* P. Lagarde (Ed.), *La reconnaissance des situations en droit international privé. Actes du colloque international de la Haye du 18 janvier 2013*, Paris, A. Pedone, 2013. On the rationale behind these rules, see however L. Aynès & P. Crocq, *Les sûretés. La publicité foncière*, 8th ed., Paris, L.G.D.J., 2014, § 636. There is indeed little room for mutual recognition or similar imperatives here, because authentication procedures for immovable conveyancing differ greatly between Member States.

29 Akkermans, 2008, p. 542; Von Wilmowsky, 1996, pp. 94-152; B. Akkermans & E. Ramaekers, 'Lex Rei Sitae in Perspective: National Developments of a Common Rule?' (May 21, 2012) Maastricht European Private Law Institute Working Paper No. 2012/14, retrieved from: http://ssrn.com/abstract=2063494 (last accessed 20 October 2017); Radicati di Brozolo, 1993, § 2; B. Akkermans, 'The Use of the Functional Method in European Union Property Law' (March 5, 2013) Maastricht European Private Law Institute Working Paper No. 2013/7, retrieved from: https://ssrn.com/abstract=2228641 (last accessed 20 October 2017), pp. 18-19 thus noting the "free movement" of property rights in the European Union. More generally for the conflict between private international law and the freedoms in the TFEU, *see* R. Savatier, 'Le Marché commun au regard du droit international privé', *Rev. Crit. DIP*, 1959, pp. 237-258; Sousi-Roubi, 1993; Basedow, 1995, p. 5; L. Gannagé, 'Le droit international privé à l'épreuve de la hiérarchie des normes. L'exemple du droit de la famille', *Rev. Crit. DIP*, 2001, p. 1.

30 Idot, 2002, § 45 and specifically for securities, J. W. Rutgers, 'Secured Credit and the Internal Market: The Fundamental Freedoms and the EU's Mandate for Legislation', retrieved from: http://ssrn.com/abstract=1099893 (last accessed 25 October 2017), p. 11.

31 Heuzé, 2005, p. 408.

been found to hamper trade even worse than the rules in the host country.[32] Moreover, the latter takes the role of a home Member State whenever its own operators are concerned. So, this reasoning actually ends up sometimes hurting economic activities instead of protecting them. The same goes for understanding freedoms of movement as pinpointing to the substantive laws best suiting the interests of the supplier, provider or investor.[33] This line of reasoning would indeed not automatically guarantee the best solution for the long-term development of economic relations. It also ignores that none of the freedoms actually personalize their beneficiaries.[34] Most striking is that it would otherwise encroach precisely upon the freedom of choice governing contract matters in private international law.[35] True, all of these contradictions evaporate if mutual recognition is not perceived as influencing conflicts of laws, but merely as a means for preserving the more or less legitimate expectations of economic agents.[36] But it then recalls a radically different method in private international law.[37] As such, it duplicates more specifically a vested rights doctrine (*théorie des droits acquis*) that transcends classic internal connecting rules.[38]

Mutual recognition, as a vested rights doctrine, struggles even harder to locate its textual source within European primary law. This could not be said to be inferred from the statement of freedom proclaimed in the principles of circulation. The contrary would imply a

32 *See, e.g.*, Judgment of 20 April 1983 in *Case 59/82, Schutzverband gegen Unwesen in der Wirtschaft v Weinvertriebs-GmbH* [1983] ECR-01217, Rec. 12 and especially Judgment of 13 May 1997 in *Case C-384/93, Alpine Investments BV v. Minister van Financiën* [1995] ECR I-01141, Recs. 26-39. The Court expressly denies reading a country of origin principle within the Treaties in the Judgment of 10 May 1995 in *Case C-233/94, Federal Republic of Germany v. European Parliament and Council of the European Union* [1997] ECR I-02405, Rec. 64.

33 Basedow, 1995, pp. 18-25; Kieninger, 1996, pp. 122-152. The supplier side is thus considered more important for the sake of economic integration.

34 *See infra* § 4; Spamann, 2001, p. 44: "it is true, of course, and economically natural, that suppliers have taken the more visible steps towards integrating the European market (…) but the suppliers could only do this because the consumers were buying. Consumers might be less willing to buy foreign products if they had to expect the application of foreign law (…) on average, it would seem that it would be cheaper to apply the consumer's law and shift the task of learning about a foreign law to the supplier. This is because the supplier usually enters into many transactions of the same kind, and can therefore realize economies of scale".

35 Audit, 2006, § 42; Heuzé, 2005, p. 409: "le principe d'autonomie ne peut être utile qu'en tant qu'il permet de déroger à la compétence de la loi du pays d'origine; ou bien, en tant seulement qu'il incite le fournisseur à ne consentir à l'application de celle-ci qu'après s'être assuré qu'elle est pour lui la plus avantageuse". This interestingly brings Radicati di Brozolo, 1993, § 4.1 to allow freedom of choice in contract matters only when the parties designate the country of origin.

36 Audit, 2006, § 26-30; Heuzé, 2005, p. 394; Fallon, 2004.

37 Idot, 2002, § 8-10; E. Pataut, 'Le renouveau de la théorie des droits acquis', *in Travaux du Comité français de droit international privé, années 2006-2008*, Paris, A. Pedone, 2009, p. 84; Audit, 2006, § 65.

38 E. Jayme & Ch. Kohler, 'Europäisches Kollisionsrecht 2001: Anerkennungsprinzip statt IPR?', *IPRax*, 2001, pp. 501-514; Ch. Pamboukis, 'La renaissance-métamorphose de la méthode de reconnaissance', *Rev. Crit. DIP*, 2008, p. 513, § 10; Pataut, 2009, p. 83; Kohler, 2013, pp. 67-68; S. Bollée, 'Les conditions de la reconnaissance, notamment à la lumière des conventions internationales', *in* P. Lagarde (Ed.), *La reconnaissance des situations en droit international privé. Actes du colloque international de la Haye du 18 janvier 2013*, Paris, A. Pedone, 2013, p. 113; Callé *et al.*, 2012; Sonnenberger, 2013.

generic statement of deregulation, aimed to prohibit any encroaching upon individual freedom, were it not specifically justified in the public interest.[39] This is obviously not the case however.[40] Member States are actually bound to limit individual freedom if it infringes upon market integration.[41] The same goes more specifically for the contractual freedom of any given economic operators.[42] And a vast recognition of whatever rights acquired abroad can intuitively not be thought of as having a positive impact on trade.[43] This is certainly true for *in rem* security, where unlimited individual freedom would induce massive uncertainty among creditors.[44] It became obvious as even publicity requirements for rendering securities enforceable against third parties got accused of restricting intra-community trade.[45] But like professor Aynès puts it in brief, "*trop de sûretés, pas de sûreté*" ("too many securities, no security").[46] As such, mutual recognition in itself cannot be considered a duty imposed by European primary law. It pops out indeed only when enabling the development of economic relations, as outcome from enforcing the freedoms established in the TFEU.[47] But the contrary could easily unfold, provided conversely the rules restricting individual freedom in the host Member State are deemed necessary precisely

39 This seems to be however the conclusion of Von Wilmowsky, 1996, p. 1.

40 J. Drexl, 'La Constitution économique européenne – l'actualité du modèle ordolibéral', *RIDE*, 2011, No. 4, pp. 435-436; Spamann, 2001, pp. 45-47.

41 De Sousa, 2015, pp. 200-214. *See, e.g.*, the ruling in the 'strawberry war', where French producers tried to physically block fruit imports from Spain, in the Judgment of 9 December 1997 in *Case C-265/95, Commission of the European Communities v. French Republic* [1997] ECR I-06959, Rec. 31.

42 Audit, 2006, note 65; Kieninger, 1996, p. 196; Drexl, 2011, p. 435: "le point de départ qui servira à décrire cette relation entre liberté contractuelle et droit de la concurrence est la prise de conscience des ordolibéraux que – comme la liberté politique – la concurrence libre, elle aussi, est affectée par le «paradoxe de la liberté»". Against such conclusion, Basedow, 1995, pp. 27-28; Von Wilmowsky, 1996, p. 40 and Rutgers, pp. 11-12 oppose the ruling in the Judgment of 24 January 1991 in *Case C-339/89, Alsthom Atlantique SA v Compagnie de construction mécanique Sulzer SA* [1991] ECR I-00107 Rec. 15. In this case, however, contractual freedom only served to clear internal law of any accusation it may be hindering trade, given that parties could have deviated from regulatory provisions. But the ECJ didn't conversely deny any possibility for contractual freedom to encroach upon market integration

43 Flour, 1977, § 118-119: "à la vérité, le principe dit du respect des droits acquis, s'il devait être pris au pied de la lettre, méconnaitrait lui-même gravement l'intérêt des tiers".

44 B. Bouckaert, 'Divergences of the Law on Securities. A Law and Economics Approach', *in* U. Drobnig, H.J. Snijders & E.-J. Zippro (Eds.), *Divergences in Property Law. An Obstacle to the Internal Market?*, München, Sellier, 2006, pp. 175-194.

45 Basedow, 2013, pp. 226-227; Kieninger, 1996, p. 181.

46 L. Aynès, 'Les garanties du financement, Rapport de synthèse présenté au 82ᵉ congrès des notaires', *Defrénois*, 1986, Art. 33779, § 2.

47 Audit, 2006, § 19-34: "la référence faite aux règles du pays d'origine des produits étaye donc le raisonnement de la Cour de justice; en aucun cas, elle ne le fonde (...) encore faut-il que la seconde condition soit remplie: l'existence d'une entrave"; J. H. H. Weiler, 'The Constitution of the Common Market Place: Text and Content in the Evolution of the Free Movement of Goods', *in* P. Craig & G. de Burca (Eds.), *The Evolution of EU Law*, Oxford, OUP, 1999, p. 367: "«mutual recognition» or functional parallelism is not a radial hermeneutic departure, but in fact a very conservative and fully justified application of the principle of proportionality".

in the interests of economic welfare. Mutual recognition of foreign security rights thus implies arguing the specific hindrances on trade brought about by opposing internal law.

Rules on *in rem* security seldom, if ever at all, discriminate on grounds of nationality, residence or whatever origin some relevant connecting factor may have. This is however not a peremptory argument against finding hindrances on trade. The ECJ relies indeed upon an extremely broad standard when assessing alleged violations. This goes back to its judgment in the *Dassonville* ruling, where the Court stated that "all trading rules [...] which are capable of hindering, directly or indirectly, actually or potentially, intra-community trade are to be considered as measures having an effect equivalent to quantitative restrictions".[48] True, one cannot overlook past attempts of limiting the *Dassonville* formula through distinctions in subsequent cases, mainly the *Keck and Mithouard* ruling.[49] In fact this decision suggested a binary classification for internal measures allegedly hampering trade. Scholars have thus justifiably tried to assess whether laws on *in rem* security fall within the scope of 'product requirements' or should rather be considered as pertaining to 'selling arrangements'.[50] The latter were only thought prohibited upon findings of legal or at least factual discrimination between internal and external traders or operations. Additionally, it was questioned whether rules on *in rem* security could amount to indirect discriminations, were they to be treated as governing 'selling arrangements'.

Still, the ECJ has progressively abandoned the distinctions established in the *Keck and Mithouard* ruling. This has been done by over-inflating the rather blurry domain of 'product requirements' and through findings of factual discrimination any time simple regulatory differences between Member States implied costs for adapting to the local market requirements.[51] Moreover, the Court has only referred to this in matters involving the movement of goods, without extending it to services or capital investments.[52] And some consider these standards altogether abandoned in recent case law.[53] Nonetheless, the distinction between 'product requirements' and 'selling arrangements' seems thus hardly significant for *in rem* security. This means at least that alleged trade restrictions here are not conditioned by some proof of explicit discrimination. Relevant internal regulations are rather to be assessed in accordance with the traditional formula stated in the *Dassonville* ruling. The Court is indeed thought of having returned to it with the newly developed

48 Judgment of 11 July 1974 in *Case 8/74, Procureur du Roi c. Benoît and Gustave Dassonville* [1974] ECR 00837, Rec. 5.

49 Judgment of 24 November 1993 in *Joint Cases C-267/91 and C-268/91, Procédure pénale c. Bernard Keck et Daniel Mithouard* [1991] ECR I-06097, Rec. 16.

50 *See, e.g.*, Wunsch, 2009, p. 324; Akkermans & Ramaekers, 2011, pp. 9-10; Kieninger, 1996, pp. 152-153; Rutgers, 1999, pp. 195-200; Von Wilmowsky, 1996, pp. 51-52.

51 De Sousa, 2015, p. 105.

52 *See, e.g.*, Judgement of 28 September 2006 in *Joint cases C-282/04 and C-283/04, Commission of the European Communities v. Kingdom of the Netherlands* [2006] ECR I-09141, Rec. 18; Picod § 70.

53 A. Rigaux in *Europe*, 2016, comm. 50 under Judgment of 23 December 2015 in *Case C-333/14, Scotch Whisky Association* [2015] Electronic Reports of Cases; Akkermans, 2008, p. 542.

market-access test.[54] Besides, this was always the only legitimate reading for the prohibitions safeguarding economic freedoms, which never limited themselves at discriminatory measures.[55] The absence of any textual basis for the distinctions laid down in the *Keck and Mithouard* decision was the main reason for its chill reception in practice and legal science.[56] It is simply that internal market principles explicitly protect interstate commerce. Any finding of restriction implies thus for the alleged burden to weigh at least in fact more on international operations than over purely internal situations.[57] Hence, the question remains whether imperatives on *in rem* security hamper insofar market integration.

The main challenge is avoiding arguments that ultimately lead back to plain expressions of legislative diversity between Member States. Such is the case for several conclusions pinpointing solely to requirements of translation or legal advice for secured lenders in international activities.[58] It is true that some case law of the ECJ almost ends up considering legislative diversity a hindrance in itself. For instance, this was found to be the case where it compelled operators "to adopt advertising or sales promotion schemes which differ from one Member State to another or to discontinue a scheme which he considers to be particularly effective".[59] There would undoubtedly be great efficiency gains if economic agents were able to organise their international activities in the most uniform way. This objective can unquestionably serve as basis for European legislative competence following Articles 114-115 TFEU, aimed at removing obstacles in the internal market.[60] But it should not be deduced that any regulatory difference to which economic agents need to adapt encroaches upon the economic freedoms. The contrary would not only raise delicate constitutional problems as to normative competences retained by Member States.[61] It would also bring

---

54 A. Rigaux, 'La jurisprudence Keck et Mithouard à l'épreuve des règles nationales de publicité', *Europe*, 2001, No. 5, chron. 4; Akkermans, 2013, p. 9; De Sousa, 2015, p. 114; A. Fromont & Ch. Verdure, 'La consécration du critère de l'«accès au marché» en matière de libre circulation des marchandises: mythe ou réalité?', *RTD eur.*, 2011, p. 717; Akkermans & Ramaekers, 2011, p. 7.

55 Weiler, 1999, p. 352; Spamann, 2001, p. 29.

56 *Case C-110/05, Commission v. Italian Republic* (note 2), Opinion of AG Bot, Paras. 90-93; A. Rigaux, 'Symphonie déconcertante ou keckophonie? À propos des dissonances de l'arrêt Morellato', *Europe*, 2003, No. 11, chron. 13.

57 Weiler, 1999, p. 360. *See infra* § 4.

58 Commission, *White paper on the integration of EU mortgage credit markets*, COM (2007) 807 final, p. 3; Stöcker, 2012, p. 211; M. Schürheck, 'Sachenrecht im Europäischen Gemeinschaftsrecht. Bestandsaufnahme, Legislativkompetenzen, Entwicklungsperspektiven', *Osnabrück JMCE Award Series*, 2011, No. 3, p. 51; Basedow, 1995, pp. 8-9; Kieninger, 1996, pp. 58-59; Wunsch, 2009, pp. 294-295; Radicati di Brozolo, 1993, § 2; Ch. von Bar & U. Drobnig, *The Interaction of Contract Law and Tort and Property Law in Europe. A Comparative Study*, München, Sellier, 2004, p. 439, recording replies by businessmen and legal practitioners on the costs of information related to different internal laws.

59 Judgment of 15 December 1982 in *Case 286/81, Procédure pénale c Oosthoek's Uitgeversmaatschappij* [1982] ECR-04575, Rec. 15.

60 *See infra* § 4.

61 S. Weatherill, 'Diversity between National Laws in the Internal Market', *in* U. Drobnig, H.J. Snijders & E. J. Zippro (Eds.), *Divergences in Property Law. An Obstacle to the Internal Market?*, München, Sellier, 2006, p. 149; V. Sagaert, 'Harmonization of Security Rights on Immoveables: An Ongoing Story', *in*

about an overwhelming deadlock when ascribing responsibility for alleged infringements. Diversity, in itself, can logically never be traced back to a single term of the conflicting elements. Losses incurred from differences between internal regulations are just as much the fault of the host Member State as of the home country. Any conclusion would thus find them both in violation of European primary law, save for adequate justification. Clearly, this cannot be the case as it would completely blur the imperative of market integration. Negative harmonization should therefore abstractly take the impact of each national rule into account, barring any comparative consideration.

3 Absolute Benchmark of Efficiency for *In Rem* Securities

It is clear at least that norms restricting the content of private law instruments do not amount to hindrances on the Economic Freedoms just because of their imperative nature. The contrary would understand market integration as a generic statement of deregulation protecting individual freedom, which it certainly isn't.[62] Nonetheless, some scholarly conclusions have attempted an abstract benchmark for assessing trade restrictions in matters of *in rem* security. This requires scrutinizing the efficiency of an instrument, taking into account its regulatory environment.[63] Such scrutiny should in turn avoid arguments exclusively based on comparisons with similar techniques of other Member States, because regulatory diversity is not in itself a hindrance.[64] Indeed, an absolute conclusion needs to be reached regarding the repercussions stemming from internal rules, with foreign references coming only as rational alternatives. But where such conclusions are achieved, their implications are intuitive. Inefficient securities obviously deter lender interest to supply

---

A. Hartkamp *et al.* (Eds.), *Towards a European Civil Code*, 4th ed., Nijmegen, ars Aequi Libri/Kluwer Law International, 2011, p. 1045; F. Verstijlen, 'General Aspects of Transfer and Creation of Property Rights including Security Rights', *in* U. Drobnig, H.J. Snijders & E.-J. Zippro (Eds.), *Divergences in Property Law. An Obstacle to the Internal Market?*, München, Sellier, 2006, p. 23; L. Vogel in *La Semaine Juridique Edition Entreprises et Affaires*, 1994, p. 592, comm. under *Cases C-267/91 and C-268/91, Keck et Mithouard, supra* note 49, § 7; Audit, 2006, § 35: "affirmer que la diversité des législations d'origine nationale est en contradiction avec les règles communautaires relatives à l'entrave aux libertés de circulation, c'est porter indirectement - mais très nettement - atteinte au principe selon lequel l'Union européenne ne dispose que d'une compétence d'attribution".

62 *See supra* § 2.

63 Schmid, 2005, pp. 61-63; Nasarre-Aznar, 2012, pp. 80-92; Akkermans, 2012, pp. 225-228; Kieninger, 1996, pp. 122-152; Wolf, 1990, pp. 1941-1943; Schürheck, 2011, pp. 1-57; Wunsch, 2009, pp. 296-300; Akkermans & Ramaekers, 2011, pp. 19-21: "the creditor may need to make costs to obtain a more expensive property security right, usually a letter of credit, to ensure his position in a cross-border setting. He may decide to sell the object at a higher price to compensate for the risk of losing his security. Any increase in price may however cause a competitive disadvantage for the seller and make the object less attractive to the buyer (consumer). Worst of all, the seller may choose to no longer do business with a particular Member State, or not to do cross-border business at all anymore".

64 *See supra* § 2.

financing. Creditors thus feel driven to withdraw from a given market or ask for additional forms of insurance.[65] And if required to do so by legally binding prudential standards, they might not even have the choice.[66] This in turn raises the financing costs, not only for them but also for the borrowers. And above all, the national rules responsible for this outcome can hardly be deemed justified under the standards set forth by the Treaties or respectively developed through ECJ case law.[67]

Consumer protection could perhaps kick in to justify prohibiting them from handling with riskier conventional securities.[68] But this only applies to their specific personal situation. Businesses or professional borrowers are not covered. Moreover, bluntly forbidding such techniques could easily be considered disproportionate or outright inconsistent with similar instruments permitted to consumers.[69] This would especially be the case if equivalent techniques allowed in other countries haven't led there to bankrupting or massively endangering the financial situation of individuals.[70] As such, the bare minimum would be to adequately inform them in advance over whatever risks may be at stake. Save for consumer protection, regulations on *in rem* security hardly justify themselves through other considerations in the public interest.

It is true that some of the suggested justifications adequately cover most imperatives applicable to *in rem* security. Professor Basedow states for instance that all internal rules in this field are necessary for protecting an established legal order in respect to property rights over tradeable goods.[71] And it seems indeed that of general interest in private law isn't necessarily the content, rather in itself the being and existence of rules aimed at arbi-

65 Akkermans & Ramaekers, 2011, p. 6.

66 Stöcker, 2012, pp. 74-75; Akkermans, 2012, pp. 233-234.

67 W. van Gerven, 'Convention de Rome, Traité de Rome et prestations de services dans le secteur financier' (hors-série juin 1993), *Banque et Droit*, § 11-20 suggests a consistent approach on justification, irrespective of the freedom involved. It is only that derogations expressly provided for by the TFEU also allow for discriminatory measures, when necessary.

68 *See* regarding the euromortgage project S. Van Erp, 'Security Interests: A secure start for the development of European property law' (November 7, 2008) Maastricht Faculty of Law Working paper No. 5, retrieved from http://ssrn.com/abstract=1297282 (last accessed 20 October 2017), p. 9.

69 Akkermans & Ramaekers, 2011, p. 12; Von Wilmowsky, 1996, pp. 148-149.

70 Weiler, 1999, p. 365: "for a Member State to insist on a specific technical standard, even if a different standard is functionally parallel in achieving the desired result, is to have adopted a measure which is not the least restrictive possible".

71 Basedow, 1995, p. 45: "im Übrigen besitzt aber die Güterordnung, d.h. die eindeutige Umschreibung der dinglichen Rechte an Handelsgütern, eine geradezu wirtschaftsverfassungsrechtliche Bedeutung für die Organisation von Märkten, insofern ist die Güterordnung Teil der öffentliche Ordnung"; Kieninger, 1996, p. 173: "der Schaffung einer bestimmten Rangfolge zwischen den verschiedenen Gruppen von Gläubigern und Sicherungsrechten, der Festlegung eines bestimmten Inhalts solcher Rechte sowie der Steuerung ihres Volumens und damit des Kreditvolumens insgesamt dienen"; Akkermans & Ramaekers, 2011, p. 12: "the forced recognition of foreign property rights upsets the balance that is achieved at a national level through the national system of property rights".

trating between individuals.[72] But Member States relying upon this argument would easily get accused of inconsequence whenever introducing reforms that abandon the formerly established legal framework.[73] Besides, the same line of reasoning could then easily be relevant to just about any other field of private law. Most of its imperative norms are indeed merely setting out necessary boundaries to the respective areas of freedom claimed by individuals. Each of these rules aims at guaranteeing a specific established order. Whatever obstacle on trade arises therefrom thus ends up as its own justification.[74] The same goes for invoking legal certainty in order to justify them. It amounts to the confidence private persons may have invested precisely in the maintaining of the aforementioned established legal order.[75] But such an argument would itself also function for any other internal measure which can be said to infringe upon the freedoms. Short of hypocrisy, any professional person is bound to know that laws change periodically, especially when encroaching upon European principles. Finally, avoiding costs or risks thereof eventually incurred by the security provider or his other creditors cannot in itself justify possible trade restrictions.[76] Those are obviously private considerations, whereas only specific reasons or motives in the public interest may lawfully trump market integration.[77] Moreover, any claim of specifically protecting debtors, security providers or even creditors as such through burdensome regulations would see itself rebuked for inconsistency.[78] That comes in view of the many other internal measures having arbitrated in favour of the other party, or even of different stakeholders. But the problem is how far-fetched this all seems. Similar argu-

72 Heuzé, 2005, p. 413: "en matière de droit privé (…) dès lors que l'Etat acteur a fait le choix d'assurer cet arbitrage, les règles au moyen desquels il s'oblige à l'opérer, par le biais de ses tribunaux, ne peuvent évidemment être exprimés sous la forme d'une alternative entre l'action et l'abstention: il doit prendre parti, en formulant une solution".

73 Akkermans & Ramaekers, 2011, p. 12; Rutgers, 1999, pp. 205-206.

74 P. von Wilmowsky, Book review of Kieninger *supra* note 5, *RabelsZ*, No. 64, 2000, p. 160: "das, was auf seine Vereinbarkeit mit den Grundfreiheiten kontrolliert werden sollte, wird selbst zum Rechtfertigungsgrund für Eingriffe".

75 It is about protecting "einer bestimmten Ordnung und des in die Integrität dieser Ordnung gesetzten Vertrauens": Kieninger, 1996, pp. 165-173 and 179-180; Akkermans and Ramaekers, 2011, p. 12; Akkermans, 2008, p. 529; Schmid, 2005, pp. 61-63; Wunsch, 2009, pp. 327-332. The ECJ has indeed stated in the Judgment of 24 May 2011 in *Case C-50/08, European Commission v. French Republic* [2011] ECR I-04195, Rec. 87 that "to guarantee the lawfulness and legal certainty of documents entered into by individuals constitutes an overriding reason in the public interest capable of justifying restrictions".

76 Akkermans, 2012, p. 34; T. W. Merrill & H. E. Smith, 'Optimal Standardization in the Law of Property: The Numerus Clausus Principle', *Yale Law Journal*, 2000, No. 110, pp. 1-70.

77 Rutgers, p. 13 however states that ECJ case law on companies from different Member States also took into consideration as such the private interests of minority shareholders, creditors and employees. But it would be inconsistent for the ECJ to do so, seeing on the other hand how rigorously it scrutinizes justifications linked to public security (*see, e.g.*, the Judgment of 11 November 2010 in *Case C-543/08, European Commission v. Portuguese Republic* [2010] ECR I-11241, Para. 85). These references more likely pertain to legal certainty and predictability required by third parties, as these considerations come intuitively closer to the general interest.

78 Von Wilmowsky, 1996, pp. 122-149.

ments could indeed suggest a breach in the principles of economic freedom whenever national law does not provide foreign economic agents with all conceivable gains of efficiency. It may theoretically go as far as to require public guarantees for the repayment of credits disbursed by creditors from another country. Indeed, the lack of such guarantees can unquestionably be a deterring factor for the pursuit of financing activities on the local market.[79]

4 Impersonal Freedoms for Generic Efficiency of Securities

The very counterintuitive solution reached above comes precisely due to how it revolved around the interests of the secured creditor. Its starting point assumed indeed that any losses in terms of efficiency on his behalf would automatically amount to hindering trade.[80] Whatever form the protection of other stakeholders subsequently took, the rule could not justify itself as necessary for considerations in the public interest. However, their interests should not only be taken into consideration during this latter stage, thus facing obvious challenges because of the mainly private interests involved. Costs and risks borne by the security provider and his other creditors are just as discouraging for them as they are for the secured lender.[81] "Parce qu'il s'agit de réaliser un arbitrage entre des intérêts antagonistes [...] il est donc impossible de donner ou de garantir à l'un sans retirer ou imposer à l'autre".[82] In theory, this may certainly drive them too at seeking or providing financing on a different market.[83] This means that conclusions only considering the specific positions of individual stakeholders entail very different outcomes on trade, following each respective starting position. But there is no self-evident or textual reason to discriminate the stakeholders involved along these lines. Indeed, such neutrality actually fits perfectly with the ordoliberal economic theories having influenced the initial wording of the Treaties.[84] Indeed, the relevant rules in the TFEU cannot be read as having personalized their beneficiaries or being required to serve the needs and freedom of specific economic agents. Moreover, any secured lender hunting for gains in efficiency assumes in turn the position

79 Unlimited public guarantees are obviously considered state aid, for the debtor at least. *See* the Judgment of 3 April 2014 in *Case C-559/12 P, French Republic v. European Commission* [2014] Electronic Reports of Cases.

80 Audit, 2006, § 67: "parmi les différents – et nombreux – intérêts mis en cause par une relation juridique intracommunautaire, seul l'un d'entre eux est pris en considération (...) celui de l'opérateur (...) on lui sacrifie la satisfaction d'autres intérêts au moins aussi respectables".

81 Spamann, 2001, p. 44; Heuzé, 2005, pp. 397-398.

82 Heuzé, 2005, p. 413.

83 Aynès & Crocq, 2014, § 408: "l'avantage considérable qui est conféré au créancier peut constituer un préjudice et pour le débiteur – dont, de surcroît, le crédit est gaspillé – et surtout pour les autres créanciers".

84 Drexl, 2011, pp. 431-439, arguing the protection of weaker stakeholders not only for generic reasons of consumer welfare, but precisely because of its economic impact on market considerations.

of subsequent or even unsecured creditor in some other deal, thus incurring precisely the losses he intended to avoid. So before considering any kind of justification, all of these various interests need to be summed up.

It is not merely a matter of general or social considerations of stakeholder protection exceeding economic issues. A summary of all interests involved is necessary precisely to exhaustively ascertain the impact of a given internal measure on trade. This should take into account all of its negative and positive repercussions.[85] Above all, these need to be assessed on a long-term basis. On short term, *in rem* security rights altogether are massively hindering the circulation of goods and capital investment.[86] Mortgaged assets for instance would intuitively sell much easier and faster if the applicable substantive rules were to render void or inefficient any pledges encumbering them.[87] This gets very close to actually quantifying the restriction in terms of volume loss for trans-border economic relations. It seemingly comes up as a very faithful interpretation of the relevant Treaty provisions. Save for explicit discrimination, national measures are prohibited only when having an effect equivalent to clear quantitative restrictions. This is expressly stated for importing and exporting movable goods, but works just as well for every other economic freedom. Thus, there must be comprehensive proof of this equivalence.[88] It should also specifically weigh more over international operations, as the principles of market integration are protecting interstate transactions, not plainly trade in general.[89] The same can be said to be true for imperative national limitations over *in rem* security.

A comprehensive demonstration as above required seems extremely challenging, especially in view of the multifaceted considerations to be weighed in the context of *in rem*

85 Spamann, 2001, p. 29 thus advises that "private law rules should be treated with the utmost judicial restraint"

86 Von Wilmowsky, 200, p. 161: "ein Mitgliedstaat, der z.B. gar keine Sicherungsrechte an Gegenständen des Schuldnervermögens zuließe und damit jedweden grenzüberschreitenden Verkehr mit Sicherungsrechten ausschlösse, wäre mit dieser Maßnahme per se gerechtfertigt".

87 Aynès & Crocq, 2014, § 7.

88 In *Case C-543/08, Commission v. Portugal, supra* note 77, Paras. 31-38 however, Portugal precisely accused the Commission of not having adequately argued the hindrance caused by the 'golden share' retained in a privatised company. But the Court only took this argument into consideration in order to ascertain whether the hindrance is justified under Paras. 68-70, thus controversially presuming its existence.

89 *See supra* § 2. Weiler, 1999, p. 360: "is a regulatory measure which merely hinders, even if appreciably, though without the ability to gauge with precision the exact effect on imports, really equivalent to a quota restricting with precision the number of allowable cigarette imports? Is not the essence of the quota, even the non-zero quota – the pre-emptory and sharp bar to access into the market of imported products which do not fall within the quota? On this reading, a measure merely hindering the marketing of a product which had free access to that market is not equivalent to a quantitative restriction (…) a regulation which appreciably affects sales but does not differentiate between imports and domestic products is really not equivalent in this sense to a quota larger than zero (…) the imported product can compete on the domestic market and, if better in quality and price, can displace all its domestic competitors".

security.[90] But at least, it could provide for the best way to read the *Krantz* judgment.[91] This decision is one of the few cases where the ECJ actually came to rule over possible restrictions on European economic freedoms incriminated within internal *in rem* security law. A reservation of title consented in Germany was at stake. However, this did not prevent Dutch tax authorities from seizing the goods in question. The secured creditor subsequently claimed such laws were hampering on intracommunity trade. His argument was nonetheless rejected. In the first instance the Court observed there was no explicit discrimination against interstate operations in the applicable laws. More importantly, the decision noted how "uncertain and indirect" it would be to consider economic agents discouraged from investing and hindered in their activities particularly because of this internal rule.[92] It is true that the judges may thus have simply proclaimed some vague threshold of value under which restrictions encroaching upon economic freedoms are not really worth sanctioning.[93] The case must certainly not be understood as excluding any hindrance on trade whatsoever stemming from internal security law.[94] But the ruling could also be thought of precisely as an inquiry for additional evidence in support of the burden claimed. It is a wrong decision, insofar as the global financial impact of the national rule was not taken into consideration. Had the judges approached its implications for all stakeholders involved, the case would have had a different outcome. Such a demonstration thus appears to be the only way for the ECJ to find out whether or not rules over *in rem* security infringe upon the principles of freedom in the Treaties. If a similar case were to be tried today, its outcome would necessarily depend on these kinds of complex economic predictions.

Summing up the effects of internal measures regulating *in rem* security amounts intuitively to a very complex challenge. Many thus believe that a comprehensive approximation of private law will rather be achieved through regulations or directives aimed to reinforce the functioning of the internal market.[95] True, these issues are somewhat intertwined.

---

90 Verstijlen, 2006, p. 35 doubts whether such evidence may be found as regards *in rem* security. More generally, Spamann, 2001, p. 27 considers that "the idea that the courts can objectively determine the precise effects of a measure is, of course, misleading. Nobody can. Just establishing the likely effect of the measure will therefore require educated guesses. In fact, if evaluating different policy options were such an easy and objective task, we could dispense with much of our philosophical and political debate and institutions". *See* however for an attempt precisely in the field of *in rem* security, the *White paper on the integration of EU mortgage credit markets*, 2007, pp. 4-6, *supra* note 58. But arguments in the white paper are to be used in political decision-making, not as indisputable proof in judiciary matters.

91 Judgment of 7 March 1990 in *Case C-69/88, H. Krantz GmbH & Co v. Ontvanger der Directe Belastingen and Staat der Nederlanden* [1990] ECR I-00583. On this case, *see* Akkermans, 2012, pp. 217-219; Akkermans & Ramaekers, 2011, pp. 15-17.

92 *Case C-69/88, Krantz* (note 91), Rec. 11.

93 *See* precisely *Case C-69/88, Krantz supra* note 91, Opinion of AG Darmon, Recs. 12-16 calling for some *de minimis* threshold in this field. But the Court of Justice traditionally excludes such a benchmark for invoking economic freedoms. *See* Akkermans & Ramaekers, 2011, p. 8.

94 Akkermans, 2012, p. 216; Akkermans & Ramaekers, 2011, p. 3.

95 J. Basedow, 'Codification of Private Law in the European Union: the making of a Hybrid', *ERPL*, 2001, No. 1, p. 47; F. Baur, J. Baur & R. Stürner, *Sachenrecht*, 18th ed., München, C.H. Beck, 2009, § 64.72; Wunsch,

European legislative competence in private law requires precisely for regulatory intervention to help removing obstacles on exercising economic freedoms.[96] This means it actually refers back to findings of hindrances in the various national laws applicable to *in rem* security. But adopting uniform rules instead of striking down specific national measures at least avoids the logical dead-ends in ascribing responsibility for regulatory differences.[97] Above all perhaps, "the idea of mutual recognition of property rights remains controversial as it touches on the national identity – as expressed through private law – of the Member States".[98] This paper confirms however that there is no categorical argument against negative harmonization of *in rem* securities through mutual recognition or invoking economic freedoms. It is only that any conclusion on this matter should attentively weigh in the potential impact for all stakeholders involved. Indeed, the principles of European market integration are generically protecting lasting interstate economic relations, without specifically presuming their beneficiaries.

2009, pp. 357-358; Schmid, 2005, p. 63; van Erp, 2008, pp. 11-12, albeit having reservations over such an ambitious task.

96 Rutgers, p. 1.

97 *See supra* § 2.

98 Akkermans & Ramaekers, 2011, p. 29. *See* also H.J. Snijders, 'Acces to Civil Securities and Free Competition in the EU. A Plea for One European Security Right in Movables', *in* U. Drobnig, H. J. Snijders & E.-J. Zippro (Eds.), *Divergences in Property Law. An Obstacle to the Internal Market?*, München, Sellier, 2006, pp. 153-164; J. Basedow, 'Federal Choice of Law in Europe and the United States – A Comparative Account of Interstate Conflicts', *Tul. L. Rev.*, 2007-2008, No. 82, p. 2119.

Maastricht Law Series

The Maastricht Law Series is created in 2018 by Boom juridisch and Eleven International Publishing in association with the Maastricht University Faculty of Law. The Maastricht Law Series publishes books on comparative, European and International law. The series builds upon the tradition of excellence in research at the Maastricht Faculty of Law, its research centers and the Ius Commune Research School. The Maastricht Law Series is a peer reviewed book series that allows researchers an excellent opportunity to showcase their work.

Series editors

Published in this series:

Volume 1: Reinhard Zimmermann, Does the Law of Succession Reflect Cultural Differences?, ISBN 978-94-6236-856-9
Volume 2: Anna Berlee, Access to personal data in public land registers, ISBN 978-94-6236-841-5
Volume 3: Marcus Meyer, The Position of Dutch Works Councils in Multinational Corporations, ISBN 978-94-6236-848-4
Volume 4: Jaap Hage, Foundations and Building Blocks of Law, ISBN 978-94-6236-860-6
Volume 5: Bastiaan van Zelst, The End of Justice(s)?, ISBN 978-94-6236-881-1
Volume 6: Lars van Vliet & Agustin Parise (eds.), Re- De- Co-dification?, ISBN 978-94-6236-900-9
Volume 7: Caroline S. Rupp, Rafael Ibarra Garza & Bram Akkermans, Property Law Perspectives VI, ISBN 978-94-6236-904-7
Volume 8: Aalt Willem Heringa, Europees Nederlands Staatsrecht, ISBN 978-94-6290-604-4

Printed by Libri Plureos GmbH in Hamburg,
Germany

9 789462 369047